Children and Society

Malcolm Hill and Kay Tisdall

Prentice
Hall

An imprint of Pearson Education

Harlow, England · London · New York · Reading, Massachusetts · San Francisco
Toronto · Don Mills, Ontario · Sydney · Tokyo · Singapore · Hong Kong · Seoul
Taipei · Cape Town · Madrid · Mexico City · Amsterdam · Munich · Paris · Milan

Pearson Education Limited
Edinburgh Gate
Harlow
Essex CM20 2JE
England

and Associated Companies throughout the world

Visit us on the World Wide Web at:
http://www.pearsoneduc.com

First published 1997

ISBN 0 582-29492-4

British Library Cataloguing-in-Publication Data

A catalogue record for this book is available from the British Library

Library of Congress Cataloging-in-Publication Data

A catalogue record for this book is available from the Library of Congress

10 9 8 7 6 5 4
06 05 04 03 02

Set by 35 in 10/11 pt Times
Printed in Malaysia VVP

CONTENTS

PREFACE

The idea for this book originated in a multi-disciplinary course initiated by our colleague, Professor Stewart Asquith, and organised by one of us (Malcolm Hill). The course was intended to give a broad but detailed overview of children's lives in relation to key policy areas, such as education, the law, health, crime and child protection. The interest aroused in the students by such an integrated *social* approach to children inspired us to propose and eventually write this volume. It is intended for professionals, students and others with an interest in children who may have detailed knowledge in one or more areas and wish to extend their breadth of understanding. Hopefully it will also be of interest to the general reader who would like to explore a number of significant issues related to children.

The main sources for the book have been empirical research, social science theories and social policy reviews, supplemented by media and advocacy agency sources. We think there is value in bringing together, in a single volume, issues which are often dealt with separately and which combine insights from a range of social science and applied disciplines. Yet we are also conscious that with such a wide coverage we have had to be selective about what is included. We have sought to discuss central issues concerning children, but inevitably our own preferences and knowledge limitations have affected choices about what to include or exclude. Doubtless important gaps or inadequacies will be apparent to specialists in any one area and during the writing we have been aware that at times we have had to deal extremely briefly with complex matters. Readers who wish to pursue these in more depth are given guidance to further reading.

FOREWORD

Some time ago, a lot of people from all over the world got together to discuss the rights of children and young people under the age of 18. This led to the UN Convention on the Rights of the Child. Article 12 of the Convention states that any child (regardless of skin colour, race, sex, background, etc.) has a right to voice his or her opinion on issues that may affect him or her. A British organisation of young people was set up in the name of Article 12 in order to pursue the rights stated above. As a member of the Article 12 steering committee, I am going to discuss the right to be heard.

It is all very well in theory to say that a child does have the right to be heard, but the reality can be quite different. Many people do not realise that children have this right and do not take children's opinions into consideration. Even when children are heard, their views, no matter how valid, are often not taken seriously. All children are entitled to be heard and their views taken into consideration in matters that concern them. Adults and children should work together to support each other in obtaining this basic human right.

It is the view of many people that because children do not pay tax, children do not have rights. This is totally untrue. There are many adults in society who also do not pay tax but still have rights. We are all members of a community whether we pay tax or not and so we should all be classed as equal. But this is not the only reason children should be listened to. There is a moral obligation as well as the legal obligation. Children and young people all have a considerable amount to contribute to the world: after all, they are the future. Adults make decisions that will affect children when they are older and, therefore, children have to live with the consequences of adult decisions.

Perhaps there should be more opportunities for children to voice their opinions. Maybe adults just aren't letting children have a say. Children should not only have an opportunity to say how they feel about major political topics that affect them, such as education, the juvenile justice system or the NHS, but also to affect smaller issues that surround their lives such as the way their local park is set out, the newspapers and magazines that they read or what is on their school's dinner menu.

After all, children have first-hand experience of their lifestyle and of issues that affect them, so why shouldn't they have a say?

This is very important, not just for the present day but for the future. Children want and need to be heard – this is their right. If adults continue to assume that children don't have valid opinions, children will never be heard. Let's rule out the saying, 'Children should be seen and not heard.' Children should be seen *and* heard.

Julia Press
Steering Group member of Article 12

For further information about Article 12, contact the following address:
8 Wakley Street
London EC1V 7QE
Tel: 0171 843 6026

ACKNOWLEDGEMENTS

We would like to thank very much our editor, Sarah Caro, for her courage in responding to our ambitious proposal and for giving support and advice during the writing process. The children's organisation, Article 12, has provided useful information and one of its members, Julia Press, took great care in writing a thoughtful foreword to this book. We are grateful to Stewart Asquith for his general encouragement and for his specific suggestions in relation to children and crime. Thanks are due to Paul Littlewood, Andrew Lockyer and Helen Sweeting, who each read one draft chapter and gave helpful feedback. We appreciated the help of Laura Lochhead and Fiona McNicol for their conscientious work on correspondence and formatting, for this as for many other projects.

Malcolm Hill and Kay Tisdall (Glasgow, 1997).

CHAPTER 1

Children's lives in social context

Children are just the same as adults, just younger and smaller.
(Girl aged ten, quoted in *Childhood Matters*, National Commission of
Inquiry into the Prevention of Child Abuse, 1996)

Introduction

This book attempts to place children's lives in the UK today within the
contexts of their personal social relationships and of the role of society
at large, through its social policies. The interests, feelings, behaviour
and personalities of individual children are crucially affected by, and in
turn affect, their key relationships – with parents, other family members,
peers, teachers and other professionals, and wider society. Furthermore,
the experiences of individual children are part of the set of relations
between children in general and adults, which shape expectations about
the appropriate and acceptable nature of childhood within society and
in particular communities. Increasingly it has been recognised that
children are not simply passive recipients of adults' models, knowledge
and values, but contribute actively to the creation of the social worlds
in which they live, both individually and collectively.

Present-day Britain offers a wealth of opportunities, but also challenges and constraints, for children. On the one hand, material standards
of living, life expectancy and health have, on average, reached unprecedented levels. Technological developments ranging from the aeroplane to
CD-Roms can potentially link children to experiences, cultures and environments across the world. Yet, as we shall see, many children live in
situations of material and social deprivation; some are physically or sexually abused. The modern or indeed post-modern world has brought new
or increased hazards, such as motor accidents, drug misuse and AIDS.

Demographic changes also impinge on children. Since the 1960s a
number of trends have occurred in the UK and indeed in most other
countries of Western Europe (Kiernan and Wicks 1990; Richards 1995;
Tisdall with Donnaghie 1995):*

* References: books referred to in the text are listed in the References on pages 262–
310. There are Suggestions for further reading at the end of each chapter, as well as
numbered footnotes.

- fertility and average family size have fallen
- children form a smaller proportion of the population
- the proportion of births to unmarried mothers has grown substantially (although many such births are jointly registered, suggesting cohabitation by the parents)
- the number of households headed by a lone parent has grown (about 90 per cent by lone mothers)
- approximately one in three marriages ends in divorce
- the numbers of remarriages and reconstituted families have increased
- ethnic diversity has increased, though today the great majority of children of ethnic minority background were born in the UK
- male unemployment has increased markedly
- there has been a substantial rise in the proportion of mothers in paid employment, though many are in part-time work.

Consequently, few children are now raised in what used to be called a conventional family household comprising a married couple and their joint children, with the father working and the wife at home, although this does still apply to some children for part of their childhood.

The diversification of households and families has implications not only for the immediate context of children's lives, but for their aspirations and transitions to adulthood. The so-called traditional goals of adulthood – full-time employment, marriage with children, forming an independent household – are not achieved by all young people today and may not even be the goals of some (Jones and Wallace 1992; Tisdall 1994; Coles 1995). Many children do aspire to work, money, home ownership and marriage, but they also see growing up as associated with freedoms, making decisions, assuming responsibilities, and coping with pressures and obligations (Lindon 1996).

The 1990s have been a time for adults to re-examine their perceptions of children and attitudes towards them. Academically, traditional approaches to childhood and the very notion of child development have been questioned. In law and policy, increased prominence has been given to children's rights and especially to their entitlement to influence decisions affecting themselves. So far, this has chiefly meant greater sensitivity to hearing and understanding the viewpoints of individual children. There has been little preparedness to confer a greater role for children as a social group to influence policy and practice in schools, local neighbourhoods and society.

The social connectedness of children's lives and development is the overarching theme of this book. Within that perspective we shall address some of the core private and public issues concerning children, with a focus on the following:

- How is childhood defined and 'socially constructed', particularly by academic commentators and service providers, or within policy formulations?
- What kinds of children's rights are recognised?
- What kinds of children's needs are identified?

In this chapter, we discuss the social contexts of children's experiences and differing conceptions of childhood. Children's rights and needs will be explored in the two following chapters. The rest of the book will examine particular aspects of children's lives, with each giving special attention to these recurrent themes. The aspects covered are:

- family relationships
- friendships and peer relations
- poverty and access to resources
- schooling
- health
- crime
- child abuse and protection
- separation from one or both parents.

Special emphasis is given to children's own perspectives and to the position of disadvantaged children.

In any discussion of children and childhood, an implicit or explicit choice has to be made about where to set the upper age limit. The boundaries between childhood and adulthood in modern Britain are multiple and indeterminate, with the teen years constituting a broad period of transition. Legal thresholds recognise different ages at which young people are entitled to partake in 'adult' activities, such as paid employment, sexual intercourse, marriage, driving and voting. The United Nations Convention on the Rights of the Child (see Appendix) defines a child as any person below the age of 18, unless majority is attained earlier under the applicable law (Article 1). Broadly we shall abide by this definition, whilst recognising that many young people do not regard themselves as children – partly because of the connotations of lower status and power than adults, which will be a leitmotiv of this book.

Children are of course a highly differentiated group of people. Age, gender, ethnicity, class, disability and other characteristics crucially affect children's experiences, self-perceptions and treatment by others. Social attitudes about these qualities often form the basis for marginalisation and stigmatisation, so that in this book we have attempted to integrate material which takes account of difference, rather than have segregated sections.

The main theme of this chapter is that children's physical, intellectual and recreational activities, as they evolve over time, are greatly affected by the attitudes, ideas and expectations of both the immediate and wider social context. Biology certainly plays a part in general patterns as infants grow into a post-pubertal young people, while genetic endowment affects differences between individuals (Rutter and Rutter 1993). Yet children's experiences are also intimately affected by conceptions of childhood which prevail in particular households, communities and societies. These conceptions are firmly located in social structures and in cultural and historical contexts which construct their meaning and significance (Jenks 1996). Firstly, we examine the concentric circles of influence with which children interact. Then we outline some differing definitions and views of children embodied in psychological and sociological thinking, before concluding with evidence about the varied ways in which child–adult relations have been manifest in different times and cultures.

The social connectedness of children's lives and development

Children – and adults – have individual wants, needs, rights and interests, but they are also intensely social in their orientations. From early babyhood, children are highly dependent on and responsive to the caregiving and interactions of others, notably parents. Indeed, infants appear to have an innate predisposition to form attachments, which are usually formed with several adults and children, to varying degrees, within the first year of life (Schaffer and Emerson 1964; Smith 1979; Howe 1996). Babies in the first few months show an interest in other babies and will smile and vocalise with a strange infant (Becker 1977; Tizard 1986). From their earliest days, children are linked into a set of informal relationships – a personal social network which evolves over the life span. A child's personality, interests and activities are neither attributes of an isolated individual nor imposed by the environment, but are firmly located in the interactions between a child and the network or system of social relationships to which each child belongs. In complex and urban societies, people's time, activities and identities are only partly rooted in their local communities, since usually their personal and formal relationships link them in various directions and connect them with a number of different places. The network provides not only an immediate context for a child's activities and development, but also a range of conduits to social resources and supports and to societal institutions, values and policies (see, for example, Bronfenbrenner 1979; Dunst *et al.* 1988; Boushel and Lebacq 1992).

Figure 1.1 Children's social networks

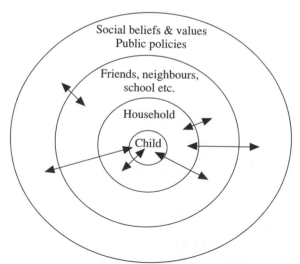

Early network members tend to be 'inherited' from a child's immediate family or household, but soon the child's own temperament and choices, as well as external opportunities and events, influence the nature and quality of network relationships. These provide both significant influences and options in a two-way process of interaction. In other words, key social relationships are both active and reciprocal: socialisation is not usually imposed on a child but emerges through a process of mutual adaptation (Waksler 1991). Of course, power relations between adults and children greatly affect the scope for children to modify or resist social influences. The actions and sanctions used by adults to instil their expectations may be intended or experienced as authoritarian.

Children's networks vary greatly in their size, structure, composition and functions (Mitchell 1969; Cochran *et al.* 1990). Some children are immersed in a large system of relationships: others have few significant contacts outside the household. However, research indicates that it is the qualities of care, support and stimulation present or lacking in networks which are crucial, and not their size (Belle 1989; Savin-Williams and Berndt 1990). Network members can help children practically, emotionally, cognitively and socially. Relatives, friends and others contribute to the care and education of children, providing access to a range of experiences and ways of life besides those of the child's parents. A developing sense of identity is crucially affected not only by identification with and reaction against parents or carers, but also by a sense of belonging to or association with wider social groupings, which may be based on proximity, ethnicity, religion, language or life-stage, for example. Less positively, networks can be the locus of conflict, pressure and discriminatory behaviour (for example, towards children who look or behave differently from most others). Close-knit networks tend to offer greater intimacy and support than looser networks but also more pressure to conform.

For most children the key relationships are mainly with close relatives and other children of similar age. Non-related people of a different age can have particular significance, especially as children grow older (Galbo 1986; Belle 1989). Some cultures and some children are mainly family-oriented, whilst for others peers and friends are more salient. Ethnic minority families tend to retain strong ties with a wide set of extended kin, though migration has sometimes reduced or disrupted contact (Modood *et al.* 1994). Sometimes children's relations with adults and with peers are portrayed as antagonistic, but in fact they are usually complementary, each providing opportunities for distinct kinds of communication and learning about the world, for example (Corsaro 1992). Peer relationships offer opportunities for children to acquire different kinds of knowledge compared with, say, parents or teachers. For example, children's school progress and formal use of language appear to be enhanced by high levels of active involvement with adults, but the adaptability of speech for use in varied contexts can be helped by interaction with a larger number of peers (Cochran *et al.* 1990; Salzinger 1990). Likewise it is usually valuable for young people to have both adults and friends to confide in, often about different kinds of issues (Coleman and Hendry 1990). These matters are explored further in chapters 4 and 5.

Children, society, the state and social policy

Children's lives and relationships are from the very beginning affected by resources, policies and attitudes beyond their immediate network and neighbourhood. For example, the quality of early care will be affected by such factors as:

• parental income
• entitlements to child benefit and other financial assistance
• access to ante-natal care
• advice from midwives and health visitors
• the quality of housing and the local environment
• availability of early years facilities (playgroups, nursery centres etc.).

These are all affected by the economy and by government policies.

Children's knowledge about the society in which they live ranges from 'very well informed' to 'relatively ignorant' (Furnham and Stacey 1991: 191). Younger children are often very well informed about their immediate environment (Matthews 1992), but their notions about the functions and connections of different social and economic institutions, including central and local government, tend to be hazy until the teen years (Furth 1980). Understanding of particular public services tends to be greater than of national political issues and processes (Furnham and Gunter 1989).

In political theory and practice, children have typically not been considered at all or conceived of as dependent on parents (O'Neill 1995). The UK has not had an explicit and comprehensive children's policy. Unlike countries like Norway, Britain has no separate ministry which deals partly or wholly with children's affairs (Leira 1993). Rather, there have been specific policies directed at particular issues concerning children, notably education. Since 1948 several Children Acts (and in the 1960s Children and Young Persons Acts) have been passed, but these have been largely concerned with children who break the law or are thought to need special care or protection. The Children Act 1989, Children (Scotland) Act 1995 and Children (Northern Ireland) Order 1995 broke new ground in integrating early years provision (day care) and more general parent–child relationships, especially those associated with divorce. Whilst these developments have been largely regarded as positive, they have occurred against a background of low government priority to social issues or inequalities, not just in Britain but internationally (Packman and Jordan 1991; O'Neill 1994; Tisdall 1996).

The role of the state with respect to financial payments and service provision with respect to children and families is discussed in several later chapters, so here we simply foreshadow key elements. The actual policies pursued by governments and commentaries thereon have been affected by both general predispositions as regards the state and specific orientations with respect to parents and children. Within Western Europe, it has been common to identify three main approaches to the welfare state, though additional types occur elsewhere in the world (Titmuss 1958; Esping-Andersen 1990; Leibfried 1991; Jones 1993a; Rhodes 1996):

Table 1.1 Types of welfare state in Western Europe

Type (Titmuss)	Type (Esping-Anderson)	Basis	Example countries
Institutional-redistributive	Social democratic	Universal provision; entitlement based on needs	Sweden
Industrial-achievement	Conservative	Selective provision; entitlement related to work record	Germany
Residual	Liberal	Safety net provision; entitlement based on means	UK

Inevitably this framework oversimplifies and the UK has some elements of each of the three models. Recent years have witnessed a shift to more residual state services, a more enabling role for local government (rather than direct provision), with a corresponding encouragement of voluntary and private provision (Johnson 1990; Leach *et al.* 1996). Scandinavia retains a greater commitment to collective provision, despite retrenchments since the mid-1980s (Ginsburg 1992; Olsson and McMurphy 1993).

With respect to children and families, there are similar contrasts in viewpoint. Some argue that it is the responsibility and right of parents to bring up children with little government support or interference, so the state should have a minimal role except in helping the very poor. Others believe that parents' responsibilities to promote children's well-being are best promoted by a range of universal supports. The present range of provision exhibits the mixed and changing influences of these different perspectives. For instance, the fluctuating nature and levels of family allowances and then child benefit over the last 50 years have reflected ambivalence about the respective responsibilities of the state and parents for the financial maintenance of children (Macnicol 1978; Brown 1992; see Chapter 8). Likewise, opinions differ on the desired role for early-years services as either targeted on families with identified difficulties or as available on demand to stimulate child development and facilitate parental employment (Chapter 3).

In the field of child welfare (Chapters 10 and 11), the state has a role not only as provider of services, but also as protector of children and 'social controller' of parenting (Hill *et al.* 1995). Everyone acknowledges a societal responsibility to safeguard children from abuse and neglect, but ideas differ as to the extent of this and on the circumstances when intervention by public agencies should override norms of parental autonomy and family privacy (Parton 1991). Some children have died as a result of parental ill-treatment, when with the benefits of hindsight it appeared that state agencies had been in a position to intervene (Reder *et al.* 1993). Other children have been removed from home precipitately and in certain instances unnecessarily (Butler-Sloss 1988; Clyde 1992). Harding (1991) identified four competing schools of thought in relation to the protection of children from ill-treatment. These embody elements of more general attitudes towards government noted above:

1 *Laissez faire* – leave the responsibility for children to parents, except in extreme cases when compulsory intervention is needed (cf. residual–liberal welfare state, Table 1.1)
2 *Protectionist* – society should intervene promptly when children are at risk and make ready use of legal sanctions (cf. achievement–conservative welfare state)
3 *Family support* – the main role of the state should be to provide material and social support to all parents, but particularly those who are struggling to care adequately for their children (cf. institutional–social democratic welfare state)
4 *Children's rights* – it is most important to give priority to the interests and especially the expressed wishes of children.

Few people hold exclusively to one of these value positions, but UK policy has seen a number of swings in emphasis, so that policy in the 1990s has inherited features of each.

Whereas the first three perspectives in Harding's framework are largely concerned with the tension between state and parent with regard to children's welfare as perceived by adults, the fourth (children's rights) recognises the importance of children's own views and entitlements to participation (Chapter 3). Attention to children's participatory rights was reinforced when the UK ratified the UN Convention on the Rights of the Child in 1991. Professionals and advocacy agencies have promoted mechanisms which seek to ensure that policies and decisions take more account of children's opinions (Lansdown 1995; Long 1996). Nevertheless, many adults remain anxious or even hostile about giving more power and influence to children. This is sometimes based on misconceptions that children's rights mean giving carte blanche to children to do what they want. In fact, their newly strengthened legal rights are to express views and influence decisions, not determine them. Also, adults can be reluctant to forgo the authority and convenience which they gain from devaluing or disregarding children's wishes. In practice, most of the recent measures to extend children's participatory rights so far have been adult-initiated and piecemeal. We return to detailed consideration of rights in Chapter 2.

Academic conceptions of children and childhood

A wind of change has also been blowing through academic writings and debates on children. Here, too, increasing value is being ascribed to children's own perspectives.

For much of its history, sociology had little to say about children, except as objects of socialisation in the home and at school, or – in the teen years – as part of youth studies. The neglect of children within sociology until recently has been compared to the earlier ignoring of women's perspectives, which resulted from preoccupation with the public world of work largely dominated by men (Ambert 1986; Oakley 1994). With a few exceptions, detailed social science study and theorising about children were largely left to psychology, psychiatry and education. Child psychology built up an impressive body of knowledge, often, though not exclusively, based on quantitative research, commonly with highly controlled methods of data-gathering. Much of this has taken a developmental approach, i.e. analysing aspects of children's learning, thinking, emotions or behaviour as they emerge in early childhood, change over time and progress towards adulthood. Commonly, childhood has been conceptualised not as a process of continuous evolution but as characterised by a series of stages, associated with particular age-spans and separated by quite sharp transitions, as in the classical frameworks of Freud and Erikson (Sugarman 1986: Table 1.2):

Table 1.2 Developmental stages identified by Freud and Erikson

Approximate age	Freud's stages of sexual development	Erikson's stages of psycho-social development
0–1	Oral	Basic trust or Mistrust
1–3	Anal	Autonomy or Shame and doubt
3–5	Phallic/Oedipal	Initiative or Guilt
5–12	Latency	Industry or Inferiority
13–18	Genital	Identity or Role confusion

Freud's stages depict a progression of focus in children's 'sexual' interests (for instance, from sucking in the early months to defecation in toddlerhood). Erikson (1963) envisaged children having a key psycho-social task to be accomplished at each stage, which could be resolved in either a positive or negative way. For example, he believed it was crucial for subsequent wellbeing whether infants develop basic trust or mistrust with adults and whether adolescents acquire a clear sense of identity or not. The stage concept has also been applied to children's thinking, notably by Piaget (see below).

Stage-based models tend to presume that later attributes and achievements are closely related to the way in which earlier stages are negotiated. Also the patterns of emotional response, behaviour or thinking associated may persist, so that some children appear to be 'stuck' in an earlier stage.

The ideas and influence of Piaget

The developmental framework proposed by Piaget has been one of the most influential in education and research. Although initially based on a comparatively narrow set of cognitive skills, Piaget's stage ideas have been widely extrapolated in pure or modified form, for example to account for the progression of children's moral and emotional development, economic understanding, sense of place and views of health (Kohlberg 1969; Berti and Bombi 1988; Harris 1992; Matthews 1992; Hartzema 1996). The Piagetian approach remains important in education, with the emphasis on facilitating active learning by the child and adapting teaching input and materials to the perceived appropriate levels of understanding. Piaget's work will be referred to at various points in later chapters, so it is helpful to review briefly his central ideas here. It must be remembered, though, that these largely deal with just one aspect of development (cognition) and they constitute only one framework within that field.

Piaget concentrated on the microprocesses of children's thinking and did not take account of macro-sociological influences. However, he did view children as actively trying to make sense of the world, not simply responding to it as many of his contemporaries contended (Smith and Cowie 1991; Meadows 1993). He was most interested in children's understanding of the physical world, although he did attend to some elements of moral and social development (Piaget 1959). He identified three main processes:

- *organisation* – the inborn capacity to co-ordinate mental operations, to classify and make sense of the world
- *assimilation* – relating new information to existing patterns of understanding
- *accommodation* – altering old structures of thinking in response to challenging or contradictory information.

Piaget concluded that the development of thinking structures was characterised by periods of stability (stages) in which a child's capacity to understand was inherently limited compared with later stages. He also saw these stages as being broadly universal in nature and timing, i.e.

there was a natural unfolding of ability common to nearly all children. Although there were a number of subdivisions, the main stages he identified were:

- *sensori-motor* (up to age two) – the world is known through direct sensing and manipulation
- *pre-operational* (two to seven years) – children use language and imagery, but are not able to carry out certain logical actions related to the ordering, conservation and classification of objects. Thinking is 'egocentric' in the sense of not being able to consider physical objects from other viewpoints (e.g. what a scene looks like from a different direction)
- *concrete operational* (seven to twelve years) – children are able to use formal thinking in relation to immediate physical tasks
- *formal operational* (twelve years and over) – children are able to carry out holistic, abstract and hypothetical thinking.

Later research has shown that Piaget underestimated children's abilities, in part because he failed to take into account the social context of adult–child communication from which he derived his results. When children have been given tasks which are more relevant to them and have more careful explanations, they have been able to perform well much earlier than Piaget stated (Donaldson 1978; Cox 1980). Short (1991) concluded that children are more able to discuss seemingly abstract controversial issues than Piaget and many teachers thought possible, provided the context and language for exploring these issues make sense to children. Nevertheless, the broad sequence of logical development identified by Piaget has been corroborated, though there is much individual and cross-cultural variability in achieving the thresholds of competence (Meadows 1993).

Within psychology, the Piagetian framework has been criticised for privileging 'masculine and Western forms of reasoning' (Burman 1994: 160), individualising assessments of children's abilities and diminishing the role of emotions and irrationality in human behaviour. Indeed a few psychologists have pointed to the near absence of daily life in much developmental psychology more generally, with its focus on discrete 'bits and pieces' of a child (Skolnick 1975). By contrast, 'there is a long-standing, but minor tradition, that has been concerned with the social worlds and daily lives of children' (Morrow and Richards 1996). Certain psychologists (e.g. Garling and Valsiner 1985) have stressed the competencies which children possess more than the limitations which followers of Piaget have tended to concentrate on. These revisions and dissenting voices within psychology pale into insignificance compared with the assault from the sociological 'reconstruction of childhood' movement, for whom Piaget is the *bête noire*, symbolising all that is worst in developmental approaches to children.

The sociology of childhood

During the 1970s and 80s, a small number of sociologists were interested in childhood, though little attention was given to children themselves and the main emphasis was on analysing how adults portrayed and treated children (Dreitzel 1973; Denzin 1977; Jenks 1982). A critique developed of the way in which children had been portrayed in most of the social science literature to date as passive recipients of socialisation, i.e. they were thought simply to learn and internalise unquestioningly expectations and practices of adult society. There was a parallel complaint that research had mostly treated children as 'objects of study' to produce correlational results and inform conceptual frameworks, rather than take seriously the subjective meanings of children's viewpoints. Moreover, children were often subsumed within families or households for the purposes of statistical information gathering and analysis, or classified according to adult variables like parental occupation (Leonard 1990; Qvortrup 1991).

James and Prout (1990: 8–9) proposed a new paradigm which included the following key features:

• childhood is socially constructed, i.e. it is not 'natural', but shaped in crucial ways by the cultural and structural context
• children's social relationships and cultures are worthy of study in their own right
• children are not passive subjects of social structures and processes, but actively contribute to their own social worlds
• childhood is differentiated by factors like gender, ethnicity and class.

Qvortrup *et al.* (1994) linked the previous low status of children in sociology to the position of children in society more generally. They portrayed children as a quintessential minority group, defined by its subordinate relationship to a dominant group (adults). Their analysis indicated that children are marginalised in adult thinking and actions, resulting in major restrictions on children's access to attention, places and resources. This marginalisation is often justified by children's need for protection, but can also be paternalistic in its effects. Qvortrup (1991) emphasised the importance of seeing children as an integral, active part of society as a whole, not simply representing a preparatory stage or product of adult society. Provocatively, Oldman (1994) has outlined a neo-Marxist analysis of the relationship between children and adults as social groups. He suggests that in many respects children's activities and use of time are ordered to suit adult needs and often to generate adult employment, as in schools and nursery centres.

The contrast in perspective between the emergent sociology of childhood and its view of conventional developmental psychology is summarised in Table 1.3. It should be recognised that many child psychologists would qualify or reject the stereotypical way in which their subject has been portrayed within the sociological discourse on childhood:

Table 1.3 Sociologists' reconstruction of childhood

Traditional developmental view of children	Sociological critique
The focus is on the development of individuals as they grow older.	The focus is on children as a 'social group', with low status and power in society.
Childhood is depicted as biologically driven.	Childhood is depicted as socially created.
Childhood is seen as divided into relatively fixed universal stages.	Childhood is seen as evolving in diverse ways.
Children's thinking and behaviour are judged as part of a process leading towards adulthood.	Children's thinking, behaviour and cultures are judged and valued in their own right and on their own terms.
Children are viewed as 'deficient' in terms of adult capabilities.	Children's positive competencies are emphasised.
Young children are regarded as moulded through adult socialisation processes.	Young children are regarded as active participants in socialisation processes which are reciprocal.
Features such as age, gender, sibling status, ethnic background and social status are seen as discrete variables with consistent implications once other factors are allowed for statistically.	Features such as age, gender, sibling status, ethnic background and social status are regarded as social constructs, whose impact depends on meaning and context.

Not all sociologists reject totally the developmental framework. For example, Tesson and Youniss (1995) blended Piaget's ideas with the theoretical framework of Giddens (1987) to offer an account of the interplay between individual agency and social structure. Giddens and others have conceptualised the linkages between macro-social systems and micro-social processes in ways which seek to reconcile the constraints of institutionalised structures in society with scope for individuals to exercise freedom and create their social worlds in interaction with others (Berger and Luckmann 1971; May 1996). The processes of cognition act as vital links between children and the social order. Evolving understandings of social structures and institutions as experienced in everyday reality depend on children's organisation of notions like intention and causality to which Piaget gave close attention. Moreover, both developmental perspectives and Giddens's social analysis emphasise openness to change and the existence of different potentials, rather than a necessarily imposed outcome of socialisation. It seems that some of the specific processes and the broad progression in understanding identified by Piaget remain relevant to an understanding of children's conceptions of social phenomena and their own social actions (Furnham and Gunter 1989; Short 1991), but experience and exposure are vital modifiers of cognitive capacities which cannot be ascribed neatly to specific age bands.

A phase of theoretical analysis in the sociology of childhood has now led on to a growing number of mainly qualitative studies, which aim to reveal and analyse the concerns, interests and priorities of children themselves (such as Mayall 1994a). This has been accompanied by a review of ethical and methodological issues in research (Alderson 1995; Morrow and Richards 1996; Hood *et al*. 1996a). Two competing principles need to be reconciled when selecting techniques which enable research to be carried out with rather than on children:

- making allowances for differences between adults and children
- respecting children's competencies and views.

It can be helpful and appropriate to make use of settings and methods of communication favoured by children (like drawing and games) in order to facilitate understanding (Moore 1986; Garbarino and Stott 1992; Hill *et al*. 1996a). Equally it is important to recognise children's communicative abilities and dignity, so that often the same techniques can be suitable for children as for adults. According to Shaw (1996), recent qualitative research adapted to children's perspectives has highlighted their perceptiveness and cultural richness, by contrast with the limitation of their understandings, ability to co-ordinate different ideas and see others' viewpoints which crude application of Piaget's ideas had previously suggested.

In these ways sociologists and others are currently exploring how adults and children, separately and together, create the experiences and relationships which constitute differing forms of childhood in Britain today. The diversity of ways in which childhood is constructed is also illuminated by historical and cross-cultural comparisons.

Historical and cultural constructions of childhood

The nature of children's experiences is greatly affected by the economy and culture in which they grow up. Onto the universal biological canvas of development, from helpless neonate to sexually mature adult, a huge diversity of tableaux have been painted by the many social groups of humankind. The wandering lifestyle of young Masai cowherds seems to bear little resemblance to the regulated schooling of their age-mates in Britain, though both are learning to assume the adult roles expected of them in their respective societies. Child-rearing practices like swaddling and wet-nursing which were once commonplace and seen as beneficial to children are now regarded as odd, if not cruel. Thus it is important to recognise and understand the ways in which childhood is and has been socially constructed, i.e. the processes whereby 'the immaturity of children is conceived and articulated in particular societies into culturally specific sets of ideas and philosophies, attitudes and practices' (James and Prout 1990: 1). Each society has its own:

- ways of defining and treating the boundaries between childhood and adulthood

- expectations about adult-child relations, children's behaviour and appearance
- subdivisions of childhood
- rites and rituals associated with transitions within and out of childhood.

Historical and cross-cultural comparisons show that conceptualisations and categories with respect to children are not inevitable or impermeable, and indicate as much about society and adults as they do about children. Some believe that the diversity of childhoods in different cultures makes impossible the application of universal prescriptions about expected standards for children's welfare (as does the UN Convention). Others think these can be adapted flexibly so that all children can be seen as having common rights (Goonesekere 1994; Burman 1996).

Historical change or continuity?

Few authors have been both lauded and pilloried in such equal measure as Phillipe Ariès, for his book *Centuries of Childhood* (published first in 1960). Now questioned for its historical accuracy and application to the past of present-day assumptions, Ariès's book was seminal in drawing academic interest to the study of 'childhood' and heightening awareness that 'childhood' itself was a category, whose meaning may not necessarily stay the same or even exist over time.

Ariès posited that medieval society did not have an idea of 'childhood'. While people in medieval society may well have had affection for children, a particular awareness that children were different from adults was said to be lacking. As soon as they could live without the constant attention of their mothers, nannies or cradle rockers (1973: 124), children mixed freely in adult society, taking part in the same activities and wearing similar clothes. According to Ariès, the *sentiment* of childhood emerged in the Renaissance and particularly the Reformation, associated with childish innocence and weakness, and the corresponding need to discipline children. Ariès's account continued until the modern day, describing how 'childhood' became further differentiated from 'adulthood' by the removal of children from the labour market into compulsory education (which led to today's emphasis on age groupings), and the removal of children from public life into the private realm of the family. Ennew (1994) elaborated the notion that children's use of time has become increasingly specialised, commercialised and subject to adult regulation.

Numerous criticisms have been made about Ariès's work. For example, his conclusions about medieval society were primarily based on studying paintings, which do not necessarily represent how society actually thought about children. He used the diary of the Dauphin's doctor, yet the future King Louis XIII was hardly representative of most children at the time. Ariès did not satisfactorily explain why changes happened nor relate them to other historical themes. His chronology was vague and inconsistent (Pollock 1983; Veerman 1992; Cunningham 1995).

One of the strongest criticisms against Ariès's work is his 'present-minded' point of view (Wilson 1980): that is, what medieval society lacked was not necessarily a concept of childhood, but our modern concept of childhood (Pollock 1983; Archard 1993). Alternative social histories have now been written, although it is important to note that they are mostly histories of Western childhood or even more particularised societies.

Stone (1977) charted a change from exploitative and authoritarian parent–child relationships in the English past to affectionate and nurturing ones today, fuelled by 'affective individualism' (p. 4). He claimed that in the sixteenth century, relations were formal and adults used brutality to enforce obedience. Children were utterly subjected to their fathers, and this subordination worsened from 1550 to 1800 with the spread of state and Protestant power. Stone believed that a general easing of political tensions led to more affectionate and permissive parenting in the period from the Restoration to the French Revolution – a later period than the seventeenth century, as Ariès had claimed. Subsequent changes in parent–child relationships have not been uniform nor linear. So, for example, the idea of the innate sinfulness of children was revived in the Victorian period, when a return to more authoritarian relationships reversed the previous permissive trend. Stone was careful to qualify these general trends by recognising class or status differences.

Hendrick (1990) delineated different models of the child that emerged from the 1800s on. He described particular types of child or aspects of childhood which were emphasised in public attention at different times. Images of the 'romantic child' of innocence inspired by Rousseau conflicted with the Evangelical pessimism about children's original sin. By the mid-1880s, the 'sinful child' representation had won. The industrial revolution created the 'factory child', who then had to be saved from exploitation. The mid-nineteenth century saw the construction of the 'delinquent child', and the reformatory and industrial schools of the time borrowed some of the Romantic imagery for their work. During this time, the idea of a child as dependent gained force. 'Childhood' and 'adulthood' became defining opposites. Compulsory education in the late nineteenth century created the 'school child', and hence created a 'truly *national* childhood' (p. 46). This finally removed children from adult society. The 'psycho-medical child' of the 1880s emerged from concern about schoolchildren's mental and physical health. The related child-saving movement created the 'welfare child'. According to Hendrick, by 1918 'childhood' was largely defined in relation to medicine, psychology and welfare.

Pollock (1983) was highly critical of most social histories of 'childhood', including those of Ariès and Stone, for three main reasons. The sources used were suspect and did not justify such dramatic generalisations; problems inherent to the sources were not considered; and some of the data used and conclusions reached were plainly inaccurate.

Pollock herself concentrated on adults' diaries and autobiographies to consider parent–child relations (reliance on such sources itself criticised by Cunningham 1995). In the sixteenth century, she found that a concept of childhood did exist, in that children were seen as different from adults and required certain protections. Pollock revealed examples of parents enjoying the company of their children at least from the sixteenth century onwards. According to her sources, the majority of children were not subjected to brutality and the parent–child relationship was often more informal than other histories had stated. Pollock emphasised the continuity of parent–child relationships, rather than change. So too did Mount (1982), who stressed the resilience of family loyalties in the face of religious and state authority.

Shahar (1992) also concentrated on continuity. Where other writers had associated conceptions of childhood innocence with Rousseau in the eighteenth century and ideas of children ruled by their drives with Freud in the late nineteenth century, she discovered instances of both in medieval Christian scriptural texts. Some medieval writers characterised childhood as a basis for adulthood and divided it into distinct stages, just like many modern psychologists. Thus many of the ways in which children are viewed today were already present in medieval society. There has probably always been a tendency to hold polarised images of children (and hence adults) as either inherently sinful, needing constraint or as well-meaning and innocent, requiring nurturance. These are what Jencks (1996) called the Dionysian and Appollonian perceptions of children. They correspond with the classification of cultures by Benedict (1935) into predominantly frenzied or harmonious, though that dichotomy is now seen as a crude oversimplification. The potential for manifestations of either are always present, as the James Bulger case illustrated, with children as both murderers and victim (Chapter 9). Ideals of childhood which portray it as a happy and innocent period serve to exclude those who are unhappy or abused, as well as those who are abusers (Ennew 1986).

Childhood in any historical period is a key locus for defining expectations related to gender. In the nineteenth century there were parallels and connections between the exclusion of children from the adult world of work and women's experience of discrimination with regard to involvement in high status and powerful positions in public life (Shorter 1976; Oakley 1994). Since then, most young children have spent far more time with women than with men. Families and networks are vital filters for values concerned with what is deemed to be appropriate masculine or feminine behaviour, as with regard to aggression and sexuality (Boushel 1994).

Cross-cultural comparisons of childhood

Comparisons between different cultural traditions indicate that certain functions and distinctions are near-universal but precise conceptions of childhood nevertheless vary in fundamental ways. For instance, Mead (1962) concluded that all societies have contrasting expectations for males and females, but any particular personal characteristic, economic function or social activity may be seen as 'feminine' in one culture and 'masculine' in another. Each culture tends to take for granted its own pattern of, say, weaning or toilet training, but the timing and nature of these practices differ widely (Barry and Paxson 1971).

Care of young children is frequently shared informally amongst a wide set of people, often female kinfolk (Smith 1980; Dahlberg 1981). It has been claimed that this is associated with less intense affection and specific loyalties, but assessments in communities in Africa and the Pacific suggest that widely shared care can be accompanied by close attachments and co-operation, both in infancy and later (Freeman 1983; Rashid 1996). There may, however, be more emphasis than in the West on family identity rather than individual personality (MBise 1990). In parts of West Africa it has been common to foster children with relatives from five years onwards. This is not seen as a parental rejection, but as a positive service to the child, who gains wider social links and specific skills, whilst retaining the relationship with parents (Goody 1970). On the other hand, in many cultures the idea of fostering or adoption *outside* the kin network is quite alien (van Loon 1990; Dickens and Watts 1996).

It has been common for children aged six to ten to look after younger children in small playgroups in places as diverse as parts of Africa, Nepal and Polynesia (Konner 1975; Weisner 1987). In some cultures, children have traditionally spent much time in activities largely separate from adults, with a great deal of autonomy (Mead 1942). Sometimes this involves considerable leisure, but often children also carry out important domestic tasks (like fetching water or collecting fuel). In many hunter-gatherer and farming communities, there is no social and spatial divide between home and work, as there tends to be in industrialised societies. Hence from an early age children are exposed to and involved in economic activities, resulting in detailed knowledge of the local environment and its resources (Katz 1993). In these ways children may establish a wide range of relationships which cut across age groups and integrate children with adult activities. In some societies there has been a gradual assumption of adult responsibilities; in others, young people have been congregated in age-sets, sometimes living in separate households, before making a sharp ritualised accession to adult status.

Patterns of parent–child relationships often appear to parallel wider political structures. For example, Ganda children are expected to show unquestioning obedience towards their fathers, whom they fear and respect, just as adults traditionally defer to their absolute ruler (Jahoda 1982). However, it is now recognised that characterisation of whole cultures in terms of single personality or relationship types is oversimple and ignores the scope for variation and modification within cultures.

Britain has always had a diversity of cultural influences, but the last 50 years have witnessed a significant increase in the proportion of the population with non-European heritages, particularly from India, Pakistan, the Caribbean, Hong Kong/China and Bangladesh. The children grow up legally British and in some ways culturally too, but with distinctive religious and cultural influences. These present multiple options for identification and sometimes segmented social lives (Cooper 1995). The children also encounter 'institutional racism' and ethnocentrism, through stereotyping, negative portrayals and discounting of the past and present contributions of non-white and non-European traditions (Gambe *et al.* 1992; Katz 1996a). Thus the experiences of British children of ethnic minority backgrounds reflect their responses not only to family customs and attitudes, but to mainstream assumptions and marginalisation, whilst white youth, too, are often challenged by exposure to different cultural practices and to racist and anti-racist ideas (Katz 1996b).

Conclusions

Each society and social group has devised its own distinct way of managing the differences, similarities and continuities between childhood and adulthood. Prevailing ideas affect how individuals manage the evolution from child to adult and also how children as a social group are treated collectively. At present, legal and social attitudes to children on the one hand and academic theorising on the other are both being challenged by questioning and debate about assumptions concerning the nature of children and childhood. It is claimed that the abilities of children have been underestimated and their views undervalued.

Law and policy attempt to strike a balance between perceived opposite characteristics of children. On the one hand, they are dependent and vulnerable; on the other hand, they are people with capacities and viewpoints to be respected. The former considerations require adults to act on behalf of children and that the latter recognise children's rights to act for themselves. The UN Convention on the Rights of the Child and recent UK legislation emphasise the responsibilities which adults have to protect children and to further their best interests, yet also accord rights to children to have their say in decisions and actions which concern them.

To some extent all societies encompass a gradual or graduated shift from protection to autonomy as children grow older, but the nature of this progression is socially constructed in myriad ways. In each case, notions of childhood, adulthood and hence the 'transition to adulthood' are inextricably connected. Conventionally the justification for separate and distinct treatment of children in terms of employment, education and social life has been dependency. Shamgar-Handelman stated that 'childhood, whatever form it may take in any given society, always determines children's dependency on adults for supplying their needs and protecting their interests' (1994: 251). One could argue, however, that it is power which is the main differentiating factor between children and adults. Children have little formal control of space and time, decisions and resources. Adults constrain children's choices ostensibly in the interests of children, but this can too readily become a rationalisation for marginalising children for the convenience of adults.

At present, 'childhood' least of all belongs to children. The study of 'childhood' remains largely a study of adults' attitudes to and practices with children (Shamgar-Handelman 1994). The growing view that children are social actors, however, has the potential to change this. Children are not merely 'human becomings' (Qvortrup 1994: 4), and they have particular views about their own status. Such thinking is fundamental to the idea that children are people in their own right and thus should be recognised as having rights. This is the specific topic to be explored in the next chapter.

Suggestions for further reading

Burman, E. (1994) *Deconstructing Developmental Psychology*, London: Routledge.

Cunningham, H. (1995) *Children and Childhood in Western Society since 1500*, Harlow, Essex: Longman.

Mayall, B. (ed.) (1994) *Children's Childhoods*, London: Falmer Press.

Nestmann, F. and Hurrelmann, K. (eds.) (1994) *Social Networks and Social Support in Childhood*, Berlin: De Gruyter.

Qvortrup, J., Bardy, M., Sgritta, G. and Wintersberger, H. (eds.) (1994) *Childhood Matters*, Aldershot: Avebury.

Woodhead, M., Light, P. and Carr, R. (eds.) (1991) *Growing up in a Changing Society*, London: Routledge.

CHAPTER 2

Children's rights

Introduction: the power of children's rights

Rights is the language of equality. Rights claims are about dignity, respect, liberty, opportunity, access to and protection from the law, and participation in one's own fate.   (McGillivray 1994: 252)

Rights, and the related concept of citizenship, constitute one of the most powerful discourses in today's world. The discourse has been used to promote widespread changes in recent British social policy. It has had a powerful effect in North America, where a wealth of anti-discrimination legislation and change has been forwarded under its mantle, for such groups as African-Americans, women, and people with disabilities. As Freeman wrote, rights are particularly valuable 'moral coinage' (1983: 32) for those without other means of power.

In the past decades, the moral coinage of rights has been applied to children, typically by adults on children's behalf. From early origins in the protectionist child-saving movement of the nineteenth century to the children's liberationists in the 1970s, conceptualisations of children's rights, and strategies to promote them, have moved on apace. One of the most powerful tools in the 1990s has been the United Nations (UN) Convention on the Rights of the Child, as countries that ratify the Convention commit themselves to operationalising its articles. The Convention, however, is not without its critics, and has its own strengths and weaknesses.

Definitions of children's rights, and debates around them, are reliant on two concepts – of 'childhood' and of 'rights' – and how these two are combined. The previous chapter explored the concept of 'childhood'. Below, the concept of rights is explored and then arguments in favour of children's rights are considered. The history of the international children's rights movement is briefly covered, and a more intensive analysis of the UN Convention is undertaken. Finally, the chapter concludes with reflections on the concepts of 'childhood' and full citizenship for children.

What is a right?

The debate on 'rights' has a long history in the Western world. Its foundations can be traced back at least as far as discussions of natural law amongst Greek and Roman Stoics. These discussions were revived, added to and modified in the Enlightenment by such philosophers as Locke and Thomas Paine. These philosophers argued for the links between natural rights, individualism and liberty; arguments taken up politically, for example, in the United States' Declaration of Independence (1776):

We hold these truths to be self-evident, that all men were created equal, that they are endowed by their Creator with certain unalienable Rights, that among them are Life, Liberty and the pursuit of happiness.

Rights' basis in nature, and their divine creation, made them fundamental and universal – and thus overriding of other values. With this philosophical heritage, the discourse of rights is rhetorically and ideologically powerful.

The idea of natural rights has faced increasing criticism over time, as more and more philosophers pointed out that rights are socially or legally constructed rather than natural or God-given (see Jones 1994). Some would say that rights are inextricably linked to a particular society, and thus the idea that rights can be universalised across societies is incorrect. For those who believe certain rights are universal, the concept of human rights has largely replaced that of natural rights, thus avoiding the theological underpinnings of most natural rights theories. Such philosophers rely on a concept of basic human needs (sometimes called the 'interest theory' of rights), to provide the basis for human rights (MacCormick 1982; Freeden 1991; Eekelaar 1992). These needs are said to be irrefutable:

Certain needs are so fundamental, it may be argued, that they should be treated as a social right and society should accept a duty to provide them to all citizens.
(Charles and Webb 1986: 71)

Such justifications relate to the literature on needs, which is addressed in the following chapter. (For discussions of such debates, see Cranston 1967; Melden 1970; Freeden 1991.)

Many hierarchies and distinctions have been made in relation to rights. A useful distinction is made between legal and moral rights. Legal rights are those set out in law, which are thus enforceable. Moral rights are not established in law, but are put forward as what ought to be. T. H. Marshall's foundational work (1949) on citizenship and rights posited three types of rights: civil, political and social. Civil rights (such as personal liberty or freedom of speech) are defined as those necessary for individual freedom. Political rights involve participation in the exercise of political power. The bundle of social rights range from ensuring a 'modicum of economic welfare and security to the right to share to the full in the social heritage' (1963: 74).

Considerable thought has been put into the relations between claims, duties and rights:

> A right is a legal capacity in one person to control or limit or require an act of another. The right resides with the first person, the duty with the second. Rights are about obligation, an obligation fixed in law or fought for on moral and legal grounds, a duty placed on someone other than the rights-holder. Rights establish and support relationships.   (McGillivray 1994: 254)[1]

Whether someone can have a right without someone else having a corresponding duty has been the subject of much debate (see Dworkin 1978; MacCormick 1982; Olsen 1992). In relation to some rights, it is relatively easy to identify who is the duty-holder and what the duty is. For example, a child may have a right to its parent's care and supervision. The child has the right; the parent has the duty; and the duty is for care and supervision. In relation to other rights, identifying the duty and duty-holder can be more difficult. For example, a child may have a right to an adequate standard of living. But who has the duty to provide the adequate standard of living? What would this duty entail? In the UK, primary responsibility for children's living standard lies with parents. But if parents are unable to meet this duty, the state has secondary responsibility. Who is the 'state'? The duty no longer is clearly on individuals, but becomes a wider collective responsibility. What if the state is unable to fulfil its responsibility? Do other states have a responsibility? At this point, the duty on others internationally becomes even more diffuse. Does the child still have the right to an adequate standard of living, if no one individual or institution is an identifiable duty-holder? Beyond the question of who the duty-holder is, the scenario also raises the question of specifying the duty. What if, even with all the international resources expended, children's poverty could not be eliminated? What would the duty then be? Such questions imply a requirement for rights that they be fulfillable. Such a requirement seems over-restrictive for moral rights, although it certainly reflects difficulties for the practical implementation of legal rights.

Rights and duties are further intertwined with the concept of citizenship: 'Citizenship is a matter of the rights and duties attendant upon membership of a specified community' (Rees 1995: 313). T. H. Marshall stated that only full members of a community have the status of citizenship (1963). People can have rights and duties in a particular community without being citizens of it (for example, refugees, migrant workers and, arguably, children). But, by Marshall's statements, such people are not considered full members of the community and usually have more restricted rights and duties (for example, limits on political rights or access to state support). They are not fully included.

Such statements beg the question of what constitutes a 'community'. In citizenship terms, 'community' in practice is usually connected with the nation state and its geographical space. 'Community' also has more social connotations, as a set of social relations and institutions with a network of obligations and privileges that proceeds from social ties (see communitarian theory on citizenship, for example, Sandel 1982; Avineri and de-Shalit 1992). Taylor (1989) argued that belonging to a community is not necessarily beneficial; communities can enforce role expectations and disenfranchise those without power. Citizenship not only defines inclusion, but also exclusion of particular groups and categories of individuals. Taylor challenged the traditional philosophical alignments between rights, liberty, equality and individuality. He advocated recognising differences and discrimination rather than assuming equality, citing the reality faced by women and people from minority groups. Liberal theory's preoccupation with liberty and privacy, for example, can ignore the abuse of women in the 'privacy' of their homes. Taylor suggested considering groups' claims rather than only those of individuals. 'Citizenship' is not neutral nor unchangeable. Struggle characterises both citizenship and rights, which can be forwarded or reversed (see also Turner 1986, 1990). Somers went a step further than Taylor in her description of struggle. Reconsidering Marshall's argument, she declared that rights are 'free-floating cultural and institutional resources that must be appropriated' (1994: 79) instead of being attached to any one social category or persons (including citizens). Rights can be revolutionary assets.

The connection between citizenship and duties is not greatly explored by T. H. Marshall. In his three pages on the subject, he said that the state not only had duties towards its citizens, but the citizen also had duties. These were fulfilled in five ways: payment of taxes and social insurance; education; military service; undertaking paid work with dedication; and vague duties about civic responsibility. The key was a 'lively sense of responsibility to the welfare of the community' (117), rather than a checklist of duties. With the renaissance of 'citizenship' in the 1980s and 1990s, the compulsory nature of citizens' duties and responsibilities has been far more emphasised. The 'active' citizen has now increasingly become the only recognised citizen in government policy: so that those who do not pay taxes, undertake paid work or take on civic responsibility risk being excluded from citizenship. Individual responsibility is stressed, freeing the family from welfare dependency and voluntary contribution to the community (see Deakin 1991).

Whether 'rights' and 'citizenship' are irretrievably and inevitably ethnocentric is unresolved. Citizenship is a Western concept and perhaps, at present, particularly one used in the UK and in the European Union. Its traditional reliance on rights, individuality and liberty can be at odds with cultures based on community and interdependence. Whether modern theorists can redefine rights and citizenship, both to keep their essence and encapsulate other cultural frames, is debatable. But there is little doubt that both 'rights' and 'citizenship' are powerful rhetorical tools, and that the concept of rights is powerful not only on a national, but international, stage.

What are children's rights?

Philosophical perspectives

In the past, most philosophers have asserted that children had either no or limited rights. Hobbes, for example, posited that children have no natural rights and are under the absolute subjection of their parents. In contrast, Locke wrote that children do have natural rights but only adults are fully rational. Thus parents have authority over children and the corresponding responsibility to educate children into reason. Mill definitely excluded children from liberty, as not being fully rational nor cultivated, but assented that parents have a responsibility to protect children. (For discussion of these and other philosophers, see Freeman 1983 and Archard 1993.) These philosophers accorded children rights (for example, to education) but were denying children rights of agency or liberty, which the philosophers considered the fundamental rights.

All three philosophers mentioned above raised the classic argument against children's rights to agency or liberty: children lack rationality. Generally, children are seen as irrational because they either lack the competence to be rational, or lack the experience or understanding to be so. Retorts to such views have either focused on children's actual competence and ability to be rational, or challenged rationality as a criterion. Psychological research demonstrates that older children at least typically show very similar competence in rational thinking to that of adults (Freeman 1983; Reppucci and Crosby 1993). Research on street children shows their capability at very young ages to survive on the street (Ennew 1995). The moral relevance of rationality has also been questioned. Rationality can be in the eyes of the beholder, and what can seem rational to one person can seem irrational to another. Adults, whatever their capacity to act rationally, do not always apply instrumental rationality consistently to their day-to-day decisions or even larger policy decisions, so why should rationality be the criterion for denying children rights but not adults? Even if all people were to act on rational judgements, other criteria might also be desirable – such as empathy with others, the eventual outcome or democratic decisions.

Purdy (1992 and 1994), for one, made a strong rejoinder to these attacks on rationality. She argued that most children and most adults do have sufficiently large differences in their instrumental reasoning to justify treating them differently. Rationality is important, she claimed, because 'A society where people routinely do that [behave intelligently and morally] clearly works better and is more enjoyable to live in than one where they do not' (1994: 229). She recognised that some adults do act imprudently, with tragic results, but the problem would only be compounded if adult rights were extended to children, '. . . the world is a mess now, largely because of adults' inadequacies in these respects. Adding many actors to the scene who suffer from even more extreme deficiencies will make it still more difficult . . .' (1994: 229). Purdy was not arguing that children should have no rights, but they should not have equal rights to adults. All children should have welfare rights or protection rights, such as the right to survival and to an adequate standard of living; in fact, they should have more welfare rights than adults (for example, the right to education).

An additional query is raised by writers such as Phillips (1996) and Harding (1996b). If children are to have rights, what are their corresponding responsibilities? Such writers raise concerns that children would be inappropriately responsible for themselves or their actions, worrying that freedom would become an euphemism for neglect. Again, such concerns seem most alarmed about giving children the same rights of agency or liberty as adults, and not about welfare rights or protection rights.

Why should children have welfare rights? Just as Locke and Mill thought parents had a responsibility to protect children and educate them into reason, modern-day writers such as Purdy and Freeman believe that children must be initially protected so that they can think and act rationally in due course. Freeman (1983) explicitly stated the goal of children's rights ultimately as the child's rational independence. Such justifications mirror the concept of 'childhood' as a preparation or transition stage. (The situation of a child with a terminal illness, who is never going to live to 'adulthood', seems to be ignored. A wider justification than a child's eventual rational independence is needed, unless such children are to be denied protective rights.) A child's liberty may be infringed in the name of paternalism, defined as 'interference with a person's liberty of action . . . by reasons, referring exclusively to the welfare, good, happiness, needs, interests or values of the person being coerced' (Dworkin, quoted in Freeman 1983: 52). Freeman recognised that such paternalistic protection can deny children the opportunity to develop the very competence and experience necessary for rational independence. For this reason, he advocated that children should gradually gain rights of agency as they gain in competence.

Except for the children's liberationists discussed below, the idea that children have rights, but not the same rights as adults, represents the majority view amongst today's children's rights proponents. Children's rights to participation and agency must be balanced by regard to their best interests. First and foremost, adults have a duty to protect children's welfare.

History of the children's rights movement

Freeman (1983) traced the origins of the UK movement for children's rights back to the middle of the nineteenth century, which was also the time of the 'child-saving movement' and the growth of compulsory education for children. Children were largely seen as objects of intervention rather than legal subjects, where protection was strongly framed by paternalism (see also Hill, Murray and Rankin 1991). The flip side to the protection of children was the perception of them as a 'problem population' (Freeman 1983: 18), which can be directly linked to the development of juvenile justice systems at a similar time.

On an international stage, manifestos of children's rights were being developed by children's rights proponents and taken on by international bodies. Aghast at the plight of children in Europe as a result of World War I, Eglantyne Jebb established the Save the Children Fund in 1919: 'It is our children who pay the highest price for our shortsighted economic policies, our political blunders, our wars' (quoted in Hammarberg 1990: 98). By 1923, the Save the Children Fund was an international presence and had drafted the Declaration on the Rights of the Child. In 1924, the League of Nations adopted the Declaration (called the Geneva Declaration). The Declaration places a high value on children: in its preamble, the Declaration states 'mankind owes the best it has to give'. The Declaration focuses mainly on children's material needs in its five principles. In 1948, the United Nations (UN) accepted a revised text of the Geneva Declaration, with two additional clauses on non-discrimination and respect for the family. The 1959 UN Declaration was a yet further expanded version, which for the first time included civil rights for children (e.g. rights to name and nationality) as well as protective rights. The 1959 Declaration introduced, on an international stage, the now ubiquitous phrase 'the best interests of the child' as the paramount consideration. Other Declarations – such as the Universal Declaration of Human Rights (1948) and the International Covenant on Economic, Social and Cultural Rights (1966) – also contain specific provisions to protect children. As Declarations, these statements had no mechanisms for enforcement and thus only had moral force.

In the 1970s, a children's liberation movement gathered momentum, promoting equal rights for children. Children should have exactly the same rights as adults (e.g. to work, to vote, to have lawful sexual relationships) and not just strengthened ones based on their vulnerability. One of its leading proponents declared: 'I urge the law grant and guarantee to the young the freedom that it now grants to adults to make certain kinds of choices, do certain kinds of things, and accept certain kinds of responsibilities' (Holt 1974: 114). Holt and others were criticised for not recognising a child was in the process of development, with limits on his or her abilities (e.g. see Freeman 1983; Purdy 1992 and 1994). As Veerman wrote, 'It is our opinion that the unlimited rights the Kiddie Libbers want to give to children withhold from them the most essential right: *to be a child*' (1992: 397, emphasis in original).

While the liberationists' school of thought is not widely accepted today, it did dramatically widen the conception of children's rights beyond protectionism. Children today themselves assert that they should have rights of agency. As one young person from Northern Ireland stated:

We should have rights, to some extent, to go where we want, rights to take part in family decisions, rights to make our own decisions about our future, rights to live our own life and not what our parents want us to do, the right to our own opinion.   (quoted in CRDU 1994: 24)

As this quotation shows, children themselves are social actors with their own views and goals, and not just objects or problems. Such a view was incorporated in the recent international statement on children's rights, the UN Convention on the Rights of the Child.

United Nations (UN) Convention on the Rights of the Child

During the International Year of the Child (1979), the Polish government proposed a convention for children's rights. The UN General Assembly agreed, authorising the Commission on Human Rights to draft such a convention. From its beginning, the Working Party of the Commission was influenced considerably by non-governmental organisations (NGOs). To an unprecedented extent, NGOs made written and oral contributions, and the numbers participating increased every year of the drafting process. The drafting time was lengthy, as the original Polish proposal was rewritten, elaborated upon and expanded. It was not until 1989 that the UN General Assembly gave approval to the final version.

The Convention states in its preamble that children have equal value to adults, but children also need special safeguards and care. For the sake of their development, children should grow up in a 'family environment' and due account should be given to traditional and cultural values. The preamble ends by stressing the importance of international co-operation in improving living conditions for children in every country.

Three key principles are identified in the background to the Convention:

- All rights guaranteed by the Convention must be available to all children without discrimination of any kind (Article 2)
- The best interests of the child must be a primary consideration in all actions concerning children (Article 3)
- Children's views must be considered and taken into account in all matters affecting them, subject to the children's age and maturity (Article 12).

Other articles can then be divided into three areas: participation, protection and provision (p. 2).

In total, the Convention brings together 54 articles concerning civil, economic, social and cultural rights (see Appendix I for the English text of the Convention. For detailed analysis of articles, see Veerman 1992). Article 1 establishes that a 'child' under the Convention is defined by age: 'every human being below the age of eighteen years', unless a child is considered an adult legally at an earlier age (age of majority).

As of 1996, all but six countries have ratified the convention, including the UK in 1991. Signatory countries commit themselves to operationalising the articles contained within the Convention (with the exception of any reservations they make at the time of signing). They must report regularly to the UN Committee on the Rights of the Child, which is composed of experts from different countries. The Committee not only comments on and discusses with states their reports, but also visits countries to learn more and disseminate information on the Convention (Reid 1994). The UN cannot enforce the rights stated within the Convention, but the mechanism of reporting puts more pressure on signatory countries to comply than a Declaration and can be useful in international law.

The Convention introduces several new rights compared with earlier UN Declarations and Conventions. Under Article 8, the state must seek to respect, and help speedily re-establish if necessary, a child's identity (which includes a child's nationality, name and family relations). The Convention goes beyond previous international statements about the duties of adults and the state towards children, to recognise children's rights to participate in decisions that affect them. Children now not only have the right to have their views heard (Article 12), but other rights such as the freedom of association (Article 15) and the right to access appropriate information (Article 17). Article 16 recognises children's right to privacy. A range of articles gives the state responsibility to support and help reintegrate a child if the child's rights are violated, such as Article 19 when a child is abused or neglected. Articles 20 and 21 specifically address residential, adoption and foster care and Article 25 requires regular reviews of children's placements in alternative care.

Joint parenting is emphasised by Article 18, which requires states to recognise that both parents of a child have common responsibilities for the child's upbringing and development. Article 4 requires signatory states to take all appropriate measures to implement the rights in the Convention to 'the maximum extent of their available resources' and within an international co-operative framework.

Advantages of the UN Convention

Franklin hailed the UN Convention as 'undoubtedly the most significant recent policy development intended to promote and protect children's rights' (1995a: 16). The Convention is welcomed by many as having a positive ideology of the 'child': children are seen as social actors and human beings with their own rights (Hart 1991; Lansdown 1994). Reid (1994) described the Convention's radical enfranchisement:

It is radical because it enfranchises a whole new cohort of population . . . a cohort which, in its pre-adolescent childhood, is regarded at best with fond patronisation by the general public; in its adolescence and teenage ranks, it is regarded with widespread uneasiness and even fear. (p. 19)

(Despite Reid's enthusiasm, children have not actually been 'enfranchised' by the Convention, as the Convention is notably silent on the right to vote. In fact, the definition of 'child' is based on not only age, but also the age of majority. This gap will be discussed later.)

Article 4 requires the *maximum* use of available resources for states to implement the Convention, not only on a national but also international scale. Given such rights in the Convention as adequate standards of living, education and health, such a requirement could have considerable financial and policy implications. Might the Convention be so radical as to oblige signatory countries to eliminate child poverty and promote child development both in their own countries and internationally?

Cleland (1995) was impressed by the balance struck in the Convention between welfare and participation. The right to be protected, and to have best interests as a primary concern, apply to all children and young people. A child's right to participate is, however, minimally qualified by the child's age and maturity. While a child's view must be taken into consideration, it does not have to be adhered to. Thus, while a child should be involved in decisions, the child is not the final arbiter.

Veerman (1992) identified two other specific advantages of the Convention:

- It brings together under one single, binding international instrument provisions of international law pertaining to children.
- It exceeds the 1959 Declaration on the Rights of the Child. Not only are children's particular needs and rights recognised, separate from those of adults, but also general human rights are reiterated for children.

Practically, the Convention provides an alternative binding instrument for states that have so far not signed other human rights conventions, but might be persuaded to commit themselves to instituting such rights for children.

Many practical benefits are seen to derive from the Convention. Lestor (1995) believed the Convention has stimulated debates within the developed world on how to interpret and implement the Convention's rights meaningfully. As Veerman wrote, as a single document it is an 'important and easily understood advocacy tool' (1992: 184), and provides a framework for international agencies and impetus for international alliances. In the UK, the UN Convention has become the touchstone for proponents of children's rights, in part because the UK government has signed the Convention and thus bound itself to operationalise it. (Further details are discussed later in this chapter.)

Criticisms of the UN Convention

The UN Convention is not without its critics, who challenge some of the concepts of childhood and rights underlying it.

The UN Convention has been criticised for its definition of a child by age. By using an age criterion, the Convention fails to address the accusations that competency is a better criterion than age to justify distinctions between children and adults. The Convention also fails to grapple with the issue of when childhood starts – and thus the thorny issues of abortion and treatment of pregnant women. It fudges the issue by stating in the preamble that the child needs special protection 'before as well as after birth' but simply defining the child in Article 12 as 'every human being below the age of eighteen years . . .'.

Feminist critiques raise some other difficulties with the Convention (see Olsen 1992):

1 Omissions are noted in the document. For example, while the Convention addresses child military service, which mostly affects boys, it fails to mention child marriage, which mostly affects girls.
2 By being 'gender-blind', it can camouflage or even reinforce sex discrimination. For example, the Convention promotes the family as the primary setting for children to be brought up in. Feminist analysis finds that traditional family life is typically patriarchal, and can further socialise girl children into subordinate roles (Datar 1995). (On the other hand, no definition of parent nor family is given, so that non-traditional families and parents fall within the Convention's articles.)
3 The Convention ignores the actual distributions of power, in its naive assumptions about choice and consent. For example, a child's choice to state his/her views is not only subject to the child's age and maturity, but 'real choice' is subject to the power the child has in relation to the law, family etc.
4 Certain writers also worried about the possibility that the UN Convention could serve to control and constrain women. As women still tend to be the primary caretakers of children, articles in the Convention could be used to justify increased surveillance of them. While obligations are placed equally on fathers in the Convention, the Convention could be used by fathers to harass women, without fathers fulfilling their responsibilities. Intrusive questioning could be legitimated regarding women's sexual behaviour to meet the right of children to their identities, in cases where mothers do not wish the fathers to be involved – such as when rape has occurred.

Olsen declared that the Convention is not only gender-centric but also ethnocentric: 'To the extent that the Convention deals with children as unspecified, unsituated people, it tends in fact to deal with white, male, relatively privileged children' (1992: 509). For example, Ennew (1995) stated that the child in the Convention is a Northern child, which has damaging consequences for Southern children who can be excluded. Considering the lives of street children, she commented on the Convention's reinforcement of the family, which ignores children's own friendships and social networks on the street. The Convention has no specific article recognising children's place in such networks (although there is an article on freedom of association). Statements on universal rights arguably overlook particular social meanings, so that protecting children from child labour is seen as beneficial in the UK but may undermine children's position in countries such as India (see Chapter

8 for further discussion of child labour). While the preamble carefully uses the term 'family', which recognises non-nuclear family units in many cultures, the articles themselves often slip into using 'parents' (e.g. Article 9 about separation from parents).

The Convention does not create a definitive hierarchy of children's rights, although a child's best interests is used in practice to qualify a variety of other rights. It thus does not address potential conflicts between different rights. For example, children's freedom of expression is protected by Article 13. Restrictions should only be to respect the rights or reputations of others, or for national security, to protect public order, health or morals. Article 38 requires states to try and ensure children below 15 years of age do not directly take part in hostilities. Olsen (1992) pointed out a potential conflict between these articles: what if children below the age of 15 might be expressing their political views in the only way they feel is effective, by fighting in irregular or guerrilla armies?

Another potential conflict lies between the prioritisation of children's best interests in all actions concerning them, and children's right to express their views (see also the discussion above). What if asking a child's view might be deemed against a child's best interests (e.g. if a child is unaware of a parent's illness but this information is pertinent to decisions being made about where the child should live)? Marshall (1995) explored the role of discretion within this issue: who should decide what children's best interests are? There are the difficulties in defining or justifying what is in children's best interests (for discussion, see Reppucci & Crosby 1993; Eekelaar 1994; Marshall 1995b). Are best interests defined with regard to the short or long term? How does one decide between seemingly equal alternatives? On what basis does one make a decision? Does the discretion of Article 3 undermine children's agency rights in general?

Many articles in the Convention are similarly vague and qualified. When Article 4 requires states to assist internationally, it is qualified by the extent of their 'available resources'. When Article 12 requires children's views to be heard, it is qualified by decisions about their maturity and age. No guidance is given on what is meant by an 'adequate standard of living' (Article 27) or a child's 'fullest potential' (Article 29). A state could evade the requirements of the Convention, even after ratifying the Convention, by simply lowering the age of majority (as Article 1's definition of the child excludes those over this age) (Toope 1996). Certain articles are weaker than in other UN Conventions. For example, Barsh (1989) pointed out that states only have to provide 'appropriate' assistance to parents (Article 18 (2)), whereas the International Covenant on Economic, Social and Cultural Rights requires 'the widest possible protection and assistance' for families.

The creation of the UN Convention itself had some considerable flaws. Considering Article 12 (due regard to a child's views), it is contradictory that children had very little input into the construction of the

Convention itself. The Convention thus remains very much what adults think children's rights should be, not what children think. The Working Group worked by consensus. While this has some considerable advantages – such as greater likelihood of it being universally adopted by states – it also meant that certain of the articles represent the 'lowest common denominator'. So while many countries supported a ban on military service for all children, the block presented by such countries as the United States made this impossible and Article 38 only forbids military service for those under fifteen years. Some attempt was made to avoid countries 'back-tracking' on children's rights, so that Article 41 states that the Convention shall not 'affect' any provisions that provide a higher standard on children's rights. Yet states can make 'reservations' to the UN Convention, so they make no obligation to abide by certain articles. The UK, for example, made four reservations and two declarations (see Appendix).

One of the greatest weaknesses of the Convention is its lack of enforceability unless it is incorporated into national law. Unlike other countries (such as Belgium), UK ratification of International Conventions does not automatically incorporate them into the UK legal system. The UN Convention thus has no legal force in the UK. This contrasts with the European Convention on Human Rights. Any European Court decision against the government causes it considerable embarrassment, and thus the European Convention itself has arguably more impact on UK law, policy and practice. Further, the 1997 Labour Government has announced its intentions to bring the Convention into UK domestic law. The International Covenant on Civil and Political Rights has a complaints procedure, both for a state to complain about the non-compliance of another state and for individuals claiming violations (with some qualifications about recognition and admissibility). No such complaints procedure is available for the UN Convention. Reports to the UN Committee are submitted by states, and states are much more likely to emphasise their positive aspects than negative ones. The UN Committee can ask for non-government organisations to provide information, but there is no requirement for an 'independent' report.

Impact of Children's Rights on Legislation, Policy and Practice

Despite its limitations, the UN Convention has galvanised countries across the world to implement children's rights. The required report to the UN Committee has resulted in signatory states examining their legislation, policy and practice in light of children's rights and provided at least moral pressure on the countries to improve. The Convention has complemented the promotion of children's rights in many countries, if not propelled it. Following chapters will investigate change in specific arenas affecting children, but here certain legislative changes and particular institutional reforms will be briefly explored.

Many signatory countries have had a boom in new children's legislation and official documents influenced by the UN Convention. In the UK, England and Wales have their Children Act 1989, and both Northern Ireland and Scotland received new children's legislation in 1995. The Council of Europe has recently passed an European Convention on the Exercise of Children's Rights, which now awaits signing by Council members. The European Parliament has passed its European Strategy for Children (Recommendation 1286). Increasingly, reference to children's rights and the UN Convention can be seen in official and influential documents.

Legislation in the UK, however, has lacked a truly comprehensive application of children's rights. While the UK government heralded the new Children's Acts to the UN Committee as fulfilling its legislative obligations, the legislation in fact largely relates to social work services, family, and childcare proceedings and, to some extent, adoption. No similar rights have yet been fully incorporated into other legislation such as education, housing or health. The European Convention on the Exercise of Children's Rights only addresses family proceedings before a judicial authority. The discourse on children's rights is still largely unheard in areas such as local government planning and foreign policy. Some countries, even though they are signatory states, have passed new legislation seen as directly breaching articles in the UN Convention (e.g. Western Australia's 1992 juvenile sentencing legislation, described in Cleland 1995 and Rayner 1995). The UN Convention has inspired new legislation, but by no means has it ensured comprehensive regard to its articles.

Increasingly, countries are appointing an official spokesperson for children (an Ombudsperson or Children's Commissioner) as a means of promoting and protecting children's rights. The Norwegian Ombudsperson for Children was first appointed in 1981. The Norwegian Ombudsperson is a politically independent, public official funded by the state; the Ombudsperson has the official remit both to assess children's situation and to promote children's interests (through legislation, regulations, and information). Other Ombudspeople have since been officially established in countries such as Costa Rica, Spain, New Zealand and provincially in Canada, with various remits and influence. The Labour Party in the UK committed themselves in their 1992 (but not in 1997) general election manifesto to appointing an independent Children's Rights Commissioner who would work with a Minister for Children. The Minister would head a new Department, with senior status and the primary responsibility to argue children's cases within government. At a more local level, several local government authorities in the UK have appointed Children's Rights Officers. These have been particularly utilised to support young people's rights in residential care, in training residential staff, acting as an informational and support resource, and especially helping young people make a complaint. Such official positions as Ombudspeople/ Children's Commissioners, Ministers for

Children and Children's Rights Officers are institutional means to ensure children's rights are recognised, promoted and protected.

Advocacy for children has been promoted in other ways as well: children's legal shops in the Netherlands and Belgium, for example, or children's ability to access legal aid in civil cases under the Children (Scotland) Act 1995. Non-legal advocates for children have also proliferated in child protection cases, in places like the United States and England and Wales. In Tunisia, child protection delegates have been appointed in all 23 governorates. In Brazil, nearly 5000 municipalities now have Children's Rights Councils (UNICEF 1996). Various initiatives have been developed to encourage children's own participation in political and policy decisions, such as Youth Strategies that feed into certain Scottish local governments' decision-making (Children in Scotland 1995), the Youth Forum set up by Glasgow Council (*The Scotsman* 6.11.96) or the proposed International Children's Parliament in Edinburgh (Colin 1996). Munich has set up 'children's advisors' to its mayor. Slovenia has a children's parliament where child representatives question high-ranking Ministers annually, although this parliament has no power over budgets or policy-making (Pavlovic 1996). Street children in India undertook a poster campaign and collected 950 usable responses as a basis for a government report. Denmark's National Council on Children's Rights obtains children's views through direct consultation with children, affiliated school classes and one day-care institution, a further network of children's groups across the country, and a free telephone service where children can record their views and identify issues (Cohen and Hagen 1997). Despite this heartening proliferation of institutionalised means to promote children's rights and particularly their participation, the risk of tokenism remains. Hart noted the difficulty of turning the rhetoric of participation rights into reality: 'Regrettably, while children's and youths' participation does occur in different degrees around the world, it is often exploitative or frivolous' (1992: 4).

To conceptualise participation types, Hart developed an eight-step ladder of participation (see Figure 2.1). The bottom three steps – manipulation, decoration and tokenism – are non-participative. He labelled the top five steps as increasingly participative: assigned but informed; consulted and informed; adult-initiated, shared decisions with children; child-initiated and directed; child-initiated, shared decisions with adults (1992: 9). Hart clearly stated at the beginning of his 1992 booklet that he would concentrate on children's participation in the public domain, but had insightful comments about children's participation in family life as well. Ultimately, Hart saw families as the primary setting for most children to develop their social responsibilities and competency to participate. He recognised that promoting children's rights without considering their families can be counterproductive (for those children with families).

Taking children's rights to participate seriously can be difficult to operationalise, both in the public and private domains, because children's

Figure 2.1 Hart's 'Ladder of Participation'

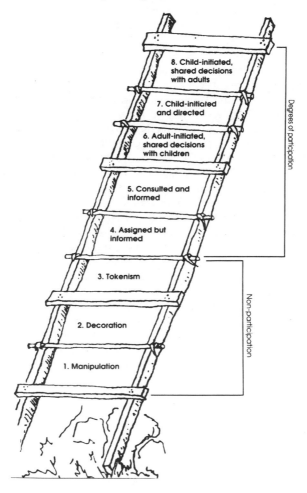

Source: Hart, R. A. (1992)

participation can threaten adult hegemony and established practice. Indeed, the government had threatened a review of the Children Act 1989, claiming that some local authorities were misinterpreting the Act by promoting children's views over those of their parents (Valios 1997). Yet the importance of children's participation is high. As one young woman exclaimed:

I never get the chance to say what I feel. They [professionals/ parents] always make up their minds before asking me. And that really bugs me, because I feel if you don't say what's on your mind, you're not human.

(quoted in Tisdall 1990: 127)

Clearly to this young person, the right to have her views heard is fundamental to valuing her as a person.

Concluding thoughts: Children as citizens?

As has been discussed above, participation, rights and citizenship are connected in the Western world with human dignity and full inclusion in a community. To what extent are young people respected and included?

Qvortrup, for one, was critical that the UN Convention does not promote children's participation through political rights:

While participation – as well as protection and provision – are foreseen in the new UN Convention on the Rights of the Child, it is also specifically said that children should not have political rights, which according to Marshall's classical definition . . . is a precondition for being a citizen. Enhancing rights in specific areas in terms of participation, provision and protection may be seen as progress, but at the same time the distance to adulthood and its 'natural' sovereignty is kept.   (1994: 19)

Certain political theorists, in particular, would disagree with T. H. Marshall and state that political rights are not just part of citizenship, but its core (Frazer 1996).

If Lister's (1990a) analysis of citizenship for women is taken, children are also excluded. According to Lister, economic participation is the central plank of citizenship, from which women have been traditionally excluded. Lister wrote of the devaluation of women's unpaid work as carers. Similarly, children's unpaid work at home (sometimes as carers themselves) or at school is not given full economic status. She elaborated on the meaning for women of financial dependence on men: lack of control; lack of rights to income; and sense of obligation towards the financial provider and on what items money can be spent. Without financial independence, Lister asserted, women do not experience full citizenship. The UN Convention puts children in a similar position of financial dependence. Article 26 states children's right to social security, but this is mediated through their carers. Just as women are traditionally excluded from economic citizenship, so are children. Lister went beyond noting that women's rights are not respected (and thus denied citizenship), to questioning the very meaning of citizenship (for example, its basis in an abstract set of rights). Should the citizenship concept be similarly challenged for children?

In another publication (1990b), Lister did not have a problem with children's dependency, because children had a restricted form of citizenship:

Although they are members of the community, children are not full citizens in the sense of political and legal rights which pertain to citizenship; the social rights of citizenship come to them indirectly through the adults responsible for their care.   (62)

To extend full citizenship to children could cancel today's social construction of childhood. This construction, fundamentally based on the dependency of children on adults (see Chapter 1), could be fatally undermined if children had extensively more control over their lives. Changes within the boundaries of children's rights and obligations can be meaningful to all those concerned with childhood, including children. But these modifications, wrote Shamgar-Handelman (1994), do not change the nature of 'childhood' fundamentally. Can today's concept of childhood exist if children were considered citizens?

Political and social exclusion for children are strongly justified by many children's rights proponents because of the need to balance protection and participation. Indeed, these justifications have considerable merit and evidence for them. What is being asked here, though, is whether the concepts of 'childhood' and 'citizenship' are compatible. This question depends just as much on how 'citizenship' is defined as it does on childhood's definition. Certainly, a definition of 'citizenship' could be made that would definitely include children. The idea of social citizenship, for example, might be widely accepted for children, recognising as it does their rights to protection and provision. But would such a definition of 'citizenship' retain the basic building blocks of the concept? Whether the concepts of 'childhood' and 'citizenship' can remain definitionally intact but conceptually paired will be pursued in later chapters.

Note

1 McGillivray (1994) previously made clear that rights 'lie beyond law' (252), and are not only a 'legal' concept.

Suggestions for further reading

Franklin, B. (ed.) (1995) *The Handbook of Children's Rights: Comparative Policy and Practice*, London: Routledge.

Freeman, M. D. A. (1983) *The Rights and Wrongs of Children*, London: Frances Pinter Publishers.

Marshall, T. H. (1963) 'Citizenship and Social Class' in *Sociology at the Crossroads and Other Essays*, London: Heinemann, pp. 67–127.

Purdy, L. (1992) *In Their Best Interest? The Case against Equal Rights for Children*, Ithaca and London: Cornell University Press.

UNICEF Children's Rights Web site: http://www.unicef.org/crc/

UN Convention on the Rights of the Child (see Appendix p. 311).

CHAPTER 3

Children's needs

Introduction

Besides notions of rights, a number of fundamental concepts recur in general discussions and documents about children. One of the most important of these is the idea of children's needs. Talk of 'rights' and 'needs' represents distinct but overlapping discourses. 'Rights' have been most prominent in legal and philosophical contexts, although they are increasingly referred to in a wide range of settings. 'Needs' have been more central in psychology and in social policy. Child psychology is concerned with the needs of individual children as they develop. Meeting such needs is generally seen as mainly the responsibility of parents and families within the private sphere of the home, although wider society has a role in supporting families to do so. The collective needs of populations or communities are part of the realm of social policy which examines the nature and extent of societal responses through provision of services, financial benefits and legal regulation.

The two concepts of rights and needs provide complementary understanding of reasons why actions or services for the sake of children may be seen as desirable. Both rights and needs entail an implication of an obligation to respond. Whereas rights are based on moral or legal status, needs are derived from human characteristics perceived to be inherent to individuals or everyone. The rights perspective tends to concentrate on mechanisms to ensure that claims can be made and met. A needs approach is interested in the nature, causes and distribution of the circumstances which appear to warrant a response. In some respects rights can be seen as entitlements to have certain needs met. It can also be the case that children have a vital need for knowledge of their rights and for appropriate legal advice. This is true for unaccompanied refugee children, for example (Argent 1996).

Beliefs or assumptions about what children need figure prominently in debates about the satisfactory upbringing of children, the responsibilities and functions of parents and families, and the nature and extent of services for children. It is commonly recognised that children have needs for food, clothing and shelter for which others and particularly parents should be responsible (Pugh *et al*. 1995; see Chapter 8). Schools respond to the perceived need for children to be informed and educated. These are examples of universal needs, deemed to apply to all children or at least to all in a particular country or society at any one time. There are also many kinds of needs which apply to some children but not to others or which apply at certain ages more than others – such as the need to be carried. In addition, groups or categories of children have been described as having 'special needs', often in relation to ill-health, disability and learning difficulties. Recent legislation has sought to target services on 'children in need', creating a new demarcated group (Tisdall 1997).

We can already begin to see that the word 'need' is used in several different ways, at times controversially. In this chapter we aim to unpack this 'slippery concept' (Weale 1983: 32) and elucidate its application to children's issues. The first part of this chapter will examine psychological views about children's needs. Next, concepts of need are explored with regard to social policies and services, both in general and with specific reference to children. In the final section, consideration is given to the concepts of 'children in need' and 'special needs', which figure prominently in current law and policy.

Psychological perspectives on children's needs

Psychologists have sought to identify needs common to all children or to specify the needs of particular types of children. For the most part, the concern has been to examine the key requirements for children in their immediate primary relationships, particularly with parents. The typical basis for identifying needs has been to examine the conditions which are statistically associated with 'good' or 'bad' outcomes for children. For example, parental warmth, moderate levels of control and use of reasoning correlate with positive social adjustment and intellectual development, whereas coldness and harsh discipline do not. Thus the former are what children appear to need from adults for optimal development (Maccoby and Martin 1983; White and Woollett 1992). A wide range of outcome dimensions may be used, such as health, education, family and network relationships, emotional and behavioural development, self-care and competence, self-esteem and identity, and self-presentation (Ward 1995).

Maslow's hierarchy of needs

One of the most. influential early formulations of universal human needs was by Maslow (1970). He postulated a pyramidal hierarchy of needs:

Figure 3.1 Maslow's hierarchy of needs

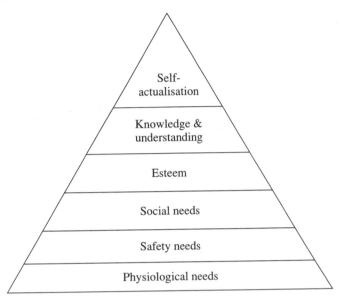

Source: Maslow (1970)

The more fundamental needs at the bottom of the hierarchy had to be met before it was possible to devote energies to higher needs. Whereas the lower needs can be completely met, the higher needs are more open-ended and individualised. Indeed they might more properly be regarded as desirable goals rather than needs, but Maslow affirmed that human life should consist of more than safety and survival.

The hierarchy is also to some extent a life-span model. Physiological and safety needs are most urgent in infancy (and perhaps again in extreme old age); social and educational needs become increasingly prominent through childhood; and, according to Maslow, full self-actualisation and intellectual development are usually not reached until adulthood. Maslow emphasised the importance to children of love and friendships; self-confidence based on achievements and positive evaluations by others; and of control over one's life through knowledge and understanding.

Maslow's six elements may be better considered alongside each other rather than in succession, since relationships, creativity, autonomy and so on are not necessarily more important for adults than for children: they may simply have different forms of expression at different ages and stages. Moreover, adult autonomy and creativity may be rooted as much in childhood opportunities to exercise these qualities as in early satisfaction of physical needs.

One of the main advantages of Maslow's approach is its emphasis on the positive and future-oriented nature of needs, rather than a pre-occupation with a narrow set of current, basic needs. This indicates that carers of children should anticipate and adapt to changes in need or the expression of need. People who are good at giving love and security in early childhood may be less good at supporting young people's questioning and challenges later – or vice versa, so may benefit from advice or help about responding to different needs at different times. Likewise, decisions about who may be the best carers for children separated from parents have to take account of long-term as well as present needs.

Four principal needs of children

A more detailed picture focused exclusively on childhood was provided by Pringle (1980) in her review of the literature on children's needs. Unlike Maslow, she saw needs as occurring at the same time, intertwining rather than forming a progression. She largely took for granted satisfaction of physiological and safety needs, partly on the basis that the great majority of children in modern Britain survive into adulthood in good health, by contrast with earlier times and other parts of the world. Even so, we shall see in chapters 7 and 11 that the health and other risks faced by children are not inconsiderable.

Pringle concentrated on children's non-physical needs, because she wished to emphasise the less obvious damage which can result if these are not fulfilled. Studies had shown that day nurseries, children's homes and even families which provided adequate physical care could still produce children who were unhappy, in trouble or both, because of failure to recognise or attend to children's social and emotional needs (Rutter 1981). Pringle grouped these needs into four categories:

- love and security
- new experiences
- praise and recognition
- responsibility.

Emotional security is seen to depend on the availability of love, consistency and responsiveness. Fahlberg (1994) suggested that satisfactory relationship patterns are set up in infancy if carers accurately identify and respond to children's needs. She described a cyclical pattern in which a child initiates interaction in response to an immediate felt need, arising from hunger or pain, for example. A sensitive adult response satisfies the need and calms the child:

Figure 3.2 **The arousal-relaxation cycle**

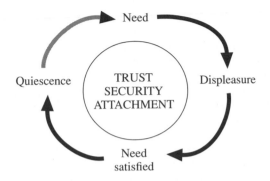

Source: Fahlberg (1994)

Repeated successful completion of this cycle helps the child to trust adults, gain in self-esteem and learn about the world, so the benefits are both emotional and cognitive. Conversely, negative cycles may develop when parents persistently misunderstand a child's communication of what he or she wants, so that they become frustrated and the child insecure (Brandon 1996).

Pringle saw loving relationships as the basis for moral development. Children are motivated to conform to the expectations of adults they are fond of and will be concerned to avoid disapproval. According to Pringle, consistent application of clear rules promotes co-operation by children.

Stimulation is required both to respond to children's curiosity and to help develop their motivation and understanding of the world and of relationships. Play is vital for this, particularly in early childhood (see Chapter 5). Later, schooling, reading and the media become more directly important. Like Maslow, Pringle stressed the significance of praise and recognition, since there is evidence that frequent criticism, complaints or neglect by others can lead to low self-image and insecurity (Rutter 1981; Harter 1983). Encouragement and a reasonable level of expectation also foster effort and achievement (Bee 1995).

Children's needs are not simply self-centred. According to Pringle, children have a social need to be responsible both for self-care and attending to others. This is also seen to benefit children themselves in the long run, however attractive it may appear in the short run to have all your wants met by other people. This need to be able to exercise responsibility is linked to notions about the importance of discipline. Research evidence suggests that firm but caring upbringing is most likely to foster social competence and concern for others, whereas both excessive indulgence and authoritarian modes of parenting are often associated with children who have social problems (Maccoby and Martin 1983).

The needs for autonomy and responsibility were portrayed by Pringle as incremental. Young children should have the opportunities to do things for themselves and make decisions on a small scale. As they grow older they require increasingly greater scope for freedom and self-care in order to develop optimally.

Pringle placed much emphasis on the role of teachers as well as parents and carers in responding to children's needs. She noted evidence that success at school is fostered by teacher enthusiasm and warmth; by links being made between general knowledge and the child's interests and understanding; and by positive feedback about progress. She also argued that pupils be more involved in establishing rules and planning their activities on the basis of the need to develop responsibility.

Not everyone will agree with all the details of Pringle's account. Some conclusions were based on good empirical support, but others were more value-laden or idealised, such as the emphasis on individual responsibility or the implication that carers can be totally consistent.

Attachment theory and children's needs

Pringle's work was much influenced by research and thinking carried out within what has come to be known as attachment theory (Parkes *et al.* 1991; Howe 1995a). Based on wide-ranging research, it asserts that children not only have a primary need for intimacy, but indeed a propensity to form close, loving relationships with responsive people in their lives, usually although not necessarily their parents and other family members (Bowlby 1969; Holmes 1993). In most cases children develop secure attachments in early life. These give them confidence in themselves and in other people that assists later relationships. Difficulties in children's early relationships not only cause short-term distress but have the potential for leading to persistent social problems (Rutter and Rutter 1993; Howe 1996b). Attachment processes can be disturbed in three main ways:

1 The child has no consistent caregiver, as formerly occurred in British residential institutions and still does in some parts of the world. This usually means that children become detached, unable to give or receive affection.
2 The child's key relationships are interrupted by prolonged separation, which may be experienced by a young child as signifying that they are no longer wanted. This can give rise to anxious or avoidant attachments, when children are uncertain of other people's love and avoid closeness for fear of further hurt or separation.
3 The child's parents or main caregivers are unresponsive, hostile or unpredictable. Then children develop ambivalent attachments, in which there is a mixture of strong positive and negative feelings.

These three forms of attachment refer to one-to-one relationships, but it is evident that children are also affected by the interrelationships amongst the people to whom they are attached. In particular, constant discord and hostility between parents or parent-figures are known to be associated with poor outcomes for children (Robins and Rutter 1991; Mullender and Morley 1994). Children with attachment difficulties require sensitive and patient love and support which is adapted to their varying capacities for closeness and independence (Downes 1992). According to Fahlberg (1994) it is often helpful to perceive a child's problematic behaviour as stemming from a need. For instance, stealing, hoarding or overeating may each be reframed as needs to compensate for a felt deprivation of love in the past or present. By this view, punishment may only exacerbate the need and the problem, whereas support and understanding should help reduce them.

Some formulations of attachment theory have been narrow and over-deterministic. Bowlby (1956) originally suggested that children tend to attach to just one main 'mother figure' and that any problem in that single relationship had ominous implications for the future. It is now recognised that infants can and do attach to a number of people and that the qualities of these multiple attachments often differ, so that one poor relationship may well be compensated for by other good ones (Smith 1980). Research has also shown that even when children do lack consistent, close relationships in early life, they can frequently recover well if their needs for love and stability are met later (Tizard 1977; Thoburn 1986). Nevertheless, there is much evidence of the emotional and social harm that can result from deprivation and dislocation of affection and support. Children who have experienced recurrent discontinuities of home and family life are likely to have major difficulties in their adolescent and young adult relationships, often associated with behaviour adults find disruptive (Black 1990; Howe 1996a, b). Conversely, the regular availability of at least one supportive person can help children to do well in spite of very adverse circumstances (Rutter 1985; Garmezy 1987). Although some of the details of attachment theory have been rightly criticised, it remains a powerful framework for conceptualising certain aspects of children's development. Some of its initial overgeneralisations have been later modified (Rutter 1981). What has become clear is that children need certain qualities from people in their early caring environment, but these do not have to be provided by the same people in each case. Children need affection, continuity, stimulation and mutuality. In practice these are often given by parents, particularly mothers, but can be provided by other relatives, adopters, foster carers and others, if need be (Schaffer 1990; Hill 1991) (see also Chapters 4 and 11).

Identity needs

A number of additions have been suggested to Pringle's list of four main needs. One of these is identity, which is a multiple concept comprising an individual's sense of self; of personal, family and community history; and of belonging to one or more social groupings (Weigert *et al.* 1986). Identity is a matter taken for granted by many, but it can be very problematic for children whose sense of who they are is threatened by negative social images, discontinuities of life experience or conflicting loyalties. Many people argue that it is necessary to have a positive and accurate identity to achieve both a holistic sense of self and high self-esteem, though others claim there is no demonstrated link between self-image and self-esteem. This has particular relevance to the debate about the desirability or necessity for black and ethnic minority children to develop a clear identification as black or with their specific ethnic heritage (Maxime 1986; Cross 1992; Tizard and Phoenix 1993).

Erikson (1963) argued that children need to emerge from childhood with a definite sense of who they are. He characterised youth as often a period of role confusion which usually leads on to clear ideas about function (occupational identity), beliefs (ideological identity) and sex role (sexual identity). This framework tends to be stereotypical both in assuming a progression of increasing certainty and suggesting a limited basis for identification. It ignores ethnicity and the situations of non-employed people, for instance. An important implication, though, is that distress tends to arise when there are major discrepancies amongst the different aspects of the self-concept: self-perceptions, ideals about self, evaluations of self and evaluations by others.

Identity tends to be a particularly salient issue for children from ethnic minority backgrounds. Like anyone else they are likely to gain in self-awareness and confidence from having a definite sense of belonging and positive appraisal of their traditions. This is enhanced by understanding of their roots and associated customs, religion and language, though this does not necessarily require full adherence (Modood *et al.* 1994; Pugh *et al.* 1995). A strong ethnic identity can be especially important when racist images and talk appear to diminish or exclude membership of the majority (white) society. Some children are comfortable with a dual identity (e.g. as Black British or Asian British), but others feel obliged to 'choose' between the identity of their family background and of the majority culture. Feelings of rejection may appear to leave no alternative but to adopt a distinct Black or Asian identity (Sanghera 1994). Children of mixed parentage often have an allegiance to both sides of their heritage (Kitwood 1983; Wilson 1987; Cooper 1995; Katz 1996a).

Children who live apart from one or both of their parents for an extended period of time or who are adopted have to deal with the issue of having two families, usually with differing roles and significance, but still both forming part of the child's history and sense of self (Wendelken 1983; Thoburn 1994). Not uncommonly, adults may wish to suppress the child's memories of the missing parent or portray a negative image, especially in the bitterness following the breakdown of a marriage or other adult partnership. This can lead to problems for a child in developing a coherent self-image (see Chapter 11).

Many, though not all, adopted children have an urge to find out more details about their original parents. Most feel very attached to their adopters, but still have a wish to know where they came from – a sense of origins (Triseliotis 1973; Triseliotis *et al.* 1997). With present legal arrangements, it is difficult for this need to find expression before adulthood, since only then do adoptees become entitled to locate birth record information. It is increasingly acknowledged by professionals that a child's relationship with adoptive parents or foster carers is not undermined by interest and understanding of her/his personal history, but enables more successful adaptation to a new home (Kirk 1981; Brodzinsky and Schechter 1990). Indeed, Ryburn (1995) argues that children who cannot stay with their original parents should still be able to maintain contacts in order to reduce their sense of loss or confusion.

The prevailing view is that black children living apart from their original families need to have good contacts with others of similar background to reduce their sense of strangeness and to enable continued ability to identify and communicate with their community of origin (Small 1991; Mehra 1996). Nevertheless, black children adopted in white families have often developed positive lives and self-esteem in spite of limited association with other black people (Simon and Altstein 1992; Zeitlin 1996).

Age, stage and need

Even if children's broad needs, like those of adults, may be similar regardless of age, the balance amongst different needs and the precise forms they take do change as children grow older. Children's needs have mostly been formulated with younger children in mind. Specialists on the teen years have typically pointed to a somewhat different set of needs reflecting the more imminent assumption of adult responsibilities for self and others (Coleman and Hendry 1990). Middle childhood has gained little systematic attention (Collings *et al.* 1995).

During the primary school years, it is commonly stated that children need to learn how to master a range of situations outside the home, to gain more independence, develop satisfactory peer relationships and take more responsibility for both self and others (Erikson 1963; Pringle 1980; Fahlberg 1994). The task of parents becomes more indirect – to prepare, guide, support and reassure. Older children have less need for overt affection, close supervision and detailed guidance, but parental love and support usually remain important to them (Youniss and Smollar 1985; Shucksmith *et al.* 1995). In the teen years, sexual needs become prominent. Both adults and children are often confused about what are appropriate forms of gratification at different ages. Most agree that sex education by teachers as well as parents and others can play a vital role in averting ignorance, anxiety and unwelcome sexual activity or pregnancy, though a minority fear this promotes immoral behaviour (Martinson, 1994). Felt needs for privacy and control of personal space tend to increase with age, at least in European-based cultures (Noller and Callan 1991).

A critique of psychological notions of need

Woodhead (1990) questioned the way in which developmental psychology has portrayed childhood as a period of need, and by implication dependency, in which the foundations for future wellbeing are laid. Also, there is a danger of assuming that children's life prospects are totally dependent on adult care, whereas children themselves actively shape their environments. Some succeed in adverse circumstances when key needs were apparently not met (Werner and Smith 1992).

Woodhead argued further that lists of definitive needs give an air of spurious certainty. In fact the best interests of children are unclear and there is much disagreement (Eekelaar 1994). Need statements appear to be descriptive, when in fact they embody prescriptive force. Observations about what children and parents typically do are commonly translated into prescriptions about needs and how these should be met. Some if not most pronouncements are derived from particular historical and cultural contexts rather than universal truths. For instance, Pringle's idea of responsibility and Maslow's of self-actualisation are very much based on Western libertarian ideals of individualistic, independent thinking. They contrast with the ideals of deference and obedience towards elders in many traditional societies and within ethnic minority cultures in the UK (Dwivedi 1996). Shifts in thinking about wet nurses, nannies and day nurseries owe more to changing mores than scientific truth about what is best for children as regards care by mothers and others (Hardyment 1983; Scarr and Dunn 1987).

Overall, Woodhead concluded it is important not to imagine that there is one single and simple set of needs, but rather 'multiple pathways' through childhood. He also argued that the conventional lists drawn up by adult researchers may omit the needs which children themselves might identify as being important in the here and now.

Children's views of what they need

Little direct information is available on children's perspectives about their needs at a general level, though some studies have looked at the particular needs of children in special circumstances (such as those who are disabled). From the research which has taken place, one of the most striking and consistent findings is that children very much want to be given attention, respect and understanding for their points of view.

As part of a study of parenthood in middle childhood, children were asked for their views on what they needed from parents and schools (Borland *et al.* 1996). They emphasised their strong wish to be loved and cared for. Some still wanted cuddles and kisses, whilst others spoke appreciatively of parents doing things for them in ways which showed they were valued:

My Mum – well she always buys me things and she always thinks of us before she thinks of herself.   (girl aged ten)

My mum, if I'm going somewhere, my mum always says I look lovely and 'I really love you', and she always says that to me.
(girl aged eleven; both quoted in Borland *et al.* 1996: 145)

Gibbons *et al.* (1995) found that the four main things which children wanted from parents were:

1 time spent with them
2 reliability (keeping promises)
3 predictability
4 supervision (they valued some form of checking).

Studies of teenagers confirm that there is commonly a wish for a combination of support and definite standards, applied with flexibility and acceptance of difference (Noller and Callan 1991).

Research concerned with children's perceptions of their emotional needs revealed a strong wish by many children for more attention from adults, including parents, and to have their deeper feelings of distress recognised (Hill *et al.* 1995). It was also important to children that adults empathised with their worries and tried to see issues through the child's own eyes:

You feel they won't understand, 'cause they are older than you and don't realise what happens to children.   (girl aged eleven)

They should try to understand you more and think when they were small. If they got bullied or something or if something happened to them, they should try and understand.   (girl aged nine, unpublished quotes from Hill *et al.* 1995)

The children also identified needs to be given more explanations of adults' own actions, worries and conflicts. Lindon (1996) also noted that children wanted open communication with adults and in particular resented being excluded from knowing key information and feelings which affected their parents and other significant adults.

In the main, children expect their needs to be met by members of their immediate social network, but direct or indirect help and support is also provided by a range of health, welfare and educational services. The nature and availability of these is also related to adult perceptions of children's needs, in ways which will be examined in the following sections.

The concept of need in social policy and allied fields

Need as a basis for service provision

Many services and policies which exist or are recommended for children and their families are justified by claims that they meet needs or are targeted at children with particular needs. Percy-Smith (1996) asserts that 'meeting needs is what public services ought to be about' (p. 1). However, what counts as a need in any given context depends on the perceptions and power of those who influence political agendas (Lukes 1974). Within political discourses, 'needs-talk' may involve competing lobbies with markedly different ideas about the extent and nature of need. For instance, 'needs' for public daycare provision can be interpreted in terms of compensating children for poverty or poor parenting, investing in children's and society's future or meeting women's needs for employment and higher incomes. Fraser argues that this does not make each need claim as valid as any other, but that 'the best need interpretations are those reached by means of communicative processes that most closely approximate ideals of democracy, equality and fairness' (1989: 312).

In most welfare states the government accepts that it has a duty to ensure certain needs are met for all children, such as immunisation or schooling. They provide universal services (notably health and education) not only to promote children's current wellbeing, but also to meet society's own needs for a skilled labour force and informed citizenry (Hill 1995a). Other forms of provision are more selectively based on the idea that the needs are confined to some children only. This may be because the need is thought to arise only for one or more categories of children (such as those with a physical disability) or because there is a general need but only some parents or families are regarded as requiring additional help to meet it (for example, because of their poverty). In the provision of local services, the terms 'needs assessment' and 'needs-led services' first became prominent in the field of community care (mainly social and health services for adults), but have been increasingly imported into children's services (Dartington 1996).

When resources are limited, it can be argued that it makes sense to target services rather than give them to everyone, including some who do 'not really need it'. Even when there is widespread demand for a service (as in relation to daytime care for pre-school children), central or local government may decide that there are only sufficient resources to offer limited provision for those deemed to have special needs. In practice, this targeting tends to be directed towards children and families with significant difficulties and problems, which in turn may lead to stigmatisation of the service and its users. Partly as a result, some of those who would most benefit from a service may be deterred from taking advantage of it. Arguments such as these have played a part in the recurrent debates in the UK about whether child benefit should remain a universal payment regardless of income or shift to a selective system with means-tested access (Macnicol 1978; Brown 1992).

Need is also relevant to arguments about the best way to respond to children who behave in ways which are socially unacceptable, like stealing, bullying or staying off school. For example, the Scottish juvenile justice system requires that responses to young offenders are based on judgements about their needs for voluntary provision of services or compulsory measures of supervision (Norrie 1995; Kelly 1996). English and North American systems focus more on the nature of the offence (Pitts 1988; Leshied *et al.* 1991). According to the welfare model which underpins the Scottish approach, a child's crime or antisocial behaviour are regarded as a symptom of wider problems – in the family or in the local environment which deprived the child of such things as effective discipline, good role models or legitimate opportunities for fulfilment. By this view, juvenile justice systems should aim to provide help to children and families so that their needs in these respects are met. As a result, the theory goes, they will then be less likely to act in antisocial ways. For instance, guided activities, including outdoor adventure programmes, may be justified as prosocial means of meeting needs for excitement and responsibility, whereas from another perspective these appear to 'reward' misdemeanours. By contrast, in a justice model, children's needs are secondary and illegal behaviour is tackled in its own right, whether by punishment which it 'deserves' or by various ways of modifying or treating the behaviour (see Chapter 9 for further discussion).

The meaning of need as a basis for societal responses

Many people in different fields have applied themselves to the complex task of clarifying what is meant by 'need'. Some have concluded that the word is so vague or ambiguous that it would be better abandoned (Thomson 1987; Hewitt 1992). Yet its use is so common that it seems more productive to understand the different senses in which the term can be interpreted. In general, a need for something can be taken to denote a gap between a person's current state and a desired state (goal), such as good health or happiness. The goal may be desired by the person or by someone else like a parent, doctor or teacher. It may involve the presence of something (like food or clothes): it may consist of the absence of something (like pain or harm).

A common first step in thinking about needs is to distinguish them from wants, satisfactions, tastes, whims and indulgences. We are likely to say that a child wants an ice cream, but needs love and affection. Footwear is regarded as a need in chilly Britain, but expensive trainers are more a matter of commercially driven desire. What a person wants can change from time to time; earlier preferences may come to be seen as mistaken, as when friendships end; desired objects of the moment (like chocolate or cigarettes) may run counter to a person's ideals or to someone else's view of what is good for that person. In contrast, what a person needs has more to do with their *long-term* interests, whether in their own eyes or someone else's (Ware and Goodin 1990). It can be argued that younger children may have particular difficulty in assessing their longer-term interests or even seeing the importance of doing so, since they have less of the relevant experience and foresight than most adults. As we saw in Chapter 1, the developmental perspective which portrays children as incompetent to assess their needs may be used as an excuse by adults to substitute their own views (Franklin 1995). In any case, adults are not necessarily good at judging their long-term interests, either. Also some needs may only be recognised by someone with specialist knowledge, as is true for many medical conditions.

Thus a need is more substantial than an immediate wish. It is something which infers necessity for a response or resource in order to achieve or maintain a desirable state of affairs – in this context children's well-being. The implication is that a want *may* be satisfied if resources or goodwill permit, but that a need *should* be satisfied, or else the child will suffer. Herein lies the strength of the word 'need', since like 'right', it implies an obligation to meet it. Consequently, those seeking resources have an interest in identifying need; anyone trying to harbour scarce resources is likely to be under pressure to minimise or deny need.

Liss (1993) identified three distinct elements in statements about needs (in relation to health):

1 the person's current state
2 the goal of the need
3 the means of satisfying the need.

There can be disagreements and value judgements about each of these. Even when there is a consensus amongst interested parties about the first two, there may be differences of opinion about the third, i.e. how the need should be met. Thus it may be agreed that a pre-school child lacks company (1) and that mixing with peers is desirable (2) but the means for satisfying that need (3) could be a self-help play group, a private nursery, a family centre run by a voluntary organisation or a state nursery school.

A distinction is commonly made between two levels of need – basic (general purpose) needs and specific needs (Weale 1983). Basic needs correspond to the minimum requirements for living. In broad terms these apply across time and culture, although the precise form they take may be highly varied. Thus infants need protection, but this may be from wild animals in one context, motor cars in another, from freezing in the Arctic, from dehydration in a tropical desert. Specific needs allow for more particular activities to be carried out (e.g. for a pen or pencil in order to write). Most commentators, including Weale, argue that basic needs in a modern society consist of many besides the physical necessities for survival. As Maslow (1970) averred, human life should and usually does consist of more than simply existing from one day to the next. In this view, needs encompass access to the wherewithal to lead a meaningful social life and to fulfil social obligations (Townsend 1979; Oppenheim 1996). For children it can be said that they need the material, personal and social resources for both current and future effective social participation. Thus, in Britain, families may be seen as needing sufficient income to afford birthday presents or a television for their children, but these are not perceived as necessities in countries where there are high risks of child malnutrition and mortality (see Chapter 8).

Doyal and Gough (1991) suggested that there are two basic needs for human beings – for survival/health and for autonomy. Autonomy involves the capacity to make significant choices as participants in social life, which requires emotional, social, cognitive and linguistic needs to be met. This corresponds in some ways to the top half of Maslow's hierarchy discussed earlier (40–2). To achieve such autonomy in a modern society, they suggest that a number of intermediate needs have to be met. In childhood these include security, education, appropriate health care and protective housing. Doyal and Gough incorporated the four needs identified by Pringle (1980) into their framework of intermediate needs in childhood. Since these are needs common to everyone, then we all have claims on society for these needs to be met.

Doyal and Gough argued that their framework of needs has universal application, although the specific ways in which needs can be satisfied are acknowledged to be historically and culturally variable. Soper (1993a, 1993b) suggested that the very generality of their framework makes it difficult to derive particular policy consequences. Furthermore, it is evident that opinions differ sharply about the role of the state in ensuring basic needs are met, as we saw in Chapter 1. It is possible for contrasting views on the role of the welfare state each to be cast in terms of needs. A residualist or minimalist perspective entails concentration of resources on those 'in need', by contrast with the majority who are assumed to be able to meet most of their needs by purchasing goods and services. An institutional or social model supports wider provision for all on the basis of common needs (and rights) (Ware and Goodin 1990; Esping-Anderson 1990). Most people also accept that there is a significant role for voluntary organisations, especially in relation to 'special needs', newly identified needs or innovative ways of providing services (Knight 1993). Across Western Europe, the number of voluntary and self-help organisations has proliferated in the last ten years: many of these seek to help children and families (Lorenz 1994; Billis and Harris 1996). The largest operate on a national or international scale (e.g. Barnardo's, Save the Children).

Parents' and children's needs

There is a complex relationship between parents' and children's needs, which means that financial and other assistance is often directed at children via their parents. Usually, parents meet many of children's needs, but it may be important that parents' own needs are met so this can happen. Parents who are dependent on income support or other low income may find it hard to provide children with daily necessities, although many women sacrifice themselves to try and ensure their children have enough (Glendinning and Millar 1987). Children's access to pre-school care and/or education is often justified in terms of children's needs for stimulation, peer contacts and so on, but children may also benefit if this enables a parent – typically the mother – to feel more fulfilled through work or other activities.

Sometimes reference is made to 'family needs' or the need for 'family support' (for example, Tunstill 1996). Family policy is a more widely recognised subdivision of social policy than children's policy. Evidently external assistance may well help the whole household, but it is also necessary to deconstruct the presumed unity of 'the family' (see Chapter 4). The needs and interests of family members are often different, if not divergent, so each should be assessed separately. Parents and other carers often act as advocates or spokespersons in relation to their children's needs, especially when children are unable to speak for themselves (or are not enabled to do so). Sometimes, of course, parents and children's perceptions will differ and even conflict. When a parent sees a need for discipline and obedience, a child may see a need for free expression. A significant minority of children experience neglect or abuse as a result of parental behaviour or inaction (Gillham 1991; 1994). In such circumstances support or alternative care is required to ensure children's survival and wellbeing (see Chapter 11).

The nature and distribution of need

Commonly policy makers seek to match the allocation of resources to perceived levels of need. In planning services five main aspects of need require consideration:

1 the relevant population to be served
2 the nature of the need
3 the extent of the need
4 the distribution of the need
5 the intensity of the need.

For example, it might be thought desirable to set up an after-school club. Amongst the questions to be asked are:

1 What is the intended coverage as regards geographical area and age group?
2 Is the purpose care, supervision, educational support or recreation? What types of activity are required? What level of adult supervision and input is desirable?
3 How many children of the appropriate age in the area would attend and benefit?
4 Where do potential attenders live? How dispersed or concentrated are they?
5 How strong is the wish for a club?

Of course, people planning to set up a service usually have their own hunches about the answers to these questions, but these could easily be inaccurate and it is not unusual for services to have a low uptake or to acquire a different clientele from that envisaged. Consequently it is desirable to obtain systematic information at an early stage.

This leads on to questions of how need is to be assessed and by whom? Bradshaw (1972) proposed a classification which has been much utilised since. He distinguished four types of need, based on the method of identifying it. These were:

1 **Felt need** This corresponds to *what people want.*
2 **Expressed need** This is demand, i.e. *felt need which is acted upon.*
3 **Normative need** This is *defined by outside experts* (professionals, officials, social scientists).
4 **Comparative need** This is established by *comparing different populations or areas* from the one under consideration.

It is important to note that this framework mainly relates to identifying people or populations in need, rather than specification of what their needs might be.

The distinction between felt need and expressed need is an important one. For example, a parent or child may feel a need for an adventure playground, but do nothing about it. Only if people make their needs known does it become a demand. Apparent demand for a service can be measured by applications, referrals or waiting lists (Jackson and Jackson 1979). These may be deceptive, since all sorts of reasons can inhibit people from giving voice to their needs, such as lack of information about appropriate resources, low self-confidence, not being aware that others have similar needs, concern or conviction that a demand will not be met (Kerr 1983). If a service has to be paid for, some people may not act on their desire because they cannot afford it. Many parents do not bother to apply for a place in a full-time children's nursery centre because they know their chances of obtaining a place are minimal. Usage of children's clinics is limited by the preferences of some mothers to obtain lay advice from relatives and friends, as well as fears about the surveillance role of health visitors (McIntosh 1992). There are issues which a child may wish to discuss with others, yet feel ashamed to admit, as in relation to sexuality or parental separation.

Bradshaw also pointed out that experts of various kinds may identify needs differently from people themselves. Doctors may diagnose health needs of which their patients are unaware. For many services or benefits it may be required that a need is certified by a medical expert, even though a person is well able to provide the information themselves. Planners and researchers may be able to spot discrepancies in demand by comparing similar areas. Comparisons between different social strata can indicate need, as in the identification of low health levels of poor children in contrast to those of children in materially advantaged homes (see Chapter 7).

Although it is legitimate to use expertise appropriately applied, there are dangers to reliance on experts (Smith 1980). Researchers' findings may be restricted by the measuring instruments they use. Professionals typically notice what they are trained to see and may neglect other aspects (Lishman 1983; Taylor and Ford 1989). There is also a tendency to define need only in terms of the existing service the professional works for, which may unduly restrict perceptions of need. For instance, many health professionals are inclined to see child safety as a matter largely of parental education, rather than housing or environmental improvement (Roberts *et al.* 1995). Social workers have usually not been vigilant about the health and educational needs of children in care (Jackson 1989). On a wider front, professionals and officials are not necessarily disinterested parties. They have power to influence ordinary people and, according to Foucault, for example, may use their system of knowledge to impose their ideas on people who are powerless to resist and to perpetuate their professional status (Hewitt 1992).

With varying degrees of enthusiasm, experts may transfer some of their power to define need to lay people. The recent history of services for children with disabilities illustrates a contemporary shift away from need determined purely by experts to shared or user-led definitions, at least at the level of rhetoric (Appleton and Minchom 1988; Oliver 1991). More often than not this may empower parents rather than children, but older children are also more involved than formerly. Recently, researchers and professionals have identified young carers of adults with a disability or mental health problem as a neglected group and their hidden needs have been brought to light. A small sample expressed their wish for more practical support and reduced isolation (Aldridge and Becker 1994, 1995; for more discussion, see Chapter 4).

Bradshaw's classification was derived with a hypothetical service in mind which would respond to the needs of the population in its area, but his fourfold typology can be applied to individual children too. A child may have a *felt need* to stop or escape from violence, but be too fearful to express that need. A young person's *expressed need* for financial or housing assistance may not fit with official criteria. Professionals may identify a *normative need* for a child to go to a residential school which may conflict with the child's wish to stay home. The *comparative need* of a child for better care and nutrition may be indicated by contrasting the child's height and weight with charts of the distribution for that age in the general population or with the same child's progress in a different context. Jasmine Beckford's physical regression when with her parents compared with her progress in foster care was an indicator of life-threatening neglect by her parents, whose significance social workers failed to see (Blom-Cooper 1986).

Smith (1980) challenged the view that it was possible to view social needs as objective attributes of individuals or populations. He argued that expert-defined needs were inevitably affected by the subjective interpretations of professionals or researchers. Further, individuals and professionals have differing predispositions when they assess need and plan or advocate for the need to be met. For example, the four levels in Table 3.1 represent different levels of possible response to parental neglect of children:

Table 3.1 Perceived unit of need and corresponding level of response

Perceived unit of need and level of response	Example: Child neglect
Individual	Child's need for care and stimulation
Family	Parents' need for education/resources
Community	Neighbourhood need for facilities
Society	Need for fairer distribution of opportunities and resources in society

Likewise, the causes of need can be perceived at different levels. So, depending on the viewpoint, when a child commits a crime, this may reflect a need for the child to be better disciplined or cared for; for the family to receive guidance; for the area to have more leisure facilities; or for society to create more long-term opportunities for young people. Community workers are trained to see collective needs within neighbourhoods which other professionals often see as individualistic. Therapists may underestimate the material shortcomings in a child's household, whilst a welfare rights adviser may not recognise emotional needs. Croll and Moses (1985) found that teachers tended to attribute emotional and behavioural difficulties to home background, other learning difficulties to factors within the child and in only a few instances reported school-based influences as significant. Smith termed these propensities 'ideologies of need'. He argued that it was important to understand how professionals apply ideas of need in the contexts within which they work, since this affects the allocation of services and resources at least as much as administrative or external criteria of need.

Assessments of individual children may also be couched in terms of individual needs, but reflect wider group or institutional needs. For example, the needs of children with learning difficulties might be catered for by adjustments within the class and school, but this poses a challenge to teachers and other pupils, so removal to a 'special' setting may act like a 'safety valve' for others (Tomlinson 1982). Likewise, secure accommodation provides placements for young people whose management is disruptive for mainstream residential homes (Parker 1988; Harris and Timms 1993).

As judgements about needs vary according to different values, perspectives and knowledge bases, it is desirable to obtain information about needs from more than one source to build up a complementary picture. A range of methods is available such as population or client surveys, service use analysis, social indicators and feedback from group discussions (McKillip 1987). Pickin and St. Leger (1993) outlined the following sources of data for assessing the health needs of school-aged children in a given area:

- census data on the age-groups of local residents
- number and type of GP consultations
- number and type of hospital admissions
- police accident records
- notifications of infectious diseases
- cancer registries
- disability registers
- education departments
- school medical services
- community dental service local survey results
- extrapolation of national figures for certain diseases and disabilities
- mortality statistics.

This illustrates the value of compiling multiple profiles from different directions, though in this case the data are confined to official numerical data which identify the extent of ill-health concerns, but not the nature of associated need or of requirements for positive health, let alone the views of children themselves. Dingwall and Robinson (1990) bemoaned the trend to rely on statistical data alone. They suggested that, traditionally, health visitors could make very good appraisals of observed and felt needs of children and their mothers at home, which could be aggregated into a picture of community needs, but this will be undermined by increased reliance on clinic-based contacts and quantifiable epidemiological information. Moreover, official data on needs tend to concentrate on what the need is, without acknowledging different perceptions of the nature of need or the range of possible ways in which need can be met.

Children in need

Certain children are seen as requiring additional assistance beyond that required to meet the needs of any child. Also, when resources are perceived to be limited, then it can be seen as most efficient to target those resources on children 'most in need', even if others or indeed all children might well have benefited. This requires mechanisms for identification of such children and channelling assistance to them. The potential benefits are that the type and scale of provision will be effectively adapted to the type and level of need. The risks are that the children and families concerned may feel labelled and stigmatised, and that some needy children will be left out because of faulty or over-restrictive targeting procedures. Two terms which illustrate some of these issues of inclusion and exclusion are 'children in need' and 'special needs'.

Local authorities in the UK have a duty to provide a range of supportive services for 'children in their area who are in need'. These are mainly provided by social services/work departments (Health Boards in Northern Ireland). This requirement was introduced for England and Wales by Section 17 of the Children Act 1989. Similar wording was included in legislation for Scotland and Northern Ireland in 1995. The 1989 Act defined 'in need' as covering three broad categories of children [Section 17(10)]:

• those requiring services to achieve or maintain a 'reasonable standard of health or development'
• those whose health or development would be otherwise impaired
• disabled children

The first category refers to situations where children's welfare is promoted: the second relates primarily to children deemed to be at risk of neglect or abuse. The Guidance to the Children Act (Department of Health 1991b) made it clear that services should not be confined to children at risk of intra-familial abuse (see Chapter 10). The broad approach has allowed different criteria to be used across England and Wales. For instance, children with HIV/AIDS are included as children in need by some authorities but not others. Also misunderstandings and disagreements in views about need have occurred between agencies, especially health and social work (Audit Commission 1994). Although the definition of need is wide, authorities are instructed to 'make decisions about the priorities for service provision' and by implication set up rationing devices (Tunstill 1995). Moreover, local authorities also have specific duties to give particular attention to those in extreme circumstances, i.e. children suffering or liable to suffer significant harm.

The Children Act 1989 in general and this section in particular had been based on dialogue in England and Wales amongst policy-makers, officials, politicians, researchers and lobby groups which had led to a near consensus about the importance of establishing more positive family support services in contrast to the emphasis in the 1980s on child protection and social control (Packman and Jordan 1991; Bullock 1993; Berridge 1995, 1996a). Previously the availability of services and support had been mainly linked to prevention of imminent removal of a child from home or appearance in court. Now it was hoped that the wider spread of circumstances in which help was to be offered would mean that problems could be averted at an earlier stage. However it can be argued that there is a tension at the heart of the legislation between the concept of a broad role for the state in family support and the notion of targeting, which in other areas of government policy has usually meant a much more 'residual' view of collective responsibility (see Chapter 1).

The importing of the concept of 'children in need' into Scotland occurred in a different context, which meant that here the new formulation arguably represented a narrowing rather than a widening compared with previous legislation. The Social Work (Scotland) Act 1968 had given local authorities a general duty to promote the welfare of children in their areas. Although this duty had mostly been used to provide material aid during family crises (Davidson 1991), as in England and Wales, there had also been scope to develop services to meet community needs without specific criteria of eligibility. These included open-access family and youth centres. Concerns were expressed about the individualisation of the new category 'children in need', which could restrict such developments. More positively, the Children (Scotland) Act 1995 included a fourth subgroup within the category, namely children 'affected adversely by the disability of another family member' (Section 93 (4)(a)).

Evidence has begun to accumulate about the operation of the new approach in England and Wales. This suggests that concentration on 'children at risk' continues, although efforts are being made to embrace both wider family support and children with disabilities. Aldgate *et al.* (1995) carried out a postal survey of 82 local authorities, supplemented by detailed interviews with key personnel in ten of the authorities. In assessing needs, most relied on their existing data about referrals and/or children belonging to certain groups, such as those on the child protection registers, on remand or looked after away from home. These represent a mixture of expressed and expert-defined populations with needs related to current high risk. Some authorities did additionally use demographic data which can provide indicators of need, but hardly any appear to have ascertained the extent and nature of felt needs. There was little consultation with current adult service users, let alone potential users or children.

Service provision was primarily concentrated on children for whom the authority already had some responsibility – usually because of risk of abuse or neglect, or children in foster and residential care. This accords with the findings of a more detailed study in eight English authorities (Gibbons 1995). In about 75 per cent of cases where there were suspicions of child abuse, preliminary investigations indicated no need for a 'case conference' to consider further intervention. In most instances the family received no further help and the case was closed. Yet most were living in severely deprived circumstances and did have childcare needs, which went unattended to.

Research in Wales has reached similar conclusions. Denman and Thorpe (1993) analysed referrals to a Welsh authority. They discovered that many children of lone parents on very low incomes were referred on the grounds of possible neglect, which was not substantiated. Despite these families' apparently high level of need, few gained any help, which was largely confined to cases with persistent concerns about abuse. Colton *et al.* (1995) found that Welsh social services departments were still using definitions of need based on previous legislation and concerned with risk. They had been very slow to set up registers of disabled children, as legally required.

All the studies suggest that in a context of limited resources managers give priority to children who have been abused or are at risk of abuse, even though they are often aware of the desirability of providing more general family support and less stigmatising services. Supporters of the new legislation had hoped that it would enable agencies to tackle threats to children's welfare on a broader front. There is a strong link between poverty on the one hand and risks of neglect and removal from home on the other (Becker and MacPherson 1988; Bebbington and Miles 1989). Whilst the root causes are linked to general socio-economic circumstances, it is possible to ameliorate conditions at local level in collaboration with residents and community organisations. This ought to result in fewer children becoming at risk, but the early signs are that services will continue to be directed mainly to those already at risk.

Children with special needs

Children may have needs above and beyond those of other children because of family and environmental circumstances, as we have just seen. When they have particular needs related to their personal characteristics, then it has become customary in several contexts to use the term 'special needs'. For instance, in the field of adoption and fostering, the category of 'children with special needs' has been associated with requirements for particularly skilled or sensitive care, extra support compared with other children and/or possibly additional financial allowances. In this context children with special needs include those with physical impairments, learning difficulties, serious behavioural/emotional problems or chronic health problems. The term replaced the earlier phrase 'hard to place' which was seen as more pejorative since it seemed to blame the child for having a deficit or deficiency. The idea of special needs is intended to place the onus more on the child's caring environment to respond appropriately. Nevertheless this term still marks some children out as 'different' and so has aroused resentment.

The main arena in which the concept of 'special needs' plays a central role, however, is that of education (see Chapter 6 for more detailed discussion). Similar dilemmas have arisen between ensuring children receive the additional assistance they need and the avoidance of stigmatising labels and assessment procedures (Beveridge 1993). Here again there has been an attempt since the late 1970s 'to reconceptualise learning difficulties not as intrinsic to the child but as arising in the context of interaction between the child and his or her environment' (Riddell and Brown 1994: 1). The path-breaking Warnock Report of 1978 stressed that there is a continuum of educational needs and that many children with learning difficulties could have their needs met within ordinary schools, though a positive role was still envisaged for separate schools. Warnock sought to shift the responsibility for the need for special educational measures away from the child alone and onto the interaction between school and pupil. More recently the use of the word 'special' has been questioned on the grounds that the needs of many disadvantaged children with attainments significantly below average are in fact 'normal' but simply unmet (Galloway *et al.* 1994).

Legislation in 1981 established the new term of 'special educational needs' both in England and Wales and in Scotland. A child is considered to have special educational needs if he or she has a learning difficulty which calls for special educational provision (Chasty and Friel 1993). Education authorities are required to carry out assessments of individual children and produce statements (England and Wales) or records (Scotland) of needs, outlining the measures to be taken to respond (Sinclair *et al.* 1995). This has produced yet another stigmatising label in England and Wales, with children divided into the 'statemented' and 'non-statemented'. The Scottish equivalent is 'recorded'.

Galloway *et al.* (1994) pointed out that the system for assessing special educational need is a political and social process, affected not only by information about the child, but also by expectations about teachers, schools and children in general. As with 'children in need', the basis for action is confined to particular individual children, whereas it may be sometimes more appropriate to target extra resources at particular classes, schools or neighbourhoods (see Table 3.1). Educational psychologists tend to tailor their views on what a child needs according to their knowledge of what kind of learning supports are available. Thus in Bradshaw's terms, needs are expert-defined and the views of experts appear influenced by factors besides their professional learning. Children themselves are rarely involved in the decision-making process and so cannot contribute their opinions about what they need. One small study with a sample of 29 gave an insight into children's perceptions of assessments. They tended to see these as negative and passive processes, with the professionals defining their faults and problems (Galloway *et al.* 1994).

Interestingly, children who pose management problems in class are referred to as having 'emotional and behavioural difficulties' (EBD in shorthand) without direct reference to needs, although they may also be assessed as having special educational needs. Armstrong and Galloway (1994) argue that there has been a shift in attitude amongst teachers, so that they are more inclined than formerly to request asessment for separate provision rather than seek to meet the children's needs within the classroom. These writers also suggest that invoking the idea of an individual child's needs to justify removal from the class or the school can serve to disguise the part played by the teacher–pupil context in generating difficulties. On the other hand, there is evidence of substantial approval by parents and children for the residential schooling provided as an alternative (Grimshaw with Berridge 1994; Triseliotis *et al.* 1995).

Conclusions

The concept of need is commonly used for informing discussions and judgements about optimal upbringing of children and for considering children's services. Talk about need can relate to an individual child, a group or a population. It signifies that a response is thought necessary in order to achieve a desired goal or status. The implication is that where a need exists something should be done, but as we have seen it is often a matter of opinion and a question of values as to what constitutes a desired goal, what levels of deprivation justify action, who should act and how.

There is a superficial attractiveness in discourses about need. The ambiguity of meaning can gain support from differing quarters, as few people would wish to oppose meeting children's needs. Nevertheless it is a problematic notion. Questions about what ought to happen (matters of judgement) are absorbed in seemingly factual questions (for empirical determination), so that the contribution of subjective, culturally and politically influenced perceptions may be hidden. Needs which all children have (like common human needs) are often very vague and general, yet more specific formulations with respect to some children often serve to stigmatise children and may restrict as well as target access to resources. Furthermore, the extent to which some needs are responded to more than others reflects the uneven capacities of individuals and social groups to mobilise resources and images in order to enter public and political agendas (Spector and Kitsuse 1987).

A right implies a legitimate claim (though one whose applicability may have to be proven), which derives from a respected status as person or citizen. In contrast, a need can all too readily be seen as a personal deficiency associated with a negative status, even when the intentions behind responses to need are rooted in benign intentions. Determining who has a need for assistance and deciding what form that assistance should take is often left to professionals and officials, whose definitions are affected by their training and organisational context. On the one hand these form the basis for their knowledge and authority, but on the other there are dangers of being constrained by currently accepted wisdom which later turns out to be wrong or at least a product of its time. Decisions may also be affected by awareness and availability of resources. Furthermore, the idea of need implies a compassionate basis for action, but in practice may mask decisions which are intended to make life easier for adults, as with respect to some placements of children in hospital or secure accommodation (Coppock 1996; Littlewood 1996). Recent policies have given parents more say, especially in relation to schools, but children's felt needs rarely figure. Unless children are involved in defining their own needs and interests, policies based on needs will be paternalistic and based on images of children as passive recipients.

Despite these drawbacks, the idea of need remains useful in conceptualising the basis for adult responses to children at universal, area and individual levels. There is much evidence about children's shared psychological needs for love and intimacy, security, continuity, knowledge and stimulation, praise, responsibility and identity. How these apply in relation to particular needs, such as health, or particular settings, such as the family and school, will be explored in later chapters. Needs-based frameworks exist for assessing the nature, extent, intensity and distribution of children's circumstances as a basis for shaping the type and allocation of resources in local neighbourhoods or within administrative districts.

In conclusion, it seems that the notion of children's needs carries risks of over-generalisation and biased prescription, but remains a valuable way of organising thinking about children, as long as care is taken to clarify the nature and sources of claims made about needs and provided that multiple viewpoints are taken into account.

Suggestions for further reading

Doyal, L. and Gough, I. (1991) *A Theory of Human Need*, London: Macmillan.

Dwivedi, K. N. and Varma, V. P. (1996) *Meeting the Needs of Ethnic Minority Children*, London: Jessica Kingsley.

Galloway, D., Armstrong, D. and Tomlinson, S. (1994) *The Assessment of Special Educational Needs: Whose Problem?*, London: Longman.

Howe, D. (ed.) (1996) *Attachment Theory and Child and Family Social Work*, Aldershot: Avebury.

Pugh, G., De'Ath, E. and Smith C. (1995) *Confident Parents, Confident Children*, London: National Children's Bureau.

Smith, G. (1980) *Social Need: Policy, Practice and Research*, London: Routledge & Kegan Paul.

CHAPTER 4

Children's family relationships

Introduction

In the next two chapters we shall examine children's relationships, activities and use of different places in their environment. This chapter will deal primarily with children's relationships within their families. The next will concentrate on children's relationships with each other and with their activities alone or with peers, mainly though not invariably outside their homes.

First, consideration is given to family relationships as a whole. Then three key relationships within the family are considered in turn – between children and parents, siblings and grandparents respectively. The concerns of many researchers have centred on relationship dynamics and outcomes for children. Hence consideration of rights (e.g. to parental guidance, freedom of expression) and needs (e.g. for love, security and stimulation), as outlined in the previous chapters, is often implicit, embedded within measures of the effects of particular aspects of family life on children.

Families and households: definitions and values

First of all, the term 'family' must be unpacked, since it is both ambiguous and emotive. We shall confine ourselves to considering families which contain children under 18, whilst acknowledging that family ties are significant in adult-adult relationships too (Finch and Mason 1993). In virtually all cultures, family has conventionally referred to a group of people to whom a person is related through birth or marriage (Fox 1977; Harris 1990). A distinction has commonly been made between the 'nuclear family', consisting of parents and children, and the 'extended family' or wider kin network, which includes grandparents, cousins and so on. However, this is an oversimplified picture, especially in view of recent changes in social mores and household patterns. For instance, family relationships may be established through cohabitation which does not involve marriage, whilst some children are brought up by adopters or following assisted reproduction so that one or both of their legal parents are not their biological parents. Divorce and remarriage also affect the boundaries and composition of the family network. Close friends and carers may become honorary family members, with titles like Auntie Susan. Thus the idea of family is to some degree a fluid one, with a mix of concepts at its core – direct biological relatedness, parental caring role, long-term cohabitation, permanent belonging.

Family is not the same as household, which refers to one or more individuals sharing the same 'home'. It is common to speak of 'lone-parent families' when what is really meant are lone-parent households, since the children still have two parents in their family (unless one has died), but are living separately from one of them. Most British households with children are limited to the nuclear family of one or two parents plus children, but sometimes grandparents, au pairs, lodgers or others do share the living unit, with varying degrees of social integration. Joint households of close kin are more common amongst families of Asian background. Children may also live in step-family households (also referred to as reconstituted or re-ordered), communal households or gay couple households.

Despite the vagueness and permeability of its nature, the 'family' is imbued with evaluative significance. On the one hand, the family is seen as uniquely suited for the upbringing of children, not only to meet their needs for love and commitment but also to create stable citizens and foster social order (Parsons and Bales 1956; Pringle 1980). The United Nations Convention states that 'parents or, as the case may be, legal guardians, have the primary responsibility for the upbringing and development of the child' (Article 18), whilst also acknowledging the role of the wider family in giving guidance and direction (Article 5). On the other hand, dangers exist of rose-tinted 'familism', in which families are seen as inherently good and 'the family' is portrayed uncritically as an institution to be supported and as a solution to social ills. In reality, family relationships can be major contributors to social problems. The family is the locus of much violence and ill-treatment, especially committed by males (Morgan 1985). Despite recent challenges and changes, even nonviolent family households have usually been conducted in ways which subordinate the interests of women and children to those of men (Dalley 1993).

Debates continue about whether or not families ought to take a particular form in the interests of children. Many think that children's emotional and social needs can only be properly met in two-parent heterosexual households. This viewpoint gains support from both New Right thinkers and ethical socialists who regret what they see as the weakening, in the late twentieth century, of enduring moral commitments in relationships (Anderson and Dawson 1986; Dennis and Erdos 1992; Halsey 1993). Others state that diverse household forms may be equally appropriate for child-rearing – lone parents, cohabiting or married heterosexual couples, homosexual couples or combined households (Saraga 1993). In later sections of this chapter, we shall examine what light empirical evidence can shed on these differing perceptions.

Theories about families

Kinship has long been a central concern of anthropology and the 'sociology of the family' has existed for many years. Until recently there has been no psychology of the family, as such, although developmental psychology has given much attention to certain aspects of parent–child relationships. Theorisation about family life has been concerned with:

1 the relationship between families and society
2 the internal dynamics of families
3 the connections between 1 and 2.

Family theories try to do several things: classify family types; explain external and internal relations; account for historical and cross-cultural variations; and describe family processes. Some stress family patterns and roles. Others emphasise the subjective experiences of family members – particularly the adults. Thus one of the key features of family theorisation is its pluralism (Cheal 1991; Klein and White 1996). That reflects the diversity of family functions and forms within society, as well as the range of viewpoints about the roles played by families within society and in the genesis of individual wellbeing and problems.

Space does not permit detailed review of particular theories, so these are summarised in Tables 4.1 and 4.2. A few key points are highlighted in the next sections and a number of the theories will be referred to again later in the book. This chapter concentrates on internal family structures and processes, whilst external relationships are dealt with in other chapters – particularly with respect to the state and government policies. Although a few of the theories about families and society take account of cross-cultural variations, most concepts and supporting data have been based on white European and North American families.

The relationship between families and society

Despite reaching different and sometimes conflicting conclusions, several theories like functionalism, Marxism and feminism emphasise that the nature of family life is crucially related to the nature of the socio-economic system, the role of government and informal social networks. Social class and gender have been at the heart of many analyses. Modern capitalism entails wage labour and the location of most paid employment outside the home. Early functionalists thought that industrialisation and urbanisation had caused a shift from extended family to nuclear family households, but it is now known that nuclear family households were common in Britain prior to this and may even have been one of the preconditions for the development of modern capitalism (Laslett and Wall 1972). The development of capitalism from the sixteenth to nineteenth centuries was accompanied by a greater division between the public world of work and the domestic sphere. Employment outside the home was often dominated by men, whereas children came to spend

Table 4.1 'Families and society' theories

Theory	Core ideas	Key references
Functionalism	Conventional nuclear family households are well suited to modern industrial society and facilitate free movement of labour. They reconcile family needs for earned income, children's needs for stable care and society's needs for effective socialisation.	Parsons 1980 Elliott 1986
Marxism	In capitalist economies, families provide unpaid work (mainly female) which services the labour force and reproduces the next generation of workers.	Secombe 1974 Morgan 1985
Post-structuralism	The modern state controls citizens largely through health and welfare professionals. They inculcate ideas about good parenting. A range of advisory, bureaucratic and legal mechanisms is used to modify deviant family patterns.	Donzelot 1980 Parton 1991 Rodger 1996
Feminism	Male power and status tends to dominate both the private world of the family and the public world of society. This is often detrimental to the interests of women and children.	Gittins 1993 Oakley 1994 Segal 1995
Family policy analyses	Governments seek to influence and support families, both implicitly and explicitly, through a range of legal, financial, service and fiscal mechanisms. There are often discrepancies between avowed aims and achievements.	Muncie *et al.* 1995 Hantrais 1994, 1995 Hill 1995a
Social network theories	Individuals and families interact with wider social networks, which vary in composition, structure and functions. Family processes are often vitally affected by support and stress from the wider social network.	Bott 1971 Belle 1989 Cochran *et al.* 1990
Ecological theories	Child development and family relations are affected by nested systems of settings, relationships, influences and values.	Bronfenbrenner 1979 Belsky 1984 Boushel 1994

most of their time at home and school, mainly cared for by women (Gittins 1993). Recent changes in work patterns and technology have begun to modify that relationship, but it remains true that the extent and nature of children's involvement with parents and other key adults in their lives is very much influenced by the physical and temporal location of paid work. Feminists in particular have emphasised the importance of considering separately who amongst men, women and children benefit from family–work relationships and who lose. Parallels have also been drawn between the position of women and of children as 'members of social minority groups . . . dominated by masculine power' (Oakley 1994: 14). It must not be forgotten that mothers and other women, as adults, can be oppressive to children, too. Oppression refers broadly to the (mis-)use of power which restricts the life-chances and choices of individuals or groups, sometimes insidiously (Dalrymple and Burke 1995). The more specific issue of child abuse will be addressed in Chapter 10.

The way children are brought up is affected by the actions of governments directly or indirectly through such measures as family allowances, schooling, early years provision and employment leave entitlements (see Chapter 1). In particular, these affect parental availability (e.g. to look after a sick child) and family resources (Moss 1988/9). Post-structuralists have suggested that the state nowadays encourages or imposes parenting standards through the advice and actions of professionals like doctors, health visitors, teachers and social workers (Parton 1991; Rodger 1996). In this way, the state governs children's lives.

The more immediate context for family life is that of the social network, i.e. relatives, friends, neighbours and others encountered in everyday interaction. These relationships can affect children directly by providing company, stimulation, support, exposure to a range of values, and so on. Relatives and friends can also mediate the consequences of parental attitudes and behaviour (Belle 1989; Cochran *et al.* 1990). From an early age, most children now spend time in some kind of group setting, so that both they and their families negotiate and make sense of the differences and transitions between home and group care well before the start of compulsory schooling (Hill 1987; Dahlberg 1996).

Theories concerned with internal family relationships

A second set of theories has been mainly concerned with the internal dynamic of families, although some also link these to wider social processes.

Several of these approaches have been developed partly or mainly as applied theories by psychiatrists, counsellors and others in order to help and change families as well as understand them. As a result, ideas based on small numbers of families with identified problems have sometimes been inappropriately generalised to other family circumstances.

Table 4.2 'Internal family relationship' theories

Theory	Core ideas	Key references
Systems	Individual actions, beliefs and attitudes need to be understood as part of the total system of family relationships and role allocation. Causation is circular not linear. Families have internal and external boundaries of varying clarity and permeability.	Burnham 1986 Dallos 1995 Reimers and Treacher 1995
Symbolic interactionist perspectives	Family members negotiate patterns of thinking and behaving through interactive processes in which shared and non-shared definitions and ascriptions of meaning are developed. People use 'common-sense' to provide understanding, explanations and rationalisations which help ease transitions like marriage, parenthood and divorce.	Backett 1982 Clark 1991 Jordan et al. 1994
Psycho-dynamic theories	Tensions between children's urges and adult expectations for socialisation are inevitable. Children's unmet needs in early childhood have long-lasting effects. Feelings derived from early relationships are often transferred or projected onto later relationships.	Clulow and Mattinson 1989 Rodger 1996
Attachment theory	Close relationships in early childhood display typical patterns (e.g. security, ambivalence, hostility, detachment). These affect children's levels of trust and confidence in later relationships. Parents may misperceive children's needs because of their own attachment histories.	Bowlby 1969, 1973 Parkes et al. 1991 Howe 1995a
Behavioural theory	The actions of both parents and children are largely explained by social learning principles. Behaviour develops and changes in response to perceived rewards, negative consequences and imitation.	Patterson 1971 Hudson and McDonald 1986 Herbert 1987
Exchange theories	The evolution of family relationships is related to the balance and exchange of material and non-material resources. These include money, power and knowledge.	Ekeh 1974 Scanzoni and Szinovacz 1980 Argyle and Henderson 1986
Transactional theories	Children modify adults' behaviour as much as vice versa, both as individuals and as sets of sisters and brothers. Important aspects are: emotional reactions; interpretations of others' intentions, needs and behaviour; mind sets.	Sameroff 1975 Bruner 1990 Rutter and Rutter 1993 Dunn 1993

For instance, in family systems theory the notion of 'collusion' between men and women was derived from observations that in some families adult partners appear to collaborate in maintaining conflict, sometimes unwittingly. In the 1980s this idea was overgeneralised within some family therapy circles to suggest that women shared responsibility for the violence of men within family households.

In different ways, family relationship theories stress the interrelatedness of actions, thought and feelings within the family. Consequently, the behaviour of individuals and particular events can be accounted for at the family level, at least in part. For instance, depending on the specific theory, a child's 'problem', such as bedwetting or school refusal could be attributed to any of the following:

• the child's role within the family as attention-seeker, scapegoat or carer
• unresolved parental tensions, or
• faulty social control techniques by the parents.

Attachment and psychodynamic theories particularly emphasise the importance of past relationships on present ones, so that parents may unwittingly expect children to satisfy needs or repeat patterns 'left over' from the parents' own upbringing. For example, adults deprived of affection or support in childhood may have excessive expectations of receiving these from their own children.

Reflections on family theories in general

Given the complexity and variety of family life and its relationships with wider social processes, it is not surprising that each theoretical perspective offers useful understanding, yet is inadequate to provide a comprehensive account since it does not include key considerations attended to by other perspectives. It is a reflection of the current mistrust of global theorising that the present tendency is to focus on specific aspects of families, rather than to integrate external and within-household relationships and influences on a grand scale, as people like Parsons and Bott did in the 1950s. It remains clear that family life is greatly affected by societal structures, employment–home relations, state interventions, social expectations and personal history, but that people also exercise choices and so are to varying degrees agents in the creation of their family patterns. Indeed present-day families and life courses are often distinguished from these of earlier times by the diversity of forms and lifestyles, with much emphasis placed on individual goals (Leonard 1990; Richards 1995; Dahlberg 1996), although options and capacities do vary according to income and socio-economic status (Oppenheim 1996).

A criticism which applies to all the perspectives outlined is the preoccupation with adults. Several so-called family theories might be more accurately called partnership or parent theories. Only recently has the role of children as active participants gained credence. Whereas the influences of social class and gender have been questioned in depth, intergenerational relations and in particular the subordinate position of children have largely been taken for granted. Attachment and behavioural theories have placed children centre stage, but mainly in terms of their passive needs – for consistent loving care and effective management, respectively. Interesting qualitative accounts exist of the views of adults (Stolz 1967; Jordan *et al.* 1994), but less attention has been given to the ways children construe family life. Therefore we shall give priority to these in the sections which follow. These concern children's relationships with parents, siblings and grandparents.

Children and parents

The following sections address several key questions about parent–child relationships from the point of view of the child:

- In which ways and to what extent do children influence the nature of parenting?
- What are children's own views and expectations about parents?
- Can children's needs be met equally well within different household forms?

Children's contributions to child–parent relationships

For a long time, both functionalist family sociology and developmental psychology characterised child–parent relationships in terms of 'socialisation'. Children were typically seen as empty containers into which families poured the customs of their society and culture, mediated by the social grouping and class to which they belonged. A minority of parents dissented from prevailing values or lacked the skills to inculcate them, so their children grew up with social problems of one kind or another. Behaviourist theory in its simplest forms has been particularly notable for portraying children's actions (such as stealing or aggression) as the outcomes of effective or ineffective parental training.

Over the last 20 years or so, it has been increasingly recognised that the relationship is not one-way. The active role of children in family dynamics has been particularly emphasised in family systems and transactional theories about the family. As we saw in Chapter 1, the sociology of childhood has reinforced the view of children as mutual creators of their social worlds. Children's influences on how parents bring them up takes two main forms. Firstly interaction is affected by the children's own personalities, communication, interests and so on. Less directly parents and other adults modify their behaviour depending on their:

- descriptive and explanatory attributions about the nature of children in general

- their ideas about the influence of factors like age, gender and birth order
- their specific perceptions of individual children.

(McGillicuddy-DeLisi 1982; Mitchell 1985)

For example, parents' willingness to leave their young children with other people depends to some extent on whether they see children as sociable and resilient or vulnerable and sensitive (Hill 1987). Fathers appear to be more likely to act on beliefs about children in general, whereas mothers, who usually have closer and more frequent contacts with their children, adapt to their more particularised understanding of each child (Goodnow and Collins 1990). Furthermore, child–parent relationships are negotiated within a collective as well as an individual context. Siblings mediate family life in major ways (see below). Peers exert crucial influences in myriad ways (for example, requests to play or spend time together; comparing expectations about clothes, pocket money and times for getting home).

Academic recognition of children's active role came from both a reassessment of correlational research and from a new perspective on the processes of interaction. Analyses of quantitative data have demonstrated a number of statistical associations between parental attributes (e.g. methods of discipline) and children's behaviour. Previously this had often been presented as meaning that parents' actions had caused the children to act that way, but it is quite possible to view the link the other way round (Bell 1970; Sameroff 1975). For example, it is known that the frequent use of harsh or inconsistent punishments by parents often coincides with challenging behaviour by their children (Maccoby and Martin 1983; Wadsworth 1986). It could be that parental chastisement leads to difficult behaviour, but equally parents may feel obliged to respond punitively or have disputes with each other when they see their child as problematic. Moreover a family systems approach would suggest that causation does not necessarily go in either direction but is circular, with each side reinforcing the other in patterns of compatible or conflictual response (Dallos and McLaughlin 1993).

Support for a changed interpretation came from longitudinal research which showed that sometimes characteristics of the child apparently preceded parental influence or enabled a child to do well despite 'poor' parenting. For instance, studies which have followed children from birth suggests that there are persistent temperamental dispositions evident in neonates, so that some children are placid or active from the start (Thomas and Chess 1977). Parents then respond to the child's character depending on their own dispositions: e.g. they may see a quiet child as easy or uninteresting, an active child as stimulating or demanding. Children who are emotionally intense and find adapting to new experiences difficult are more likely than others to evoke parental criticism and hostility. This in turn fosters resentment and aggression, so that a vicious circle of difficult relationships can be set up (Rutter and Rutter 1993; Fahlberg 1994).

Long-term studies of children have also identified some who seem to be particularly resilient. Most children who experience major parental rejection or discord have poor outcomes, as judged by such things as school performance, involvement in crime and self-esteem (Rutter 1981). This fits with what would be expected according to attachment theory (see also Chapter 3). Yet some children do well despite apparently problematic upbringing. There seems to be a cluster of factors which enables resilient children to overcome adversity, including both internal and external factors. Intelligence, high self-esteem and a sense of self-efficacy are valuable assets, as is access to at least one supportive adult (Antonovsky 1987; Garmezy 1987; Herrenkohl *et al*. 1994; Fonagy *et al*. 1994). Doing well at school can also offset poor home circumstances. This probably results from a combination of personal factors and access to encouragement and opportunity.

From a different direction, observational studies – particularly of young children and mothers – have also questioned the image of parents imposing their will on children. These have revealed that from a very early age children are often initiators. Most mothers adapt what they do both to the varying actions of the same child and to the differing behaviour and communication of siblings (Dunn and Kendrick 1982; Bruner 1990; Trevarthen 1992; Cohen 1993). Indeed many parents set out to offer choices and agree mini-contracts with their (pre-school) children about how time should be spent. Dahlberg (1996) noted that this has the potential both to promote children's control over their lives and to subtly impose adult management over children's spontaneous wishes. Infants imitate adults, but mothers also copy their children, sometimes with elaborations to extend the child's use of language or play. Moreover, children respond selectively to parental actions:

During play the mothers provided the children with a constant flow of suggestions; the children, however, appeared quite systematically to select from these only the ones that fitted in with their own capabilities. (Schaffer 1992: 113)

Through such processes children learn not only practical and linguistic knowledge, but also principles of human interaction, such as how to take turns. They gain insights into what pleases, distresses or irritates others. Through such two-way processes, moral rules are learned about fairness and reciprocity, while social skills are acquired, such as how to comfort or provoke others (Dunn 1993).

Children's perceptions and expectations of parents, family and home

Most accounts of parenting and family life are derived from parents' own perspectives or the views of academics and professionals based on the evidence they have perceived or gathered about outcomes (Pugh *et al*. 1995). Systematic accounts of children's own views are rare, but a few exist. A recent study in East London revealed that many children retained conventional expectations about nuclear family households (O'Brien *et al.* 1996). Primary and secondary schoolchildren were asked to label a range of household configurations as 'a family' or 'not a family'. Many indicated that the presence of children was necessary to make a family. Most regarded an unmarried couple living together with children as not being a family. Older children were much more likely than younger ones to regard a lone-parent household as a family. In drawings of their own families, primary school children usually included only the people they lived with, though sometimes a relative who visited frequently was also portrayed. As children grow older, however, they tend to define family more in terms of emotionally significant relationships rather than co-residence (Newman *et al.* 1993). The drawings of children in reconstituted families revealed how some saw the households of both parents as integral parts of their 'family', while others depicted themselves as in the middle of two separate parts to their family (Levin 1995).

When asked, children of primary school age nearly all indicate that parents and close family are central in their lives. They value love and security, but often talk about their expectations and satisfactions in material terms, e.g. being well-fed and clothed, receiving presents (Williams *et al.* 1989; Hill *et al.* 1995). This does not mean that they necessarily experience relationships only in those terms, but may find it easier to respond to adult questions with concrete illustrations.

A small qualitative study concerned with middle childhood elicited the views of some Scottish primary school children on the nature and tasks of parenthood (five group discussions, nine individual interviews). The quality they valued most in parents was love (Borland *et al.* 1996: 153–4). One described this as a prerequisite of the job of parenting:

They wouldnae really be parents to you if they didnae love you.
(Girl, aged eleven)

Another pointed to the long term consequences of withholding love from children:

If your parents didn't show you love then you would grow up and you wouldn't show your children love and then it would be that you weren't a very nice family. (Boy, aged eleven)

According to the children, parental love is not just shown through overt affection, but embodied symbolically in the provision of meals and gifts, wrapping the children up warm, providing comfort during ill-health or accompanying them to places which might entail risk:

My mum – well she always buys me things and she always thinks of us before she thinks of herself. (Girl, aged ten)

In many ways the children's views embodied an idealised view of the family, but for the majority this was rooted in their own broadly positive experiences of family life thus far. Nevertheless, many also recognised that parenting is stressful and involves sacrifice:

(My mother) used to be an accountant but she went and gave that up once she had my little brother. So it was quite hard for her to give up something that she had worked hard to achieve. (Girl, aged nine)

Children may also recognise that their own behaviour can contribute to stress:

I irritate my mum sometimes 'cause, say she's trying to sort out her money for the bills, I'm always asking her these questions. And I'm always asking her for food and I'm always talking about Christmas during the summer . . . (Boy, aged 11)

A ten year old in a different study listed some of the ways he might make his parents 'cross':

Smash a window. Pinch money out of a purse. Be nasty, be lazy. Don't do anything. (Quoted in Williams *et al.* 1989: 46)

Children use a range of techniques including bargaining, badgering and bemoaning their deprivation compared with other children to try and gain parental consent for activities and purchases (Middleton *et al.* 1994).

Children are often sources of support as well as stress for their parents. Some highlight the reciprocity of the child–parent relationship. Examples of children acting in a caring way for their parents include a boy opting to play indoors with his Dad who dislikes the cold, an eight-year-old girl massaging her mother who has back pains, and another doing chores when her mother is unwell (Borland *et al.* 1996). Children are often very perceptive about adults' worries and offer emotional help:

I knew my Mum was really upset because Grandad died. I said to her in the end 'It's all right, Mum, I know you've been crying. You don't have to pretend.' (Eight-year old, quoted in Lindon 1996: 68)

Most children accept that they should take on increasing responsibilities for self-care and domestic tasks as they grow older, as Pringle advocated (Chapter 3). This may be welcomed as signifying greater recognition of their abilities and opportunities for self-reliance, though it can be resented as a burden or restriction:

You have to change your clothes and get dressed. (10-year old)

I have to tidy my room. (11-year old)

Your parents say 'If you're grown up enough to do that, then you're old enough to help with the washing and the cleaning'. (14-year old)

I have to babysit the younger ones and they play me up. (14 year old; all quoted in Lindon 1996: 110)

In certain circumstances children take on major household or care responsibilities, when a parent's capacities are restricted, for whatever reason. Some children with a disabled parent resent as a burden the practical work entailed in doing housework or lifting. This can also result in social isolation and their schooling can be affected by responsibilities at home (Aldridge and Becker 1994). In a study of children whose parents had alcohol difficulties, children took on a variety of emotional roles, such as confidant, mediator or protector of the non-drinking parent, but also sometimes physical care of a drunken parent:

I was carrying her and then I fell (while helping his mother into bed). *When she had the DTs, I used to go into bed with her, so she could sleep instead of getting up and walking about.* (Quoted in Laybourn *et al.* 1996: 64–5)

Hard work may be combined with emotional stresses:

I used to get very very angry. I wanted to be like a normal family. I think the worst thing is seeing someone you love, someone active who becomes tired of walking. (Quoted in Garratt *et al.* 1997: 49)

Based on experiences such as these, the category of 'young carers' has been created in the last few years (see Chapter 3 concerning the social construction of needs). The accompanying literature highlights the practical and emotional difficulties which can result from the reversal of usual roles between parents and children, mainly with respect to physically disabled parents. Questions are raised about caring responsibilities conflicting with children's rights – to autonomy, services and education, for instance (Aldridge and Becker 1995). However, it is important that such children's needs are met in ways which respond to their particular wishes and abilities, and also which do not devalue their parents' roles as carers too. Some children see the extra work as enhancing their competencies, a source of satisfaction or a fair return for their parents' love and help in other ways (Reed 1995; Keith and Morris 1995; Garratt *et al.* 1997). Evidently thinking about this issue needs to take account of preconceptions about children's abilities and rights, different dimensions of parent–child relationships (parenting is not just physical care) and the diversity of expectations about appropriate levels of responsibility which children can and should take on at different ages.

The majority of children in the upper primary age range are positive about their relationships with parents and indeed other adults, whom they generally find supportive and understanding, though of course there are exceptions (Williams *et al.* 1989; Hill *et al.* 1995). Parents, especially mothers, are also the people with whom most children first wish to share positive feelings (e.g. about school activities, sporting success) or their worries. However, many also convey a sense of not receiving enough attention from adults, though they are often sympathetic to parental time constraints and stresses. Here is an excerpt from a group discussion with children aged nine to ten:

I asked my Mum to play with me and she said no, she was too busy doing the washing.

My Mum said she would play Monopoly with me three days ago – she hasn't played since because she's doing so much stuff for my sister.

I don't ask my Mum to do anything, cos she's got the baby to feed.

. . . My Mum and Dad are too busy.   (Quoted in Hill *et al.* 1995: 70)

A different group made similar remarks:

They're so busy they don't notice.

When you're sitting down and you want your Mum and Dad to talk to you and they're too busy.   (Quoted in Hill *et al.* 1995: 71)

The teen years are often thought to be time of serious conflict and tension between young people and their parents. Although this is true for a minority (perhaps one in five), the majority report reasonable satisfaction and harmony (Fogelman 1975). Besides, some degree of disagreement helps young people to clarify their thoughts and attitudes, and so reflects 'psychological growth rather than discord' (Rutter and Rutter 1993: 252). Unfortunately, when there are severe difficulties with parents, this is associated with a host of other problems which tend to persist, such as suicide attempts and drug abuse (Petersen 1988).

Adolescents tend to dislike both authoritarian and permissive parental styles (Coleman and Hendry 1990). They do not want rigid and harsh discipline, but neither do they want to be given complete freedom – well, at least that is what they say to researchers! Fortunately, most parents do adopt approaches which combine rules, guidance, flexibility and negotiation (Shucksmith *et al.* 1995). Generally young people see parental constraints and controls as a positive sign of concern, especially over major lifestyle and risk issues. On the other hand, young people do resent parents' strictures on matters which they see as trivial or a question of taste, such as personal appearance. They also want parents to recognise that expectations derived from their own childhood need adapting to present-day circumstances:

Sometimes they don't seem to realise that it's the nineties. It's not the same as when they were our age.   (13-year old, quoted in Lindon 1996: 14)

In families of Asian and Chinese backgrounds, parents tend to be seen as more protective. Although this can lead to tensions, deference to elders is often accepted on both sides as a positive basis for restricting young people's autonomy in ways which enhance educational and work achievements (Shams and Williams 1995; Brannen 1996).

Although teenagers do increasingly turn to friends as confidants and supporters as they grow older, this does not supplant the role of parents, whose advice and approval is usually still welcomed (Youniss and Smollar 1985). Older teenagers often value the moral guidance and practical help which parents have given them, so feel a sense of obligation in return (Allatt 1996). Even young people who have experienced separation from home or been in serious trouble with the law often continue to see parents as their main sources of support and representation (Triseliotis *et al.* 1995).

The quality and intensity of relationships with mothers and fathers are frequently quite different. Most young people, both male and female, communicate more openly and more often with mothers than fathers (Anderson and Clarke 1982; Buchanan *et al.* 1991). In one sample of young women, nearly half said they confided fully in their mothers, but only a handful in their fathers (Monck 1991). Mothers are also generally seen as more understanding and fathers as more remote, especially by girls (Noller and Callan 1991). Within two-parent households, teenagers tend to look to fathers for approval and guidance but mainly with respect to a few practical areas (e.g. about careers, money issues, sports). They talk to mothers about a wider range of issues and have more emotional exchanges with them (Youniss and Smollar 1985; O'Brien *et al.* 1996).

Different ways to meet children's needs

The growth in non-marital cohabitation, divorce and remarriage means that a much higher proportion of children spend part or all of their childhoods in a household which does not contain both their biological parents. The proportion of lone-parent households has grown considerably, with the largest percentage resulting from separation and divorce. The 1991 Census showed that one-fifth of households with dependent children were headed by lone parents (21 per cent) and 4 per cent by cohabiting couples (Haskey 1994b). About 90 per cent of lone-parent households are headed by women, 10 per cent by men. Haskey (1994a) estimated that about 8 per cent of all dependent children were living in stepfamilies. Of these one-quarter were the couples' own children and three-quarters were stepchildren. As a result of such changes in parents' relationships, increasing numbers of children experience a sequence of different types of household structure (Tisdall with Donnaghie 1994; Richards 1995).

Throughout history there have been debates about the 'best' way for children to be brought up, but the diversification of family and household patterns has evoked anew questions as to the effects this may or may not have on children. For instance, does it matter if increasing numbers of children are being brought up by mothers alone or in stepfamilies? This section reviews evidence about three significant issues relevant to family care. These concern the effects on children of:

- household form
- parental employment patterns
- parenting styles.

It will be seen that it is not easy to draw clear-cut conclusions, for a number of reasons, including:

* large variations occur *within* as well as *between* different family/ household forms
* research findings sometimes conflict
* family and household characteristics interact with other factors like poverty and social class
* changes over time mean that the nature and proportion of, for instance, dual-career families and lone-parent households are very different now compared with even 20 or 30 years ago
* the measures used to assess outcomes may be limited and open to varied interpretation
* even if significant contrasts are identified, these are still only differences in proportions and there is always some overlap in patterns.

Household form

It is often assumed that it is best for children to be brought up jointly by both their birth parents, but it must be remembered that these 'intact' households include some where children are subject to violence or conflict. We shall see that the evidence suggests the nature of the household is in itself not usually a significant consideration – each type works well or poorly depending on the quality of the relationships. For instance, children brought up jointly by several kinswomen remain well attached to their mothers and may even benefit cognitively from the wider range of stimulation (Smith 1979, 1980; Schaffer 1990). Reflecting wider concerns, some researchers have set out to assess whether children reared by a woman alone or a man alone have special difficulties in their sexual identity. Apparently, the answer is 'No' – they do not differ from their peers in this respect. Also a study of lesbian-headed households revealed no special problems in the children's emotional, social and psychosexual development (Golombok *et al.* 1983; Schaffer 1990).

Over the years, studies have shown that a higher proportion of children in lone-parent households have scholastic or emotional/behavioural difficulties compared with those living with both parents, though the majority in both types of household do well (McLanahan and Booth 1989). However, this apparently consistent and significant difference disappears when families in similar material circumstances are compared. In other words, it is because lone-parent households are much more likely to be poor that their children are more vulnerable. In the UK, higher percentages of lone mothers are dependent on state benefits (three-quarters) than in countries with better support and incentives for employment (Roll 1991; Long 1995). A cluster of factors means that many, though not all, lone parents seeking to manage on Income Support encounter difficulties. These include economic hardship, increased likelihood of experiencing negative life events and lower chances of having access to social network support.

Ferri (1984) compared children living in stepfamilies with those with both birth parents. On average the former experienced more difficulties and poorer educational achievement but the differences were mostly small and linked to material circumstances. Kiernan (1992) found that children in stepfamilies had high incidence of early completion of schooling and leaving home early. On the one hand, both children and adults in reconstituted families may be affected by folk myths like that of the wicked stepmother (Hughes 1991). On the other hand, there is a paucity of culturally sanctioned expectations and rituals in Britain to guide the establishment of parent–child relationships which start after infancy and outside blood kinship (Burgoyne and Clark 1984). As a result, parenting difficulties often arise (such as ineffective discipline and role confusion). Children can be resentful when a well-meaning step-parent seeks to become emotionally involved or engage in activities which, from the children's viewpoint, usurp the place of the parent who has died or separated (Ochiltree 1990).

Schaffer (1990) concluded 'there is no indication that departures from the conventional norm of family structure are necessarily harmful to children' (189–90). Further, Campion (1995) argued that the crucial factors in the care of children are not household characteristics, but the sensitivity of parents and the availability of support to compensate for any difficulties they may have, including prejudice and stereotyping. This claim is supported by evidence that it is family functioning and parenting styles and not family structure which are correlated with positive or negative outcomes for children in terms of self-esteem, psychological wellbeing and physical symptoms (Sweeting and West 1995).

Mothers and fathers

We have seen so far that the absence of a father from the household is not necessarily crucial for children, except in as far as it is associated with lower earning potential. Nor indeed is mother absence, judging by the success which can be achieved by lone fathers or adopters, provided the adults concerned can offer loving, consistent and stimulating care. This is not to deny that children will have questions and feelings about the reasons for the loss of one or both parents, but these effects will depend very much both on the circumstances and the responses of all concerned. Particularly important will be the child's understanding of how and why the parent died or left home – does the child feel in any way to blame, directly or indirectly? To what extent does the child identify with the absent parent? Is the child worried about inheriting the parent's illness, difficult behaviour or whatever other characteristics are associated with the loss? (Bowlby 1988).

There are nonetheless more 'fine-grained' implications of 'mother-care' and 'father-care', which stem in part from differing social expectations about the two parental roles. As far as we know, all societies differentiate between male and female roles, but the particular expectations as regards economic, social and emotional functions have been highly varied, with apparently few tasks other than childbirth and breast-feeding assigned universally to one rather than the other (Mead 1962). Western (mainly American) research suggests that men and women do typically treat their children in different ways. For instance, men have been found to be more sex-stereotyped in their play and expectations, are likely to be more punitive towards boys than girls, and engage in more rough play with sons (Parke 1981; Beail and McGuire 1982; Lamb 1987). Some of the gender differences are related to the amount of time and timing of interaction, so that women usually assume more respons-ibility for physical care, emotional comfort, social control and educative play with younger children, whereas men spend more time in fun play (Lewis and O'Brien 1987; Parke and Stearns 1993). Of course, there are many individual exceptions to these generalisations. Despite these differences, fathers and mothers show similar ranges of responsiveness to the needs of new-born babies and can be equally competent in caring for them (Lamb 1987; Moss 1996). Many infants appear to be as attached to their fathers as their mothers, even when the former undertake little practical care giving (Schaffer and Emerson 1964; Schaffer 1990).

Parental employment patterns

This issue has usually been discussed in terms of 'working mothers', either to express or rebut fears that children are neglected in comparison with 'homemaker' mothers. Similar concerns are not expressed about working fathers (only sometimes about *over*working fathers). This results from traditional, though receding, assumptions about women's primary role in childcare. In this context, the notion of 'working' has excluded unpaid work at home.

In practice, no sharp distinction exists between the working and non-working mother. Particularly in children's early years, many women's paid employment is part-time or discontinuous. Some work at home or do work where children can accompany them (Hill 1987; Hakim 1996). Women's work need not mean that children are cared for outside the nuclear family or household, since some women arrange their work around the availability of the father (usually by working evenings or weekends), whilst some parents employ au pairs and daily helps. The rise in male unemployment has increased the still small numbers of 'role-reversal' households in which the man stays home and the wife works (Moss 1996). It seems that unemployment frees some men to become more participative parents, but others feel constrained to main-tain traditional roles (Binns and Mars 1984).

There are two types of relevant research about 'working mothers' – comparisons of different work patterns and assessments of daycare arrangements. The latter are only partially relevant, because working par-ents do not necessarily use formal daycare provision and, conversely, care facilities are used for several reasons other than employment. Research comparing the outcomes for children of working and non-working mothers have usually not taken account of the precise care arrangements and have tended to assume that children with non-working mothers do not have alternative carers, which in fact is rarely the case since nearly all children spend time apart from their parents from a young age (Hill 1987). With these qualifications in mind, the evidence is that children are not harmed when both parents work. Studies by Hock (1978; 1980) suggested that the level of development and quality of attachment of infants was not related to the mother's employment status, but was affected by role satisfaction. On the whole, children did well when their mothers were happy to be home full-time or happy at work, but showed more signs of anxiety when their mothers were discontented in either role. Similar conclusions have emerged from following up families over a number of years (Schaffer 1990).

Likewise it has been shown that, by and large, children who attend nursery groups are not adversely affected, provided that the quality of care is adequate (Scarr and Dunn 1987). Indeed, there are often short-term benefits socially and educationally, while participation in intensive programmes is associated with long-term gains in scholastic achievement (Gold and Andres 1978; Hawthorne-Kirk 1995).

As many parents realise, whatever the household form and care arrangements, children in the same family often turn out very differently. It is time we looked at the other core relationship for children in the nuclear family – with sisters and brothers.

Sisters and brothers

There have been two main phases of research concerning sisters and brothers (siblings). The first examined influence of sibling structure, i.e. the number, age-spacing and gender distribution of siblings. The second has focused more on general differences between siblings and the processes of sibling relationships.

Position in the family

The investigation of sibling structure mainly consisted of statistical comparisons of children's characteristics according to their family size or birth order. In the main this yielded few significant conclusions. Brief reflection indicates some of the reasons for this. One is the sheer complexity of sibling structures, once account is taken of gender and sibling spacing. For example, the following are all second-borns aged six in two-child families, but they have very different family patterns:

- six-year old boy with an older brother aged 8
- six-year old boy with an older sister aged 15
- six-year old girl with an older brother aged 8.

Further complications could be added – such as including children in larger families or step-sibling relationships. Secondly, position in the family will affect children through a variety of mechanisms, including parental perceptions, sibling interaction and changes in family income, employment or social network (e.g. death of a grandparent).

Partly to simplify comparisons, studies usually confined themselves to two-child families or else compared first borns with later-born children (Sears 1950; McArthur 1956; Sutton-Smith and Rosenberg 1970). These did reveal some significant *average* differences between first borns and other children. Characteristics found to be more common amongst first borns included:

- smaller birth size
- greater anxiety about success
- conformity to adult expectations
- weaker orientation to peers
- early language development
- high achievement motivation
- better performance at school and university.

Zajonc and Marcus (1975) explained the non-physical differences in terms of the first born experiencing a period of sole adult attention and hence developing a particularly close relationship with adults. Others argued that the findings were a statistical artefact resulting from the fact that more families with later-born children have low incomes. Indeed, once comparisons were confined to those at a comparable socio-economic level, often the differences disappeared.

Closely spaced siblings tend to have more quarrels and conflicts than those with a wider age gap (Abramovitch *et al.* 1982; Wagner *et al.* 1985). Several studies have found that same-sex pairs tend to have more positive relationships than opposite-sex pairs, especially when both are girls (Dunn and Kendrick 1982; Berndt and Bulleit 1985). As might be expected, more conflicts and resentments are reported between step-siblings than birth siblings (Ferri 1984; Funder and Kinsella 1991).

The differences amongst siblings

Since the 1980s, attention has shifted from family-position influences on children to consideration of processes and interaction. At the same time, the theoretical and practical significance of sibling differences have been emphasised.

Common sense would suggest that children having a shared genetic inheritance and brought up by the same parents ought to turn out quite similar. Furthermore, children's behaviour is often explained by their family and environmental characteristics, which if true would mean that siblings ought to be affected in the same way. Yet what is striking about sisters and brothers is just how different they usually are. Assessments on a range of dimensions like temperament, personality traits, interests and psycho-social adjustment have shown that, apart from twins, brothers and sisters are no more like each other than any other children. They are more similar in cognitive abilities and academic achievements, but even then the mean difference between siblings on these dimensions is still quite large (Dunn and Plomin 1990).

Genetic differences have been shown to make a contribution to these wide variations between siblings (Scarr 1992), but much emphasis has also been given to their *non-shared environments*. In other words, despite sharing the same parents and household, siblings have very different experiences (Dunn and Plomin 1990). Even when brothers and sisters share involvement in the same event, like moving home, they do so at different ages (apart from twins and some step-siblings), so it is likely to have a different meaning and impact. Amongst the main micro-environmental influences are variations in:

• parental treatment
• selective responses by the children to available roles and activities
• interaction between the children
• exposure to life events (e.g. death of grandparent; parental change of job; moving house)
• external experiences (e.g. friends, teachers)
• social network changes

For example, a mother encompassed several interacting factors in explaining the different reactions to separation of her son and daughter:

I know they are differing natures, but when he went along to nursery he found it a lot harder, because he's been, well you know, just a baby, whereas she had more contact with other children. And her going along to nursery before it even started (accompanying her older brother), she took it a lot easier.
(Quoted in Hill 1987: 263)

Scarr and Grajeck (1982) offered a transactional explanation which integrated several of the factors noted above – genetic influences, parental treatment and children's choices. They argued that parents adapt to inborn differences between their children and those same differences mean that children select different aspects of their family environment to respond to (i.e. they occupy different niches within the family). In this way, one child in a family may become very musical, another be mainly interested in sport, and a third may concentrate on academic achievements.

The processes of sibling relationships

In order to understand these variations and also the meanings of relationships, it is helpful to take a systemic or transactional perspective, examining how sisters and brothers interact with their parents, each other and the extra-familial world over time.

At an early age, the relationships between parents and different siblings may be affected by events specific to one child such as a difficult labour, prematurity or illness, as well as wider changes in the material and social circumstances of the family. Social construction theories emphasise that it is the *meaning ascribed* to these experiences which is crucial. Similarly, as noted above, parents treat children differently according to their *perceived* personalities and needs (Miller *et al.* 1993). Parents tend to be more anxious about their first child. With later children they are usually more relaxed and also modify their expectations and care in the light of experience (Lasko 1954; Backett 1982; Dunn and Kendrick 1982).

I wouldn't have left a nine-month baby with a friend had it been a first one, but by the time the third one arrives you realise it's really quite good for them to get away from you for a couple of hours.   (Quoted in Hill 1987: 262)

Especially when children are closely spaced, mothers spend less time with second and later borns because they now have to divide their attention between more than one child.

Once first children are joined by others, parents and relatives sometimes now relate to siblings as a pair or group rather than individually. It becomes necessary to establish rules for sibling interaction as well as individual behaviour. Dunn and Munn (1986) found that when there were disputes between children, parents were more likely to punish the older child and distract the younger one.

Consideration of how children respond to their parents vis-à-vis their siblings has been dominated by the idea of sibling rivalry. This notion dates back at least to the story of Cain and Abel, and was prominent in the psychoanalytical ideas of Alfred Adler. He believed that older or eldest children feel pushed off their pedestal by the arrival of a new baby who suddenly takes away parental attention. This 'dethronement' leads to hostility towards the younger sibling and to enduring effects on personality. Whilst Adler's claim about the long-term consequences is unproven, short-term negative reactions are undoubtedly common. In the first few months after the new birth, first borns often show naughty or demanding behaviour, clinginess and increased conflict with their mothers compared with before. Negative reactions are also sometimes evident during the pre-birth period (Nadelbaum and Begun 1982; Dunn and Kendrick 1982). Usually the resentments are directed more at the parent than the baby, but when strong hostility to the other child occurs, it tends to persist. Despite the sudden diminution in parental attention, first borns still tend to have more direct interaction with parents and other adults than do their younger siblings (Baskett 1984).

The quality of sibling relationships is also influenced by the nature of the parental relationship and the perceived attitude of parents. Many children are hypersensitive to parents' differential treatment of themselves and siblings, yet also want personalised attention. For parents, the difficult trick to pull off is to treat their offspring individually without being seen as favouring.

Parents shouldn't compare you with your sister or brother.

You get blamed when the younger one does something.

I watch her getting to do all the things that I want to do.
                                        (10- to 14-year-olds, quoted in Lindon 1996)

Attachment theory has been preoccupied with child–parent relationships, but siblings are usually very important attachment figures for each other. They become mutually attached very quickly and at about the same time as to parents. They often miss each other when apart, seek the other out when distressed and feel more comfortable in an unfamiliar situation when accompanied by a sibling (Schaffer and Emerson 1964; Stewart 1983). Children who have a trusting relationship with their parents also tend to be securely attached to their siblings, whilst tension between siblings is most apparent when there is insecure attachment to both parents and/or when parents are in conflict (Hetherington *et al.* 1985; Stocker and McHale 1992; Vandell and Bailey 1992). Thus in many cases parent–child and child–child relationships reflect and reinforce each other, either positively or negatively.

Relationships between sisters and brothers have special qualities which Dunn (1988) suggests are vital in development (though, as we shall see below, this claim is challenged by evidence that 'only children' do not appear to be disadvantaged at all). One of the crucial aspects of most sibling relationships is ambivalence, that is, the experience of strong negative and positive feelings in the same relationship. Warm relationships are typically accompanied by frequent quarrels (Boer 1990; Kosonen 1994, 1996a). This mix of feelings is more readily expressed than in relation to parents because there is not the same dependency and power differential. Thus, sibling relationships give early opportunities to come to terms with a person whose actions are less motivated by a desire to meet his/her needs than parents usually are. Moreover, children see everyday sibling conflicts as largely a matter for themselves to sort out, with parental intervention often seen as ineffective or even counterproductive (Prochaska and Prochaska 1985).

Dunn (1988) also concluded that sibling relationships are of considerable significance cognitively for young children – a corrective to the view that only parents and other adults contribute to early learning. Younger children can learn through imitation of older siblings and gain from them information about the world, while an older child can learn early forms of responsibility for others. Both can learn to empathise through their intimate knowledge of each other. Young children seem to be expert at both comforting and provoking their siblings not only through heedless actions but through sensitive appraisal of what will help or irritate the other. Furthermore, language and reasoning skills are amply practised in sibling disputes!

Especially in middle childhood, a process of *de-identification* is common in sibling relationships (Bryant 1982). Children feel a need to differentiate themselves from each other and develop a separate identity. They do not want to be seen as clones and treated the same. Hence they often seek deliberately to accentuate differences by choosing different interests or subjects to concentrate on at school. Having separate domains helps to avoid rivalry and unfavourable social comparisons. De-identification is another factor in making brothers and sisters diverge and links with the niche-selection theory outlined above (Scarr and Grajek 1982). Of course, some siblings do like to share similar activities and interests.

Twins are particularly conscious of expectations that they should feel and be treated the same. Many resent other people's stereotyping of twinship, though are also disappointed to feel less close than everyone assumes. Some develop rigid role differences in order to resist others' tendencies to lump them together and to achieve a separate identity (Ainslie 1985).

Disabled children tend to spend more time with siblings than other children do and usually have positive relationships:

We get on very well. If we have an argument we're back to normal in five to ten minutes.   (Quoted in Anderson and Clarke 1982)

Children often feel supportive towards disabled siblings and take on caring or advocacy roles (Macaskill 1985; Bluebond-Langner 1991). They may also experience more worry and stress than usual, but much depends on their understanding of the condition or disability (Laybourn and Hill 1994; Summers 1994; Roeyers and Mycke 1995).

In many societies older siblings from seven or eight years onwards play a major role in looking after younger children without adults being present (Weisner and Gallimore 1977). This can be seen as an important means for children to learn and take responsibility, but concern has also been expressed that this exploits the caregiving children and may restrict the development of the children looked after (Weisner 1987). Kosonen (1996b) asked a sample of 64 Scottish children aged 9 to 12 about their experiences of sibling caretaking and found all but a few reported instances of this happening. Many enjoyed this:

It is fun and their friends come round.

He plays me games.

They are really kind sometimes.

On the other hand, some disliked being annoyed and bossed around. One in five said they had been bullied, punched or 'battered' by a sibling.

Children who do not have a brother or sister

The point at which a household can finally be considered to contain only one child is often uncertain, especially to an outsider, since it can take a long time to be sure a family is complete. In the UK about one in 10 households with dependent children have an only child, though smaller proportions of children are 'only children', and the preference by adults for having only one child is growing in popularity (Laybourn 1994).

Negative stereotypes are common about only children (for example, that they are selfish, spoilt and/or lonely) and these have often been given as one of the reasons for having a second child (Busfield and Paddon 1977; Laybourn 1994). In fact, no general differences are apparent between only children and others as regards sociability, popularity or happiness. On the other hand, only children tend to have above-average intelligence and educational achievement (Falbo 1984; Laybourn 1994). It would seem that only children need and are entitled to be freed from false assumptions about their personalities.

Grandparents

Little systematic information is available about aunts, uncles, cousins – though they are very special to many children (Hill 1987; Williams *et al.* 1989). In the last decade, though, there has been an upsurge in academic interest in one extended kin relationship – grandparenthood. The grandparent, parent and grandchildren relationships operate at the interface between two intimately connected nuclear families and embody strong feelings transferred from one childhood to another. The children may have at best a hazy awareness of the complex dynamics, which draw on personal histories before they were born. Concepts of systems and subsystems, transference and displacement help understanding (Bronfenbrenner 1979; Bengston and Robertson 1985).

For many young children, the most important relationship outside the nuclear family is with a grandparent. Even when grandparents live at a distance, considerable effort is usually made to sustain the relationship by means of visits, letters and phone calls. There is quite a choice of special words for children to call their grandparents (grannie, grandma, nan, nanna, nannie; grandpa, granddad, pop, poppa, papa), as well as occasionally affectionate terms unique to an individual family. Different terms are used in other languages, which often differentiate maternal and paternal grandparents (and other kin, too).

Contrary to common images of frailty and grey hair, grandparents are often fit and active, especially when children are young (Smith 1991). The average person becomes a grandparent at about 50 and will be a grandparent for the last third of their lives (Smith and Cowie 1991).

Occasionally, grandparents act as surrogate parents especially in relation to young single mothers. In many families, grandparents are the preferred secondary carers for children, whether in relation to parents working or for evening baby-sitting (Martin and Roberts 1984). Other roles include – companion; source of gifts, pocket money or payment for errands; mediator in conflicts with parents; confidant; conveyor of family history. There is also a common expectation that grandparents are entitled to indulge children more than their parents. This can become a source of tension when parents feel spoiling is excessive. Generally the two adult generations negotiate a trade-off so that grandparents are entitled to spend time with their grandchildren, but try not to interfere (Kahana and Kahana 1970; Blaxter and Paterson 1982; Hill 1987). In families of Asian and Afro-Caribbean backgrounds, grandparents more often have a co-equal relationship with parents towards the children (Campion 1995).

Most children regard grandparents with affection (Furman and Buhrmeister 1985), although more problematic interaction includes unwanted advice and remarks by grandparents which make the children feel bad about themselves (Eisenberg 1988). Many children themselves appreciate the patience and unconditional listening of grandparents (Battitstelli and Farneti 1991). 'Grandchild status' can affect the amount and type of attention by grandparents. This refers to a child's position with regard to other grandchildren (oldest, youngest, only girl etc.), which may make that child special. This can be different for the two sets of grandparents and may affect how prominent the grandchild is, so that contacts are likely to be more frequent with grandparents who have no other grandchildren when the other set of grandparents have a large number (Hill 1987). However, gender-based expectations mean that contacts with mothers' mothers are commonly the closest and most frequent (Kahana and Kahana 1971; Eisenberg 1988).

Conclusions

This chapter has concentrated on children's relationships with significant family members, mainly parents, siblings and grandparents. It is important to remember that those relationships are greatly affected by wider networks and government policies and services – an issue to which we shall return in the final chapter.

It has been possible to pick out only a few of the key issues from our understanding of the child-family nexus. In both sociology and psychology, childhood was formerly seen as a period when adults transmitted their expectations and culture by moulding children into desired shapes, with the family as the primary site for socialisation (Jenks 1996). No longer is the family seen simply as a means of instilling parental and societal knowledge and values. Children contribute in major ways to the nature and variety of family life through reciprocal interactive processes. They respond selectively to the available 'niches' within the family; parents and others adapt to perceived differences between children; children help and care for other family members as well as vice versa. The changed academic view corresponds with legal and social developments towards less dictatorial and more negotiated parent–child relationships (Dahlberg 1996). Recent British children's legislation has in many respects substituted the concept of parental responsibility for that of parental right, to convey the idea that what parents do for and to children derives not from possession of a child but from their duty of care.

Children's needs are usually perceived as satisfied through living within family households. The majority of children and young people appear content with how they are treated by parents, and even the teen years are negotiated by most with only minor ups and downs. That does not mean that household members meet all the needs, as the significant contributions of grandparents (or teachers and peers) illustrate. Nor does the household have to conform to any single pattern, despite common views that two married parents and at least two children are optimal. Each household form can have good or bad outcomes depending on the particular circumstances and relationships. Of course, not all families serve children well and we shall examine in later chapters some of the problems which occur when children suffer and cause others to suffer.

Until recently children's participative rights within the family have received little attention in policy, law or research. A common wish expressed by children is to be listened to more attentively and have their views taken seriously, by parents and others (Hill *et al.* 1995; Lindon 1996). The UN Convention indicates that children have a right to be consulted about decisions affecting them and that the proper exercise of parental responsibilities and rights is contingent on enabling children to have a say, according to their evolving capacities (Articles 5 and 18). Research reviewed in this chapter suggested that those capacities have been frequently underestimated. Most children accept and understand the reasons for limitations on their autonomy, though they also cherish being trusted and having freedoms. They are sensitive to the needs, stresses and wishes of parents, too. The Convention takes a strong stance not against parents, but against authoritarian parenting (Children's Rights Office 1996). Again this is supported by studies which indicated that adherence by offspring to desired values is more likely to be forthcoming when parents are firm but flexible and fair, rather than punitive and unbending.

Many adults remain uncertain or antagonistic about children's participatory rights, which they fear threaten their authority. More dialogue is needed within families and between families and children's rights advocates to develop the debates about when and how children's views should influence or hold sway in the family arena (Borland *et al.* 1996).

So far, British governments have generally seen children's participation in family decisions as a matter for parental discretion rather than state regulation. Ideals of family autonomy sit uneasily alongside the discourse of children's participatory rights, so that law and policy have conceded only restricted entitlements for children as individuals to make choices contrary to the wishes of their parents. The Children Act 1989 limited the right to be consulted on major decisions to public welfare settings: both home and school were omitted (Lansdown 1996). However, Section 6 of Children (Scotland) Act 1995 does state that anyone in the position of parent must give due regard to children's views when making major parenting decisions affecting the child (as in Finnish law). It will be fascinating to see how this may or may not affect exchanges within families when differences in viewpoint occur between parents and children on matters as diverse as choice of diet, moving house, selecting school or religious affiliation.

Suggestions for further reading

Borland, M., Laybourn, A., Hill, M. and Brown, J. (forthcoming in 1997) *Middle Childhood*, London: Jessica Kingsley.

Brannen, J. and O'Brien, M. (eds) (1996) *Children in Families*, London: Falmer Press.

Dunn, J. (1993) *Young Children's Close Relationships*, London: Sage.

Hill, M., Hawthorne-Kirk, R. and Part, D. (eds) *Supporting Families*, Edinburgh: HMSO.

Lindon, J. (1996) *Growing up: From Eight Years to Young Adulthood*, London: National Children's Bureau.

Muncie, J., Wetherell, M., Dallos, R. and Cochrane, A. (eds) (1995) *Understanding the Family*, London: Sage.

CHAPTER 5

Children's peer relationships, activities and cultures

Introduction

In adult thinking, it has been common to fuse childhood 'into the family institution to such an extent that it becomes an inseparable unit, which hampers the social visibility of its weaker part', i.e. children (Makrinioti 1994: 268). Yet significant proportions of a child's life are usually spent away from the family and, to varying degrees, apart from adults altogether. This chapter is largely concerned with what children do when they are outside the home and away from direct involvement with adults. It concentrates on children's autonomous activities and cultures, whilst recognising that these interact with the social worlds of adults. It will be seen that children develop their own practices and values, some of which are transmitted from generation to generation, adapting to social, economic and technological changes.

After infancy, children typically spend increasing amounts of time in ways which are not directed, structured or witnessed by the key adults in their lives. In the early years most British children nowadays attend informal or official playgroups or nursery settings, organised by adults but with opportunities for 'free' play with age-mates. Subsequently they attend school whose regime and timetables are largely determined by adults, but in addition more time is usually spent outside home and formal settings – alone or with friends playing, exploring, moving from A to B etc. Indeed nowadays it is commonly accepted that children have a need for a certain degree of autonomy in order to develop confidence and competence in social interaction with peers, self-care and effective mobility (Pringle 1980; Ward 1995). Rights to self-determination are also thought to evolve gradually with age (Lindley 1991). Yet parents, teachers and others are very conscious of children's rights to protection from human and other hazards in their environments. Hence adults seek to impose or negotiate rules and limits, adjusted over time, aimed at reconciling children's freedom and security (Collings et al. 1995; Borland et al. 1996). The nature of the local environment and the availability of formal recreational services, ranging from parks to clubs, crucially affect how children negotiate their relationships and use of space outside the home.

Children's time spent in unpaid work at school and in paid employment are dealt with in Chapters 6 and 8 respectively, so here we concentrate on social relationships and recreational activities. The rest of the chapter will cover four inter-related themes:

• children's peer relations and friendships
• play
• children's use of space
• youth culture.

Thus we shall progress from consideration of children's personal relationships to consideration of their activities and use of their local environments – each of which influences the other. The final section examines the interface between childhood and adulthood as expressed in youth subcultures and cultural activities. While play has been investigated chiefly when it involves younger children and use of space during middle childhood, youth culture has been usually linked with the teen years. However, partly through media influences, certain manifestations of young people's culture (like music and dress) have penetrated younger age groups.

Much of the relevant research has been carried out within a cognitive –developmental paradigm, although contributions have been made of a more anthropological and phenomenological nature. Theorising about children's interactions with peers, objects and environments has often either followed a Piagetian framework or proffered an alternative as a critique of Piaget (see Chapter 1). Most emphasise the interaction between developments in children's understanding of the world and their social and experiential opportunities. Piaget believed that certain mental thresholds had to be overcome before children can carry out such social tasks as seeing matters from another's viewpoint or reflecting on their relationships. In contrast, Vygotsky reversed the order by suggesting that children learn thinking skills through imitating and working with peers (Jones 1995). An equally important sociological perspective is to understand and value children's autonomous 'cultures' as creations in their own right, regardless of their developmental significance.

Relationships with other children

Peer relationships

This section will focus on relationships amongst non-related children. It is common to talk about 'peers', meaning those roughly similar in age. In most Westernised societies, children's interactions and friendships tend to be finely age-graded because associations are so much affected by yearly cohorts into which schools and pre-school groups are normally organised. In addition, cross-age relationships are often subject to negative stereotypes by adults. They presume immaturity in the case of an older child mixing with younger ones or suspect vulnerability to undesirable influences when a young child belongs to a group of older children. Nevertheless, many children do have important relationships with others outside their immediate family who are much older or younger, usually with cousins and the friends of siblings (Hill 1987). As with siblings (Chapter 4), peer relations outside the family are important for children, because they give opportunities to exercise skills and to negotiate rules and routines on a reciprocal basis with 'equals' rather than with more powerful adults. The number and quality of contacts with peers are affected by a host of personal, family and social factors. Confidence and security within the household generally promote self-assurance and trust with other children, too (Miller 1993). Children who are placed early in nursery settings understandably tend to be more 'peer-oriented' in their interests than others (Moore 1975). There is evidence that in early childhood, more children in middle-class families and neighbourhoods have wider circles of peer contacts (Hill 1987; Cochran *et al.* 1990). Relationships are also more often formalised (e.g. as regards invitations to play in each others' homes). These differences reflect access to resources like cars, larger accommodation and gardens as well as differing social expectations.

Contacts with peers are usually more open to choice and voluntarism than kin relations are. They become structured by patterns of liking and dislike, power and hierarchy. It is valuable to distinguish friendship from popularity. Friendship embodies strong two-way affection, whereas popularity is based on the number of others who express liking or admiration. A child's degree of popularity within groups is only loosely related to the number and significance of that child's friends. Some children who are widely liked do not have intense reciprocal friendships (Erwin 1992).

Friendships

Friendship tends to be differentiated from other social relationships by the strength of mutual liking, the amount of time spent together and its duration (Allan 1979; Duck and Gilmour 1981). They are also characterised by contacts in more than one setting (e.g. playing at home as well as meeting at school or at a club). From an early age, children differentiate peers they are especially close to and soon learn to refer to them as friends.

Friendships are important in their own right, because of the amount of time children spend with friends and the value they place on those relationships. The loss of a close friendship (e.g. because of a move away) can have profound effects on children (Rubin 1980). Friends are also significant sources of information, support and normative influence. They affect a child's identity and self-concept, by offering behaviour and ideas to imitate or react against, and by providing feedback and evaluations (Hartup 1992). Friendships also afford opportunities to evolve and practise social and cognitive skills like practical and emotional sharing or conflict management. Hirst and Baldwin (1994) found that the majority of disabled people had a 'satisfactory' social or friendship network, but a large minority had a restricted friendship circle and found difficulty socialising with their non-disabled peers. Those who were more socially active were also those reporting more satisfactory friendships.

In order to sustain a close friendship in the early years, frequent meetings and a meshing of interactive motivation and styles are required (Maxwell 1990). In a series of related studies, Berndt (1986) asked American children about their perceptions of friendship. The main qualities they identified in friends were – playing together; mutual liking; helpfulness; talking about intimate matters; support; and loyalty. Older children were much more likely to refer to intimacy and trust, reflecting a growing recognition of friendship as sharing thoughts and feelings as well as activities.

Children (like adults) tend to choose as friends people who are similar to themselves, as regards gender, race, academic achievement, social-class background, attitude to school and interests (Berndt 1986). Not uncommonly, friendship may be based on similar experiences which facilitate mutual confiding and understanding. Thus children whose parents are divorced or drink heavily find it helpful to confide in and compare experiences with others who have had similar experiences (Mitchell 1985; Laybourn *et al.* 1996).

Disagreements do occur between friends, of course, but compared with disputes between non-friends, these tend to be more calmly negotiated, generally without aggression (Miller 1993). When friends do fall out they sometimes use standard formulae for seeking a reconciliation, such as an invitation to join in a game or showing a new possession. Other children often intervene, either to help patch things up or to provide an alternative playmate (James 1993; Hill *et al.* 1995). Children are able to articulate clear rules and rationales for avoiding and handling relationship difficulties (Bigelow *et al.* 1996).

Developments in peer relationships with age

It has sometimes been assumed that babies or even toddlers have little interest in peers, because of self-absorption and preference for solitary play (Parten 1932), but young infants do often indicate interest in an unknown child (Becker 1977). Pre-school children usually have a smaller number of friends than older children and the relationships are often short-lived (Bigelow and La Gaipa 1980). However, strong preferences for the company of special friends can occur over an extended period (Vandell and Mueller 1980). Conversations are mostly concrete and about immediate circumstances. Nevertheless, young children are able to show great sensitivity to the situations of others, empathise with distress and offer help to an upset child (Tizard 1986). Of course, there are often conflicts and mismatches of wants and expectations, but these afford opportunities for young children to develop their communication, negotiation and self-control skills. Children soon become aware that having friends is not simply a matter between two individuals, since it confers a role and status within the wider social group:

In the infants when we wanted someone to do something, we would say 'I'll be your best friend', like it was a prize.

(12-year-old girl, quoted in Lindon 1996: 135)

During the primary-school years the size of both the adult and peer sectors of children's networks usually increases (Feiring and Lewis 1992). The number of friends also increases to an average of five to eight (Tietjen 1982; Hartup 1992). The criteria for friendship usually alter as children grow older, too, affected by children's increased mobility, growing opportunities to choose who they meet and interact with, and cognitive changes (Bigelow and La Gaipa 1980; Foot *et al.* 1980). At first, proximity and availability are important, so that friendships are usually with children living in the street, known to parents or met at a group. Gradually, more choice is exercised, with personality and shared interests playing a greater part, although allocation to a class or set in school and even seating arrangements can be influential.

Close relationships tend to become more stable. They also develop greater reciprocity, sharing and understanding of each other's viewpoints and emotions. By middle childhood, children have usually become more able to adapt to friends' wants and needs (Maxwell 1990):

He's helpful, generous, doesn't lie and helps me when I'm bullied.

She never minds when I'm in a mood.

(10- and 11-year-olds, quoted in Williams *et al.* 1989: 47)

Being with friends and having them to stay (if accommodation permits) is often a major source of pleasure. Correspondingly, falling out with friends can be a primary cause of distress, whose significance children feel adults underestimate. When close friendships end, temporarily or permanently, other children are frequently the main confidants and sources of comfort:

Me and R. are best friends and I get upset when R. goes off with other friends.

(9-year-old girl)

The angriest I've ever felt . . . One of my friends . . . we were going to play in the park and then go back to his house, and he never came.   (11-year-old boy)

My friend . . . she really comforts me . . . when I go to play with her, if I tell her, like a secret or something, I know that she'll keep it.

(11-year-old girl, all quoted in Hill *et al.* 1995: 48)

During the teen years peers are prominent, but do not normally displace the importance of parents or adults in general. Teenage friendships have greater intimacy, selectivity and duration than those of younger children. Shared self-disclosures and reliability are significant considerations in making and keeping friends. Loyalty is a prized quality (Savin-Williams and Berndt 1990) Youngsters with stable, close friendships tend to have high self-esteem. Correspondingly, self-confident individuals are usually more popular than others (Fischer *et al.* 1986).

From about 10 to 14 years of age, children tend to associate in quite large cliques, especially boys. Later on, mixed groups may go around together, which act as a setting in which teenagers may test out relationships with the opposite sex and begin to pair off (Hendry *et al.* 1993).

Parents are often particularly worried about their children's peer relations during the teens (Coleman 1992). Most teenage activities which parents disapprove of tend to develop in a peer context. Much smoking, law-breaking and substance abuse is carried out by small groups rather than by individuals. However, peer support and communication plays a vital positive role in learning about the world and developing a personal and social identity (Coleman and Hendry 1990). One young woman explained:

I can talk to my friends about things I can't really talk to my parents about, because well – they seem to understand me more, and my parents don't really listen to me, and my friends do, because they've been in the same situations as me. (Quoted in Tizard and Phoenix 1993: 72)

Gender differences

Most studies have found little or no difference in the average number of friends boys or girls have, but there are strong tendencies to associate with others of the same sex (Thorne 1993). Even in the pre-school years, friendships begin to show a gender bias (Hill 1987). In nurseries, playmate choices divide about 2:1 in favour of same sex (Smith and Cowie 1991; Archer 1992), so there is marked preference but not exclusivity. Sex segregation becomes even stronger by age six and reaches its peak in the early teens, after which to varying degrees interest in pairing off with someone of the opposite sex usually takes over, though not invariably.

From middle childhood onwards, girls' relationships are usually more intensive and boys' more extensive (Hartup 1992). Most girls spend more time with one or two particular friends towards whom they have intense loyalty sometimes interspersed with sharp conflict (Waldrop and Halverson 1975; James 1993; Ganetz 1995). Boys tend to form larger but looser friendship groups, sometimes hierarchically organised. This is partly linked to their keen interest in team games (Archer 1992). There is also some evidence that boys are more concerned to establish social status and hierarchies, whereas girls are more concerned with co-operation. In their conversations with friends, females tend to place emphasis on relationships, thoughts and feelings, while boys concentrate on activities and status (Lees 1993). These differences can be seen as precursors to different role expectations for, and performance by, women and men, with the former generally being more interested, and skilful, in relationship issues.

Wulff (1995b) concluded from her anthropological research in London that young women are more likely to mix with young people of different cultures than young men.

Differentiation, exclusion and abuse

Peer relationships embody conflict and differentiation as well as harmony and integration. For peer networks this results in cleavages and hierarchies, whilst for individuals it has implications for status, acceptance and self-esteem.

There have been many studies examining the degree of group approval and disapproval for children, mainly relying on sociometry (children's rankings of others in the group) and observation of group processes. These have mostly taken place in the classroom context and much less information is available about relationships outside school. The ratings suggest that popular children tend to be assertive and have leadership skills, yet use these qualities democratically rather than autocratically by taking account of others' wishes and feelings. When seeking to join a group, children who wait and respond to the observed interests and activities of others tend to be readily accepted, whereas sudden gate crashing is unpopular (Dodge *et al.* 1986). Physical attractiveness also seems to elicit popularity (Erwin 1992). In the main, children who are liked by the majority of their peers are also popular with adults, but some individuals gain popularity and status within groups that adults disapprove of as anti-social.

Lack of acceptance can be based on visible characteristics, such as obesity, ethnicity or disability. A child's manner of social presentation may overcome or reinforce negative attitudes based on stereotyping (Coie 1991).

When considering less-popular children, it is common to distinguish a neglected or isolated child (who is neither liked nor disliked by classmates) from a rejected child (who is disliked by most others). Neglected children tend to be those who are insecure, lacking in confidence and engagement skills (Asher and Renshaw 1981). They often make little attempt to mix. There is a link between anxious attachment to parents and social isolation (Lafreniere and Sroufe 1985). However, it is important to remember that peer behaviour may be situationally specific, so that a child who is withdrawn in one setting may be confident in another. In contrast, rejected children seek to join in group activities, but do so in an aggressive or disruptive fashion. They often try and impose their wishes on others in a way which is out of tune with the wishes and expectations of their peers. Rejection by peers tends to be more persistent than neglect (Malik and Furman 1993). Children who are disliked by the majority are not necessarily friendless or isolated, but their friends tend to be unpopular too – both with peers and adults. Such children often feel alienated in secondary school and leave as soon as they can. The combination of low peer acceptance and high aggression is a predictor for problems in adulthood, such as criminality. In extreme cases it seems that a number of factors reinforce each other – family relationships, individual behaviour patterns, peer rejection, teacher displeasure (Parker and Asher 1987; Asher and Coie 1991; Hartup 1996).

Aggression and peer rejection are linked to another aspect of peer relations – bullying. This involves the 'systematic abuse of power' in order to gain compliance (Smith and Sharp 1994: 2). Bullying may be seen as an extreme form of the common social processes of differentiation and exclusion. It is discussed more fully in Chapter 6.

Play

The meaning and functions of play

Play is a primary mechanism in which both peer associations and differentiations flourish. Play is also one of those words whose meaning most of us take for granted but whose precise definition is remarkably elusive. It refers to activities associated with fun, relaxation or even frivolity, and which do not have obvious immediate functions in terms of survival. Play is often contrasted with work, a serious business concerned with making or sustaining a living. Yet the same activity may count as play in some contexts and serious paid employment in others (for example, football or drama). Play can also provoke conflict and unhappiness as well as give pleasure.

In modern society, play is often seen as one of the defining features of childhood. Whereas adults take part in games, act in shows and engage in leisure or recreational activities, it is primarily young children who have playgroups, play school, play time, playbuses and so on. At times, adults have adopted somewhat pejorative attitudes towards children's play as trivial and purposeless, whereas others have claimed paradoxically that play is children's work, namely the main way they learn and prepare for adult tasks and responsibilities. Children themselves soon acquire the view that play and learning are inextricably mixed (Karrby 1990). Children's removal from the labour market was partly based on a presumed right to 'play' (and learn) rather than do paid work. In the twentieth century experts have come to see play as a major component of education, especially in the early years (Smith 1990). Claims for resources to be devoted to pre-school facilities have often emphasised children's need for play and stimulation if they are to develop optimally.

Through play children can learn and develop their own representations of the social and physical worlds. It is a primary medium for the creation of social networks, with their associated norms, and of personal identity (Denzin 1977). If adults are directly involved they will often seek to transmit values, rules and traditions to children. When children play together without adults they enjoy and perpetuate a child-based heritage of games, sayings, songs and so on. These embody techniques, rules and customs which promote social integration, problem solving and the avoidance or management of disputes (Burroughs and Evans 1986). Children acquire such skills as how to initiate interactive play (such as by making persuasive suggestions for dressing up) and how to join an ongoing activity. Evidence suggests that academic achievements are facilitated when play is structured and reinforced by skilled adults (Goldschmied and Jackson 1994), but certain social competencies are assisted by interaction with others of the same size and status, providing models for co-equal as opposed to subordinate relationships (Bruner 1990; Dunn 1993). Even when playing alone, children can be both practising and modifying actions they have observed or learned from others, as in their creative activities with dolls, building blocks and other toys.

Whilst play can thus be a form of learning or rehearsing, there are dangers in seeing it mainly as an opportunity to prepare for the 'serious' world of adults (Denzin 1977). Play is of intrinsic interest and value, regardless of any role it may have for a child's future. Opie (1993: 15) noted the paradox and advantage of play as being both serious and inconsequential – 'A game is a microcosm, more powerful and important than any individual player; yet when it is finished it is finished, and nothing depends on the outcome'.

Types of play

Children's play can involve objects, other children, adults or combinations of these. The nature of play has been classified in various ways, depending on the relative significance of physical and mental activity and on the degree of planning or organisation. For example, Smith (1990) refers to the following:

• practice play
• symbolic play
• games with rules
• socio-dramatic play
• constructive play
• physical activity
• rough and tumble.

An early classification of play in groups involved three levels of social interaction which were seen as forming an age-based progression (Parten 1933):

- *solitary play* – self-absorbed activity
- *parallel play* – activity alongside another child
- *co-operative play* – joint activity.

By the age of three or four, children in groups often enjoy make-believe play, in which they will often parody adults. They have also typically learned to name and express feelings as well as refer to things. By this time they can usually distinguish between appearance and reality, and are also well able to pretend that an object stands in for something else, as when a ruler is treated like a knife, for instance (Cohen 1993). Thus, cooperative play enables children to represent and comment on both their own social worlds and those of adults.

Theories of play

Cohen (1993) recognised three main psychological perspectives on children's play:

- *cognitive* – relating changes in children's play to distinct stages of intellectual development and competence
- *psychoanalytic* – stressing the role of play in emotional expression and healing
- *educational* – focusing on how children's learning can be shaped by play.

Piaget's cognitive theories (outlined in Chapter 1) were largely based on children's play with objects (and experimenters' manipulation of objects). Piaget emphasised the reciprocal relationship between play and children's reasoning powers (Gilmore 1971; Donaldson 1978). Children's manipulation of objects helps to develop understanding of reality, to practise and fix mental as well as physical abilities. Over the years, ideas about when children can perform or understand various tasks has progressively lowered the thresholds and emphasised the diversity of individual progress. For example, nowadays psychologists recognise that children's capacities to pretend or take the perspective of another can occur as early as two years, much sooner than Piaget asserted (Cox 1980; Cohen 1993).

Erikson (1963) also saw early play as a means of 'mastering reality', but with a more emotional component. He suggested children often engage with their worries through pretence and fantasy. This usually alleviates worries, but may occasionally reinforce them. In fantasy play, repetition of feared situations (like being orphaned, or encountering a fierce animal) enables children to rehearse practical and emotional ways of coping (Gottman and Parker 1986). According to psychodynamic theories, toys and objects may 'stand in' for other people or indeed the child. For example, children gain comfort from a favourite possession when separated from a loved one (Winnicott 1957). A child can vent anger on a substitute object without the repercussions of doing so with the real target of animosity. In these ways, play can be an important safety valve or coping mechanism for dealing with intense feelings and setbacks.

Children's play activities when on their own

Understandably, much early research on children's play concentrated on places where children were most easy for adults to observe – often in nurseries and schools, less often in the home. These are settings which to varying degrees are under adult supervision, orchestration and control. Although children are often 'free' to choose what and who to play with, the context and range of play objects is predetermined. The nature and implications of play are different when children have more liberty to determine their own activities – in the streets, in parks, fields and woods, or in the playground.

The detailed observations by Iona and Peter Opie of children's activities in streets and playgrounds provided fascinating insights into geographical and temporal variations. They revealed a rich child-based culture, half-remembered by adults but largely independent of them. Many songs, sayings, jokes and games had been handed down for years and in some cases centuries. 'Knock, knock' jokes are at least 60 years old and elephant jokes started in the 1960s. Alongside the seemingly timeless are the latest fads:

It's a craze. We do it all the time now. Skipping might come back later, but it's Bottle Tops now. (Quoted in Opie 1993: 145)

Many traditional games involve racing, hiding, seeking and chasing, which encourage exploration, handling fear, and making choices about risk and safety. Others entail more verbal activity, such as in guessing, answering riddles and role play. Some involve sharing and jointness (rhymes and songs), whereas in others children take on different or reciprocal roles. The sexual content of jokes, teasing and stories is very prominent (Pollard 1985; Opie 1993). This indicates that primary-aged children have ready access to information about adult sexual activities outside formal sex education classes. Another prominent feature of conversation is food, reflecting both the immediacy of hunger and the social significance of eating choices and habits (James 1993; Opie 1993).

The interaction of children's and adults' social worlds

For the most part, the games children play are different from those of adults. The main exceptions are ball games, particularly football, which appears now to be the most popular playground activity of boys (Blatchford *et al.* 1991; Opie 1993).

Many of children's practices, rhymes and sayings are learned from other children and form self-sustaining subcultures with their own social stock of knowledge. Satisfaction can be gained from pursuing activities which are largely unknown and poorly understood by adults

(Opie and Opie 1959). Children's own cultures enable them to pursue autonomous interests which disregard adults. James (1993) noted how rarely children's conversations outside the home make reference to family and domestic happenings. At the same time, through play and age-mate conversations children develop strategies for coping with the adult world (Pollard 1985). Sometimes adults are mimicked or mocked. This allows for the expression of resentments which children feel afraid or powerless to vent directly. Also rehearsal of roles like doctor or astronaut helps prepare for the future. Children's games and stories have always adapted with the times and incorporated current events. Increasingly, the media (especially television and films) have prompted developments, ranging from Popeye jokes to disco dancing (Opie 1993). In this way, children take elements of the adult world and modify them for their own purposes.

Social integration and control

Particularly at school, but also elsewhere, children spend much of their time in groups and associations. Any group activity entails mechanisms for enabling group members to co-operate, for reconciling individual wishes and aims, and for achieving the group's purposes. Organisational and social skills of a high order are displayed in child-directed games which often embrace over twelve individuals (Boulton 1992). Opie and Opie (1969) observed how children valued repetition and standardisation in their games. This provides both familiarity and shared expectations, which help minimise disputes or misunderstandings. Commonly 'random' methods are used to decide what game to play, who should pick sides, be the leader, chaser or chased. These embody ideas of equity, expressing a commitment to give everyone an equal opportunity to take on cherished or unpopular roles. Likewise children have conventions which are deployed before embarking on a role-play, exchange, bargain or private revelation (Opie and Opie 1959). Such informal standard contracts avoid the need to negotiate agreements afresh on every occasion, since it can be assumed that the requirements and sanctions are well known.

When potential or actual difficulties arise, then standard words and phrases – like 'bagsee' – are available to allow for time out to discuss differing expectations or to withdraw from a situation in a way which preserves friendship (Sluckin 1981). It could be argued that in these ways, children's communication is often more openly negotiated than that of many adults, although of course sometimes the rules break down and some children may be excluded from the shared understandings.

Hart (1979) stressed that children's neighbourhood activities often entail quiet watching and playing. The Opies believed that children become more aggressive when they are confined to more restricted areas, like playgrounds. Even then skilled verbal tactics are used by children to defuse threats and conflicts by redefining situations and actions in ways that make it possible to back down, agree to disagree or change the subject without loss of face (Sluckin 1981; Gottman and Parker 1986).

Conformity and differentiation

The smooth running of children's play interaction may depend on hierarchical processes as well as the harmonisation techniques just described. Deference to recognised leaders, suppression of dissenting individuals or the marginalisation of disfavoured individuals and groups help sustain conformity. Status within the group may be achieved, at least temporarily, by leading or suggesting activities, sporting prowess and having access to new ideas, jokes and tricks. High status can confer entitlements, such as determining the activity to be undertaken, choosing who does what and deciding about requests for entry by new-comers, although often leadership is bounded by consultation and the equal access rules noted above (Sluckin 1981; Opie 1993).

Not uncommonly, children use insults or refusals to play to exclude or marginalise certain others. The effects can be deep and lasting:

Name-calling grinds away. What's supposed to happen is you ignore them and it's supposed to wear off, but it never wears off.

(Boy aged ten, quoted in Butler and Williamson 1994: 54)

Appearance and clothes form a common focus for teasing, which can be very upsetting:

And when me and my friends have fun, you know, [playing tig] they kind of comment and stuff and go 'That's so babyish' you know, and go 'Oh look at your trainers', you know, start teasing you.

(11-year-old, quoted in Hill *et al.* 1995: 49)

While ascription of negative status can be based on individual appearance, personality or interaction style, it is also typically related to generalised external signs of difference, whether on the grounds of skin colour, obesity, disability or wearing spectacles (Gottlieb and Leyser 1981; James 1993; Hill *et al.* 1995). A 13 year old with spina bifida described her emotional pain and resentment:

People skit me all the time. Sometimes they shouted 'spastic' which really upsets me.   (Quoted in Appleton 1995: 110)

Learning difficulties as well as physical disability can result in insults and segregation:

They think I am stupid.   (Girl aged eleven)

(They dislike me) because of my arm and leg.   (Girl aged twelve)

I walk like a duck.

(Boy aged seven; all quoted in Wade and Moore 1993: 112)

Racial origin was another common focus for differentiation revealed in the Wade and Moore survey, though an observational study in one school found that being white or black did not seem to form a basis for exclusion from games, but being a girl or a boy was used as a justification to exclude (Sluckin 1981).

Not surprisingly, in view of such pressures to produce acceptable appearance and behaviour, children employ a range of self-presentation techniques to minimise differences. Apparently mundane examples include conformity in dress and hiding or throwing away the contents of packed lunches likely to evoke disapproval. More substantial disguising occurs when children keep secret major family processes like parental separation.

Males and females not only tend to play separately, but also commonly engage in different kinds of activity. In general, boys in playgrounds have been observed to play games which emphasise physical activity and competitiveness (Sluckin 1981). They also tend to dominate the use of space, especially by playing football (Blatchford *et al.* 1991; Boulton 1992). Girls more often play games with larger verbal components. In primary school, rhymes, songs and skipping are popular with many girls, but rarely involve boys (Opie 1993). Girls' activities on the street can be often different from the boys. Research by Foster (1990: 107) indicated that girls are less inclined to be aggressive. She cited observations of two young girls aged nine and 11:

They sat on the steps of the block of flats playing banks, talking, and singing songs. This was in marked contrast to the behaviour of the boys, who spent much of their time being destructive, smashing bottles and windows, for example. Even in the older age group, the girls would sit and talk quietly amongst themselves about boys, clothes and babies.

Children and their local informal environment

While the school playground has been the primary location for adults to observe children's self-governing play, children spend time unsupervised in an increasing diversity of places as they grow older. In this section we concentrate on children's knowledge and use of their local environments outside the home, with particular reference to the middle years of childhood. At that stage there is typically a marked increase in the time children spend away from home and beyond the purview of adults (Collings *et al.* 1995). According to Moore, this period represents the 'apex of childhood' when children 'have the greatest chance to strike out, alone or with peers, to explore an ever-expanding repertoire of reachable places, in search of new experiences and adventure' (1986: 12).

We shall be mainly concerned with children's use of space outside formal institutions like schools, clubs, shops or hospitals. The intention is not to devalue children's interactions with adults or use of formal settings, but to highlight those activities which involve a high degree of autonomy for children.

The concept of *territorial range* has been used to depict the area which a child is familiar with. The range may alter or extend abruptly following events such as: starting or changing school; moving house; acquiring a new friend. Three levels have been recognised (Moore 1986):

- *Habitual range* – where a child spends most of the time, often near to home
- *Frequented range* – places further afield visited regularly
- *Occasional range* – locations encountered once or rarely.

On average, the territorial range increases with age.

Children's use of their local environment is affected by external factors, such as the seasons and weather; the landscape and facilities nearby; distance from family and friends. Also important are their perceptions, preferences and fears, and negotiations with parents, peers and significant others. Children may be deterred from going to places which they perceive as defended by custodians like park-keepers, janitors or watching neighbours (Moore 1986). Other 'barriers' to outdoor activities include domestic responsibilities and lack of playmates (Garling and Valsiner 1985).

Parents usually seek to impose or negotiate rules about territorial limits and prohibited places. Parental anxieties about their children's safety are high in the primary school years, at the same time as children's entitlement to greater independence is recognised (Roberts *et al.* 1995; Borland *et al.* 1996). Parents are concerned about

- 'unsafe' objects and events like falls and traffic accidents
- 'dangerous' people (Ward 1978).

Often territorial rules incorporate a distinction between a free-range area and other places for which special permission is needed, perhaps with reporting back conditions. There are usually different requirements about going out alone, with siblings or with friends. Injunctions can vary greatly in their details and flexibility of application, even amongst families in the same small area. Most children are aware of parents' worries and able to cite rules about keeping safe, but do not always abide by limits set (Hart 1979; McNeish and Roberts 1995). They also want to be trusted and, within reason, allowed to make and learn from mistakes:

They have to give you a chance. You can't learn unless they let you do things.
(10 year old)

It's no good adults getting cross. You can't learn unless you make mistakes.
(12 year old, both quoted in Lindon 1996: 15)

In general, parents give boys more freedom than girls to roam on foot or by bicycle and so they have a wider territorial range, on average (Naylor 1986; Hillman 1993; Walmsley and Lewis 1993). In fact boys are more at risk from injury and harm, perhaps partly because of their greater freedom (Katz 1993). Income and social class affect both the scope for travel and parental attitudes towards supervision.

Preferred places and use of space

A distinction is commonly made between places where children stay (territories) and the routes by which they travel from one place to another (pathways). Children with impaired mobility or sight may have difficulties negotiating certain pathways, so that their access to territories is also limited, even when these are adapted to take account of disability. Territories can also be divided into formal locations, planned by adults for children to use, and informal locations, with different purposes.

Whilst many children do enjoy going to formal playgrounds and parks, other kinds of space are often equally or more favoured, as shown both by children's expressed preferences and the kinds of places where they actually spend time. Non-designated and interstitial areas like waste ground, small woods and waterside sites are particularly attractive for children (Hart 1979), though inner-city areas may have few of these. When asked, many children express a wish for access to trees, bushes and varied terrain. These provide opportunities for climbing and hiding (Naylor 1986). Often it is the 'wilder' part of parks which are preferred (Opie and Opie 1969). Certain pathways are also popular as play areas. Pavements and streets close to home have the advantages of accessibility and familiarity. On the other hand, less visible trails, alleys and short-cuts can serve as valuable arenas for avoiding adult oversight.

These preferences demonstrate children's desires to engage with 'real' rather than artificial environments. They like to create their own play environment, whether imaginatively or through using and moving materials provided by nature or left by adults. Some children develop their own names for special localities like 'the Dump' or 'Charlie's field' (Matthews 1992). These can embody a sense of ownership by children. Hart (1979) found that when he accompanied children they showed him small favourite haunts which they had not mentioned when interviewed. This illustrates how adults may gain a false impression of children's place preferences by reliance on limited methods for understanding children's worlds. On the other hand, ethical concerns arise if adult researchers seek access to children's secret or private spaces.

Berg and Medrich (1980) found that the play patterns and use of space by 11- to 12-year-olds in Oakland (California) varied greatly according to the nature of the local environment, type of housing and child density. For example, in one area children played mainly with siblings and immediate neighbours in their own yards, since they were surrounded by busy roads. Elsewhere, children went further afield to play, often walking in groups to undeveloped or open land, wherever they could find it. The children 'craved the opportunity to get around on their own' (p. 343) and to shape environments for their own purposes. The authors concluded that mobility and autonomy were special needs of pre-teenagers and these needs were largely unmet in many urban settings. They also regarded it as a basic right of childhood 'to experience and explore the world around them safely, spontaneously, and on their own terms' (p. 344). Yet children are not considered prominently, let alone consulted, in most decisions about the design and use of space.

Places which children find scary tend to be dark, enclosed, uninhabited or associated with a mythical or actual frightening incident (Hart 1979; Hill *et al.* 1995). Frightening and dangerous places may attract as well as repel children, offering opportunities for status within the peer group, bravado and mastery of fears. Traffic tends to be the greatest source of anxiety for most young people when moving about their local area (Hill and Michelson 1981). Until the age of about 10, children usually have significant difficulties in judging the distance, direction and speed of an approaching car and in assessing where and how to cross roads safely (Ward 1978; Ampofo-Boateng and Thomson 1991). Many children, especially girls, also avoid certain areas because of fears of certain types of people (such as drunks, gangs, muggers, drug-users).

As well as favouring or avoiding certain micro-locations, children often have strong views about different kinds of area. Whatever the home environment, children usually develop some sense of belonging and loyalty to the neighbourhood they live in. As with groups of people, there is a tendency to characterise the familiar as positive and regard the unfamiliar less favourably. Evidence from North America suggests that children of minority ethnic backgrounds living in territorial enclaves tend to have more restricted mobility, a strong local identity and fears of entering 'white' neighbourhoods (Gould and White 1986), but there has been little attention in the UK to the influence of race and ethnicity on the use of space by children. In certain towns and cities, experience of racism and violence has led some young people of Asian origin to see 'white areas' as too risky to enter:

Asian areas are safe – we know each other and we stick together.

I stay in Asian areas. No one will attack me, because they're the same people as me, they're normal.   (Both quoted in Webster 1996: 19)

When children are asked about satisfaction with where they live or with ideals, suburban and rural environments with more open space tend to gain most approval, provided that there are sufficient peers around to avoid isolation from playmates (Berg and Medrich 1980: Homel and Burns 1985).

Children's knowledge and representations of their environments

When academics have sought to understand children's knowledge of their environments, there has been a tendency to focus on children's deficits or inaccuracies in perception compared with the adult view-point. At least two dangers arise from this. Firstly, the way in which children communicate, whether in words, with diagrams or maps, may disguise their level of comprehension. If children are asked to describe places in words or draw maps, they tend to communicate less proficiently than if they use models, sand and water or aerial photos (Downs and Stea 1977). Also pre-school children may be able to recognise places and retrace routes effectively long before they can verbalise how they do so (Walmsley and Lewis 1993). Secondly, children may have an orientation to their environment which is different from that of most adults, but not inferior to it. Children tend to be very concerned with the minutiae of the micro-environments where they spend most of their time. They may notice and recall details overlooked by adults.

Typically, small children identify prominent landmarks first, then recognise routes and only later develop overall mental maps which link the separate places they know (Hill and Michelson 1981). Young children are often uncertain about the relative sizes, locations and distances of places they have experienced or heard of. Only gradually do they develop an understanding of how places they are familiar with are embedded and distributed within larger spaces (Hart 1979; Piche 1981). This is partly a matter of learning and differentiating adult labels (for example, Paris is a city, France a country, Europe a continent), but also seems related to the increased capacity to conceptualise size and abstract relations. Nonetheless, Matthews (1992) suggested that young children's geographical skills have been previously underestimated. Also he claimed that the development of environmental knowledge is incremental rather than following distinct stages as in a Piagetian model (see Chapter 1).

Despite the difficulties about measurement and judgement just noted, there are some indications that access to varied environments enhances children's spatial abilities and sense of effectiveness (Hart 1979; Matthews 1992). Furthermore Kegerreis (1993) claimed that the opportunities to explore alone and with peers promote self-esteem and a positive identity. They also promote access to shared peer cultures, which are subject to national and international as well as local influences.

Youth culture

Youth subcultures

Children's autonomous activities and use of space often cause anxiety and alarm in senior generations. Their worries may reflect protective concern about children's welfare, but can also result from feelings that adult values, comfort and safety are under threat. This is particularly apparent when certain groups of young people have subcultures which contrast with prevailing norms and appear to challenge them. These subcultures may be seen to coalesce into a universal youth culture, distinct from and in some respects oppositional to adult culture.

Young people are perceived as particularly vulnerable and malleable to the influences of popular cultures, which are thought to threaten morality and lead young people into crime. Campaigns against various forms of popular culture have ranged from banning dime novels in nineteenth-century America or comics after the war in Sweden (Boëthius 1995) to restricting films and worrying about violent videos today. Criticisms of the new media and consumerism are consistently linked with criticisms of youth culture and young people themselves. With the rise of computer technology and the Internet, along with the world-wide market for music and other popular culture, youth culture is seen as increasingly globalised – and thus out of (adult) control.

A minority of young people have long been a subject of adults' vitriolic disapproval, generation after generation. British examples include alarm about 'street urchins' (Victorian times), 'teddy boys' (1950s), 'mods' and 'rockers' (1960s), skinheads, punks and football hooliganism (1970s and 80s) (Cohen 1972; Hebdige 1988). In the 1990s, British adults became so alarmed about the growing 'rave culture' that strict controlling measures were introduced by the Criminal Justice and Public Order Act 1994. Headlines about the associated drug use remain frequent.

In academia, attention has similarly focused on a minority of youth, with the emphasis on 'youth subcultures'. Widdicombe and Woofit (1995: 28) provided a common-sense definition: 'By youth subcultures we are referring to highly visible, named groups of young people who are apparently characterised by their style and hairstyle, music preferences and beliefs: punks, gothics, hippies and skinheads, for example'. Youth subcultures are typically perceived as new and entirely separate from the adult generation.

Subcultures have been highly theorised, particularly due to the influential work of the Centre for Contemporary Cultural Studies (CCCS) at the University of Birmingham, beginning in the mid-1950s. To generalise, CCCS promoted a Marxist, structuralist and semiotic perspective and concentrated on male working-class, white youth culture. Working-class boys were seen as temporarily fighting a symbolic class war, which they eventually lost and of which they became victims. Their resistance was expressed in subcultural styles (see also Chapter 6). Such studies of youth subcultures took on a determinedly political analysis (Dunn 1986), typically standing against public condemnation of them. Widdicombe and Woofit (1995) accused CCCS of ignoring the negative aspects of working-class youth subcultures, and obscuring young people's personal responsibility. Certainly, CCCS neglected studying those who were not working-class, white males, with the notable exception of McRobbie's work on young women (for example, McRobbie and Garber 1991). Also generally excluded from CCCS studies were the influences of family breakdown and poverty (MacDonald 1989).

Widdicombe and Woofit put forward two further criticisms: one methodological and one theoretical. First, CCCS theory was based on little empirical data and was overreliant on the case study by Willis (1977). Second, CCCS overemphasised the self-generation of subcultures, and underemphasised subcultures' interdependence with commercial and media enterprises. Thus, postmodern theorists like Widdicombe and Woofit, or Thornton (1995) presented theories that combine society and the individual, and emphasise differences within youth subcultures, as well as conformity.

Young people's leisure

Despite their dominance of the literature on youth culture, youth subcultures have usually involved a minority of young people as active participants. What do we know in Britain about young people generally? In their extensive survey of young Scots, Hendry *et al.* (1993) reported that a third of young people attended a sports event at least once a fortnight, with young men more likely to do this than young women. Weekly involvement in sport decreased after age 15. Involvement was highly correlated with whether young people were in school and, if not, whether they were employed. Little difference was associated with class (as defined by father's occupation).

Young people (aged 16 to 19) read as often as other age categories (OPCS 1995). They watch a considerable amount of television and videos in their homes (Hollands 1990; Hendry *et al.* 1993). Young people go to more films than any other age group, but Thornton (1995) suggested that the cultural form closest to the majority of British youth is actually music. Ninety-six per cent of 16 to 19 year olds listen to records and tapes, the highest percentage across all age categories (OPCS 1995). Style and fashion are often seen as crucial to youth culture and to young people's search for identity and belonging (see Chapter 8). Young women may create their style in department stores' fitting rooms (Ganetz 1995) or their bedrooms (McRobbie and Garber 1991). Both are spaces that are protected and free from parental surveillance. Researchers, however, strongly assert that young women have more than their 'bedroom culture', but have a presence outside the home (Ganetz 1995; Wulff 1995a).

Hendry *et al.* (1993) identified three stages in young people's leisure activities:

- *organised*: (up to age 14),
- *casual*: (ages fourteen to 16),
- *commercial*: (post-16 years).

Casual leisure ('hanging about') is common between the ages of 14 and 16 because of lack of money and commercial places to go:

There is a very definite lack of places in town where young people (under 18) can meet, without going into pubs. This leads to many people illegally drinking and showing false ID. Why can't there be 'cafés', or something of that sort, open 'til late? (Jane from Edinburgh, quoted in Hendry *et al.* 1993: 47)

Many disabled young people's leisure activities can be restricted by such constraints as inaccessible buildings, limited transport and lack of money. Young people in rural areas and certain urban areas can also find their opportunities constrained by the absence or infrequency of public transport. Young people without employment or other means of funds can find it difficult to participate in the 'consumer culture'.

Even though the legal drinking age is 18 in Britain, more than half of 13 year olds drink alcohol on a regular basis (Stephenson 1995). Fifteen to 19 year olds are the most avid clubbers and ravers (Thornton 1995). Dance clubs are another type of 'free space' for young people, writes Thornton, where their rules largely prevail and they can indulge in 'adult' activities. Merchant and Macdonald (1994) reported on the now big business of raves, defined as:

a long period of constant energetic and stylistic dancing exhibited by a large group of people in a hot, crowded facility providing continuous loud House music and an accompanying strobe-light show.
(Newcombe, quoted in Merchant and Macdonald: 18)

According to Merchant and Macdonald, raves differ from more conventional nightclubs because they are not 'pick-up' joints, and tend to be less aggressive, masochistic and violent. Raves are strongly associated with taking drugs, like Ecstasy and newer variants. While prompting a 'moral panic', rave culture is distinct from past subcultures that instilled moral panics in that it crosses classes; it tends to be restricted to weekends; includes younger and older age groups; and is popular with a large minority of young people. In fact, these writers argued, rave culture is scarcely a 'sub'culture at all (Merchant and Macdonald 1994; Stanley 1995).

Alongside their use of drugs and alcohol, young people's sexual relations are another source of adult anxiety. Wellings and Bradshaw (1994) found that black people reported a median age of first sexual intercourse at eighteen for women and seventeen for men, Asians at age twenty-one and twenty respectively, and white people at age eighteen for both sexes. In face-to-face interviews, 4.6 per cent of male respondents (aged sixteen to twenty-four) said they had had an 'homosexual experience', compared to 2.4 per cent of young women (Wellings *et al.* 1994). Young people who are sexually active tend not to 'sleep around' with different partners, but to have one sexual partner until that relationship ends (Netting 1992; Hendry *et al.* 1993). Hirst and Baldwin (1994) reported that in terms of dating, 42 per cent of young disabled people said they had never had a boy- or girl-friend compared to 30 per cent of young people generally; it appears that their survey did not ask a direct question about young people's sexuality.

Youth culture and the need for identity

Sexuality, according to Netting (1992), is part of delineating a personal identity and hence a critical issue in youth culture. Almost all aspects of youth culture reported above – leisure activities, consumption, style, music, friendships – have been depicted as critical to young people's nascent and developing identities. Leisure is seen as the space for young people to experiment, to move outside their family to socialise with other peers and adults: '. . . it is in the realm of leisure that young people truly become themselves' (Hendry *et al*. 1993: 2).

A number of writers have expressed concern that young people find it harder today to create their own identity (e.g. Giroux 1994; Holstein-Beck 1995). Traditional means of young people's socialisation, such as family, school and community, are seen as becoming much weaker and the influence of peers and media much stronger. According to such writers, young people are faced with so many messages, so many contradictions, so many options and freedoms, that they can feel lost and disoriented. As noted in Chapter 1, if young people do not successfully cope with the challenges of adolescence, they may face negative consequences (Erikson 1963; Arnett 1995). So may society.

Particular worry has been expressed about the identity of young people from ethnic minorities in the UK, who may experience particular tensions between identification with their families and with local or wider peer cultures. For example, inter-generational tension is feared, between parents who wish to maintain the culture and beliefs of their former country, and young people who feel more akin to UK culture. Whether these fears are justified is a subject of much debate. Modood *et al*. (1994) did find considerable differences between the generation that first settled in the UK, and the 'second' generation born and brought up in the UK. But such differences depended on the particular culture, religion or ethnicity. For example, religion was far more important to people who had originally lived in the Caribbean or Asia, than for the second generations, except for those who were Muslim. Some children of 'mixed' parentage may feel torn between two cultures, though only a minority appear to find this problematic (Tizard and Phoenix 1993). One boy described his feelings:

It's not that I've ever actually wanted to be white, I'd never, never want to be, actually. But there are occasions when you think, if I were white, then this wouldn't happen.   (Quoted in Tizard and Phoenix 1993: 56)

This boy made the connection between ethnic identity and discrimination, which was also addressed by Modood *et al*. (1994). Ethnic identity, according to Modood *et al*., is a plastic and changing membership produced by a number of forces. The negative forces include social exclusion and stigma, and resistance to them. Positive forces comprise awareness of distinctive heritages and new forms of culture, loyalties and coalitions of interests.

Youth transitions to adulthood

Hendry *et al.* (1993) linked the development of identity in adolescence to the aspirations and demands associated with adulthood. A common framework used in the literature to connect these issues when considering older teenagers and young adults is that of *transitions* (Banks *et al.* 1992; Jones and Wallace 1992). This life stage is seen as negotiating the change from childhood to adulthood along four main dimensions, each with its associated goal:

Table 5.1 Youth transitions: dimensions and conventional goals

Dimension of transition	Goal
Family of origin to adult (sexual) partnership(s)	Personal independence
School to work	Occupation/career
Parental income to own income	Financial autonomy
Family home to own household	Householder status

While the literature on youth subcultures emphasises the distinctions between childhood, adolescence and adulthood, transitional theory emphasises the links between them.

The transitions into adulthood are increasingly problematic as a result of social structures and policies which have reduced employment opportunities and access to independent income for young people (Hollands 1990; Coles 1995; Borland and Hill 1997). Increasing proportions of older children thus face prolonged periods of dependency (financial and otherwise), perhaps well into adulthood. Many young people with disabilities face particular obstacles and difficult transitions (Ward *et al.* 1991).

Youth unemployment and the perennial concern about youth subcultures combine in negative public images of youth, which can become self-fulfilling. The sociological literature on youth culture constantly states that the public only pays attention to youth when they are perceived as a problem. According to Hebdige (1988), the only real power of young people, and particularly young people without jobs and living in inner cities, is to discomfit and to pose a threat. As Bennett and Westera (1994) wrote, adults are far more likely to be outspoken about young people's risk behaviours than to lobby with young people for greater recreational resources. The public's negative image of youth was not always so: after World War II, there was also a sense that the young people represented the future, that they had new opportunities and new affluence, that they 'never had it so good' (Clarke *et al.* 1976).

Conclusions and implications

Children have cultures, activities, rules, places and terminology of their own. Many of these are common to most children, but there are also local and subgroup variations. Childhood cultures overlap with and draw on adult practices in ways which often aid preparation for later life-stages, but there are also many aspects which are autonomous and related to the here-and-now interests of children. Knowledge and skills are frequently imparted by other children, rather than copied or learned from adults. Thus childhood socialisation is not only about preparation for the future, but also about acquiring a sense of self as a child, belonging to peer-based groups and developing child-based norms and practices.

Adults are ambivalent about children's free or bounded associations with peers. On the one hand, it is recognised that most children have a strong orientation towards their age-mates from an early age and that social interaction fulfils many positive functions, including social support and the facilitation of learning. On the other hand, concerns have often been expressed about children's involvement with groups of peers undermining family loyalties and social discipline, whether through early full-time group care or 'delinquent' or destructive subcultures in the teen years. The cultures of children and young people include elements which evoke adult alarm because of their seeming alienation and deviation from adult norms, but also entail activities and tasks which mark the transition into adulthood.

A **rights-based** approach suggests that children are entitled to freedoms of association, provided this does not contradict their entitlement to protection from adverse influences. Enabling children safely to explore diverse relationships and contexts may be seen as an entitlement, regardless of whether this can be demonstrated to have beneficial consequences or not. The rights to play and to a stimulating environment are part of the United Nations Declaration of the Rights of the Child (Moore 1986). There is no specific entitlement to friendship or access to friends (Ennew 1995), though this can be regarded as implied by the right to free association and peaceable assembly in Article 15. Holden (1996) illustrated how children themselves can devise rules which balance the rights to freedom and protection of majorities and minorities in playgrounds. She cited a list compiled by one group of nine year olds which includes rights to:

• be free from bullying
• choose games to play
• have safe play equipment
• be in a quiet place
• be alone.

The provision of pre-school and after-school care has been partly premised on the needs of working parents, but also justified by appeals to children's needs for company and stimulation which promote social competence and cognitive learning (Petrie 1994; Hawthorne-Kirk 1995). In addition to these claims for adult-organised provision, several writers have conceptualised independent use of space as part of children's environmental needs (Ward 1978; Hill and Michelson 1981; Matthews 1992).

Although formal designated play areas are seen as desirable, these are not sufficient. It is argued that children need more opportunities for access to space which they can determine how to use. This both satisfies their own wishes and develops a wider repertoire of environmental understanding and skills.

Specific needs have been identified for spaces which:

- children have some control in shaping and owning
- can be modified to suit different children
- provide variety and 'wild' elements
- enhance exploration and manipulation of the environment
- are safe and have safe access routes.

When adults are willing to listen and give support, children can participate in planning and even running community facilities (Henderson 1995; Hogan 1996).

By and large, these formulations have been made with a 'universal child' in mind, usually the urban child. Particular care is necessary to ensure that similar access is available to disabled children and that safety measures take account of different kinds of impairment. The gendered nature of play and use of space raise questions about limitations experienced by girls and about risk-taking and aggression in boys. Bjorklid argued that environmental designs can 'reinforce sex-bound activities rather than encourage children to extend their range of activities' (1985: 102). Sensitivity is needed to cultural traditions (e.g. to enable Muslim girls to swim in mixed bathing contexts when they have dress restrictions).

While most children prefer plentiful opportunities to be alone and with age-mates, they should not be excluded from adult activities and places. Noschis (1992) argues that more informal child–adult dialogues should be encouraged, to help children engage more with the adult world and to build unobtrusive protection for them. Along with the family home, the principle site for adult–child interaction is school, which is the subject of the next chapter.

Suggestions for further reading

Cohen, D. (1993) *The Development of Play*, London: Routledge.

Erwin, P. (1992) *Friendship and Peer Relations in Children*, Chichester: Wiley.

Henderson, P. (ed.) (1995) *Children and Communities*, London: Pluto Press.

Hendry, L., Shucksmith, J., Love, J., and Glendinning, A. (1993) *Young People's Leisure and Lifestyles*, London: Routledge.

Matthews, M. H. (1992) *Making Sense of Place*, Hemel Hempstead: Harvester Wheatsheaf.

Roche, J. and Tucker, S. (1997) *Youth in Society*, London: Sage.

CHAPTER 6

The schooling of children

Introduction

In his foundational history of childhood, Ariès (1973) equated the development of modern schooling with the ascendancy of the modern concept of 'childhood'. Children were seen as unready for life and needing to be treated specially in a 'sort of quarantine' (p. 396). Children were segregated from adult society, shut up in schools that had increasingly severe discipline systems. Schools became institutions for the young (first only for boys and then for girls as well), which aimed to provide children with a 'training for life' (397).

This chapter will address children's education and, more specifically, state-funded, day schooling for children of compulsory school age. Parents have the duty to ensure children between the ages of five and 16 are educated, but can choose whether to do this at home, through state schools or the private/independent sector. The vast majority of children do attend state schools, with only a minority of the school-age population educated in the private/independent sector:

- 8% England
- 2% Wales
- 1% Scotland (Gorard 1996).

In recent years, education policy has become increasingly politicised and turbulent. Scarcely a year has passed without another education bill going through Parliament. Behind this politicisation lies the continued debate about the purpose of schooling. Down one path are ideas about developing every individual's potential, which match articles in the United Nations (UN) Convention on the Rights of the Child. Another path extends beyond schooling to work, seeing schooling as adding to 'human capital' and thus improving economic efficiency and well-being. This link to the labour market is projected as advantageous by the politicians, but analysed as oppression and stratification by some Marxist sociologists. A third path similarly emphasises the transition from childhood to adulthood, but more broadly in terms of socialisation. Schooling is seen as one of the three key sites of positive socialisation (along with families and peer groups), by which children can become committed to society's values and to their specific roles within society's structure.

This chapter will begin with a brief description of recent policy changes in Great Britain. Although similar in some key respects, the Northern Ireland system has such significant differences that it cannot be given justice in this chapter. (For further information on Northern Ireland, see Osborne *et al.* 1987; McEwen and Salters 1995). The contours of the three different purposes of schooling described above will then be explored, by considering children who test the boundaries: children with 'special educational needs'; children who are excluded from school; and children who bully. How schools deal with such children provides means by which to judge state education. Are schools ensuring that *all* children's potential is developed? Are schools preparing *all* children to contribute to the labour market? Are schools socialising *all* children into good citizens?

The socialisation role of schooling will then be further examined, considering how schooling 'trains' children for citizenship. Within this discussion, children's method of 'voting with their feet' – truanting – will be highlighted as well as other means of protest. The chapter will conclude with reflections on how schooling constitutes 'childhood', children's rights and children's needs.

Recent changes in educational policy

Schooling has radically changed in past decades, with England and Wales often blazing the trail, with Scotland and Northern Ireland following more reluctantly. Economic liberalism has been brought into educational provision, with its accompanying ideas about markets and competition. Budgets and decisions have been decentralised down to individual schools and school boards (Scotland) or school governors (England and Wales). Central government has taken increasing control over policy – making local authority[1] control more and more marginal in both provision and policy-making. Standardised national curricula have become required for state schooling. Students must be regularly assessed and the aggregate results for each school published. Parents are the designated consumers of education, with a range of powers to increase their choice and say.

The market has been introduced into education in numerous ways. For example, in Great Britain, schools are now formula funded, and the bulk of the formula relies on the individual school's student numbers. Schools are thus rewarded for attracting pupils and penalised if their rolls decrease. As a result, schools are encouraged to compete for pupils to obtain more money, and their attractiveness is affected by the publication of performance tables on truancy and test results. Different types of schooling are increasingly in competition. The Education Bill which was introduced into Parliament in 1996 would have allowed further expansion of schools' freedom to select their pupils on ability or aptitude, thus creating further pressure against comprehensive schooling (which remains strong in Scotland but has never been prevalent in Northern Ireland). Financial help is available so that children can attend independent schools, through the means-tested Assisted Places Schemes now to be phased out. Technology Colleges and Schools have been encouraged by the government, directly funded by the state, but run by educational trusts closely linked and partly sponsored by industry (Walford 1990; DfE and Welsh Office 1992). With the support of parents, schools can 'opt out' of local authority control to become 'grant maintained schools' (England and Wales) or 'self-governing schools' (Scotland). In Northern Ireland, 'opt-out' legislation was transformed from its market-orientation to a morally ideological one. Schools opt out to become Grant Maintained Integrated Schools, where Protestant and Roman Catholic pupils are educated together. Parents now have a range of different types of schooling, as well as possibly different local schools, from which to choose – that is, unless their children attend school in remote areas.

Expanded parental choice has a longer legislative basis in Scotland than elsewhere in the UK. The Education (Scotland) Act 1980 as amended established the right of parents to choose their child's school, albeit with a lengthy list of reasons a local authority can refuse parents' choice. Research on the impact of these provisions showed movement towards a two-tier system, as popular schools continued to improve and attract pupils whilst unpopular schools risked becoming 'sink' schools in 'sink' communities (Adler *et al.* 1989). Provisions for greater parental choice were introduced in England and Wales through the Education Reform Act 1988. Legislation to introduce voucher systems for pre-school education was promoted by the Conservative Government as providing parents with the power to choose as consumers (Scottish Office Education Department 1995). Parental influence in schooling has been encouraged by their presence on schools' governing boards and school boards.

In all these developments, children have been perceived as passive recipients of state schooling, not as active consumers with rights of choice and influence. Choice of school lies with parents, and not with children, in education legislation. Children's ability to be school governors was specifically removed from education law by the Education Act 1986. Children have no right to education in law, which instead specifies the duties of the state (i.e. local authorities) to provide education, and the duty of parents to ensure their children receive education. Children are treated as the 'objects' of education law rather than the 'subjects'.

Central government is taking increasing control of what is taught in schools, through national curricula. England's and Wales' National Curricula are by far the most deterministic, but all curricula lay out required areas of study that take up most of schools' teaching time and require regular assessments. The 5–14 Development Programme in

Scotland is less prescriptive, but does seek to set national standards and required areas of study. While the subject of considerable controversy, results of these assessments are being increasingly published, with the justification that they provide information for parents to make an informed choice about their children's schooling.

Changes in educational policy in the 1980s and 1990s have thus promoted:

- consumerism and market competition over public service
- selection over comprehensive schooling (particularly in England and Wales)
- 'back to basics' in national curricula over child-centred learning and
- decentralised management and centralised policy-making.

The discourse has favoured parental rights and been largely silent on children's rights. The reported impact of these changes will be integrated into the discussion of schooling's purpose.

Individual flowering: the test of children with disabilities

What is education for? Measor and Sikes stated their view:

Although this is a controversial view, it seems to us that schools are or should be about more than just qualifications. Some writers have seen education as important for citizenship and crucial for maintaining a democratic nation. Humanist thinkers have seen education as having an unique function in liberating the individual and enabling us to achieve our full potential.

(1992: 2–3)

Such a humanistic view seems to be the basis for the specific educational rights in the UN Convention (see Appendix). Article 28 articulates a child's right to education, emphasising the rights of progressive development and equal opportunity. Article 29 states five aims of education, all set out in terms of development and preparation of the child. The first stated aim is the most general and has the most individualistic slant: 'The development of the child's personality, talents and mental and physical abilities to their fullest potential'. Article 23 is dedicated to the specific rights of children with disabilities. Education is mentioned twice, with the requirement on states to extend assistance 'to ensure that the disabled child has effective access to and receives education . . .' (23 (3)) and to provide information on education to improve provision in other countries (23 (4)).

The need for the UN Convention to underline disabled children's rights specifically is demonstrated by the historical exclusion of disabled children from UK state provision. Until 1980s legislation, young people labelled as 'defective' were considered 'uneducable' and the state had no duty to help them 'develop their potential'. The influential Warnock Report (1978) strongly disagreed with this exclusion, by appealing to a human rights perspective:

... [education] is a good, and a specifically human good, to which all human beings are entitled. There exists, therefore, a clear obligation to educate the most severely disabled for no other reason than that they are human.

(1.7)

The education acts following the Warnock Report formally extended state schooling to all children. But has the legislation and following implementation delivered the Warnock Report's promise?

A new system was created for evaluating disabled children's needs, through statementing (England and Wales) and recording (Scotland). The process requires numerous stages and professional assessments, and results in a written statement/record. Local authorities are then legally obligated to meet the stated needs.

All has not gone smoothly in the statementing and recording processes. In England and Wales, the Audit Commission/Her Majesty's Inspectorate (HMI) for Schools (1992) heavily criticised the lengthy delays parents and children were experiencing in the statementing process. Thomson *et al.*'s (1995) national sample of Scottish records revealed considerable disparity between local authorities on numbers recorded, with the largest differences appearing for young people with 'emotional and behavioural difficulties'. The process has been described as heightening professional rather than parents' control (Fulcher 1989). Local authority staff have felt caught between the restrictive resource pressures of their local authority, and their professional obligations to the child to evaluate and report on the child's needs (Education Committee 1996). Children reported to Armstrong *et al.* (1993) their confusion as to the purpose of their psychological and medical assessments, and their anxiety: for example,

I was dreading going. I don't know why. I was nervous and dreading going.
(Susan, quoted on p. 124)

Some of the children saw the assessments as punishment for past failures and behaviours. Yet such confusion, anxieties and (mis)interpretations were often unaddressed by professionals, so that children's behaviour and willingness to state their views were greatly affected in their assessments.

The term 'special educational needs', as laid out by the Warnock Report, was intended to move away from medical categorisation and underline the part played by the school in generating a child's special needs – and thus the school's responsibility to adapt. This responsibility has been largely unfulfilled (Fulcher 1989). Statements and records are mainly used either to provide children with access to segregated schools or for special assistance. They do not require schools to alter their ethos, physical environment or policies. Special educational needs tend still to be located firmly in the individual child, and not her/his school or family environment (Armstrong *et al.* 1993).

According to the Warnock Report, one in five children could be expected to have special educational needs sometime during their school careers (3.17), but most of these needs could be met without the formal procedures. Local authorities are required to make provisions for all children and statements records are for those whose special educational needs require continuing review and are pronounced, specific or complex. Without a statement/record though, meeting a child's special educational needs can be a matter of wide discretion. The changes in formula funding and the increased competition between schools have caused considerable worries for such unstatemented 'special needs' children, particularly in England and Wales. Children with 'special educational needs' are likely to be more expensive to most schools. With funding largely based on pupil numbers rather than needs, schools distributing their own budgets may not want to 'divert' money from the bulk of children, whose performance the schools' ratings will depend on (Hadley and Wilkinson 1995). Despite the promotion of parental choice, parental requests can be refused by recourse to a lengthy list of reasons, many of which could be easily applied to someone with perceived behavioural or learning difficulties. Research by Levačič (1993), however, reached less gloomy conclusions about the impact of formula funding and competition on schools. Schools that lost budgets over the two years of research did not have a higher proportion of special needs pupils (although 'special needs' was defined very widely in Levačič's research).

In the late 1980s, the recording process seems often to have been used as a means for children to gain access to segregated schooling rather than for support in mainstream schools (Thomson *et al.* 1990). The inclusion movement has since gathered force, and Thomson *et al.* (1995) found that children beginning in mainstream schools now tend to remain in them after recording. The debate, however, has not been concluded between segregated and inclusive schooling. Arguments continue to rage over whether state education for disabled children is truly 'developing their potential'.

Those who support special (i.e. segregated) schools for at least some disabled children point to the specialist education and therapy skills, which mainstream education lacks the resources to provide. When policy advocates integration, it can be a 'smokescreen' to make savings in educational budgets (Lewis 1995), and integration can be tokenistic:

the only time I feel different is when/ of a Wednesday afternoon/ periods seven and eight/ year eight/ all the other kids do sport/ now they go all to various other schools to play cricket/ at basketball/ where we have to stay back and do lessons . . . I just feel that/ even if we could just go and watch/ I just feel that/ why should we have to stay back and do work if they're out having fun and stuff.
(Peter, 15-year old, quoted in Wade and Moore 1993: 87. Peter wrote this account, and the slashes represent line breaks.)

Special schools can provide a protected and accessible environment, where a child can build confidence and self-esteem without constantly feeling disadvantaged in comparison with able-bodied peers. But to those who oppose special schools for any disabled child, such segregation does not represent positive support, but negative discrimination:

> To be special is to have the negative attribute of being non-normal. Once in special education, the processes will stress, explicitly or implicitly, the negative aspects bound up with handicap or needs – the *in*capacity, the *in*ability or *dis*ability . . . In terms of the examination-oriented values of modern industrial society, everything about the special curricula is negative.
>
> (Tomlinson 1982: 121–122, emphasis in original)

Many recorded/statemented young people continue to leave school worse qualified than their non-disabled peers, and disadvantaged in the labour market (Hirst and Baldwin 1994). Young people can find it difficult to make friends with non-disabled peers (Hirst and Baldwin 1994), as exemplified by Keith's words:

> *I feel different because when you go to a mainstream school that is in your area so you can see your friends but when you go to a handicapped school you have to traval [sic] from home on a bus so when you go home at night you don't get to see your friends.*
>
> (14-year old, attending a special school, quoted in Wade and Moore 1993: 86)

A significant number of disabled adults, as well as others, feel that special schools set children on the path of exclusion and stigmatisation (see Pearson 1994).

Children with disabilities are not the only children for whom the professed goal of 'developing the potential of each child' has been at risk. While discrimination is officially forbidden, considerable research has reported on how girls as a group are disadvantaged in numerous ways (Delamont 1990). Recently fears have been expressed about the educational achievement of boys, children from certain ethnic minority groups (Brown and Riddell 1992; Children's Rights Development Unit (CRDU) 1994), gypsy and traveller children (CRDU 1994) and children who are 'looked after' (Sinclair *et al.* 1994). The disadvantages of working-class children have a more extensive research history, an area which is further explored in the next section. The right to equal opportunity – whether in access to schooling or in outcomes – does not seem to have been actualised for a large number of children.

Serving the labour market: the test of troubled and troublesome children

As Tomlinson's quotation indicated above, educational values are not necessarily focused on individual development. Schooling can be seen as directed by the economy – either through the approving lens of increasing human capital or the more accusatory Marxist lens of subordinating labour.

Schooling's role to serve the economy is openly stated by politicians. For example, in the 1980s government proposals sought to encourage and extend work experience for young people in school. The Technical and Vocational Educational Initiative (TVEI) was set up in 1983 to increase expertise for vital areas of the economy. In 1995, education and employment were merged into single government departments in Great Britain. Scheme after scheme has been introduced in vocational training (Youth Opportunities Programme, Youth Training Scheme, Youth Training), with the official purpose of helping young people gain vocational skills, and new vocational qualifications have been introduced (e.g. National Vocational Qualifications, General Scottish Vocational Qualifications).

Bowles and Gintis (1976) would agree with the politicians that education increases human capital, but they took a less benign view of economy's use for education. Developing a Marxist analysis, they wrote:

. . . education helps defuse and depoliticize the potentially explosive class relations of the production process . . . Schools foster legitimate inequality through ostensibly meritocratic manner by which they reward and promote students, and allocate them to distinct positions on the occupational hierarchy. (11)

Evidence can be found in the UK to support Bowles and Gintis' claims. Britain does have highly stratified and exclusive assessment systems, with a much larger proportion of students leaving school without any qualifications than other European countries (Lees 1994). To correct this, various new qualifications have been introduced across the UK. In Scotland, for example, Standard Grades replaced Ordinary Grades in 1992 with the explicit intention to certificate all children (Littlewood 1997). Regular testing is required as children progress through national curricula, and children will gather 'records of achievement'. Young people are very aware of the importance of qualifications. For example, Robert Nielson, aged 15, explained:

Just now it's my standard grades and if I don't get the marks I need it will alter my future and if I don't get accepted into college then it means I'll have less chance of getting a job when I've finished college. (1996)

However positively or negatively one views these assessment changes, they can be perceived as more sophisticated means by which to differentiate between students, which ultimately are likely to 'track' them into particular jobs or unemployment.

Marxist theory such as that of Bowles and Gintis risks ignoring individual action, and interactions between groups. Such criticisms are somewhat addressed by research such as that by Willis (1977), who applied Marxist theory to an ethnographic study of working class 'lads' in school (see also Chapter 5). The lads were not transformed into docile, dependable workers, but rebelled against the school culture, curriculum and authority that failed to value their working-class, shop-floor culture. But by creating a disruptive, anti-school culture, the 'lads' failed in school. And with this failure, they directed themselves to manual jobs and limited prospects. The school itself was not the sole cause of social reproduction; the 'lads' were actively involved in it.

Theories such as those articulated by Bowles and Gintis or Willis become even more complicated in today's world, as education is increasingly itself a 'market economy', impelled by its own financial and structural needs. Today, much attention has focused on young people who are perceived as so against school culture and discipline, that they are excluded from school.

The official numbers of excluded young people are small, although they have been increasing in recent years. Official statistics, however, are likely to underestimate exclusions substantially. Exclusions can be 'unofficial': e.g. parents can be pressured into 'voluntarily' withdrawing their child to avoid the stigma of official exclusion (Bennathan 1992) or children being encouraged to stay off school for extended periods of supposed illness (Stirling 1992). Research demonstrates that exclusions are not equally distributed amongst the school population or among schools (Imich 1994). African Caribbean young people are over-represented, according to English research. While African Caribbean students constituted two per cent of the school-age population between 1990–2, eight per cent of permanently excluded students were African Caribbean (reported in Audit Commission 1996). One young person explained why:

They would rather pick on a black person so you end up getting blamed a lot. By the time I got to my third year I was expelled.
                                    (18-year-old, quoted in CRDU 1994: 154)

Boys are between four and five times more likely to be excluded than girls (Blyth and Milner 1994), although the difference seems to lie in the processes which trigger exclusion rather than differences within the exclusion processes themselves (Copeland 1994).

In-depth research of one large local education authority by Imich (1994) showed that three-quarters of exclusions were over issues of pupil management or control – and not violence against teachers, which has been given prominence in the media. When Gersch and Nolan (1994) spoke to six excluded pupils, five of them felt they had received few warnings before they had been excluded. They frequently indicated that they had difficulties with school work, behaviour, teachers and pupil relationships stretching as far back as primary school, for example:

Nearly every day me and the teachers used to row. The work wasn't too good, it was really hard. Everyone used to call me 'thicko' and the teachers did nothing about it.

I only do it if I'm bored and no-one is listening to me and then I cause trouble. It's like in music the only time I get any attention is when I turn the keyboard on full blast.   (39)

Difficulties were not just reserved to the school context; all the pupils had experienced some type of family disruption, such as parental separations or interrupted care.

Although the state retains a duty to provide education for excluded pupils, 'exclusion units' that do exist may be poorly staffed (Parffrey 1994). The alternative of one-to-one home tuition rarely meets the required minimum of three hours education per week (Stirling 1992). Social work and education services have been accused of trying to pass on the responsibility to each other, leaving the child without education:

I left care and went home and as soon as that happened, social services wanted nothing to do with me and education wanted nothing to do with me. The pair of them thought: good, he's off our hands, pass the buck to someone else. It was brilliant living at home again and I wanted to go to a normal school again but once you have got the reputation of being chucked out of school a lot of schools won't accept you. (14-year-old, quoted in CRDU 1994: 153)

On the issue of educational exclusions, the UK government was criticised by the UN Committee on the Rights of the Child for failing to meet children's rights to participate. Excluded children under 16, for example, cannot appeal against their exclusion; only their parents can appeal. Few parents do formally appeal and, even when they do, they rarely succeed. Children's own perception of why they are excluded is not required for official records (Blyth and Milner 1993). Gersh and Nolan (1994) found that pupils had very little idea about what would happen after they were excluded, were unsure about the general process and procedures, and often anxious:

I was starting to realise that things were pretty bad. I thought something was going to happen but I didn't know what. (40)

Many researchers have explained the rise of exclusions by the effects of education's 'market economy':

'Naughty' children are bad news in a market economy. No one wants them. They are bad for the image of the school, they are bad for the league [performance] tables, they are difficult and time-consuming, they upset and stress the teachers. (Parffrey 1994: 108)

Excluding pupils can improve a school's performance tables. It can be a speedy alternative to the lengthy process of statementing (Sinclair *et al.* 1994). As money has increasingly gone to schools directly, so local authorities have less scope to offer support services. Teacher workloads have increased, partially because of the National Curriculum, so they have less time to devote to children's particular needs.

Worry about exclusions goes beyond concern for individuals' education or schools' images. It is feared that exclusions may foster the excluded students' delinquency (Stirling 1992; Audit Commission 1996) and their future social, economic and civil exclusion (Blyth and Milner 1994). Excluded children do not have their 'human capital' increased, though they may serve capitalism by being 'reserve labour', the lowest rung on capitalism's hierarchy. Yet, by excluding young people from the schooling system, does society risk these young people refusing to accept their future roles as adults and workers?

Socialisation: the test of school bullying

According to classical functionalist theory, school is a vital agent of positive socialisation, able to develop students' commitments and capacities essential for their future roles. An overwhelming majority of children report that they enjoy and value school (Jeffs 1995). Most young people feel that a good education is 'important for doing well in life' (Hughes and Lloyd 1996: 106). And school is not all adult-directed. School is a place to meet other children, to make friendships and to have fun. The peer group is another important site of socialisation. Nicola Gaylard, age 11, reported:

The best thing about school is breaktimes and lunchtimes because I can play with my friends. Playing is the best thing in the world.   (Guardian, 1996)

School's socialisation of children into good citizens is threatened by bullying. For example, Olweus (1991) found that 60 per cent of bullies as children were later convicted of criminal offences by age 24; and 24-year-old adults, who had bullied as children, were four times more likely to have committed three or more offences than peers who had neither bullied nor been bullied. Such research supports Smith and Sharp's concern that those who bully others, if unchecked, learn that they can get their own way by abusing power in their relationships (1994).

Worry has also been expressed about the socialising effect of bullying on victims. Social isolation and victimisation appear to persist from childhood to adulthood, and children who are victimised often have parents who were themselves victims of bullying (Farrington 1993). Olweus (1991) suggested that, if adults did not intervene, victims' social values would be adversely affected. Victims tend to have low self-esteem and some have or develop mental health problems. In a few well-publicised cases, bullying may even have contributed to victims' suicides (Smith and Sharp 1994). Educationally, bullying may affect victims' ability to learn, as they may find it difficult to concentrate (Smith and Sharp 1994) or may absent themselves from school (Carlen *et al.* 1992).

Research on bullying suggests that approximately one-quarter of students in primary schools have been victimised by bullies sometimes or frequently, and around ten per cent in secondary schools. Fewer children are bullies: research finds between ten and 20 per cent of younger children and four per cent of secondary school pupils (Mellor 1990; Smith and Sharp 1994; Boulton 1995). In a survey of Sheffield schools, one-quarter of pupils reported being bullied recently, with one in ten once a week or more (Whitney and Smith 1993). Bullies and victims differ by a variety of characteristics. For example, girls are less likely to be bullies and rarely bully boys; bullying generally decreases by age; Asian pupils are more likely to be 'racially' teased than white pupils, and Asian boys are more likely to be considered bullies than white boys (Boulton 1995). The playground is the most likely place to be bullied, with the classroom the second most likely. Bullying also occurs when children travel to or from school, and in other parts of the school (Mellor 1990; Smith and Sharp 1994). The most frequent form of bullying is general name calling, followed by hitting, threats or spreading rumours. Less common types of bullying are racial teasing, being ignored and having belongings taken. Girls are more likely to receive verbal forms of bullying than boys, and boys more likely to be bullied physically than girls (Whitney and Smith 1993). Children with 'special needs' seem to be more likely to be bullied than other children (Lewis 1995). Says Robert, aged nine and who has a disability: *'Friends are good but enemies make fun of you because you're different'* (Wade and Moore 1993: 102).

According to research, many children are hesitant to report bullying to adults: for example, Mellor (1990) found that 47 per cent of children reported bullying to their parents and 31 per cent to their teachers. Whitney and Smith (1993) wrote that around one in five children said they would do nothing to help when they saw someone being bullied, because it was none of their business. Some bullies say the bullying is the victims' fault:

Bullying is brought upon the person by himself . . . He might start acting smart and the group might keep on slagging him and hitting him.
(Boy, quoted in Mellor 1990: 5)

Such evidence suggests at least some children are socialised into seeing violence as an inevitable (and acceptable?) reality of schooling.

Schooling and citizenship

Jeffs suggested that fundamental change would be needed to combat bullying:

The protestations of teachers that they are wholeheartedly opposed to all manifestations of bullying are as empty and hypocritical as those of army officers. For the structures of the organizations they operate within are based upon the denial of basic human rights to those who occupy the lower echelons. The survival of both organizations in their present form of the staffroom and officers' mess is a carefully elaborated charade providing a temporary retreat from the harsh and often brutal world of the playground and lower decks.
(1986: 58)

Jeffs perceived schooling as fundamentally undemocratic. Yet part of the socialisation task is expressed by some as training for citizenship (Adams 1991; Hannan 1996). As one young person said:

. . . in the very place which is supposed to promote positive learning, and give the children a wide education on all different aspects of life, little is done to treat the children as individual, thinking, human beings.

(quoted in CRDU 1994: 163)

For example, most schools allow students little or no say in the structuring of their day and the curriculum (Gersch *et al.* 1996). In a survey of 115 mainstream primary and secondary schoolteachers, Wade and Moore (1993) found that less than one-third took account of their pupils' views. Many of the teachers saw consultation with pupils as time-consuming, irrelevant and with no value, only leading to problems and wasting time. One of the few places in educational policy where children's participation is clearly required is special educational assessments (and those later required for students with statements or records, as they reach school leaving age). The Code of Practice on the Identification and Assessment of Educational Needs (Department for Education (DfE) 1994) is a statutory instrument, and is obligatory as educationalists interpret the Education Act 1993 in England and Wales. This code requires children's involvement. Although it lacks the same legal status, the revised circular on assessment and recording in Scotland (The Scottish Office Education and Industry Department 1996) similarly makes regular reference to children's involvement. Whether these requirements are translated into practice is a topic for research.

Staff do not always model the values they expect students to follow:

He's always on about help thy neighbour and that and you try and do that in his lessons and you're out. He's always on at us for talkin'. I mean they're hypocrites. I mean you go to the staffroom for somat and they don't even open the door. They leave you standin' there for ages they're so busy talkin'.

(Dave, quoted in Dunn *et al.* 1989: 186)

Few schools involve students in creating their written rules or consult students on the rules (Merrett *et al.* 1988; Merrett and Jones 1994). School councils provide a mechanism for consulting children but are relatively rare. Those school councils that do exist may have little power:

Some schools have school councils with representatives from the student body, but more often than not these appear to be mere tokens, rarely being consulted and only on trivial matters. The fact is that every effort should be made to consult the pupils of the school on each issue that concerns them. This would obviously take a great deal of work on the part of the staff, as well as the pupils, and I am aware of the pressures of time, but I do believe that in the long run it would be worthwhile, with the pupils responding to the responsibility that they have been given.   (Young person, quoted in CRDU 1994: 164)

An example of a more powerful student council has been reported, to be found at Highfield Junior School, Plymouth (Willow 1997). In this school, the council has a budget and has been involved in the recruitment and selection of staff. Students may have little formal power in schools, but they are far from inactive. In ethnographic research of a primary school, Pollard (1985) identified three types of peer groups: 'good' groups, 'gang' groups and 'joker' groups. Each group had a different means of 'negotiating' with the classroom teacher: 'good' group members were conformist, seeking to 'please the teacher'; 'gang' group members rejected and resisted the schooling experience, treating it as an attack on their self-esteem; and 'joker' group members used humour to balance their concerns with the teacher's. For example, 'jokers' reported 'having a laugh' as an essential way to counter classroom requirements:

It's boring being in general studies, when we have to stop and think; you're looking around the room, you've nothing to do, thinking, wondering what to do, run out of ideas, looking at the paper, sighing and can't think properly, thinking of something else and can't concentrate on what you're doing – you need to have a laugh. (Quoted in Pollard 1985: 69)

Teachers reported preferring the 'joker' group members, who in turn had the higher educational results and participated more in school activities. Pollard's research thus lightens Jeffs' dismal portrait of schools; rather than children who were highly conformist to the system, the children who provided some dissent within the structure seemed the most successful by school–adult standards.

What are described as 'discipline problems' in the classroom can be reconceptualised as the *protests* of some pupils:

If people aren't listening to what you say reasonably, then the easiest way to get attention is to be disruptive.
(Kirsty McNeill, 16-year-old, quoted in Khan 1996)

A study by Adams (1991) of schooling protests yielded fascinating examples from both the past and present. As far back as the 1660s, children's protests led to a 12-year-old presenting a petition to Parliament, describing the suffering of children under school discipline. In 1987, London Borough of Camden schoolchildren went on strike to save their teachers' jobs, with the protest spreading to other areas of London. Most protests, however, have rarely been recognised as such by research and the media. The authorities seek to find explanations of student disorder in psychological problems of individual children, wrote Adams, rather than children actively expressing their views.

One of the ways children can express their dissatisfaction with schooling is not to attend[2]. The White Paper for England and Wales, *Choice and Diversity* (DfE and the Welsh Office 1992), identified truancy as a priority for the 1990s. Not only did children who truant fail to maximise their own educational opportunities, but truancy undermined the educational system. The White Paper recognised that the success of the National Curriculum, with its tightened standards and requirements, was particularly vulnerable to children not attending. The White Paper was concerned about the poor outcomes for young people who truant. Casey and Smith (1995) found a positive correlation between young people who truanted and poor outcomes in education, training and labour market at age 19, although they noted the relationship was not necessarily causal. Similarly, a positive correlation can be found between truancy and delinquency (e.g. 23 per cent of young offenders of school age, sentenced in youth courts, have truanted 'significantly' (Audit Commission 1996)), but research evidence is not conclusive on the causal connection (Graham 1988; Graham and Bowling 1995). But the linkage between delinquency and truancy continues to be raised in policy documents like the White Paper, the Education Bill put forward in Parliament in 1996 and the Audit Commission (1996).

Almost one in ten pupils may be truanting more than once a week, with nearly one in five saying they truant once a month or more (Stoll 1994). Truancy increases as children near school-leaving age. An 18-year-old offered this explanation:

By the time I was 14 or 15 I'd already decided who I was and so I was not concerned about their [school staffs'] attitude, because I was never going to come into contact with them ever again. It was false for me to stay there and say, 'Yes sir, no sir', when I had no respect for these people.

(Quoted in CRDU 1994: 157)

Students say they truant primarily because of particular lessons (Pasternicki *et al.* 1993; Stoll 1994). Many of those who had truanted felt that changes in lesson content and choice, and in some teachers' conduct of lessons, would help stop truanting (Pasternicki *et al.* 1993) – in other words, an answer may lie in giving students more say in their education, as advocated by Jeffs above.

Certain background characteristics are correlated with truanting. Children are more likely to truant if they have parents belonging to 'lower occupational groups', they live in council housing, live with only one or neither of their parents, and are 'black' (although the correlation with ethnic group did not hold for frequent truants) (Casey and Smith 1995). According to Carlen *et al.* (1992), social exclusion in other contexts (lack of income, unemployment, poor housing) could result in children excluding themselves from school:

Being a free dinner child, not being able to pay for the ingredients for domestic science lessons, skipping a school trip through lack of money, being unable to provide PE kit (or avoiding showers because of the state of one's underwear) are all factors that, no matter how sensitively handled by the school, *affect self-perception and bear heavily on the children of the poor.*

(166, emphasis in original)

Carlen *et al.* felt that the investigation, care and support of children who truant and their families was part of the 'problem' of truancy, and not its solution. They weakened the ties amongst family members and between families and their communities, and labelled and stigmatised children and their families. They pointed out that, after all those interventions, few truants actually returned to mainstream education, which at least superficially was the main point of their interventions.

The 1992 White Paper proposed that truancy should become a performance indicator for schools. The accuracy of truancy tables published, however, is highly suspect. Schools are unlikely to want to publicise themselves as having high truancy levels and thus have every incentive to minimise reported numbers. The distinction between truancy and authorised non-attendance can be slim, as parents can provide children with excuses (Munn and Johnstone 1992). If students truant for only part of the day, this is typically not recorded. John explained his strategy:

What I did, I would go in for registration in the morning, like late when none of the other kids were there. So the teachers would think I was in school and then I'd go. So all the other kids think I'm not in school – see? (Because I came in late and weren't there then and they'd already gone to lesson.)
(Quoted in Carlen *et al.* 1992: 156)

Attempts have been made by central government to tighten procedures.

Children do not commit a crime when they truant from school. In Scotland, school non-attendance is first referred to an attendance committee, and is a ground for referral to the children's hearings. This system worked for Sharon:

The school didn't chase me up for notes, because they knew I was dogging it anyway. The attendance officer talked to my sister and gave her a monitoring slip which was supposed to be filled up. Then they gave me into trouble. I was sent to the Children's Panel and that was why I stopped dogging it. They shouted at me. (15-year-old, quoted in McBain 1995)

In England and Wales, truancy is not a ground for care proceedings. The Education Supervision Order (ESO) introduced by the Children Act 1989 allows for social service supervision of a child, for one year. Both systems are based on concerns about children's welfare, and involve official recognition of children's right to have their views considered in decision-making. Along with special educational needs assessments described above, ESOs are one of the few opportunities at present for children under the age of 16 to have their views considered in their own education (Whitney 1994).

Childhood, children's needs and children's rights

Under educational policy, children are generally not seen as independent of their parents, but as extensions of them. Parents are given the statutory right to choose their children's school in education legislation. Only parents can appeal against their child's exclusion, if the child is under the age of 16. No children's charters have been published for education, although there are parents' charters. Parents, not children, are described as the consumers of education. School councils are relatively weak. Parents can serve as school governors or on school boards, but not children.

All the commonly cited purposes of schooling – individual development, serving the labour market and socialisation – are based on a version of *childhood* as a 'human becoming'. Jeffs (1995) even goes so far as to see schooling as a factory to mass produce a product. Schooling separates children from adults, setting them apart in time, space and activities in controlled, supervised and selective institutions (Näsman 1994). The goal of positive socialisation quite overtly posits adult views, goals and values as predominant over children's, and schools are firmly structured through rules, routines, curriculum and policies for adults to be in control. Schools can be seen as conspiratorial indoctrination programmes, with those in power (adults, and most especially representatives of the élite) perpetuating their power into the future; families begin to seem like enlightened child-centred alternatives. According to these latter views of education, 'childhood' becomes not only defined by dependency on adults, but oppression by them.

Children who challenge the smooth running of the schooling institutions become the subject of considerable attention, concern and intervention. Historically, children with disabilities had often been excluded from state schooling altogether. Today, their individual rights to schooling are recognised, but the perceived needs of other students, as a group, can still overrule parents' choice of school for their child with 'special educational needs'. While the shift in terminology to 'special educational needs' ostensibly recognised schools' partial generation of such needs, implementation has still generally posited the problem as predominantly the child's and not the school's. Access to schooling and assisting resources is often, and perhaps increasingly, through extensive professional assessment.

Schools can deal with 'disciplinary' or 'learning' problems by excluding children or encouraging them not to attend. Writers such as Adams and Jeffs consider learning or behaviour problems as protests of children in institutions that are generally undemocratic. Pupils' truancy can be seen as a form of consumer democracy – they are 'voting with their feet' (Stoll 1994). More often, however, such problems are seen as individualised ones. The consistent causal connection made between truancy and delinquency in public fora (despite lack of research evidence) further stigmatises, blames and marginalises children who truant. Teachers' unions express considerable public concern about discipline and violence towards them in school; the solutions offered are more control and behaviour management in the schools, and haranguing parents for lax family control.

The idealised, protected nature of 'childhood' is threatened, as the public increasingly recognises that children are bullying other children. Children are not being properly socialised and, as future adults, the use of violence and intimidation may well continue. Yet, adults may be contributing to the 'normalisation' of bullying for children. Children see such violence (whether physical or psychological) treated as less significant than (nondomestic) assaults. The term bullying could be seen to devalue children as individuals worthy of respect:

Every young person at some point gets abused by other people whether it's by adults or people of their own age and there's no support mechanism for them to deal with it in schools, and it's just seen as something that happens like falling over and banging your head. It's not seen as a form of abuse or a big problem.   (Young person, quoted in CRDU 1994: 168)

In part, compulsory schooling was instituted to protect children from the labour market (see Chapter 8). The UN Convention takes a similar approach to *children's rights*. Indeed, the discourse of the Convention can be seen as largely protective – education rights, as with all the articles, are phrased in terms of states' duties to children.

Judged against the Convention, the UK's record is at best mixed. UK legislation does state that local authorities must provide full-time education for all children in their areas, from at least the age of five until the age of 18 (although with some exceptions, such as those detained under the Mental Health Act (CRDU 1994)). Equal opportunities to education exist on paper, but research in relation to gender, race, class, disability and so on continues to show discrimination and differential outcomes. Pressures of the market, curriculum and funding risk leaving certain children out of state schooling altogether – such as children with disabilities, children who are seen as disciplinary problems and those who truant. State schooling is, on the surface, funded publicly, but pressure is growing on families to contribute directly to their children's schooling. If families cannot afford this, children may feel or be unable to participate and may exclude themselves. Constraints of the National Curriculum, parental opt-outs for sex education and religious studies, all limit the options provided for students for full information.

In UK legislation, a child has no right to education. Irving and Parker-Jenkins (1995) posed the provocative question of whether a child should have an inalienable right to education. Do children who choose not to attend school, or create so much difficulty for schools that places are hard to find, make themselves justifiably 'ineducable'? However, the UN Convention does not give children a choice to refuse education, just as the compulsory nature of education in the UK provides no opportunity for children under age 16 to opt out (officially) from education.

Schooling also demonstrates a potential conflict between the rights of children as a group, and the rights of individual children:

My friends from other schools say that their motivation and their desire to learn is totally sucked away from them because of recurring problems with discipline.   (Kirsty McCarroll, 17-year-old, quoted in Khan 1996)

How should the educational rights of a child, who is being violent, be weighed against other students' rights to safety and education? The UN Convention is consistently expressed in terms of individual children's rights, but provides no guidance about potential conflict between different children's rights.

Schools are undoubtedly important sites for children. Children spend considerable time there, both in terms of weekly hours and years. Their social lives are often organised around peers met at school; schools aim to provide knowledge and skills to students; and schools funnel children into particular future pathways. Schools can thereby meet numerous *needs of children*: from identity formation to intellectual development to social relationships. Whether schools meet all the needs of all children is more problematic. In legislation, duties are phrased in terms of education but with no obligations towards children's welfare. Children with certain characteristics appear consistently to be disadvantaged compared with others.

On the other hand – or at the same time? – schools are also often described as meeting the needs of others. The aim of 'socialisation' clearly values societal needs (even above an individual child's needs). Policy states that schools should serve the economy's needs, while Marxist sociologists would say schools help perpetuate the capitalist class structure. Schools can be used like warehouses, which meet adults' needs to have somewhere to leave their children. Schools are large employers, with considerable investments of professionalism and bureaucracy involved. Adults have a considerable investment in schools: they are not only places to meet children's needs.

While much writing on education paints an undemocratic and even tyrannical picture of education, numerous suggestions for change have been made. For example, Slee (1995) suggested a whole programme to alter discipline in schools; Hannan (1996) summarised a programme for 'equality assurance' in schools; Croce *et al.* (1996) recorded students' views of their innovative school, where all school members make decisions including students. Even Jeffs (1995) did not suggest abolishing school as an institution – just that schooling should no longer be compulsory.

I think it's right that we have to go [to school], but it doesn't have to be such a dictatorship when we get there.   (Boy, quoted in Chamberlain 1989: 105)

Notes

1 During this discussion, the Scottish term 'local authority' will be used. In England and Wales, the local education authority is the equivalent. Northern Ireland is more complicated, with several different bodies given decision-making and management powers, which have considerably less involvement of elected representatives.

2 Some of the literature is sensitive on the terms used: 'non-attendance' is a wider category, which can include parent-abetted non-attendance, for example, while 'truancy' is a particular type of non-attendance undertaken by the child.

Suggestions for further reading

Carlen, P., Gleeson, D. and Wardhaugh, J. (1992) *Truancy. The politics of compulsory schooling*, Buckingham: Open University Press.

Children's Rights Development Unit (CRDU) (1994) *UK Agenda for Children*, London: CRDU.

Gersch, I. S. and Nolan, A. (1994) 'Exclusions: What the Children Think', *Educational Psychology in Practice* **10** (1): 35–45.

Smith, P. K. and Sharp, S. (eds) (1994) *School Bullying. Insights and Perspective*, London: Routledge.

Wade, B. and Moore, M. (1993) *Experiencing special education. What young people with special educational needs can tell us*, Buckingham: Open University Press.

CHAPTER 7

Children and health

Introduction

According to Ariès (1973) the progress of hygiene and public health measures were a defining feature of the creation of modern 'childhood', alongside the development of schooling. For much of history, and still today in many parts of the world, children have faced a hazardous journey towards adulthood, with many having their lives cut very short. Debilitating diseases and malnutrition affect millions of children in developing countries. Only in modern times has it become the normal expectation that nearly all children will not only survive, but experience predominantly healthy lives. 'Our forefathers would have been astonished at the elimination or control of common fevers, which they regarded as one of the inescapable burdens of childhood' (Court and Alberman 1988: 9). Notions of health and youth are commonly associated in people's minds and children are the healthiest group in the population, though as we shall see below a considerable proportion of young people do report longstanding illnesses. Since childhood is now widely presumed to be a healthy state, those who are seriously or chronically ill or disabled tend to evoke heightened anxieties and are vulnerable to greater social disapproval or marginalisation.

A significant consequence of changed health patterns is the present perception that behaviour is a major contributor to health and hence the key target of health policy. Vaccination, hygiene and other measures have to a considerable degree countered 'external', non-human health threats to children, so that eating, drinking, smoking, drug-taking, lack of exercise and sexual activity have emerged as defining areas for health improvement. Since many 'unhealthy activities' are pleasurable, scientific pronouncements readily blur with moral prescriptions, as 'healthy' comes to be identified with 'good' and 'unhealthy' as reprehensible (Backett 1992). Childhood is a key site for attempts to influence behaviour, since this is the time when it is thought many habits are formed that have far-reaching health consequences. Hence health promotion strategies directed at childen often have as goals the prevention of poor health in adulthood.

There has always been a tension between society's legitimate interest in public health and the rights of individuals and families to behave in private as they wish, but the centrality in modern health policies and campaigns of everyday activities sharpens the issue. As we saw in Chapter 4, from a Foucaultian point of view, health professionals have been portrayed as major actors in the establishment of state social control over behaviour within families. The so-called psy-complex – a set of understandings derived from medicine, psychology and psychoanalysis – is conveyed by health and allied professionals mainly to parents but also to children in order to promote healthier child-rearing (Mayall 1996). Increasingly children themselves have been the subjects of both general health education and specific campaigns (e.g. about dental care). Such social control need not be malign in intent or impact, but does raise questions about power, choice and autonomy. Children's weak position to challenge or resist adult influences makes them especially vulnerable. Moreover, the history of child health advice and treatment indicates frequent contradictions and changes, exemplified by volte-faces about the desirability of breast-feeding (Hardyment 1983; Meadows 1988; Gottlieb 1993). Hence it is reasonable to doubt whether all current 'truths' will still be accepted as such in future years.

The chapter begins with considerations of the meaning of health – firstly to adults, then to children. Next issues of health risk are examined, followed by responsibilities and rights with respect to health care. Finally the nature and relevance of health services for children are briefly reviewed.

What is health?

Traditionally health has been seen as the absence of illness, but nowadays that is seen as an overly negative standpoint. The prevailing professional view is that health should be viewed more widely to include positive health and to embrace mental or psychological as well as physical health. The oft-quoted definition of the World Health Organisation refers to health as a 'state of complete physical, mental and social well-being and not merely the absence of disease or infirmity' (Downie *et al.* 1990).

In many ways it is laudable that health policies and professionals adopt a broad view of illness and health, recognising the close interrelationships between the body, the mind, emotions, lifestyles, cultures and social structures. On the other hand, it can become difficult to identify what distinguishes a person's 'health' from the totality of their lives. Emotional and social issues become medicalised. The 'assimilation of social movements and cultural influences into the health agenda' may deflect 'social protest into technologies for their management and administration' (O'Brien 1995: 195), although many health professionals themselves recognise the importance of social and environmental conditions for health.

Where mental health is concerned, there is little consensus about the meaning of the term (Tudor 1992; MacDonald 1993). The main image of the 'mentally healthy person' portrays an autonomous, self-actualising individual, though such qualities are not perceived as normal or desirable qualities in all communities and cultures (Sartorius 1992; Harris 1992). The conventional medical view maintains a sharp distinction between normal children and those with a psychiatric disorder. Emotional difficulties and behaviours unacceptable to adults, which in other contexts are regarded as social problems, educational issues or special needs (e.g. Chazan *et al.* 1994) become perceived as symptoms of mental or psychiatric disorder (Rutter and Rutter 1993). Whether or not children come to be regarded as in need of psychiatric help depends to a considerable degree on the professionals and organisations they happen to be referred to. Consultation with a general practitioner (family doctor) is more likely to lead to a medical response, whereas concerns arising at school may lead on to special educational measures. Moreover, shortage of social services facilities has resulted in an overspill into the comparatively better resourced health sector. Yet children in psychiatric institutions are particularly vulnerable to abuses of their civil liberties, including the use of drugs to control them rather than providing positive treatment (Malek 1991; Coppock 1996).

The relationship between disability and health is a complex and contentious one. The example of pregnancy shows that it is not necessary to be ill to be able to benefit from medical care, but equally 'medicalisation' may have drawbacks and be resented as subverting or sidelining other kinds of social and emotional care and control (Oakley 1980). Children with some kinds of disability benefit from medical treatment. For example, medication can control the frequency and severity of fits for children who have epilepsy. For other disabled children, and especially those with learning difficulties, the need is much more for a range of educational and social inclusion measures (see Chapter 6). For many years, significant numbers of so-called 'mentally handicapped' children were kept in long-stay hospitals, largely cut off from the outside world. This is no longer seen as appropriate or acceptable. In recent years it has been possible for many children with cognitive impairments to stay in or move to family settings, partly as a result of changed perceptions of their needs and capacities. Such arrangements are more in keeping with Article 23 of the United Nations Convention which states that a disabled child should live 'in conditions which ensure dignity, promote self-reliance, and facilitate the child's active participation in the community'.

Children's perceptions of health

Evidence suggests that British children share with health educators a view that health is primarily to do with diet and certain kinds of behaviour. This is not a coincidence, given the dissemination of such messages in schools. When asked to talk or draw about the main elements or requirements for their health, primary school children mostly focus on three main issues (Williams *et al.* 1989; Mayall 1994c; Oakley *et al.* 1995):

- food and nutrition
- exercise
- dental hygiene.

For example:

We brush our teeth and we ... we ... I drink lots of milk to keep my teeth nice and white. (Rita, aged five, quoted in Mayall 1996: 92)

Indeed some young people with health problems or disabilities regret the lack of attention in schools to the understanding of childhood illnesses and conditions, as this young person with epilepsy illustrated:

You talk about smoking and things, and you could (discuss epilepsy) then. I think we should do things about diseases.
(Quoted in Laybourn and Cutting 1996: 36)

Like adults, children often acknowledge or show discrepancies between the views they express about what they should do to be healthy and what they actually do. Most children seem to be quite well informed about the negative effects of eating too much food with high sugar, fat and salt contents. They also describe fresh salads and fruit as desirable, though not necessarily desired (Backett 1990; Morrison 1995). Nevertheless, for the majority of secondary school children, health considerations rate far below taste, appearance and price as factors in food choice (Brannen *et al.* 1994). As many as half of 15 and 16 year olds in one study admitted to eating junk food daily (Oakley *et al.* 1995). Young children too deploy a range of strategies in order to gain access to 'unhealthy' foods like sweets and crisps. Trading the contents of packed lunches is one way of subverting parents' dietary intentions (Prout 1996).

When asked, children affirm that physical activity promotes fitness and deem sedentary activities like watching TV as 'unhealthy', but they also report TV watching as a favourite pastime. Judgements and stereotypes about whether other children are healthy or unhealthy are mostly based on appearance (slim or fat), eating habits (especially the volume of sweets consumed) and athletic prowess (Backett and Alexander 1991; James 1993).

Particularly in adolescence, gender-based expectations about appearance and health impinge significantly on eating patterns (Brannen *et al.* 1994). For girls and young women, slimness is perceived as a vital social asset and restricted eating the main way of achieving this:

I tend to sort of worry about how I look ... I just watch what I eat and weigh myself every now and then to make sure I'm still around that weight.

I think boys don't really care what they eat, they'll just eat anything they want. Whereas girls sort of think about it and think 'Oh, should I be eating this, will it make me fat?' (Both quoted in Morrison 1995: 251, 255)

Some females question cultural stereotypes regarding body image and the desirability of dieting, however:

I've seen 'Home and Away' and there's this girl Shannon and she thought she was too fat. And she was doing exercises and not eating her food and she was getting skinnier and skinnier and she wouldn't eat. And I thought it wasn't good to do that cos it doesn't matter what size you are.

(Girl, aged eight, quoted in Borland *et al.* 1996)

Children recognise smoking as a significant threat to health (Oakley *et al.* 1995). In one study involving primary aged children, key facts were widely known – that nicotine is an addictive substance; causes a number of types of cancer, affects the respiratory system and can kill (Borland *et al.* 1996). Yet the level of regular smoking remains significant amongst children in their mid-teens – about one in five (Power 1995).

Children's understanding of illness

Research in this area has been of two kinds:

• Asking mainly healthy children about illnesses in general
• Asking children about a specific illness which they (or a sibling) have.

Very young children often find it hard to specify the precise location of pain and discomfort. American studies revealed that children often describe illness in terms of behaviours of the sick person and others (Eiser *et al.* 1983), for example:

• Want to lie down
• Irritable
• Don't go to school
• My mother gives me medicine
• Doctor gives me a shot   (Quoted in Campbell 1975)

The range of children's definitions did not vary greatly by age and was not dissimilar to the definitions of mothers. However, older children mentioned more specific symptoms and diagnoses. They also showed greater awareness of social aspects of illness. In comparison with their often detailed knowledge about health promoting behaviour noted in the last section, children nowadays are often confused or lacking in their knowledge of the symptoms of even relatively common illnesses and of the role of injections (Eiser *et al.* 1983; Oakley *et al.* 1995). This may well be true of many adults, too.

Pre-teen children tend to see illnesses as having four main types of cause (Vaskilampi *et al.* 1996):

• contagion (microbes, viruses)
• association with dirt and pollution

- overeating and poor diet
- being outdoors with inadequate clothing.

Young children often explain illness through contagion from nearby objects or people, though the precise mechanism for this can be vague:

If I have an illness and go near someone, they might catch it.

Someone has it first, then it goes to someone else.

(Quoted in Wilkinson 1988: 122)

The explanations of illness given by well childen have often been interpreted within a standard-stage framework based on Piaget (see Chapter 1). Broadly a three-fold progression was identified (Bibace and Walsh 1980; Eiser *et al*. 1983; Wilkinson 1988):

1 Under age seven – ideas that illness has 'magical' causes (e.g. the sun, trees, God in the sky), or is a form of punishment for wrongdoing
2 Seven-11 year olds – vague mechanical explanations are offered for illnesses, with many children thinking that nearly all are caused by germs
3 Teen years – greater recognition of the interaction between body, mind and environment; more specific connections made between particular conditions and body parts.

The stage-based pattern implies inherent limitations of children's thinking, but some elements can be regarded alternatively as reasonable conclusions drawn by children about their social worlds. Certain of young children's 'misunderstandings' about illness as punishment can be seen as logical inferences from adult warnings about the dangers of breaking social rules (such as 'eating food too quickly' quoted in Wilkinson 1988: 151). A more fundamental problem with stage frameworks is that several studies have revealed little difference according to age in children's perceptions. The results seemed to depend more on the type of sample and the way questions were framed (Eiser 1989). Further, children with direct experience of an individual illness are often better informed about its nature, causes and prognosis than the average adult. It may be inferred that exposure to details is at least as important as any age-related differences in cognitive ability. Most children know much more about lung cancer than any other kind of cancer, because health education has devoted so much attention to the link with smoking (Oakley *et al*. 1995).

This debate has important practical implications. If young children are incapable of understanding illnesses in similar ways to adults then there is a justification for not attempting to explain or for offering special kinds of explanation (e.g. comparing invisible processes to more concrete daily events in children's lives). On the other hand, if children's understandings are more affected by experience, information and observation, then straightforward communication not only respects children's abilities, but avoids dangers of children drawing possibly false inferences from adults' behaviour or being confused by the use of complex analogies (Eiser 1989; Yoos 1994).

The knowledge and understanding of children who are seriously ill – or with a sibling who is ill

Even more than with adults, it is commonly presumed that children with serious or life-threatening conditions should not be kept informed of the nature and course of their illnesses, either because they will not understand or because they will be unduly distressed. Consequently, 'children are often so poorly informed that they are unable to make as many decisions regarding their own health as is considered desirable' (Eiser 1989: 94). However, sensitive research carried out with children dying of cancer found that they were much more knowledgeable than adults assumed, often drawing conclusions about their status from detailed observations of behavioural changes in doctors and nurses (Bluebond-Langner 1978). Although comprehension tends to increase with age, it is affected even more by access to information and the care taken to communicate effectively, e.g. using lay terms, giving concrete examples (Ireland and Holloway 1996).

Studies have shown that children with serious illnesses feel less stressed when they gain an understanding of the diagnosis, prognosis and treatment. Conversely, children are not protected from distress when adults try to keep secret the seriousness of their condition (Claflin and Barbarin 1991). Information and experience can demystify and give a greater sense of mastery over events:

It's much better now that I know what is going on.   (8-year-old)

I like to sort of feel like I have some control over a decision . . . I like to know what is going on. It's my life.
(Ten-year old, quoted in Hockenberry-Eaton and Minick 1994: 1028)

Children with cancer reported gaining support from relatives and staff, but also took coping action themselves, particularly by pursuing their positive interests (Hockenberry-Eaton and Minick 1994). Typically the young people with cancer aimed to maintain as normal an appearance and lifestyle as possible:

I just decided to go on with life and forget about what I looked like and do the best I can and people will forget.   (Quoted in Rechner 1990: 141)

Similarly, children are able to recognise how calmness and relaxation may reduce asthmatic symptoms (Ireland and Holloway 1996). Besides behavioural coping, children also use cognitive strategies, such as reminding themselves that painful treatment will soon be over or identifying strengths in themselves, their families and friends (Claflin and Barbarin 1991).

As with other potentially shameful phenomena, many children prefer not to tell other people about serious illnesses, apart from close friends and relatives (Hockenberry-Eaton and Minick 1994). Visible signs of ill-health threaten secrecy, and challenge personal and social identity:

Losing my hair was a hard thing to put up with. I looked at myself and thought 'Wow! there is something' and everyone else looked at me and said 'Yes, there is something seriously wrong with him'.

(16-year old, quoted in Cadranel 1991)

Appearing 'imperfect' can be acutely distressing in a society that places so much value on health and good looks, as defined according to cultural norms.

Bluebond-Langner (1991) investigated the perspectives of well children on their siblings with cystic fibrosis. This is a degenerative illness – 'the most common fatal inherited disorder in childhood' (Cadranel 1991: 240). They too reported how the salience of the disease reduced markedly as care tasks, hospital visits and treatment became a regular part of everyday life:

Most of the time I forget she has it 'cause the things become quite routine. Like, you know, we're having therapy in the morning is, like, I don't even think about it anymore'. (14-year old, quoted in Bluebond-Langner 1991: 137)

In the early stages of the illness, they invested effort in thinking about their brother or sister as being 'like everyone else' and presenting this image to peers and others. Not only did this minimise feelings of difference and stigma by association, but 'well siblings felt justified in making demands for attention, privileges and special foods like the patient gets' (Bluebond-Langner 1991: 139). Typical sibling concerns about favouritism arose:

Since he's come along, it's like we don't even exist. (14-year-old)

You can't let him get away with everything just 'cause he's sick. (12-year-old)
(Quoted in Bluebond-Langner 1991: 1340)

As the disease became progressively disabling, its impact on family life became increasingly pervasive and the attempts at normalcy harder to sustain:

It's in your thoughts all the time.
(16-year-old, quoted in Bluebond-Langner 1991: 1340)

Even when able to acknowledge that the illness is terminal for children in general, several clung to hopes of a miracle recovery for their own sibling.

Risks to health

We turn now from the subjective meanings of health and illness to considerations of children's differential exposure to health hazards.

Illness and injury have been increasingly referred to as risks to health, thus forming part of a wider risk discourse which characterises much of present-day life (Beck 1992; see also Chapter 10). Children's health risks include:

- dying in childhood
- falling ill
- being involved in an accident
- premature death in later life as a result of illness or behaviour starting in childhood.

About 10,000 children die in the UK each year, rather more than half of them aged under one year (Woodroffe *et al.* 1993). The infant mortality rate is often cited as an index of national health levels. Although the UK rate is very low compared with 100 years ago, it is significantly higher than in much of western Europe (Kurtz and Tomlinson 1991). The most common causes of children's death in England and Wales in 1991 were sudden infant death syndrome for infants and injuries/poisoning for older children, with congenital abnormalities and neoplasms significant at all ages (Botting and Crawley 1995).

Suicide is rare below the age of 12, but significant numbers of teenagers kill themselves, accounting for one-tenth of all deaths in that age group. Four times as many males as females kill themselves each year and the number has risen sharply since the 1970s – thought to be due to increases in youth unemployment and parental divorce rates (Woodroffe *et al.* 1993).

Fortunately, life-threatening conditions and actions are rare in childhood, but ill-health is more widespread than many people think. Half of a sample of over 500 12-year olds expressed concerns about their health, especially their diet and body shape (Brannen and Storey 1996). In another large-scale survey, one in five children in their early teens reported that they had a long-standing illness (Ecob *et al.* 1993; Sweeting and West 1996). Just under one in ten were affected by a condition which they said limited their activities. The most common conditons reported were allergies, headaches, skin complaints, chest problems and asthma. If various emotional/psychological problems are also taken into account as 'mental health' issues, then the number of young people who are not in good health becomes considerable. Referring to teenagers, Bennet (1985: 11) spoke of 'the widespread but misguided belief that they are a fit and healthy group'.

The most common reasons recorded for children visiting their general practitioners are respiratory conditions (including asthma and bronchitis), which account for about half of consultations for children under five (Botting and Crawley 1995). Several studies indicate that the increase in recorded consultations and hospital admissions for asthma represents a real spread of the illness and is not simply a matter of changed diagnostic practices. Since the prevalence of asthma is quite evenly distributed across the child population, it is likely that the cause of the increase is environmental, although the commonly quoted suggestion of air pollution is just one of several possible factors under investigation (Anderson *et al.* 1995).

About one child in 600 develops cancer, of which the most common forms are leukaemias and brain tumours. The past 25 years have witnessed a sharp improvement in survival rates. Although infections are a frequent cause of minor ill-health, they now rarely cause serious illness or death (Botting and Crawley 1995). High rates of vaccination have contributed to large falls in the incidence of several infectious diseases (e.g. diphtheria, measles) and of related deaths. However, AIDS is 'a new disease to which children are at risk through infection transmitted during pregnancy, delivery or breast feeding by an infected mother' (McCormick and Hall 1995: 168). Slightly more than half of the children known to be HIV-positive have become so as a result of blood transfusion or other blood related transmission.

Accidents and risk

Accidents are the most common cause of hospital admissions for children (Jarvis *et al.* 1995). Accidental injuries and poisoning account for 24 per cent of deaths of children aged one to four years, rising to 60 per cent for 14 to 19 year olds (Woodroffe *et al.* 1993). The most common types of fatal accidents are caused by road traffic, fire and drowning. Two-thirds of child pedestrians who die in road accidents are boys and even higher percentages of cyclists killed are male (Polnay and Hull 1993). This is partly linked to the greater freedom of movement afforded to boys than to girls (see Chapter 5).

Large numbers of children are admitted to hospital each year as a result of less serious injuries. Accident statistics indicate that exposure and vulnerability are affected by age, gender, environment and social class (Woodroffe *et al.* 1993). Falls account for half of all accidental injuries inside the home. Accidents outside the home become more common as children grow older and typically spend more time apart from adults.

The great majority of injuries to children are deemed accidental. The term 'accident' implies randomness and lack of responsibility, but within the discourse of risk analysis 'the accident becomes patterned and predictable' (Green 1995: 117). It then becomes possible to identify the circumstances in which accidents are more likely to occur and alter them. It is also a short step to saying that the victim should have predicted the accident and taken avoiding action. Children have learned that one way to stop accidents happening is to:

Be very, very careful. (Amelia, aged eight, quoted in Green 1995: 129)

Yet they recognise that most accidents result from an interaction between a person and the physical world which has an unexpected outcome:

*We was sliding down the stairs and I was on her lap and then suddenly I fell
down and she fell on top of me.*
                                    (Maria, aged eight, quoted in Green 1995: 127)

Differing ideas about the causes of health needs affect the kinds
of solution suggested. A study in a deprived area of Glasgow revealed
that health professionals tended to think that children's exposure to
accidents was largely due to faulty parental guidance, which they therefore tried to modify with advice about teaching children 'safe' behaviour. Parents, on the other hand, saw the risks as stemming mainly from
poor housing and environmental design (e.g. unsafe wiring, balconies or
roads). Their proposals were to make the environment safer and restrict
traffic (Roberts *et al.* 1995). Preventive measures at societal level can
be effective, as illustrated by the reduction in burns following regulations about flame-resistant nightclothes and the decline in poisoning
associated with the introduction of medicine containers with more secure
lids (Golding *et al.* 1988; Woodroffe *et al.* 1993). Sweden initiated a
national policy for accident prevention in the 1950s, with the material
environment as prime target of intervention (Court and Alberman 1988).
It was recognised that children's understanding of their environment
can be very good, but before the age of about ten they have difficulties
in assessing traffic distance, speed and direction and in adapting safely.
Rather than make children responsible for hazards from adult-driven
vehicles, it was acknowledged that they had a need and right to protection, e.g. through better separation of traffic (Garling and Valsiner 1985).

Behavioural health risks

Several of the most significant health and death risks for children do
not derive from illnesses, but are related to behaviour and 'lifestyle' (for
example, smoking, drug-taking). The main targets with respect to children of the *Health of a Nation* White Paper and the report *Scotland's
Health* in the early 1990s had little to do with childhood illnesses, but
concerned accidental death, smoking, drug and alcohol misuse, dental
health and teenage conceptions.

Very few young people suffer immediate or short-term negative consequences from consumption of cigarettes, alcohol or drugs, but professionals are concerned that habits formed in youth carry significant risks
of ill-health in later life (Smith *et al.* 1996). In several of these respects
children's health risks have increased over the last decade (e.g. drug-
taking). Self-reports about behaviour known to evoke adult disapprobation are open to doubts about accuracy, even when given anonymously.
Such information suggests that about one-quarter of 15-year olds smoke
regularly and about one in three have an alcoholic drink at least weekly
(Woodroffe *et al.* 1993; Power 1995). Despite the decline in the number
of adults who smoke cigarettes, the proportion of schoolchildren who
smoke regularly has remained stable (Roker 1996). Far fewer children of

Asian backgrounds smoke and consume alcohol, compared with whites and Afro-Caribbeans (Brannen *et al.* 1994). Cannabis use is common amongst secondary school children (Barnard *et al.* 1996). It seems that *average* levels of physical activity by school-children have declined, whilst sugar and fat intakes have remained static (Jackson 1995). Over half of young people have had sexual intercourse by the age of nineteen and it appears that as many as half did not use a contraceptive on the first occasion (Millstein and Litt 1990; Brannen *et al.* 1994).

The health of children is also affected by actions of their parents. Parental heavy drinking heightens the likelihood of violence within the home and of car accidents. Smoking by parents not only exposes children to the effects of passive inhaling, but also increases the chances that the children will acquire the smoking habit (Woodroffe *et al.* 1993). Conflict within the family also has a number of adverse health or welfare consequences for children (Sweeting and West 1995).

Risk-taking

Risk refers to the probability of something happening – in this context a negative health event. 'Risk-taking' denotes more active processes of engaging in activities which have high risk for negative outcomes, such as drug-taking or 'joy riding'. Young people are often depicted as risk-takers par excellence, although many are in fact cautious or anxious about many risks (Plant and Plant 1992). Some young people perceive themselves as 'invulnerable' to the risk under consideration and may also feel overconfident about their knowledge (e.g. of contraception, drug risk). However, this is not necessarily a feature of their age-group, but may reflect social circumstances or personality (Millstein and Litt 1990). Peer pressure is often cited as encouraging risky behaviour, though generalised images and expectations may be as significant as direct incitement (Mitchell and West 1996; Roker 1996). Sometimes peer influences discourage 'risky' behaviour. For example, having close friends who are reliable contraceptive users is associated with 'more responsible sexual attitudes and behaviours for both adolescent men and women' (Milburn 1996: 10).

One public health strategy aimed at reducing risk-taking has been to ensure people are aware of the risks. Usually increased knowledge proves to have little or no effect on behaviour (e.g. in relation to unprotected sex, drugs and smoking). For example, extensive knowledge about AIDS and the use of condoms does not necessarily lead to young people practising safe sex. Reluctance to use condoms is affected by power and self-image, as young men's sensitivity about their masculinity and young women's wish not to appear like a 'whore' can prevent open communication about safe sex (Henggeler *et al.* 1992). Young people are often well aware of the risks they take – indeed that can be part of the attraction. Actions which adults may perceive as health-threatening can appear pleasurable or stress-reducing to young people (Hurrelmann and Losel 1990). They perceive any risks as small, not applicable to themselves or so far in the future as not worth worrying about (Furnham and Gunter 1989; Smith *et al.* 1996). Often the short-term risk for any individual is low, whilst rational choice may be submerged by social and emotional considerations (Plant and Plant 1992).

Health differences: health inequalities

Health risks are not evenly distributed. Many forms of ill-health in childhood are markedly over-represented in families with low incomes, especially those living in inner-city areas (Kurtz and Tomlinson 1991). 'A child in the lowest (unskilled manual) social class is twice as likely to die before age 15 years as a child in the highest (professional) social class' (Woodroffe and Glickman 1993: 193). Many features of child-hood mortality, morbidity and development have been shown to be closely and negatively related to income and social class (Townsend *et al.* 1992; Woodroffe *et al.* 1993; Long 1995). These include:

* perinatal and post-neonatal mortality rates
* birth weight
* height
* dental health
* respiratory illnesses
* traffic accidents
* deaths from fire.

Since the appearance of the Black Report in 1980, which docu-mented marked socio-economic differences in health (Smith *et al.* 1990; Townsend *et al.* 1992), debate has raged on the extent to which this results from statistical artefact, health selection (people in poor health being less able to obtain good jobs and high incomes) or social causa-tion (poverty leads to ill-health). The evidence is complex, but there is support for the argument that deprivation directly or indirectly is a major contributor to ill-health. For example, a clear link has been estab-lished between damp housing and bronchitic symptoms (Woodroffe and Glickman 1993). Lack of money is the main reason parents in poor households give for buying little fresh, healthy food (Dobson *et al.* 1994; Dowler and Calvert 1995; Ward 1995: also see Chapter 8). Certain parental behaviours like smoking impact on children's health and these in turn are related to indices of social class and are often a means of coping with stress (Spencer 1990; Graham 1996). Children whose parents are unskilled are least likely to be taken for immunisations and other health services (Townsend *et al.* 1992).

The poverty–health correlation is strongest in the pre-teen years and emerges again in early adulthood, but class differentials are negli-gible during youth (Macintyre *et al.* 1989). Sweeting and West (1995) found only a minor influence of material deprivation on self-assessed health and self-esteem for Glasgow youngsters aged 15 and 18. This is the period when immediate health risks are smallest, so that family and lifestyle patterns seem to be much more influential in accounting for variations. However, certain specific conditions and impairments, as well as deaths from accidents, do show social class gradients at these ages (Townsend *et al.* 1992).

Gender influences the pattern of some illnesses and health-related behaviour. For example, anorexia nervosa is 12 times more common among females than males, which is clearly connected to cultural expectations about eating referred to earlier. Twice as many boys as girls aged 11 to 18 take exercise or engage in sport (Woodroffe *et al.* 1993). These are 'healthy' pursuits, though they carry risks of injury and strain. Whereas more boys experience chronic illnesses in early life (including asthma and migraine, the two most common), by mid-adolescence the pattern has reversed (Sweeting 1995). Significantly more young women than men report having health difficulties and worries. Use of prescribed medicines is also higher (Brannen *et al.* 1994; Triseliotis *et al.* 1995).

Some specific problems (e.g. sudden infant death syndrome) are less common amongst children from ethnic minority backgrounds. Others (e.g. tuberculosis) occur more frequently, though incidence depends on the specific population grouping (Black 1985; Woodroffe *et al.* 1993; Raleigh and Balajaran 1995). Cultural explanations such as 'Asian diet' have sometimes been used inappropriately to explain ethnic variations in ill-health. In a few instances, there is a genetic component (e.g. sickle cell disorders). More often material deprivation plays a significant part, as it did for white Britons earlier in the century (Mason 1995).

Whereas health 'differences' may be seen as acceptable, application of the term 'inequality' implies social concern and an impetus for policy action. Significant health inequalities are not just unfortunate for the individuals concerned. They also have societal consequences, such as health service costs, reduced employment prospects and hence economic contributions, and public health consequences (Vagaro 1995). This implies need for action at the societal level (for example, to reduce poverty, or alter attitudes to the female physique). Townsend *et al.* (1992) called for the abolition of poverty to be adopted as a national goal, but government responses have instead taken the form of declaring poverty not to exist, rather than practical action to deal with deprivation. The strategies embodied in the *Health of a Nation* White Paper (Department of Health 1992) mainly focused on behavioural change (e.g. in relation to childhood accidents and teenage pregnancies) and failed 'to recognise the role of poverty and social disadvantage' (Spencer 1996a, b: 150).

Responsibilities and rights in relation to childrens' health

Responsibilities for health

Generally, mothers assume the primary role as physical and psychological carer, cook, cleaner and so on, which lays the foundations for a child's health status (Mayall 1986). They are usually the first to notice or be told that a child may be ill, drawing on culturally shaped knowledge about what is normal or deviant to differentiate substantial from passing or spurious health concerns. Mothers are also much more likely than fathers to notice and recall symptoms, provide basic care when a child is sick and organise contacts with health services (Mayall 1994c; Brannen *et al.* 1994). Approaches to general practitioners are not made lightly, since mothers are concerned not 'to bother busy doctors, nor to be seen as neurotic or overreacting' (Cunningham-Burley and McLean 1991: 38). Children's sicknesses are often treated by means of domestic remedies like rest or hot drinks, perhaps abetted by non-prescribed drugs (Ahonnen *et al.* 1996).

Even at the age of 16, young people often seek advice from their mothers about whether to go to the doctor or not. Mothers are more likely to accompany teenage daughters than sons to the surgery, whilst fathers rarely go with either (Brannen *et al.* 1994). Children are more likely to attend the dentist if their mother goes on a regular basis. Several studies have shown that mothers are also children's main sources of information about health and related behaviour (Farrell 1978; Sex Education Forum 1994; Sharpe *et al.* 1996). Other relatives like a sister or an aunt can also serve as role models or sources of advice about diet and exercise (Borland *et al.* 1996).

As children grow older they accept more responsibility themselves, although parents retain a role to check and supervise:

We're keeping ourselves healthy by doing things ourselves. It's my body, so it's my job.   (Tim, aged nine, quoted in Mayall 1996: 94)

If you just go and sit around and do nothing, that's not going to improve your health. So it's up to you.   (Quoted in Mayall 1994c: 47)

Children perceive themselves as having a role in the prevention and treatment of minor illnesses, e.g. by resting, taking an aspirin, being careful in food choice (Bush *et al.* 1996). Children with disabilities or chronic conditions can take responsibility for self care and medication (e.g. proper use of an inhaler for asthma; using appropriate creams for eczema or tablets for hayfever) and for monitoring (e.g. fits chart, sugar level) (Lindon 1996). In general, the more serious the illness, the less scope there is for children to influence what happens in the face of adult–child and medical–lay power hierarchies. Most also have a high level of awareness that use of pharmaceuticals is a matter for doctors to prescribe and (usually) mothers to supervise (Prout and Christensen 1996).

Friends have an important role in discussing health care, supporting a child after an accident or referring to adult help (Mayall 1996). They can be important helpers for children with conditions like diabetes or epilepsy – especially when they have been warned what to do when unusual behaviour or a fit occurs:

Dan starts doing stupid things – not like him at all. Or else he just stops in the middle of the road. So we get him out of any kind of trouble, then we make him eat something. He's told us what to do.

(16-year old, quoted in Lindon 1996: 122)

Disclosure and explanations by young people themselves help friends to be less anxious and offer appropriate help:

It doesn't worry my friends now because they know what to do . . . I had to tell then what to do, like cos you're unconscious, so you have to put them in the recovery position and things like that.

They're a lot calmer now (during a seizure). Some friends were hysterical and crying and stuff, but now they just basically know what to do and they are really calm about it. (Quoted in Laybourn and Cutting 1996: 16)

One class of nine-year olds stated that the main locales which enable them to keep healthy are the home and neighbourhood (sports centres, parks), with formal health services having a secondary role, while school barely figured at all (Mayall 1994b). However, school does influence children's experience and knowledge. Teachers and school secretaries act as gatekeepers to parental or medical attention if children report feeling unwell. Teachers are often concerned to discourage attention to what they regard as low-level or false claims to be ill. These are interpreted as 'fussing' or excuses to evade educational requirements (Prout 1986; Mayall 1996). There is clearly scope for misjudgement, though some children do indeed feign illness by changing their behaviour or appearance. Then legitimation may be needed when they feel really ill:

I told them I was ill, but sometimes we say it to get out of school. So I was taken to the GP's and he said I had gastric flu.

(Quoted in Brannen *et al.* 1994: 91)

On the other hand, some children are reluctant to tell teachers they feel unwell. When a classmate is ill or has an accident, other children often take on roles of messenger, supporter in help-seeking, comforter and protector of space or activities which the sick child has to leave (Christensen 1993; Mayall 1994b; Hill *et al.* 1995).

Schools also purvey deliberate and unintended health messages. Children can become aware of practices that contradict health education advice promoted in the formal curriculum, both as regards appropriate healthy behaviour and notions that children should take responsibility. In one study children 'regarded school as detrimental to health . . . It provided poor food and placed restrictions on eating and drinking and exercise' (Mayall 1996: 107). In secondary schools, pupils value choice but also recognise that the quality of food available in canteens and especially from machines is often 'unhealthy' (Morrison 1995). In many cases, little account is taken of vegetarian requirements or of needs and wishes of children with non-British traditions:

They don't do any Indian cooking or any other sort of cultural meals.

(Quoted in Morrison 1995: 256)

Most children recall coverage in class of topics like dental hygiene, smoking and diet. Nevertheless some are critical of the extent of the input:

Sometimes teachers tell you when you've got to keep healthy but I think they should explain it more and what you should do. Sometimes they are just too busy with other things.   (Girl, aged 11, quoted in Borland *et al.* 1996)

Surveys of schoolchildren indicate that their priorities for health and social education are often very different from adults' preoccupations with drugs, sex and abduction. For instance, primary schoolchildren show much concern for pets, issues of separation and of bereavement. Fitness and physical activity are of particular importance for boys as is preparation for parenthood for girls (Regis 1996).

The media, especially soaps, influence children's ideas considerably. Oakley *et al.* (1995) found these provided the main source of information. Children can absorb a range of health messages in this way:

Some soaps tell you a lot about alcohol. Like I watch Coronation Street and this guy called Jack, he was drunk and everything – he was pure mental. I thought 'What if that was my Dad?' So it made me more aware of the dangers.   (Girl, aged 11, quoted in Borland *et al.* 1996)

Children's rights in relation to medical treatment and health records

As with education, health policy and services have usually accorded parents authority in relation to their children's health. Discussion of children's ability and legal autonomy to consent to medical treatment usually begins with the Gillick case, which – perhaps unhelpfully – also involved attitudes about sexuality, since it concerned access to contraceptive advice and provision (Archard 1993). The 'Gillick' principle enunciated in this case established in English and Welsh common law that children under the age of 16 should be able to make a decision about such matters as medical treatment or contraception, without parents needing to know, once they are judged to have 'sufficient understanding' (Children's Rights Office 1996; Lansdown 1996). This still leaves adults the discretion to decide when a child's level of understanding is sufficient, but the onus is there to accept the child's choice whenever possible. However, subsequent cases modified this support of self-determination. While it was accepted that a 'Gillick competent' child can give consent (i.e. opt in), later judgements held that if a child refuses to agree to a course of action (i.e. opt out) this can be overridden by the consent of anyone with parental responsibility. Such paternalism may make it impossible that 'a child or young person with a mental health label could ever refuse treatment' (Coppock 1996: 59).

The Gillick principle has not been incorporated in English statute, but the Age of Legal Capacity (Scotland) Act 1991 specified that 'a person under the age of 16 shall have the legal capacity to consent on his own behalf to any surgical, medical or dental procedure or treatment where in the opinion of a qualified medical practitioner attending him, he is capable of understanding the nature and possible consequences of the procedure or treatment' (Section 2(4)). (Scottish law retains the anachronistic practice of subsuming females within 'he' and 'him'.) Whether a child's refusal can override consent by someone with parental responsibilities has not been tested by any Scottish cases to date.

Silverman (1987) argued that age and presumed rationality do affect doctors' willingness to perceive children as decision-makers, but this also depends on the nature of the issue. Although previous research had suggested that even older children were often 'cast as incompetent and subordinate' in medical consultations (p. 187), doctors in a cleft-palate clinic were at pains to ensure that teenagers were central in decisions about corrective surgery.

Alderson (1990) found that young people had definite views about when they would or could not give consent to surgery and when they preferred to delegate this decision to parents. For children with life-threatening illnesses or undergoing painful treatments, access to information and involvement in decisions seems to help them bear the suffering and, if necessary, prepare for dying (Bluebond-Langner 1978; Mayall 1995).

In recent years, medical services have increasingly encouraged families to hold the health records of children. This is partly influenced by consumer rights considerations, but health education is also part of the motivation. The parent-held Personal Child Health Record has become the main health record for every child under five. Studies have shown parent-held records to be popular and well-maintained, at least in the early stages with babies when motivation is likely to be highest (Polnay and Roberts 1989; Cobbett 1993).

Some areas have arranged for older children to keep their health records. A 'health fax' was introduced for school medical records in a number of south London secondary schools in 1993. The majority of children liked the fax, but some felt it was aimed at children younger than themselves, whilst others found it difficult to understand. Many wanted further details included (McAleer 1994).

Health services and children

Nowadays governments to varying degrees accept responsibility (with parents) for monitoring and promoting children's health. Article 24 of the United Nations Convention is concerned with health and health services. It concentrates on rights to survival and provision, although the general participatory right of Article 12 covers children's entitlement to express opinions on health matters affecting them. Article 24 requires governments to make available medical services, with an emphasis on prevention and primary care. Stress is also placed on informing parents and children about 'child health and nutrition, the advantages of breast-feeding, hygiene and environmental sanitation and the prevention of accidents'.

Some of the earliest developments in the British welfare state were concerned with the health needs of pregnant women and young children. Midwives, health visitors (specially trained community nurses), community paediatricians, health clinics and school health services make up an impressive system of universal preventive measures in relation to child health. Yet for some time 'children have not been a focus of policy' (Kurtz and Tomlinson 1991: 211), in part because of the shifts in demography and public concern towards the other end of the age spectrum. Official health policy (as expressed in the White Paper *The Health of a Nation*) does assert the need for action in all policy areas and with respect to developing healthy surroundings. On the other hand, policies affecting housing, income, roads, alcohol and the tobacco industry often appear to run counter to the health needs of children (and adults) (Smith *et al.* 1996). The Department of Health has recommended reduced sugar and fat intakes for children, yet the Education Act 1980 ended the universal availability of school meals, abolished nutritional standards and restricted access to free school meals.

The holistic views of health discussed at the beginning of the chapter are at variance with the fragmentation of health services. In policy and organisation, education, pre-school and health services have been largely separate (Mayall 1996). Moreover, within the health service, the provisions and medical specialities for those who become ill tend to be distinct from those which seek to promote the health of the whole population (MacFarlane and Mitchell 1988; Polnay and Hull 1992). To these long-term fissions within health provision were added the market reforms of the 1980s, which led to the creation of more differentiated and complex systems, including GP fundholding and hospital trusts. The closure of some local hospitals has resulted in increased travel time for children and their parents to attend appointments or to visit during hospitalisations, especially in rural areas (Hawthorne-Kirk and Part 1995).

By and large the delicate advisory/surveillance role of health visitors when they give advice is welcomed by mothers, although a minority resent their intrusiveness (Mayall 1986). The goal of school health services have 'been largely defect-spotting, with children referred on to a curative service if necessary' (Mayall 1996: 23). In primary schools contacts with nurses and, even more so, doctors are infrequent. They mainly provide 'a quick inspection service at fairly rare intervals, it is not geared to listening to children's concerns' (Mayall 1996: 29). In other countries, children are more able to take the initiative to refer themselves to the school nurse or dental service – or not (Wilkinson 1988).

Schoolchildren have the lowest rates of hospital admission and GP consultation of all age groups (Kurtz and Tomlinson 1991). There have been significant changes in children's experiences of hospital over the last 50 years. Rather later than in other spheres, it has come to be seen as desirable for children not to be placed with adults, although this still happens (Belson 1993). It is now routine for parents to remain with young children who stay overnight and for visiting to be 'unrestricted' (Rutter and Rutter 1993). Play provision is common and play specialists are employed not simply for recreational purposes but to prepare and support children in relation to treatment procedures. The National Association for the Welfare of Children in Hospital drew up a charter of rights which has been incorporated in policy by many health authorities. These include rights to information and respect, to have personal clothing and possessions, and to be cared for with other children (Belson 1993).

Hospital admissions for surgery have been much reduced by the ending of routine tonsil and adenoid operations, so that 'long-term in-patient care for children is now unusual' (Levitt *et al.* 1992: 151). This does not apply to some children with serious illnesses. For them, the pain of treatment is the worst part of their experience (Claflin and Barbarin 1991). This may become almost intolerable. Here a 14-year old recounts her response to chemotherapy for cancer two years previously:

When that vile yellow tube was linked to my arm I could make myself sick by just watching it ooze down the tube and into my body . . . if I could have stood up I would have killed myself. The feeling of utter hopelessness, frustration and boredom led to a desperation I never, ever want to experience again.
(Anonymous 1990)

Over the years, medical education and practice has placed increasing emphasis on understanding 'the whole person' – taking account of the patients' views and context. In relation to child patients, though, there has been a tendency to rely on parents to act as substitutes, at least pre-teens (Bernheimer 1986: Silverman 1987). Children are often given little opportunity to contribute to medical consultations in which they are the primary focus. A Swedish study in relation to children aged five to 15 revealed that, on average, the child contributed eight per cent of the conversation, compared with 58 per cent for the hospital doctor and 34 per cent for the parent(s) (Aronsson and Rundstrom 1988). Much of what children did say was elaborated or mediated by parents. When doctors engaged directly with children they sometimes used a joking style which reduced the seriousness and status of the communication. In a UK survey, hardly any children aged 12 saw a doctor alone and 25 per cent reported that the doctor spoke mainly to the accompanying adult (Brannen and Storey 1996).

In one study, about two-thirds of the sample of 16-year olds reported satisfaction with their general practitioner, about a quarter were dissatisfied or unsure and the rest claimed never to use their GP. Long experience of being spoken about or down to made it difficult for many to express themselves (Brannen *et al.* 1994). This may be particularly so for those with learning difficulties. Young people have reported concerns about confidentiality and doctors not understanding (Mayall 1995).

Conclusions

Compared with later life stages, childhood in the UK is a period of relative good health, yet a primary target for health education and promotion about behaviour with longer-term health risks. Thus health strategies have concentrated as much on future as current health needs. The focus has been on behaviours which predispose to wellness or ill-health in later life, such as diet, exercise, smoking and alcohol consumption. On the whole, children are reasonably well informed about official health messages about diet, exercise, smoking and drugs, but this has had only a limited impact on their actual behaviour. Health education conveys comparatively little information about common illnesses or conditions affecting children currently. Even increasingly widespread conditions like asthma are not prominent in the national health strategy, yet children themelves want more information on common physical ailments such as asthma, acne, migraine and diabetes (Jowett 1995). Enlightenment about physical impairments could not only help the children directly affected, but enlighten their peers.

Implicit in health education programmes is an image of children as important and autonomous actors in relation to their own health, yet only recently have attempts been made to make these messages relevant to the concerns and constraints experienced by children. A health strategy devised by children might include quite different priorities, such as the provision of more recreational areas, protection from stray dogs and drunks, safe road crossings (Kalnins *et al.* 1991). Whereas education targets children directly, in individual and family consultations with health professionals, parents are often seen as the main mediators and guardians of children's health. Hence, the formal and informal rights of children to information relevant to themselves and to participate in decisions are weakly acknowledged in many instances.

Child health policy has concentrated on surveillance, curative medicine and health education. Yet poverty and local environment still have a major impact on children's health and life chances. This is only likely to reduce when there is concerted action and advocacy across a range of policy areas to tackle material conditions and commercial interests, as well as the behaviour of children and their parents (Spencer 1996a). The next chapter examines more broadly the significance of access to resources for children and their families.

Suggestions for further reading

Botting, B. (1995) *The Health of Our Children*, London: HMSO.

Brannen, J., Dodd, D., Oakley, A. and Storey, P. (1994) *Young People, Health and Family Life*, Buckingham: Open University Press.

Brannen, J. and Storey, P. (1996) *Child Health in Social Context*, London: Health Education Authority.

Bunton, R., Nettleton, S. and Burrows, R. (eds) (1995) *The Sociology of Health Promotion*, London: Routledge.

Mayall, B. (1996) *Children, Health and the Social Order*, Buckingham: Open University Press.

Spencer, N. (1996) *Poverty and Child Health*, Oxford: Radcliffe Medical Press.

CHAPTER 8

An adequate standard of living

Introduction

A young person described the experience of living on state benefits:

I get £29.50 a week. I pay £4 to top up the rent, £5 for bills, £5.70 for a bus pass and £15 for food. This left me as a total cabbage in my own flat with no money and nothing to do. Obviously I was not going to go without food, so I ended up getting behind on the other bills and eventually my electricity got cut off.

(16-year old, quoted in Children's Rights Development Unit (CRDU) 1994: 75)

This young person would doubtlessly be surprised by the Government's repeated declarations in the 1980s and 1990s that poverty no longer existed in the UK. For example, in 1996, the Secretary of State for Social Security announced that the UK already has 'the infrastructure and social protection systems to prevent poverty and maintain living standards'. According to him, poverty was principally an issue for 'underdeveloped countries' (Johnstone 1996). These statements were countered by practitioners, researchers and charitable organisations, who argued that at least one in four children live in poverty in the UK, and one in three children in Scotland. Child poverty has been seen as such a problem in the UK that UNICEF commissioned Bradshaw to investigate child deprivation in the UK. He declared:

During the 1980s children have borne the brunt of the changes that have occurred in the economic conditions, demographic structure and social policies of the UK. More children have been living in low-income families and the number of children living in poverty has doubled. Inequalities have also become wider. There is no evidence that improvements in the living standards of the better off have 'trickled down' to low-income families with children.

(Bradshaw 1990: 51)

Different political priorities and values can partly explain the apparently contradictory statements above. The contradictions can also be partly explained by the different definitions of poverty used. The young person spoke experientially of the inadequacies of government benefits; government ministers could point to improved housing, health and education since the beginning of the century; Bradshaw considered how many children live on the Government's version of minimum income. Debates about poverty definitions in the UK have been intense and hard-fought. This chapter will briefly explore these alternative definitions, and document some of the literature on child poverty.

Parents are seen as primarily responsible financially for children, and rarely is the distribution of family resources between adults and children examined. Little is known about children's way of living in more financially advantaged families. Exceptions include research done with children which has asked them about their role as active consumers or as paid workers. These subjects will also be explored in this chapter. We conclude with a reflection on how the literature and policy on children's resources conceptualise children's needs, rights and 'childhood'.

Definitions of poverty

At its simplest level, the debate has been divided between those promoting an 'absolute' definition of poverty, and those with a 'relative' definition. 'Absolute' poverty definitions are based on various minimum criteria. At their simplest, definitions use a concept of basic survival needs, typically including food, water, clothing and shelter. Townsend, in his influential 1979 book, argued that poverty definitions should go further to incorporate not only physical but social needs:

Individuals, families and groups in the population can be said to be in poverty when they lack the resources to obtain the types of diet, participate in the activities and have the living conditions and amenities which are customary, or are at least widely encouraged and approved, in the societies to which they belong.
(Townsend 1979: 31)

Townsend recommended a comparison with societal standards – the criterion is whatever is 'customary' or 'widely encouraged and approved'. The justification is a notion of 'belonging' and of being able to 'participate'. Townsend himself developed such criteria (a 'deprivation index'), refined through research.

Townsend's deprivation index is consistently referred to as an example of 'relative' poverty definitions, although he actually made a distinction between his index and a relative income standard. The latter addresses inequality. In the UK, for example, a common definition of poverty identifies people who earn less than half of average income as poor.

Sen (1984), however, did not find such a relative standard adequate. He pointed out that, with such definitions, people can exist – or die – in deprivation, yet be equal with each other. Sen developed the idea of 'capabilities' as closest to the notion of 'standard of living'. What matters is what people *can do* (their capabilities), not what they possess nor what they actually do. With this theory, Sen sought to dissolve the debates between absolute and relative poverty: '. . . *absolute* deprivation in terms of a person's *capabilities* relates to *relative* deprivation in terms of commodities, incomes and resources' (1984: 326, italics in original).

The United Nations (UN) Convention on the Rights of the Child appears to take on the notion of capabilities, in its focus on development:

State Parties recognize the right of every child to a standard of living adequate for the child's physical, mental, spiritual, moral and social development.

(Article 27 (1))

(Other articles take on a more minimalist approach, such as a child's 'inherent right to life' in Article 6.) Similarly, in the UK the idea of a child's development (and health) is used in the category 'children in need' (see Chapter 3). In both Article 27 and UK children's legislation, children need the *capability* to reach a certain standard of development.

In the past decade, the UK Government has tended not to accept relative definitions of poverty, and thus has tended to opt out of European Union (EU) definitions. EU policy initiatives have focused on poverty as exclusion:

Poverty is not just an absolute lack of basic needs. It is also exclusion from goods, services, rights and activities which constitute the basis of citizenship, so the eradication of poverty is inseparable from the promotion of social inclusion.

(David 1994a: 42)

Such a definition argues against a reliance on finance alone to measure poverty, to include other types of social or individual poverty. The definition is reminiscent of Townsend's, except that the EU makes an overt association between poverty, rights and citizenship.

Most definitions of poverty, whether labelled 'absolute' or 'relative', are reliant on underlying assumptions of need (see Chapter 3). Absolute poverty is based on concepts of 'basic needs'; relative poverty tends to incorporate these needs, but also include comparative elements based on the needs for, say, self-respect and community participation. Both types rely on someone to determine what are the needs in question. Generally, the determiners have been policy-makers, academics or professionals who are not considered poor by any definition. Exceptions which have involved 'poor' people include Breadline Britain surveys (see Roll 1992) and Middleton *et al.* (1994)[1], while Mack and Lansley (1985) assessed public opinion. The power to define 'needs' is strong indeed, because the discourse of 'poverty' has a powerful pull on society's sense of responsibility (Piachaud 1987) – and usually a considerably stronger pull than a political claim to equality.

Impact of poverty and social exclusion on children and their families

Using a variety of poverty definitions and measurements, an immense research literature has accumulated on the effects of poverty on children and their families. Beyond the implications already inherent in definitions (e.g. deprivation, impaired development or even death for absolute poverty; social exclusion, fall of self-esteem for relative poverty), research has outlined a lengthy list of disadvantages correlated with children's poverty:

- poor health (higher infant mortality, childhood deaths and morbidity, mental health problems, poorer diets)
- poor cognitive development, poor self-esteem, stigma and isolation
- poor education, lack of qualifications, illiteracy
- behavioural problems, truanting, high rates of offending, use of drugs and alcohol
- lack of parental support, child abuse or neglect, experiences of domestic violence
- homelessness, poor housing conditions, poor environment (e.g. for play or leisure).

Concern is typically raised for children's future prospects in terms of:

- health
- (un)employment
- early child-bearing for young women
- criminal careers.

(Bradshaw 1990; Chafel 1993; CRDU 1994; Long 1995;
Jones 1996)

Writing in the European Community journal *The Courier*, David perceived a detrimental impact on the society where children are growing up:

Poverty and exclusion lead to an undermining of conventional values and traditional forms of solidarity, to social breakdown, to a fear of the future and therefore, to the emergence of people who are inward-looking and susceptible to extremism in all its forms. (1994b: 40)

Economic repercussions on society are also feared, as poverty can negatively affect future 'human capital' (i.e. the quality of the workforce) and future financial contributions through taxes etc. (Commission of the European Communities 1994; Barham *et al.* 1995).

Research has demonstrated that the general category 'poverty' hides people's different experiences of poverty, dependent on poverty's duration, prevalence, repetition and severity (Ashworth *et al.* 1994). Duncan *et al.* (1994) concluded that the effects of persistent poverty (as measured by age-five IQ) are roughly twice as large as the effects of transient poverty. They also declared that the effects of poverty are cumulative – that is, one disadvantage can build on another. Garrett *et al.* (1994) had similar findings, but added that episodic poverty can also have devastating consequences on children.

Research also suggests, however, that the effects of poverty can be modified by a variety of protective factors for children: inherited individual differences of children; number and timing of stresses; parental support; family social competence; family social control; extended family support (e.g. see McLoyd and Wilson 1991; Hutson *et al.* 1994; Long 1995). As the list above demonstrates, parents' resources and capabilities make a considerable difference to their children's reactions to, and experiences of, poverty.

How can children have an adequate standard of living?

Family resources

The UN Convention underlines that parents, or others responsible for the child, have the 'primary responsibility' to provide an adequate standard of living (Article 27 (2)). Such a view has been strongly promoted in the UK, particularly in the 1980s and early 1990s (e.g. see Social Work Services Group 1993). In this way, children's standard of living is first dependent on their parents' ability and willingness to provide.

In the UK wage economy, employment is the commonly expected means for parents to earn money for themselves and their children. High rates of unemployment, however, have jeopardised this source. For those who are employed, the employment can still be insecure, short-term and low paid. People from ethnic minorities on average have considerably lower wages, and are more likely to be unemployed (although Jones (1993b) showed considerable variation by ethnic group). Women's employment has changed considerably over the past 20 years, as an increasing percentage of women with children are in paid employment. However, female workers are more common in poorly paid, part-time work. Lone parents (who are predominantly women) and their children can find themselves in a 'poverty trap', where the poor quality of available employment means they would earn less working and paying for childcare than remaining on benefits. Poverty statistics identify 'lone-parent families' as the most likely family type to be in poverty: using the definition of households with below 50 per cent of average income, 58 per cent of lone parent households were poor compared to 24 per cent of dual parent households (1992/93, from Long *et al.* 1996).

The Child Support Act 1991 was supposed to address the poverty of single parents and their children, by strengthening the requirements of non-custodial parents to support their children financially. Whereas previously a parent's responsibility for child maintenance was decided individually in court, the maintenance is now decided by a standardised but complex formula. The Child Support Agency (a government agency) makes the calculations of what maintenance is required and administers the system. Benefit claimants (of income support or family credit) must use the Agency, or risk being penalised financially. The system has been widely unpopular since its introduction. Non-custodial parents (usually fathers) have complained about the considerable hikes in maintenance, which have not taken into account the costs of visiting the children, second families, or initial divorce/separation settlements of property etc. (Social Security Committee 1993). While the process has been slightly amended, to allow some relaxation of the formula in hardship cases, dissatisfaction remains widespread (Hernon 1996). Mothers who fear violence from their partners, or their former partners' involvement in the children's lives, are worried that maintenance claims will result in increased contact. Moreover, the money recovered has often not benefited families, as the maintenance amount has been subtracted from income support benefits. Hence, the single parent on income support rarely has any real increase in income.

Many families rely on family and community support to survive financially. Families and communities may not only provide financial support, but also vital support in-kind. For example, childcare is often provided by relatives so that mothers can be employed (Brown and Tait 1992). As Middleton *et al.* (1994) concluded: '. . . the wider family and community support, far from being a long-dead historical ideal, remains crucial to the financial survival of many families in Britain today' (120).

The state

Hill (1995a) identified four main mechanisms by which states can intervene in family life: regulation; services; financial payments, or indirect financial assistance (such as tax relief to employers or employees). This typology illuminates the somewhat artificial division between family resources and the state used in this chapter, for the two are intertwined: for example, the state tax system will affect family resources, just as parents' employment and spending affect the tax income of the state. But countries clearly differ in their attention to these interactions, and to what extent they deliberately intervene for children and their families.

Under the UN Convention, carers of children have the first responsibility to provide an adequate standard of living. States have a responsibility to assist parents and others taking care of children and in ensuring children do have an adequate living standard. Such assistance can be either material or through support programmes (Article 27 (1)). If this is taken with Article 4 (i.e. state implementation of the Convention 'to the maximum extent of their available resources'), such a state responsibility could be strong indeed.

During the 1980s, government policy in the UK became particularly concerned about 'welfare dependency' and increasingly made direct state financial support a residual option. Benefits to everyone, including those for families, have often not kept up with inflation; most benefits have shifted from being universal to being selective and means-tested. Ironically, when benefits have been equalised across groups, it has typically been to the lower benefit. For example, the government's budget announced in the autumn of 1996 that all single people receiving housing benefit, and not just young people under the age of 25, will only receive enough for a shared tenancy. The same budget took away virtually all increased benefits for lone parents and their children. Criteria for benefits (such as the jobseekers' allowance contract for seeking employment) have been tightened, or groups have been excluded (for example, most 16 to 18 year olds from income support).

Like all EU countries, the UK does presently have an universal child benefit. Nearly all families with a child under sixteen years, or with a child aged 16 to 18 in full-time non-advanced education, can receive this benefit. Child benefit is higher for the first child and presently somewhat less for additional children. The money is typically paid directly to the mother, whether or not she is the official head of the household, and the benefit is widely recognised as being intended for spending on the children (Hill 1995a).

The UK has a bewildering array of other state benefits, most of them dependent on the applicant's circumstances. Parents who are employed, but on low pay, may be eligible for family credit (577,700 families and 1,179,600 children, 31.10.94 (Department of Social Security (DSS) 1995)). A parent may be eligible for income support if s/he is working less than 16 hours per week. Except for certain categories, such as single parents or disabled people, income-support recipients must still be available and looking for work. The number of children living with families who receive this benefit grew from 1,186,000 in 1990 to 1,504,000 in 1994 (DSS 1995). Receipt of income support is a precondition for other benefits, such as housing or council tax benefits. Parents on income support may be able to receive loans from the Social Fund, which can be used for exceptional outlays such as furnishings. Other benefits, with even more specific criteria, may also be available to families with dependent children. Despite this benefit variety, criticism has been virulent about the failure of government benefit policy to alleviate child poverty in the UK – and indeed, the UN Committee on the Rights of the Child (1995) expressed its concern at the high number of UK children living in poverty.

State services can be another way by which states can ensure children have an adequate standard of living. Some of these, such as the National Health Service and education, were explored in earlier chapters. Local authorities provide a targeted service with public housing, and have certain duties under homeless legislation. Households with children, and particularly single parents with children, have tended to have priority for public housing allocations, and for short-term support when homeless. This prioritisation is presently under threat, particularly in England and Wales, with recent court decisions and the Housing Act 1996 (Thompson 1995). It may also be threatened in Scotland, when it receives its revised Code of Guidance on Homelessness.

Many houses in the UK are of poor standard. For example, one in 13 homes in the UK are 'unfit' to be lived in, with Wales particularly disadvantaged (11.8 per cent of properties) (Leather *et al.* 1994). If a house is left because parents consider it unsafe or unhealthy for their children, they can be deemed 'intentionally homeless' and thus not receive emergency help and be a low priority for rehousing. If parents are unwilling to expose their children to the trials and risks of sleeping on the streets or poor-quality bed and breakfast, and manage to find a floor to sleep on in someone's home, they can be considered housed rather than homeless.

Access to state support can depend on geographical location and stability. Certain children who do not fit neatly into the geographical criteria can find themselves excluded. For example, the Asylum and Immigration Act 1996 sought to deny refugees, and their children, state support if refugee status is not claimed as they enter the UK. Only certain parents, and thus their children, can claim benefits and receive services. Gypsy and traveller children have difficulty accessing basic health care, education and welfare services (CRDU 1994). Existing official sites typically have extremely poor amenities, and the Criminal Justice and Public Order Act 1994 is likely to increase evictions of gypsies and travellers from unofficial sites. Even though most gypsies and travellers are legally resident in the UK, their rights and citizenship status appear in question when they do not live in a community fixed in a geographical area. In part, claims to state support – the social rights of citizenship – appear to be based on geography.

Young people

The consideration of family resources and state support above has largely been based on families with younger children. Benefits for parents are typically available until their children are 16, and sometimes extend until their children are aged 19 if the children are in full-time education. With compulsory education ending at age 16, young people may be taking on employment, seeking independent housing, forming new families, or applying for benefits themselves.

While the UK is facing high unemployment generally, young people have been particularly vulnerable. In 1995, 19.6 per cent of young men and 14.8 per cent of young women (aged 16 to 19) were officially unemployed, compared to 10.1 per cent of men and 6.8 per cent of women generally (Central Statistical Office 1996). Youth employment is also unequally distributed. Young people in certain rural communities can find it particularly difficult to find work, as can young people with disabilities. Young women in employment receive, on average, lower wages than full-time male workers of the same age; as a group, young people from ethnic minorities face higher risks of unemployment and are less well paid than their white peers.

The Government offered Youth Training (formerly YTS) to combat youth unemployment and provide skilled workers. Youth Training (YT) provided educational and vocational schemes for school leavers. Like its predecessors, YT has not proved an overwhelming success in channelling young people into employment. Young people have complained about the poor quality of many schemes:

YTS is cheap slave labour. They just use you until you get to the right age and they have to pay you extra, then they get rid of you and get another on YTS.
(19-year old, quoted in CRDU 1994: 236)

The Labour Government of 1997 will replace the youth training programme yet again, with a new programme 'Target 2000.'

Young women, people with disabilities and people from ethnic minorities have often been disadvantaged and discriminated against; research has identified such problems as a lack of interesting choices, harassment, and poorer quality schemes (Amin 1992; Mizen 1995).

The YT wage, however inadequate, may be the only alternative to absolute destitution or family support. While young people can work at age 16, since 1988 legislation most are no longer eligible for income support if they are unemployed. Young people deemed without family support can receive income support or severe hardship allowance, but even then they receive less than people over age 25. As one 17-year old said:

How can someone who is 17 or 24 need less money for their home than someone who is over 25? The amount of money you need is the same, you can't spend less money because you are younger, you need a certain amount of money to survive. That's one of the main problems of the benefit system.
(Quoted in CRDU 1994: 75)

If young people were unable to find employment or a suitable place on Youth Training, the official government views in the 1980s and 1990s saw young people even if their parents refused to support them. Young people who have been 'looked after' by the state can be even worse off than other young people (e.g. they are 70 times more likely to be homeless (see Tisdall with Donnaghie 1994)). Once homeless, young people can find it difficult to find a solution to their homelessness:

If you're on the streets you can't get housed. And you can't get housed if you've not got any benefits. But you can't get any benefit if you're on the streets. It's like one circle. You can't win. (Peter, 16-year-old, quoted in Carlen 1996: 110)

I went for a job interview, and he stereotyped me just because I'm living in a hostel. (Sharne, 17-year-old, quoted in Carlen 1996: 96)

Young people are punished more than once for being homeless, even though their homelessness may have been through no fault of their own or the best option out of several very bad ones.

At the age of 16, young people with disabilities can apply for a range of disability benefits themselves. On average, young people with disabilities can be financially better off than their peers in the short-term. This financial advantage, however, soon wears off as the young people age. The lower educational qualifications, lower employment and, if employed, lower pay, of a large minority of disabled people all lead to low incomes, whereas other young people are usually gaining as they take on employment and increased wages. Further, the young disabled people's initial financial advantage is erased once the extra costs of disability are taken into account (Hirst and Baldwin 1994).

Hidden within the household: costs and contributions of children

Children tend to be perceived as, and required by policy to be, dependent on their parents. Their roles in income generation and distribution thus tend to be hidden behind statistics about families or households. Some research has been undertaken on 'the cost of children' to families, but even less done on children's role in distributing or earning family income.

Estimating the cost of children has typically been part of a search for a 'basket of goods' or a minimum budget, often in research into 'absolute' poverty. Oldfield and Yu (1993) constructed a minimum budget. They compared it to the available amount of income support for a similar family, which is seen as the Government's identified minimum income. Oldfield and Yu found that income support only met 78 per cent of their most basic budget. Their budget was formulated on experts' compilation of families' needs. Middleton *et al.* (1994) undertook a different approach. They brought together groups of mothers, some on income support and some not, to determine what they thought a minimum budget should be. Although the parents' budget was 26 per cent higher than Oldfield and Yu's, and thus even more above benefit levels, the mothers could not envisage managing on less for their children.

Other attempts to identify the costs of children have sought to compare the expenditures of households with different characteristics, and arrive at an 'equivalency scale'. The first child is estimated to add about 25 per cent to a couple's costs, with decreasing amounts added with additional children. Family income declines by nearly 40 per cent, on average, if a mother stops working after having her first child (Wintersberger 1994). Dickens *et al.* (1996) calculated that a child under 11 in an one-parent family costs half as much more as the same child in a two-parent family (reported in *Community Care* 1996: 31). From such calculations, children are expensive costs on families indeed.

The Office of Population and Census Surveys (OPCS) sought to find out the additional costs of disabled children, on their families, and discovered that, on average, families were spending above six pounds per week (in 1985). As families of disabled children already tended to have lower incomes and employment, 28 per cent of families were found to have half or less of the average available resources. This compared to 15 per cent of all families (Smyth and Robus 1989).

Just as the cost of children is typically hidden within household statistics, so is the distribution of income amongst family members. Exceptions for children include research on contributions by young people over 16 years, child employment and children's pocket money.

For example, Jones (1992) reported on the results of the first cohort of the Scottish Young People's Survey: a ten per cent sample of all pupils in their fourth year at secondary school in 1983–4 (average age 16.75 years), followed until 1987. Jones found that 90 per cent of 16-year olds who had left full-time education paid their parents for their board. Young women contributed both in cash and in kind, if they were living at home and in employment/ training, although this was differentiated by class. Jones concluded that housework is expected by parents of working-class daughters as a supplement to cash board payments, while middle-class parents consider housework an alternative to cash payments. Young men tended only to pay cash.

For younger children, however, little is known about the extent of their domestic and caring work. Morrow (1994), in her research with 11- to 16-year olds, found that 40 per cent undertook some form of domestic labour (about 50 per cent of girls and 30 per cent of boys) and ten per cent worked in family businesses. Schoolwork by children is also uncosted and unrewarded in the immediate term: yet, as Qvortrup suggested, schoolwork could be considered the equivalent of research and development work by adults (quoted in Wintersberger 1994). What has gathered considerable concern both in the UK and internationally is the issue of 'child labour' – a term typically referring to children's paid employment outside the family.

'Child labour' is an emotive issue, which exemplifies adults' changing views about 'childhood', children's needs and their rights. In the nineteenth century, public concern was mobilised against the horrendous conditions of children working in factories and up chimneys. This concern led to a series of protective acts for children, which regulated and constrained children's paid employment. At the same time, legislation was also extending compulsory education, and thus keeping children out of paid employment. Presently, legislation in the UK limits the hours, ages, types and times of children's paid work.

Internationally, both the United Nations and the International Labour Organisation (ILO) have been concerned about child labour. In the UN Convention, Article 32 specifies children's right to be protected from economic exploitation. Children should be protected from any hazardous work, or work that would interfere with their education or development. States must set minimum ages, regulate hours and conditions and provide penalties or other sanctions. The ILO estimated that 250 million children between the ages of five and 14 were working in developing countries, and 120 million were working full-time (1996).

In the UK, child labour research has been undertaken in a number of locales. Bringing together their research across Scotland and Northern England, McKechnie and colleagues (1996) found that 35 to 50 per cent of children between the ages of 14 and 15 were currently employed. Further, almost 70 per cent of school pupils had had jobs at some time. Rates of pay tend to be low: Lavalette (1994) found that the majority of children were working for £1.50 or less per hour. Surveys did not demonstrate great differences between rural and urban locations (McKechnie *et al.* 1994).

Research has uncovered the potential risks to children's health and safety, due to children's employment conditions. Almost all of the children's jobs were breaking the existing legislation:

Children reported working outwith the legal hours, for longer than the law permitted, in jobs that were deemed inappropriate and, for the vast majority, without the legally required work permit. (Lavalette 1994: 216–17)

Lavalette also found sharp gender differences. Girls were employed in a wider range of tasks whereas boys were more likely to be employed in a narrow range, covering delivery work and more manual tasks. UK surveys consistently demonstrate that there are distinctive 'children's jobs', such as milk and paper delivery, and door-to-door commission selling.

The literature on child labour can be vociferous. At one extreme, child labour is described as a battle against child abuse, '. . . the abuse of children's innocence, vitality and vulnerability' (Reddy 1995: 207). At the other extreme, children's liberationists such as Holt (1974) believe that all children have the right to work. Somewhere in between, child employment (note the common change of phrase) is seen as contributing to a child's wellbeing and transition to adulthood. When suitably regulated, employment can provide opportunities for money and independence, and for young people to learn societal values: about commitment, effort, achievement, and the management of money. Employment can be socially rewarding:

Where I work, it's enjoyable. All my friends work there and you get paid while working and enjoying myself.
(Young woman quoted in Hutson and Cheung 1992: 59–60)

It can also be part of intergenerational 'give and take' (e.g., see Song 1996 for discussion of children's labour in Chinese family businesses). Particularly in poorer communities, young people's income can be essential to family survival (Grootaert and Kanbur 1995).

Part of this debate circles around *where* children should be and *what* they should be doing. For those who argue against child labour, children should not be in the labour market but in education or at home. The negative impact of paid employment on children's education is consistently raised. For those who argue for child employment, a balance is usually suggested. Children should be in education but also have opportunities for employment. In 1996, the Secretary of State for Education, promoted increased work experience for 14- to 16-year olds with the aim of 'improving young people's awareness of the world of work and motivating them . . .' (Department for Education and Employment 1996).

The part-time employment of 'young people' over 16, as distinct from 'children', is less emotive and more accepted. Hutson and Cheung (1992) investigated part-time work of young people aged 16 to 17 in education. They found high proportions of young people working: 77 per cent of young women and 51 per cent of young men (South Wales) and, in London, three-quarters of both sexes. Part-time working was distributed widely across all class groups, which Hutson and Cheung felt demonstrated how part-time earnings have become part of life for people of this age who are involved in education. Rather than worrying about the effect on the young people's education and health, Hutson and Cheung raised the concern that young people being used as a source of cheap labour, disadvantaging adults competing for the same jobs.

Hutson and Cheung found that most of the income from part-time work was spent by the young people on leisure and luxuries, which was acceptable to the parents. Parents still gave money regularly to their children (82 per cent, with the most common weekly allowance between £6 and £10). Amounts did not vary consistently by the father's social class or whether the young person was earning. The young people rarely gave money to their parents (12 per cent did so). Such findings contrast somewhat with those of Jones (1992) who found that, at age 16, only 69 per cent of young women and 65 per cent of young men were regularly helped financially by their parents. The differences between the studies could be partially explained by their different respondents: Hutson and Cheung's being in full-time post-compulsory education whereas Jones used a more diverse cohort.

In research with younger children, Middleton *et al.* (1994) and Hill (1992) reported that relatives or neighbours may also provide children with one-off or regular pocket money. Middleton *et al.* (1994) found that poor parents are less able to give their children regular pocket money (although no class differences were found by Sweeting and West (1995)). Hill (1992), in an exploratory Scottish survey of 41 ten- and 11-year olds, found that almost all said they received pocket money from parents. The lowest amount given was £1 per week, with the most common amounts between £2 to £3. Children reported that pocket money was often given as a reward for domestic work or other errands. Children said that pocket money was sometimes used by parents to influence their behaviour: for example:

'[Getting pocket money] depends if I'm good' and *'We get money taken off [for bad behaviour] and if we sort of tidy up the rooms, then we might get some back.*   (Quoted in Hill 1992: 42)

Pocket money seems to be used, in part, by parents to control their children socially and/or morally.

Children are active consumers themselves. As children have gained spending power compared with the 1940s and 50s, so have markets for young children and young people developed. The 1995 Walls survey found that children (aged five to 16) spent their money on:

• ice cream, sweets and crisps (85 per cent of children);
• comics (55 per cent); and
• music (22 per cent).   (Robertson 1995)

Although children did make such spending decisions, Hill (1992) found that the financial autonomy of children was only partial. Children said that most parents wanted to know where children had been and what had been done with the money. Nonetheless, and although a relatively small amount, children are spending a portion of family funds. Children are also active in influencing parents' spending on them:

Yeah, I'm working on them [his parents]. Keep asking them, saying, 'Will you get me a Gameboy for my birthday?'
(11-year old, quoted in Middleton *et al*. 1994: 89)

The power of children as direct or indirect consumers is recognised by advertising, which uses television as a favourite means to target children (Kline 1993). Ninety-nine per cent of families have a television (OPCS 1995). Middleton *et al*. (1994) found that children thought advertising did influence them. Most children, however, were at the same time able to evaluate advertisements and discriminate between them. Middleton *et al*. told of a 'certain scepticism, even cynicism' that children develop when they are disappointed by products bought as a result of advertising (86).

Peer pressure is another influence on children's spending. At the age of seven, Ben was already well aware of the need to 'fit in':

If you just wear plain clothes, like you don't wear jackets with them, you just wear plain, they think you've just got plain clothes and you haven't got no clothes like.... Sometimes they say, 'Look at the horrible clothes that he's got on'.
(Quoted in Middleton *et al*. 1994: 52)

Children did not differ by class in what possessions they valued or most wished for, suggesting a 'common culture of acquisition' (28), according to Middleton *et al*. (1994). Pressures to be fashionable appear to increase in secondary school, and apply to affluent children as well as the less affluent. By 16, young people believed they were more resistant to pressure and made more individual choices. Young women, for example, limited their buying as they became more responsible for spending:

Because like now, I buy most of my own clothes and you realise you can't afford to buy everything you want, everything with designer names on.
(16-year old woman, quoted in Middleton *et al*. 1994: 56)

Miles (1996) suggested that the relationship between individuality, inclusion and peer pressure is more complicated. After undertaking research with 285 young people (aged 16 to 20) in West Yorkshire and Strathclyde, he concluded that young people are pulled between a culture where: (a) peer relationships are considered important, and consumer goods are central to these relationships and (b), at an individual level, peer influence on consumer choices is seen as entirely negative. This tension between individuality and social conformity is encapsulated within the words of one young woman:

I hope that it [clothes] says that I'm quite fashionable! Other than that the item is basically the sort of fashion I go for, I like indie music and hate dance music, so I hope this kind of shows in the clothes I wear.
(Quoted in Miles 1996: 20)

Miles, and others such as Willis (1990), suggested that young people construct who they are in relation to their peers, in a large part through consumer goods. These constructions in turn influence their self-perceptions. Young people use consumer goods as a way to communicate with each other. Such communication is particularly significant for young people, because they may not be involved in other arenas – such as employment – which provide them with other identities.

Children's needs, children's rights and childhood

The literature on children, resources and standard of living has been dominated by investigations of the extent and impact of child poverty. The literature on child poverty has itself been dominated by concern about *children's needs.*

Investigators of 'absolute' poverty compare the cost to provide for children's (basic) needs with families' ability to pay for them. 'Relative' poverty adds on the comparative dimension of social norms to the definition of 'absolute' poverty, but attention to norms is usually still justified by recourse to children's needs: the need of children to 'fit in', the need of children to be able to participate in society, the need for children to have opportunities.

The literature has contrasting emphases, depending on whether it addresses young or older children's poverty. For younger children, much research has asked about the secondary effects of children's poverty: for example, considering how failure to meet basic needs effects the need for education, the need for mental health, or the need to develop children's potential. For older children, research has placed a greater emphasis on the impact of young people's poverty on society, and its needs. For example, writings on youth unemployment worry about young people feeling marginalised and excluded, and thus more likely to commit crime. The EU is concerned about how social exclusion of young people threatens social solidarity.

The relatively small sociological literature on young people's active consumerism, however, retains a focus on young people's needs. Miles' research explores how young people's needs for a positive identity, the need to communicate and build relationships with their peers, is met through consumer goods. The literature on younger children's consumerism also considers children as social actors: the curtain is drawn on the family, and children's role in directly purchasing or influencing parental purchasing is revealed.

The UN Convention does not address the *rights of children* as active consumers themselves (e.g. rights to complain, rights of contract). The Convention implicitly makes a claim for children on parental resources, but asserts no specific right that they should have a portion of family income to spend as they wish, no specific right to decide with other family members how income is spent, nor a right to income that they earn. In fact, the Convention limits children directly achieving the usual means to be active consumers, through restrictions on child labour. The Convention does assert children's right to have their basic needs met in order to survive. The Convention contains a wider right, for children to have an adequate standard of living; this is necessary so that children can develop to their fullest potential. Such rights fit more broadly into ideas about 'human rights', as described in Chapter 2.

What type of *childhood* does the literature present? Statistics, policy and research tend to perceive parents as primarily responsible for providing for their children's needs. Statistics tend to be gathered on the basis of households, benefits usually go to the head of household and always to an adult (until the child is over 16), and research about children is typically also research on family poverty. This underlines and promotes children's dependency on their parents and their immersion in the family.

Some children's poverty is seen separately from their parents'. Children not living with parents gain some attention in the literature: street children, in other countries, for example. Homeless young people have garnered media concern, as in the UK numbers of young people sleeping rough have sky-rocketed in past decades. Young people between 16 and 18 are allowed to contribute financially and practically to society, as adults, but they do not have similar claims as adults to the benefit system. For example:

- On reaching age 16, young people can be eligible for certain benefits in their own right.
- Young people are legally allowed to leave school and start work in the UK at 16.
- Most young people cannot receive unemployment benefits until they are 18.
- Even once they are 18, income support is less for young people until the age of 25.

Young people's access to resources – or lack thereof in the UK – demonstrates the uneasy transition between childhood and adulthood that is primarily based on age.

Only children's liberationists think children under 16 should be active, full members of the labour market. The prevailing view is that children should be in education or training, not in work. They must be protected from the rigours of employment, and their future potential protected. In today's UK, children's income is not perceived as an essential and expected part of families' income. Education and training are identified as distinct from labour; children's domestic work in the family is rarely examined. Children (at least before they legally leave school) are categorised as financial non-contributors to their families.

When the ILO does support children's work, their reasons are based on children's inclusion in society and the transfer of knowledge between generations (David 1994c). The majority of justifications for children's employment in the UK are based even more strongly on children learning useful skills, for when they are adults. This concentrates on children as 'human becomings'.

The idea of 'human becomings' is repeated in the literature on children's poverty. Worries are often expressed about the effects of poverty on children's futures, as future adults. Concern about children's poverty is also described in terms of worry about society's future, when children are seen as a form of 'human capital', an investment in the future. Conversely, arguments are made that a lack of investment today is storing up trouble for tomorrow – such as the research on risk factors for juvenile delinquency.

The literature about children's poverty is almost always about deficit. The blame may be differently located – whether in genetics, poor parenting or cumulative disadvantage – but poverty is almost inevitably seen as negative. Children's claim for resources in the poverty literature tends to come from ideas of their perceived weakness, rather than as citizens claiming their rights. Only rarely are the adaptive strengths of children experiencing poverty, or the initiatives of parents the central concern of research (for some exceptions, see Musick 1993; Thrasher and Mowbray 1995).

Whatever their claim through needs, rights or their status as children, in practice children's claim to an adequate standard of living is weak. Children are overwhelmingly amongst the UK's (and the world's) poor. There is more evidence of withdrawing benefits, programmes and help for children than extensions in the UK. Children may be our 'investment for our future', but the UK has so far failed to pay for it.

Note

1 The book *Family Fortunes* reports on research undertaken by Middleton *et al.* The book's chapters are all written by different people. To avoid confusion to the reader here, references to the book will be referred to as Middleton *et al.* (1994).

Suggestions for further reading

Carlen, P. (1996) *Jigsaw – a political criminology of youth homelessness*, Buckingham: Open University Press.

Children's Rights Development Unit (1994) *UK Agenda for Children*, London: CRDU.

Lavalette, M. (1994) *Child Employment in the Capitalist Labour Market*, Aldershot: Avebury.

Middleton, S., Ashworth, K. and Walker, R. (eds) (1994) *Family Fortunes: Pressures on Parents and Children in the 1990s*, London: Child Poverty Action Group.

Oldfield, N. and Yu, A. C. S. (1993) *The Cost of a Child. Living Standards for the 1990s*, London: Child Poverty Action Group.

CHAPTER 9

Children who commit crimes

Introduction

Concern is rife throughout British society about children who commit crimes. Scarcely a day passes without news coverage of a young offender. Periodically, a crime by a child catches the media headlines, causing a furore of condemnation, soul-searching and vitriol – for example, the 1993 murder of the three-year-old Jamie Bulger by two ten-year olds. Politicians of all parties put forward their solutions to the 'blight' of youth crime, from electronic tagging of young offenders (Conservative Government policy) to curfews for children (a Labour politician's suggestion). Virtually every year in the 1990s new legislation on criminal justice has passed through Parliament. Public surveys no doubt influence the politicians, as the surveys place crime first on people's list of worries (Jowell *et al.* 1995). The research community has produced an immense literature on juvenile crime and juvenile delinquency in the past century, seeking to find the causes of such offending, to analyse and suggest policy responses.

Why are we so concerned? The issue of child crime seems to encapsulate many fraught issues for society. Children who commit crimes bring into question society's ideas of 'childhood' and of 'adolescence', gender roles, the 'proper' socialisation of young people, people's sense of safety, of community, of morals. They seem to symbolise anxieties about the state of our society. But while children who commit crimes are at the centre of many and recurrent post-war 'moral panics' about the 'crisis of order', they are perhaps the most disenfranchised group in society – 'by the very act of committing a crime a young person forfeits even those limited and previous rights and privileges which are held by other young people' (Adams 1986: 99).

As suggested above, there is in-depth and extensive consideration of what should be done about juvenile crime. In this chapter, the debates around definitions and statistics will be briefly explored. This chapter will then consider the three main approaches to juvenile justice (justice, welfare and restoration), considering the justifications for and criticisms against them. Brief attention will be given to crime prevention and discrimination within the criminal justice system. The chapter will conclude with a consideration on how our approach to children who commit crimes presents particular views of 'childhood' and to what extent it meets children's needs and rights.

Definitions

Terminology is illuminative. In legal and academic circles, the term 'juvenile delinquent' remains common. In English, the noun 'juvenile' is used almost exclusively to refer to a young person who has committed an offence (and 'juvenile', as an adjective, tends to be a derogatory description of immaturity). Different legal systems identify different age limits for 'juveniles', which perhaps explains the United Nations definition of a juvenile as 'a child or young person who, under the respective legal systems, may be dealt with for an offence in a manner which is different from an adult' (1985). A juvenile is thus defined in contrast to an adult, in a particular context – the legal system – rather than by a specific age. This distinction between juveniles and adults also lies behind 'status offences': because of their younger age, young people can be guilty of an offence for which adults would not be.

'Crime' is a kind of behaviour generally disapproved of by the community, which elicits legally sanctioned penalties. Sometimes the term 'crime' is used for behaviours not presently included in legal codes, but arguably in order to suggest that the behaviour should be included. In this chapter, 'crime' and 'offence' will be used interchangeably, although in Scotland there is a legal distinction between a crime (more serious) and an offence (less serious).

'Delinquency' is another term almost exclusively applied to young people. The term incorporates crimes but goes beyond to include such behaviours as truancy or antisocial behaviour. In the background is a presumption that delinquency when young can lead to a criminal career in the future – a presumption particularly important to the rehabilitative/ welfare answer to juvenile crime discussed later.

Statistics

What is the extent of juvenile delinquency and crime? No one really knows. Three main methods are used to gather quantitative information: self-report surveys; victim surveys; and official statistics on those involved in the criminal justice system. But all methods have their drawbacks. For example, self-report surveys of young people may over-emphasise minor delinquent acts. Since the surveys are usually administered in schools, they miss young people who are not attending (who may be more likely to offend). Victim surveys will miss 'victimless' crimes, and behaviours that victims do not perceive as crimes. (See Smith 1995 for further discussion of survey deficits.)

When compared to victim or self-report surveys, official statistics underestimate crime vastly, since they only refer to crimes that come to the attention of the criminal justice system. According to a Northern Ireland self-report survey of young people, police only detected three per cent of their crimes (McQuoid 1996); an even lower number than official statistics, which state that 19 per cent of young people's offences were recorded by police in 1994 (Audit Commission 1996). Official statistics are strongly biased by ethnic minority background and socio-economic class (see later in this chapter). Self-report surveys routinely find that the ratio of male to female offenders is around three to two (McQuoid 1996), but UK official statistics show a ratio closer to four to one. Official statistics are also biased towards certain ages and certain crimes. For example, crime is presented as a youth problem, with most crime being committed by young men between the ages of 15 and 25. Two out of every five known offenders were under the age of 21, in 1994, and one-quarter were under 18. In 1994, the peak age of offending was 15 for women and 18 for men (reported in Audit Commission 1996). Yet this statistical age curve is questionable. The younger the offender, the less likely s/he will be convicted. Young people under a certain age (age ten in England, Wales and Northern Ireland, age eight in Scotland) cannot be considered criminally responsible, and thus are not part of official criminal statistics. Rutter and Giller (1983) pointed out that it can take some time before criminal activities can be detected and this creates a time-lag in age in official statistics. At the other end of the curve, Graham and Bowling's self-report survey (1995) found that many people shifted crimes as they aged – away from offences that were more often detected, such as violent assaults, to those less often detected, such as fraud. The age curve may be much higher and flatter as people age than official statistics suggest.

What almost all surveys miss is the extent to which the population of young people not only commit crimes, but are often the victim of crimes. Only child-abuse statistics regularly highlight children's victimisation, for children of all ages. In a UK-wide survey of 12- to 19-year olds, 86 per cent of young men and 78 per cent of young women reported being victims of crime (McNeish 1996). The British Crime Survey similarly reports on children's victimisation from the age of 12. But little is known about the victimisation of even younger children.

The Audit Commission (1996) estimated that public services spend around £1 billion dealing with young offenders between 10 and 17 years old. Sixty-six per cent of this money is spent by police, and 22 per cent by social services. With most offences by young people being property-related, manufacturers and retailers are estimated to lose over £1 billion a year due to crime. The estimated cost of crime generally exceeds a staggering £16 billion for public services and victims each year. What these numbers do not tell are the non-monetary costs to victims, young offenders, or their families, nor the costs/ benefits to young people of being involved in crime and/ or the criminal justice system.

Responses to juvenile crime

Western societies have agonised endlessly over how to deal effectively with young people who commit crimes. These debates have been
fuelled by the lack of consensus on the causes of crime, which makes
decisions on effective responses particularly difficult. Over the past
century, the pendulum has swung back and forth between two main
approaches: 'justice' and 'welfare' (also termed 'restitutive' and 'rehabilitative' approaches, respectively). A third approach has recently been
much promoted, called the 'restorative' approach. While described
here below separately, most systems combine aspects of these different
approaches.

The justice approach

The justice approach is founded on the following presumptions:

- Crime is a matter of individual choice, of free will; an individual has
  the capacity to control his/ her own behaviour; crime is an individual's
  response to opportunity
- If criminal behaviour is a rational response to certain situations, then
  the individual can be reasonably held responsible for his/her actions
- The sole justification for the criminal justice system to intervene is
  the commission of a criminal offence; interventions should be based
  on the nature of the crime not the offender's family background
- Crimes should be clearly defined
- The accused should have 'due process' (e.g. legal representation, fair
  hearing, access to appeals) in the criminal justice system, so that s/he
  receives formal justice
- Sentences for those found guilty should be determinate (i.e. have
  fixed time-frames), and those who commit like offences should be
  treated equally.
       (description based on Freeman 1983; Morris and Giller 1987)

At its most extreme, the justice approach perceives young people
as no different from adults. Punishment, wrote Allen (1996), is central
to the UK adult criminal justice system and a common partner to a
justice approach. Punishment has three aims: deterrence of future offending (both for the offender and as a warning to all); retribution against
the offender; and, for some offences, incapacitation (which usually means
prison). The present system, however, is ineffective at meeting any of
these three aims. The possibility of criminal penalties seems to hold
little deterrence to offenders (Mulvey *et al.* 1993), in part because the
chances of detection are so small, the time delays are so long, and not
all crimes are carried out 'rationally'. Reoffending is high for sentenced
offenders. For example, 90 per cent of young men aged 14 to 16,
sentenced to custody for less than one year, were reconvicted within
two years of being released (in 1993, reported in Audit Commission
1996). Genders and Player (1986) found that almost three-quarters of

women and girls learned new offending techniques while in prison. So do young men:

You learn stupid little things like how to get into houses, the easy way to do it, like how to get into a car with a windscreen wiper, silly things like that, which you'd never think of before. So being in here makes it easier.

(Young man in prison, quoted in Little 1990: 128)

What some young offenders learn are the disadvantages of being caught – so they change their methods or type of offending – rather than a lesson about not offending (Foster 1990). Victims are routinely dissatisfied with the response of the criminal justice system (Walgrave 1995) and the media often report on victims' or their families' anger at a sentence perceived as too lenient. Certain sentences can incapacitate offenders in institutions for considerable time, but most offenders are going to leave the institutions at some time – and, as stated above, are highly likely to offend again.

According to opponents of the justice approach (e.g. see Asquith 1983; Allen 1996), the justice model is particularly inappropriate for children. Most young people plead guilty to their offences, and the court procedures based around decisions of guilt/ innocence can be seen as largely redundant for them. Child development theory would suggest that children's moral, cognitive and conative competencies develop over time (see Chapter 1): children are different from adults in ways fundamental to the justice approach. Children may have difficulty operationalising their legal rights, so while having 'due process' on paper they can lack formal justice in practice:

I was young and I just didn't understand; your feet are swept away from under you and you are carried off with no power to stop it. You just feel so weak and helpless. (Young person, quoted in CRDU 1994: 219)

Without adequate concern for children's welfare, experiences of 'justice' can be horrific, going directly against protective articles of the United Nations (UN) Convention on the Rights of the Child and the Beijing Rules (UN 1985):

I was only just turned 15 and they remanded me into Swansea prison. It is a really bad environment for someone so young. They don't care about you. I was Williams 3542 and nothing else. I could not comprehend why I was there and by the third day I was suicidal and started to bang my head against the wall and so the other person in the cell hit the alarm button. I needed someone to talk to, to listen to me and to tell me why I was there and why my local authority or my mother would not take me, what I didn't need was to be stripped and locked in another cell with a camera on me.

(Young person, quoted in CRDU 1994: 220)

As they cannot vote, children have little choice in the formation of social rules, but yet are expected to adhere to them. Holding children to account for rules they did not agree to may be considered unfair (Adams 1986). Children have had little choice in their social and economic circumstances, which may be strong causal factors for their offending. Formal justice considers such social justice issues irrelevant to its process and decisions.

In recent years, English and Welsh government policy has revived the idea of holding parents criminally responsible for their children's offences. Parents can be required to pay their children's fines or be 'bound over' and fined if their child should reoffend. While this may recognise that children are not fully competent and that parents have a responsibility to care and control their children, these possible court responses fail to recognise that the very children most likely to offend tend to live in families where parents have difficulty supervising, communicating with and relating to their children and tend to be disadvantaged socially and economically. Financial penalties will only lead to more economic deprivation, which in turn is likely to increase strife in families and weaken parents' ability to control their children. Further, such a response sees children and parents as a unit, rather than as separate entities. Justice is not being based on the individual. The Audit Commission (1996) reported that these provisions, in fact, have been little used.

Diversion

A 'twin-track' approach has gained credence over the last 20 years in more justice-oriented systems. The justice approach described above is largely confined to 'serious' or 'persistent' young offenders while the majority of young offenders are diverted from the criminal justice system. This approach is based on the (official statistics') evidence that most young men 'grow out' of crime, that involvement in the criminal justice system increases the likelihood of further offending ('labelling' theory) and appears to do little to reduce reoffending. Indeed, a great many offences do appear to be undertaken by a small number of young men: of the young men surveyed (age 14 to 17), five per cent committed at least two-thirds of the offences in the previous twelve months, as reported by the whole sample (Graham and Bowling 1995). However, identifying the 'serious' or 'persistent' offenders for intervention is difficult, as few young people offend very frequently for more than short periods (Audit Commission 1996).

The twin-track approach matches the UN Convention requirement to use prison only as a 'last resort'. The increased use of police cautioning in England and Wales, for example, diverts young people from the courts, and does seem to have at least a sobering, immediate effect on some young people:

I feel like crying just now . . . the Inspector said I will be taken to court and sent away if I get into trouble again next time.

(Young person, quoted in Allen 1996: 38)

The Audit Commission (1996) reported that seven out of ten first offenders cautioned by police were not known to reoffend in two years;

however, after three police cautions, the effectiveness of cautions decreased in reducing reoffending. Despite cautioning's apparent success in England and Wales, measures introduced by 1991 and 1993 legislation are likely to result in more custodial sentences for children (CRDU 1994).

Diversion is not without its critics. It is based on administrative decisions, usually requiring children's admission of guilt. Are children's rights to due process being respected? Are they being pressured to admit guilt, with the hope of avoiding formal processing? Bell and Gibson (1991) worried that the dramatic success of diversion in England and Wales may 'have been at the expense of a hardening of attitudes towards young adults and, even more particularly, young men' (99). Young people who do become involved in the courts may be treated more harshly. When diversion from the justice approach is to welfare provision, diversion is often accused of 'net-widening'. Young people's offending that would previously have been ignored or dealt with completely informally may now be picked up by officials, and the young people diverted to the welfare system. The criminal justice system may be dealing with fewer young people, but the welfare system may be dealing with more.

The 'welfare' approach

The 'welfare' approach bases decisions on the perceived best interests, or welfare, of the child. It has the following presumptions (Morris and Giller 1987):

- The causes of delinquent behaviour and child abuse/neglect are the same, so little distinction is made between children who offend and children in need of care and protection
- These causes can be discovered, and then treated and/or controlled
- Without treatment, delinquency can worsen
- The primary (or, in some models, paramount) concern in decisions is the child's welfare; this requires discretionary power of decision-makers and children who commit similar offences are not necessarily treated similarly.

Just as diversion has been accused of 'net-widening', so has the welfare approach because it tends to include not only 'crime' but 'delinquency' (see discussion, page 178).

The children's hearing system in Scotland exemplifies such a welfare approach. The system is based on the assumption that all children appearing before it, whether because they are in need of care or protection or because they have committed offences, are all exhibiting symptoms of the same kind of difficulties:

... the true distinguishing factor, common to all children concerned, is their need for special measures of education and training, the normal upbringing process having, for whatever reason, fallen short. (Kilbrandon 1964: 13)

The system was legislated for by the Social Work (Scotland) Act 1968, and implemented in 1971, with a fundamental premise: that the judiciary should deal with decisions on guilt and innocence, but that decisions on what will happen to the child (the disposal) should be decided by a separate system, the children's hearings. Except for serious, specified crimes, children under the age of 16 who commit crimes go through the children's hearing system; young people aged 16 to 18 may be dealt with under the children's hearing system if they are already under a children's hearing supervision order or at the court's discretion.

The children's hearing system has three key actors: the Children's Panel; the Reporter to the Children's Panel; and the chief social work officer. Lay people volunteer to become part of their local community's Children's Panel and, if selected, receive training. The Reporter is responsible for examining cases brought to her/his attention (referrals). S/he assesses whether a referred child is likely to need compulsory measures of supervision and should therefore be brought before a children's hearing. The chief social work officer of the local authority is managerially responsible for making inquiries on behalf of the Reporter and for implementing any measures of supervision imposed on a child by the hearing.

A children's hearing is an informal tribunal with three panel members (one of whom acts as chairperson). The panel members, the child and his/her family discuss the background and circumstances of the child referred by the Reporter, in light of the information gathered by social workers and others. Then the hearing makes a decision as to whether any compulsory measures of supervision are necessary and, if so, what such measures should be. Appeals against the grounds of referral or the children's hearings' decisions are heard by the Sheriff. (For further description of the system, see Hill, Murray and Tisdall 1997.)

Under the Children (Scotland) Act 1995, the child's welfare is the paramount consideration of the children's hearings (except when the public is judged at risk of 'serious harm'). The legislation has confused the fundamental separation of justice and welfare decisions, by giving Sheriffs a new right to substitute their own supervision requirements for those of the children's hearings, on appeal. The children's hearing may increasingly become a hybrid model between justice and welfare itself. The welfare approach has been threatened before: in the 1960s when the children's hearings were being legislated for in Parliament (and the similar White Paper in England and Wales was being neutered by opposition), and in the 1970s by advocates of the justice approach.

Research[1] has found that some children's hearings did not respect children's and parents' procedural rights and that panel members avoided sensitive but crucial issues such as child abuse (Martin *et al.* 1981). While to the professionals the welfare response may seem relatively benign, children and parents often see it instead as punishment (Campbell 1977). In this light, the panel's decision can be seen as unfair, since children committing the same offence can have widely different 'sentences';

children can be treated indefinitely (but with reviews), with no end in sight for the end of the welfare intervention (Morris 1974). Alternatively, some young people see children's hearings as an 'easy' court system:

I think the children's panel is a court with a jury where you don't get so severely punished.

I just swing back in my chair and look out of the window until it's all over [the dressing down by panel members].   (Quoted in Gallagher 1996a: 13–14)

The welfare approach has been accused of ignoring children's responsibility for offending. Panel members feel they have few resources to deal with older children – particularly 16 to 18 year olds (who, perhaps as a result, are often dealt with by adult courts) (Lockyer 1992). Social work services are expected to deal with extremely challenging behaviour, which they sometimes find difficult to do.

Not all research findings have been so negative. Martin *et al.* (1981) found that, when hearings did adhere to rules of procedure, they were very often the most successful in achieving high levels of family participation. The response of most children and parents is generally favourable to the hearings. Children and parents usually see the members as genuinely interested in what they have to say, as trying to help them and as treating them with courtesy and respect (Erickson 1982). Although some young people feel excluded or alienated, most young people feel able to communicate their views in their hearing (Triseliotis *et al.* 1995; Freeman *et al.* 1996). Some young people have reported feeling unable to speak because of their parent(s) sitting beside them:

I was stuck in the middle of my Mum and Dad as if we were a cosy wee family. Nobody seemed to see the pressure my Mum and Dad were putting on me just by a movement or a look . . .   (Quoted in Scottish Office 1994a: 4)

With the new Children (Scotland) Act 1995, parents can now be excluded from a hearing to allow a child to speak. Some separation is thus seen between parents and children.

Such separation has not been apparently considered for access to reports, however. Following an European Court of Human Rights' decision, parents now must receive all reports made for the children's hearings. This new right has not yet been definitely extended to children. Further, the provision does not yet recognise a potential danger for children – if they state their views to professionals, which are then written in reports, young people may once again feel 'caught in the middle' if they wish to reveal things their parents want suppressed or to ignore.

Young people and families can bring along someone to support them to their hearing. This provision has been little utilised, and young people have said they had not been aware of such a provision (Milne 1992). Young people do want 'someone specifically for me', 'to argue my corner', 'to help me think out what to say' (quoted in Scottish

Office 1994a: 5). Children now have the right to attend their own children's hearing (whereas before they could only be told to attend). Neither children nor parents have the right to legal representation during a children's hearing (although they would in court *and* they can bring along a 'supporter' to a children's hearing), which was a specific reservation made by the UK Government to the UN Convention (Article 37 (d)).

Ironically, the children's hearing system places Article 3 of the UN Convention (a child's best interests) at its core, but as a result, it fails to meet basic presumptions of 'due process' of legal representation in the hearing. The UN Convention does not see the two as incompatible, but the children's hearing system does (e.g. because of formalising the procedures, creating an adversarial process). This discrepancy highlights the difficulties and disagreements of what *are* children's best interests.

The 'causes' of delinquency

The original thinking behind the children's hearings system has been much criticised for medicalising delinquency and, even if that could be refuted, presuming that causes could be identified and that they could be treated (Morris and Giller 1987). This has not stopped considerable international research attention and money being spent on finding such causes.

Biological factors have been identified by research: 'hyperactivity, attentional defects, low autonomic reactivity (for example, low pulse rate even when stressed), impaired avoidance learning in response to punishment (involving reduced anxiety and low response to pain), and a greater than normal need for stimulation' (Smith 1995: 433). These factors, however, are the basis of an antisocial personality into adulthood and thus do little to explain the bulk of official crime – which at least in official statistics is committed by young people (Smith 1995). A more complicated causal model is needed, which incorporates personal and social characteristics.

Research has identified an extensive list of such characteristics, which include:

- *behaviour*: aggressiveness, impulsiveness, antisocial behaviour, use of alcohol and illicit drugs
- *school factors*: truancy, poor attachment to school and academic achievement, school exclusions
- *family*: poor parental control, poor child-rearing, poor parent–child relationships, history of family criminality and family substance abuse, family instability and marital conflict
- *social-economic*: social and material disadvantage, housing difficulties or homelessness, unemployment, disadvantaged neighbourhoods, child abuse, social exclusion/ marginalisation
- *peers or culture*: involvement in delinquent peer groups and/or youth subcultures, consumer culture.

Risk factors are often seen as cumulative, leading to exponential risks of delinquency and other problems. At the same time, 'buffer' or 'protective' factors – such as strong family social controls, positive school management, or early years education – can mediate such risks.

This list skates over the numerous explanatory theories and links between risk factors. For example, Merton's 'strain' theory (1957) postulated that people offend because they are unable to achieve socially valued goals through socially accepted means, so they take opportunities to achieve these goals through illicit means. Cloward and Ohlin (1961) expanded 'strain theory', saying that not only must legitimate means be blocked, but that illegitimate opportunities must be available. On the other hand, Hirschi's social control theory (1969) declared that people offend because the offender's ties to society are too weak, usually due to poor socialisation by families and schools. The list also places together certain factors that are disputed, are seen as replacements for each other, or are merely correlational. For example, Smith (1995) made a strong case that poverty, unemployment and housing problems may explain an individual's propensity to crime. But these problems cannot explain historical crime trends, given that crime has risen in times of relative prosperity and high employment, and fallen in times of increased poverty and unemployment. Another heated debate rages over whether parental divorce and lone parenthood cause juvenile delinquency. Recent research suggests that underlying reasons are poor parental child-rearing and social/ economic disadvantage, rather than actual family structures (Bright 1996; see Chapter 4).

While it may describe itself as being 'welfare based', the children's hearing does not address the major social justice issues surrounding poverty and unemployment. It does, though, in theory look to the possibility of strengthening parental–child relationships – thus the insistence on having both child and parents at a panel. By providing services through compulsory measures of supervision, the children's hearings can hope to strengthen protective factors for children. Increasingly, measures such as cognitive–behavioural skills training are being used to work with young people who commit crime, as rehabilitation advocates have fought back against the 'nothing works' debate to demonstrate that indeed, something does work with offenders (see McGuire 1995 for further description of 'nothing works' debate).

Combining justice and welfare approaches

Historically, youth (with its presumed relationship with irrationality etc.) was often a 'mitigating' factor in court decisions (King 1984). In the past 150 years, ideas about welfare and the need to treat children differently from adults have taken root in the UK (for an historical overview, see Morris and Giller 1987; Pitts 1988). The UN strongly promotes such separation, required in the Beijing Rules and repeated in the UN Convention. Juvenile offenders have the right to 'due process', but also to be dealt with separately from adults and with the juvenile's welfare as a primary concern. The attempt is thus made to combine the justice and 'welfare' approaches. Most Western juvenile justice/care systems do combine aspects of both welfare and justice approaches. Juvenile courts, for example, are often separated from adult courts. Regard to a child's welfare is often written into legislation on juvenile crime. Whether such combinations are successful has been questioned. Such attempts have been described by some as confusing and taking the worst of both approaches (Morris and Giller 1987), and by others as inevitably contradictory (King and Piper 1990).

The 'restorative' approach

More recently, the longstanding justice–welfare debate has been accused of being too narrow. A third alternative has been suggested as a more effective approach. Walgrave (1995) and Allen (1996) outlined several components of the restorative approach:

- Crime is seen as an act against another person or the community, and can be controlled primarily through relationships in the community
- Responsibility for crime has both social and individual dimensions
- The approach emphasises restitution of wrongs and losses, both of physical property, social injury and mental suffering; restitution may be restrictive of freedom, a hardship and educative, but these are side-effects rather than ends
- It includes three interests: the community the victim; and the offender
- It is evaluated by the satisfaction of these interests.

These components can also be the basis of 'mediation' between offender and victim. However, Walgrave is wary about equating mediation with restoration. Mediation has been incorporated into rehabilitation, he wrote, to become an 'alternative treatment', or mutated by justice to serve its aims. Further, mediation can be a component of the restorative approach, but the approach can also include other interactions such as compensation or community service.

Braithwaite (1989) firmly supported a restorative approach. For him, a key element was reintegrative shaming:

The first step to productive theorizing about crime is to think about the contention that labelling offenders makes things worse. The contention is both right and wrong. The theory of reintegrative shaming is an attempt to specify when it is right and when wrong. The distinction between shaming that leads to stigmatization – to outcasting, to confirmation of a deviant master status – versus shaming that is reintegrative, that shames while maintaining bonds of respect or love, that sharply terminates disapproval with forgiveness, instead of amplifying deviance by progressively casting out the deviant.

(1989: 12–13)

Braithwaite did not claim reintegrative shaming is a satisfactory approach to all crime. It fails to work well when agreement is lacking on whether a particular behaviour is deviant, and does best with behaviour on which there is a strong consensus.

The Family Group Conferences (FGCs) in New Zealand and similar conferences in Australia have been held up by Braithwaite (Braithwaite and Mugford 1994) as exemplary implementations of his theory. Introduced in 1989, the FGCs reflect disillusionment with aspects of the welfare approach – to the extent that FGCs have no remit to consider welfare issues when it comes to offenders (there are separate child protection FGCs). The FGCs are based on a number of fundamental principles: the needs and rights of indigenous people should be taken into account; families are placed in the centre of decision-making about their children; and young people and victims can have a say in the response to their offending. FGCs are part of a bigger criminal justice system, so young people who do not admit guilt have access to a youth court. Accountability and responsibility are emphasised, along with diversion from formal procedures, deinstitutionalisation and community-based penalties.

FGCs are composed of:

- the young person who has offended
- his/her advocate (if one has been organised)
- members of the family and whoever they invite
- the victim or his/her representative
- the police
- the social worker (if one has been involved with the family)
- the youth justice co-ordinator (who organises and chairs the conference).

If they wish, the family and those they invite can deliberate in private during the FGC and the FGC can be held wherever the family wishes. Decisions at FGCs are to be made by group consensus, if possible. The FGCs' agreed plans and decisions are binding (if the case has gone to court, the court must also accept the decisions). (Description of FGCs is based on Morris and Maxwell 1993.)

How effective are the FGCs? While keeping in mind their relative newness, the FGCs seem successful on many accounts. As a result of using these diversionary measures, only ten per cent of a sample of juvenile offenders went to the youth court. Most young offenders agreed to perform tasks that seemingly recognised their accountability for their actions. This early research showed that 58 per cent of FGC plans were completed fully and 29 per cent in part. Two-thirds of parents reported feeling involved in the decision-making process and party to the decision (Morris and Maxwell 1993). More recent research has been less favourable, however: 72 per cent of plans broke down or were never fully implemented and four out of five children reoffended (reported in Allen 1996).

More negatively, Morris and Maxwell (1993) found that both young people and victims were often sidelined in the process. Only about one-third of young people felt involved and only 16 per cent felt they had been a party to the decision. Just under half of victims were satisfied with their FGC. Morris and Maxwell were concerned that young people were pressured into admitting their guilt, and that there were breaches in 'due process' (such as advocates inadequately advising their clients). Welfare issues were not generally dealt with by the FGCs. Although FGCs were not supposed to consider welfare, their avoidance left glaring issues unresolved. Professionalism was at times creeping into FGCs, destroying their informality and emphasis on family decision-making.

Procedures have been tightened in New Zealand, and research generally remains positive about the approach. But the familiar criticisms of lack of 'due process' made against the welfare approach can again be thrown against this restorative model. Braithwaite was quite sanguine about the possibility of 'false confessions' by those accused: while people could feel pressured into admitting an offence they did not do, at least they were quickly included back into society. He suggested that 'punishment should be visible, newsworthy' (1989: 11) as a deterrent message. This certainly clashes with a child's right to privacy as protected in the UN Convention (although it should be noted that the UN Convention is based on a justice–welfare model rather than a restorative one). While founded on the inclusion of the young person and family, the restorative model has the same problem as the children's hearings with including them truly in practice.

Prevention

Braithwaite and Mugford (1994) did recognise that FGCs cannot deal with fundamental inequalities. European policy and UN statements have increasingly focused on the social exclusion and marginalisation of young people; they advocate comprehensive crime prevention policies considering a full range of interventions in education, employment, housing and recreation as well as in the criminal justice system. Crime prevention strategies, though, remain largely fragmented, uncoordinated and poorly financed. Targeted policies are far more common that those combating social exclusion. Targeted policies were conceptually divided by Bright (1996) into:

- measures that make crime more difficult to commit: e.g. reducing opportunities; designing out crime in terms of physical environments; preventive policing; preventing revictimisation
- measures that reduce young people's inclination to offend: e.g. strengthening families; enhancing education/ recreation; revitalising communities; creating training/ employment; preventing reoffending.

Policy often ignores the desperation of some young people, who can see no other way to survive but to offend:

When I get hungry, I do shoplifting. I can't live without food.

(Liam, 17-year-old, quoted in Carlen 1996: 132)

I used to offend just to get into the police cells. Used to wait for a cop to come, just put a window through or something.

(Simon, 19-year-old, quoted in Carlen 1996: 133)

Both Liam and Simon were homeless when interviewed for Carlen's research. Of the 100 young people interviewed, 83 had broken the law in some way prior to the interview (although for some this crime was begging itself).

Research on young people's criminal careers shows how most young people begin by committing opportunistic offences, like shoplifting, for 'a laugh' or out of boredom (see discussion in Coles 1995). Young people frequently offend in groups of two or three rather than alone (reported in Audit Commission 1996). As one young man explained his joyriding:

I'd always liked cars, I love driving. I think it was a mixture between that and boredom, there was nothink really to do. Tommy, the bloke I used to hop school with, his cousin was always doin' it. Tommy started through his cousin and then I started goin' out with Tommy. It was mainly cos I like driving and because of the boredom that started it off. (Quoted in Foster 1990: 127)

Some young people who first offend for such reasons then go on to become more persistent, more serious and more calculating offenders (Little 1990). Providing more recreational opportunities for young people is an obvious preventive solution (Hendry *et al.* 1993). Twenty-three per cent of young offenders on supervision orders thought that jobs would help stop others offending (Audit Commission 1996).

A more draconian 'preventive' measure has been revitalised in the United States and floated in the UK. Curfews are being imposed on all children in certain geographical areas, to restrict their presence in public places at night (and, less often, during school hours). A curfew has been tried in North Tyneside. Although it was abandoned, the failure may have been due more to poor design than the idea itself (Jeffs and Smith 1996).

Curfews are typically justified in three ways:

1 to protect children from being victimised
2 to reduce crime; and
3 to help parents in supervising their children (Jeffs and Smith 1996).

Yet, strong grounds exist to refute each justification:

1 Why should a potential victim's freedom be restricted, rather than that of the perpetrator?
2 Should anyone's freedom be restricted on the basis (however statistically likely), that they might offend – given the person has not yet offended? If the desire is to reduce crime in public places, the curfew is unfairly targeted (usually on ten- to 16-year-olds and, in the UK, suggested for under ten). Statistically, young men aged 15 to 25 are the most represented in official statistics. Males are considerably more likely to commit offences than females.

3 If a parent has trouble supervising a child, the relationship is unlikely to improve if a child is at home with little to do. Some cities in the United States have coupled a curfew with the provision of supervised recreational programmes, which seems more positive. But such programmes could be offered without curfews and other means are far more likely to help parental supervision than curfews: such as parenting-skills training, and addressing the 'stress' factors of parenting, such as poverty and unemployment/ overwork.

Curfews are startling overt examples of discrimination on the basis of age. As Jeffs and Smith wrote: 'Similar legal intervention which criminalised individuals on the basis of sex or ethnicity would not be acceptable in a civilised society and discrimination on the basis of age should also be rejected as unjust and indefensible' (1996: 11). Yet such an argument has found no purchase in the United States, despite its Bill of Rights, and now 77 per cent of cities with over 200,000 people have curfews (Ruefle and Reynolds 1995). Is this a trend for the future?

A more positive trend is the increased attention to early multipurpose intervention, seen as the greatest opportunity to protect and improve children's potential (Asquith 1996). The Perry Pre-School Project in the USA is often cited as a model. Combining pre-school and parental support, the programme has had some dramatic results: compared to control groups, the programme cohorts have had significantly higher school-completion and employment rates and substantially fewer arrests by age 27 (Schweinhart *et al.* 1993).

Prevention policies can also learn from the reasons why some people stop offending. From their self-report survey, Graham and Bowling (1995) concluded that women seem to stop offending when they successfully make the 'transition to adulthood' (e.g. finished full-time education, left home, formed a new family unit). Men appear to desist for other reasons (or because fewer make a successful transition?). Factors that stopped young men from further offending are living at home into their twenties, being successful at school and avoiding criminogenic influences, such as peer groups that offend, and drug use. Graham and Bowling therefore advocated supportive programmes for young men such as 'foyers' (that provide temporary accommodation with training and employment), and better preparation for fatherhood.

Discrimination and biases

The criminal justice system, both in theory and in practice, has demonstrated considerable discrimination. Worries have been voiced about the implicit middle-class 'norms' of family background in decisions made by such fora as the children's hearings and the juvenile liaison panels in England and Wales (which decide whether to refer a young person's case for prosecution or not) (Macmillan 1991). While self-report surveys do not demonstrate a class or ethnic minority bias in offenders, those of a lower social class and/ or from an African-Caribbean background are distinctly more likely to be accused in the UK criminal justice system. Young people themselves think the system is discriminatory (McNeish 1996).

Young women and girls have traditionally been excluded or demeaned by theory and ignored in official policy – as being statistically irrelevant – while often receiving widely disparate responses compared with male offenders, in practice. From influential writings stretching back to Lombroso and Ferrero (1895) to Pollak (1950), three critical and influential ideas took hold in the theory of female offending: that female offenders were innately irrational and immoral; they needed special protection (particularly from their sexuality); and they received greater leniency and protection from the criminal justice system (the 'chivalry factor'). While offending was thought of as common, normal and natural for young men – part of growing up, of adolescence – offending for women was seen as unusual, pathological and unnatural. This tradition perhaps explains the present media hype about 'girl gangs', which through constant repetition is reaching the level of accepted truth even though it lacks systematic and comprehensive UK research to support it.

Research demonstrates the continuing influence of these ideas in other areas. For example, far more girls than boys are referred to children's hearings under the grounds of 'moral danger' (Scottish Office 1994b). Analysis of penal institutions shows the medicalisation of women's criminality (Dobash *et al.* 1986), the increased repression compared to men (e.g. far more reports of prison indiscipline), and the control of girls' sexuality and imposition of 'femininity' (Kersten 1990). Boys may also suffer from gender stereotypes. Kersten traced the ways in which young men in institutions were 'only allowed to enjoy their bodies in a competitive way, which very often borders on violence . . .' (1990: 489).

Whether the 'chivalry' factor results in greater leniency for female offenders is questionable. Official published statistics are infamously difficult to disaggregate. In analysis of Scottish statistics, it appears that (once some account is taken for seriousness of offence and past criminal record) young women are more likely to be treated leniently than young men for less serious criminal justice dispositions, but more harshly for more serious dispositions. Young women are more likely to be sent to the welfare system of the children's hearings, than young men (Samuel and Tisdall 1996). Some evidence can be found that if young women commit crimes that do not fit a 'feminine' stereotype (such as violent crimes) they may be treated more harshly than young men (Willemsen and Van Schie 1989; Samuel and Tisdall 1996).

Discrimination may not be so simple as a gender divide. Research on women offenders suggests that factors such as ethnic minority background and marital status must also be considered, along with gender and legal factors such as criminal record and the seriousness of the offence(s). Such analysis should be replicated for young women – perhaps exchanging marital status with the perceived extent of familial control. Beyond the fears of increased violence by young women, and the unsuitability of male-dominated community-based programmes for young women, too little is known about young women's and girls' offending and experiences of the criminal justice system.

Childhood, children's needs and children's rights

Crime by young people threatens society's views of an innocent, dependent, passive '*childhood*'. We have historical amnesia, as each adult generation points to a supposed increase and worsening of young people's criminal activity (McNeish 1996). Children who do commit crimes are commonly demonised by the media, as exemplified by this evocative quotation from the *Daily Express*:

At one time our image of youthful callousness and cruelty was of children amusing themselves by pulling wings off hapless flies. Not any more. Who are these monsters, bereft of thought of conscience, who now prowl our streets? Simple. They are our children . . . (5.1.96, quoted in Allen 1996: front page)

Society feels at a loss at how to deal with children who are seen as 'out of our control', as policy and politicians repeatedly try new responses to react to their offending. Our fears about children's crime in public places exemplifies society's requirement for an 'indoors child', which will not only keep children but also the public safe. Attention is rarely given to children's own rights to access public space, and to socialise with those outside their families and schools (see Chapter 5). Rarely is the question asked why children may loiter around public areas in the first place.

The discourse around children and crime is illuminating. While seen as abnormal for children, delinquency is seen as normal for 'adolescents' – or at least for young male adolescents. Adolescence is seen as a time of psychological and physical turmoil, of transition between the social controls of family and school to adult relationships and the labour market, of testing social rules. The term 'delinquency' both undervalues the seriousness of crimes that can be included under that category (say, violent bullying) and overvalues behaviours that would not be considered crimes for adults (status offences). Rarely is the term 'child crime' used, but 'youth crime'. Rarely do children offend, but 'young people' do (although this does reflect the predominance of older children in official statistics). While we can easily associate with children of all ages as victims – albeit usually as victims of child abuse and not other crimes – we have difficulty putting the concept of children together with that of threat.

As the UN Convention and Rules require, in the UK children who offend are typically dealt with in a separate system from adults. But the

UN Convention defines children up to the age of 18, and in Scotland most young people over 16 are dealt with by the adult system. All UK systems have exceptions – children who are accused of very serious crimes – who bypass the juvenile system altogether. These children's offences cancel out their categorisation by age; their offence is more important than their childhood.

The welfare approach to children particularly recognises their need for special protection, their differences from adults in terms of culpability and rationality, the primacy (if not paramountcy) of their welfare. The approach is based on meeting *children's needs*. Within its welfare focus, it can seek to address young people's needs for development, education, health etc. What the welfare approach can particularly fail at is regard to 'due process'. In being protectionist, the approach can fall into paternalism. Young women may be particularly vulnerable to this, arguably receiving more intervention, intrusion and repression if they are perceived to deviate from femininity and social control. With some irony, the justice approach gives more respect to children's rationality and competence than does the protectionist nature of the welfare approach.

None of the most common approaches to (juvenile) crime consider much beyond the individual offender's situation. While the welfare and restorative approaches tend to have particular room for families, none of the approaches actually address possible causal factors lying in general social and economic conditions – whether they be poverty, unemployment or consumer culture. Such a comprehensive, concerted approach has not been coordinated in the UK, although interesting examples have been tried in places such as France (Bailleau 1996). The UK's reaction to young people's crime does not address such fundamental needs of children. In its responses to young people's crime it may even work against meeting their needs, as research demonstrates young people's lowered educational achievements and health problems when they are institutionalised for offending (CRDU 1994). Crime policy is increasingly used as a weapon against social problems – while doing very little to address their causes.

For some, the constant debate between justice and welfare approaches has been abandoned for a new approach of restoration. While recognising that it cannot be applied to all people who offend – for example, some children are too immature to be held responsible and participate in negotiations, and some offenders are too dangerous to the public – the approach has the possibility of reintegrating people who offend into their communities rather than casting them out (and thus increasing their future offending). Offenders are seen as *citizens* of their communities, and the restitutive approach as 'citizenship ceremonies of reintegrative shaming' (Braithwaite and Daly 1994: 193). Thus, if children are involved in such ceremonies, they are being seen as citizens.

The idea of separation between adults and juveniles can be turned on its head. Rather than the debate about whether the juvenile criminal justice system needs to incorporate more of the punishment and due process of the adult system, perhaps the adult system needs to become more like a juvenile justice system. The question may not be whether children have the same rights as adults, but should adults have the same rights as children?

Note

1 Note that since Martin *et al.* (1981), no full-scale research on the children's hearings system has been reported. The Scottish Office commissioned research in 1993, which at the time of writing was not yet available.

Suggestions for further reading

Allen, R. (1996) *Children and Crime, Taking Responsibility*, London: IPPR.
Audit Commission (1996) *Misspent Youth: Young People and Crime*, London: Audit Commission.
Children's Rights Development Unit (CRDU) (1994) *UK Agenda for Children*, London: CRDU.
Foster, J. (1990) *Villains: Crime and Community in the Inner City*, London: Routledge.
Walgrave, L. (1995) 'Restorative Justice for Juveniles: Just a Technique or a Fully Fledged Alternative', *The Howard Journal of Criminal Justice* **34** (3): 228–49.

CHAPTER 10

Child abuse and child protection

Introduction: risk, needs and rights

In the early chapters of this volume, we examined two of the main ways in which children's issues are currently debated, that is, in terms of rights and needs. A further type of discourse about childhood has become prominent in recent years, namely that of 'risk'. The previous chapter reviewed the example of children seen as putting social order at risk: here we consider risks faced by children themselves. The perspective shifts from children seen as threats to children as actual or potential victims, requiring vigilance and protection by adults. As we shall see, preoccupation with children's 'passive' right to protection by society has dominated child welfare policy and practice, sometimes overriding attention to children's active rights to influence the manner in which protection is undertaken. In a memorable phrase, the Cleveland Report (Butler-Sloss 1988) on public interventions with respect to child sexual abuse spoke of children being treated as 'objects of concern' rather than as active participants.

A series of high-profile incidents has heightened public awareness that children are at risk of ill-treatment and even death as a result of the actions and inaction of other people. The murder of Jamie Bulger and the Dunblane massacre were extreme examples of danger from strangers. School campaigns about 'saying no' to strangers and media reports of child abductions have contributed to the feelings of many parents that families are surrounded by diverse threats, which need to be constantly guarded against (Borland et al. 1996; Hood et al. 1996b). At the same time, revelations by children and adults have shown that suffering 'at the hands' of close family members is much more widespread than had been generally thought. For significant numbers of children, the family home is not a comfortable haven or hearth (Lasch 1977), but a place of danger and unhappiness (Dallos and McLaughlin 1993).

Since the 1970s the social construction of child abuse and child protection has been a selective process, deeming certain situations of risk for children as a major social problem and defining that problem in a particular way, whilst other risks and other potential ways of protecting children have been marginalised. In particular, the notion of child abuse has, apart from a few dissenting voices, been confined to the ill-treatment of children in their own homes and the concept of child protection has become synonymous with the responses by official agencies to suspected and identified intra-familial abuse. This chapter examines how and why this has happened, and reviews some of the implications for children. First we consider how awareness and definitions of abuse have altered and remain contested, then review official responses which have come to be known collectively as 'child protection'.

Child abuse: a disputed and evolving concept

The evolution of child abuse as a social problem

The ill-treatment of children by parents or carers has occurred throughout much of recorded history (DeMause 1982; Boswell 1991). In the nineteenth century it was conceptualised as cruelty. Voluntary societies for the prevention of cruelty to children were established in New York, London, Glasgow and elsewhere. Legislation was passed which defined penalties for ill-treatment and authorised the removal of children as a result (Heywood 1978; Hill *et al.* 1991; Hendrick 1994).

However, for a large part of the twentieth century, mistreatment of children was not a prominent issue. This began to change in the 1960s when the concept of 'battered babies' was introduced. Injuries to young children formerly thought to have been accidental were, with the help of new radiology techniques, re-diagnosed as deliberate. At one blow, it might be said, the notion of parents as the natural protectors of children was fatally undermined by the realisation that significant numbers of children are seriously hurt or even killed by their parents. Parton (1985) documented how developments in medical technology and increases in professional status went hand-in-hand with the new perception that parents under stress and with low impulse control might injure and even kill their own infant offspring. This could happen to older children, so that the less emotive phrase 'non-accidental injury' (NAI) soon usurped references to battered babies.

It was in 1973–4 that the present era of child abuse and protection began in Britain. In 1973 a seven-year-old girl called Maria Colwell died as a result of injuries from her stepfather. In the period leading up to her death she had experienced severe neglect in the care of her mother and stepfather whilst she was supposed to be supervised and protected by social workers under a court order. What sociologists call a 'moral panic' ensued – an ever-present issue suddenly evoked intense media, public and political alarm as a threat to the social order, leading to demands for action and reform (Parton 1985). A public inquiry was set up, which was to be followed by over 30 major inquiries about child deaths over the next 20 years. While each inquiry had individual points to make, there have been common themes, mostly related to the failure of public authorities to remove children from life-threatening situations with their families (Reder *et al.* 1993; Munro 1996).

During the 1970s and 1980s, policy-makers and professionals were preoccupied with physical ill-treatment of children. Then sexual abuse suddenly entered the public agenda in 1987 when over 100 children from a comparatively small area in Cleveland were diagnosed by doctors as having been sexually abused. Magistrates made court orders and social workers removed the children from their homes. Most of the alleged abusers were male members of the children's families. Inter-agency tensions came to light, as members of the police questioned both the diagnostic techniques being used by paediatricians and the numbers of children being labelled as abused. Many parents protested, too, as did the local member of Parliament, so the situation received widespread publicity. The conflict of opinions served not only to highlight child sexual abuse as a social problem, but also at the same time cast some doubt on how widespread it was (as claimed by many professionals and commentators). Subsequent child abuse inquiries have mainly been concerned with child sexual abuse, too (see later in this chapter for details pp. 207–9). As a result of over 20 years of high-profile inquiries, ways of tackling physical abuse, neglect and sexual abuse have become central in government policy and local authority responsibilities.

Official definitions of child abuse

Ideas about the nature of child abuse are not simply a matter of academic interest, since the definitions used in official documents and by professionals act as the triggers for formal interventions into family life. Scottish Office Guidance (1995: 8) offers an example of an official definition of child abuse, which contains three elements:

- demonstrable harm occurred
- this was due to action or inaction of the parent or carer
- the harm was avoidable.

In the official view, child abuse is confined to harm caused by a parent or carer, so that ill-treatment by strangers or even someone known to the child but not looking after him or her is dealt with separately. In such cases, it is presumed that parents themselves normally take responsibility for any action, together with the police if a crime may have been committed. Consequently, threats to children by strangers have had a lower policy profile than intra-familial abuse, despite high levels of public anxiety. Likewise, abuse by young people have been dealt with separately and at times with labels having different connotations, such as bullying or sexual experimentation.

Official definitions of child abuse embrace both acts of commission ('ill-treatment') and omission ('neglect'). Neglect ranges from leaving children unattended to allowing a child to starve. In fact, children who have been seriously harmed, including Maria Colwell, often experienced both physical injury and failure to provide adequate physical care. Some people believe, however, that neglect should be excluded from considerations of abuse, on the grounds that it is less severe or unintentional, and so less blameworthy. Thorpe (1995) argued that the term child abuse should not be applied to neglect cases involving impoverished and stressed parents, whose main needs are for material and financial help and not the moral disapprobation implied in the word abuse. For child-protection purposes though, the most important consideration may simply be the effects of 'abusive' situations. Parents may be well intentioned, but nevertheless incapable of caring for children according to the minimum standards deemed to be required. Parents who misuse alcohol seriously or are addicted to hard drugs may at times be warm-hearted and capable, but at other times unable to nurture and safeguard their children, so that public action may be justified (Lambert *et al.* 1990).

A further issue concerns how serious harm needs to be in order to qualify as abuse. The Children Act 1989 established the notion of 'significant harm' as 'the major site . . . where the boundaries between state intervention and family life are redrawn' (Hardiker 1996: 105). This Act defines 'harm' as either ill-treatment or impairment of health and development, as do the corresponding statutes for Scotland and Northern Ireland. The harm need not be physical, but may be psychological (Norrie 1995). Significance is to be determined by judgements about whether the care of the child and the resulting level of health and development could have been 'reasonably expected for this child in comparison with a similar child' (Hardiker 1996: 107). It appears that the more serious is the allegation, the more conclusive is the evidence that judges expect, so that, ironically, legal support for action may be harder to achieve when a child's need for protection is greatest (White 1994; Spicer 1996).

Alternative perspectives

In the mid-1990s, a number of researchers suggested that the concept of child abuse as currently applied to families was too broad, exposing families to unnecessary intrusion (Gibbons 1995; Thorpe 1995). A more minority viewpoint is that sexual abuse is a social construction (developed mainly by feminists) that denies children's sexual interests (Glaser and Frosh 1993; Evans 1993).

Others have suggested that the concept of abuse should be widened so that similar intensities of public disapproval and collective effort would be applied to any kind of action or inaction which prevents children from achieving desired levels of well-being. This could include the neglect by governments to ensure proper levels of health and development for their child citizens (Gil 1970; National Commission into the Prevention of Child Abuse 1996). At one level it has been argued that common practices like corporal punishment, bullying and verbal abuse should be deemed abusive in order to register strong social disapproval (Newell 1991; Commission on Children and Violence 1995). For example, children can feel devastated by humiliating and rejecting remarks, illustrated by these examples from two teenagers whose parents shouted at and threatened them when drunk:

She says 'You're going into a home'. I know she'll never do it ... she says things to me ... it's terrible, I don't feel like staying here.

She can bring me down to all sorts of sizes (but) nobody's done nothing to her.
(Quoted in Laybourn *et al.* 1996: 56)

Kennedy (1995) pointed to practices experienced by disabled children which would not be tolerated for able-bodied children, such as force feeding, over-medication and segregation. Several writers have drawn attention to the fact that men's violence towards women is traumatic for children involved and often accompanied by child abuse (Bennett 1991; Ericksen and Henderson 1992; Mullender and Morley 1994).

Critics have observed that the depiction of child abuse and protection as covering only certain types of risk and response has marginalised public attention towards other important threats to children's safety which have not prompted similar degrees of concerted governmental and professional action:

We seldom consider, say, road safety training, environmental legislation, subsidised cycle helmets, ante-natal care, anti-bullying strategies, school meals, free prescriptions or restrictions on alcohol and cigarette sales as dimensions of child care *or* child protection. (Harris 1995: 28)

As noted in Chapter 7, dangers to children from traffic and environmental hazards in the home and outside have evoked only piecemeal and low-key policy responses (Roberts *et al.* 1995).

The social construction of child abuse

No consensus exists about the definition and hence the scale of abuse. Social constructionist perspectives emphasise that child abuse is not a fixed phenomenon, but the result of negotiated processes which alter with time and culture (Parton 1991; Rogers *et al.* 1992; Rogers and Rogers 1994). Definitions of acceptable punishment and sexual activity interact with awareness and actual behaviours in families to produce experiences whose scope and significance depend to some extent on viewpoint and epoch. Both at societal and individual levels, there can be changes in whether a certain behaviour is seen as acceptable or not. Caning and strapping used to be the norm in British schools, but such 'punishments' are now seen as inappropriate violence towards children. Many parents and teachers in the UK and North America think that smacking small children is acceptable and understandable, whereas several European countries have made it illegal (Newell 1991; Tite 1993;

Creighton and Russell 1995). If this were to be regarded as abuse, then few British children would remain non-abused. Views of sexual abuse are affected by prevailing interpretations, too (MacLeod and Saraga 1988; Evans 1994).

Parton (1996b) argued that a social construction approach makes concern with precise identification of risk pointless and opens up the possibility for child abuse to be 'reconstructed as children in need' (p. 7). He wanted to see a corresponding change from investigations of risk to enquiries about need for services. However, Parton criticised an emergent 'twin-tracking' approach in which severe assaults and mistreatment are treated in terms of danger whilst the majority of cases are dealt with according to needs (as with child offenders, see Chapter 9).

Incidence and explanations of child abuse

Given the contested nature of what child abuse is or should be, it is not surprising that understandings about its extent and causation are variable and sometimes contradictory.

Incidence and prevalence

Precise understanding of the extent of child abuse is hampered not only by varied and ambiguous definitions, but also the fact that it is often hidden. Norms of family privacy can make abuse invisible to outsiders. Fears and inhibitions may prevent children from telling others, either at the time or later. Official data exclude cases that do not come to light, are not formally substantiated or do not fit agency criteria. More comprehensive information has been gathered retrospectively from surveys of adults, but the results are highly variable as a result of differences in sampling method, definition of abuse and response rate (Creighton 1995a; Pilkington and Kremer 1995).

During the 1970s and 1980s a large increase occurred in known cases of child abuse, as measured by local authority registers of children about whom abuse is a cause for concern. It is probably impossible to determine whether there was a real change in ill-treatment or simply a growth in awareness. In the early 1980s sexual abuse figured to only a small extent in official data, but by the mid-1990s it had risen to account for up to one-quarter of registered cases. Nevertheless, physical injury continues to be the most frequent primary reason for registration (Creighton 1995a; Strathclyde Region Social Work Department 1995). Some studies have reported that over 20 per cent of women and perhaps half as many men have been sexually abused as children in incidents involving direct contact (this excludes self-exposure or sexual taunts, for example). When non-contact abuse is included, the proportion of women reporting being abused as children rises to 40 to 60 per cent (Creighton 1995a). Sadly, different forms of abuse often go together. In many instances, sexual abuse is accompanied by threats or use of force (Gomes-Schwartz *et al.* 1990; Waterhouse *et al.* 1994).

Explanations of child abuse

Whilst the way abuse is defined and constructed is complex and highly variable, it is clear that some parents and carers treat children in ways that most members of the society think harmful. Explanations for this are multifarious (Parton 1985; Corby 1993; Saraga 1993), but may be grouped into four main types, which correspond with several of the theoretical approaches to the family outlined in Chapter 4.

Table 10.1 Explanations of child abuse

Explanatory framework	Implications for preventing or reducing abuse
Individual pathology Particular people ill-treat children because of, for example, personality disorders, faulty social learning	Screen and treat individual abusers
Structural/ecological Abuse results from stress in families and neighbourhoods which is caused by poverty and social deprivation	Change society, the local environment and/or income levels
Family systems Certain families have 'distorted' relationship patterns (for example, sexuality crosses intergenerational boundaries; parents collude in ill-treatment of children)	Modify family structures and processes
Feminist/power Physical and sexual violence in families results from imbalances and misuse of power between males and females, adults and children	Alter male-female relations, socialisation and power distribution

The first two frameworks have been applied mainly to physical ill-treatment, whereas the last two have been invoked chiefly to account for sexual abuse. Structural approaches are generally opposed to individualistic perspectives, while most feminist accounts are highly critical of systems theory, though a few writers have sought to reconcile these two approaches (for example, Masson and O'Byrne 1990).

Individualised explanations attribute child abuse to deficiencies in the character or upbringing of the abusers. Certainly, some adults who abuse children have been diagnosed as mentally ill or psychopathic (impulsive and aggressive), but this applies only to a relatively small minority. The tendency to abuse has also been seen as running in families to form a cycle of abuse. This idea became especially popular with politicians at the time of Maria Colwell's death (Parton 1985).

Structural and ecological accounts point to the evidence that identified physical ill-treatment (though not sexual abuse) has been consistently found to be correlated with such factors as low income, poor housing and social isolation (Parton 1985). Poverty produces stresses which increase the chances that parents give vent to frustrations through violence towards their children (Browne 1995). Poor families are also less able to pay for supports and relief-care arrangements. More of them are in contact with health or welfare services, so that situations which professionals construe as abusive are more likely to be discovered, whereas materially advantaged families are less visible to the authorities (Rodger 1996).

The family systems perspective holds that abuse must be considered within the complex dynamics of family life, so that it is the dysfunctional family which promotes and sustains the tendency to abuse (such as through scapegoating, failure to recognise appropriate intergenerational boundaries, or use of sex to avoid or manage conflict) (Furniss 1991; Glaser and Frosh 1993). Systems ideas can help us understand how some families operate to initiate and sustain abuse, but this approach has been much criticised for absolving individual abusers of responsibility, ignoring wider networks and influences, and being relevant to only certain types of abuse (Corby 1993).

Whereas systems theorists state that abuse is caused by deviations from the conventional family, feminism argues that the roots of abuse lie at the heart of typical family relations (Jenks 1996). According to feminist theory, the tendency for men to seek and be given dominance in societal and family relations predisposes them to expect their wishes (including sexual desires) to be met by women and children, and to use force when their demands are thwarted. Male domination not only fostered sexual violence, but also helped make it invisible for so long (Parton 1991; McLeod and Saraga 1991). This helps explain why the great majority of known sexual abusers are men and also why more men are involved in physical abuse than their usual involvement in care of children would predict. An extension of such ideas accounts for female abuse of children in terms of adult rather than male power. Both men and women in their roles as parents have traditionally had entitlements to direct and chastise children as they think fit. This accords with a concept of childhood as an age-defined category of oppressed people.

The British 'Child Protection System'

Official responses to child abuse have in the main addressed individual cases, with only occasional glances at the wider contributory factors which structural and feminist theories have drawn attention to. The last 30 years have witnessed the development in Britain of a coordinated system consisting of agencies and arrangements that respond to suspected intra-familial child abuse. There are certain legal and procedural differences within the UK (notably the distinct role of reporters and hearings in Scotland outlined in Chapter 9), but the main elements are to be found in similar form throughout the country (King 1994; Wilson and James 1995). These are:

- coordinated or joint social work–police investigations
- inter-agency meetings and case conferences
- local authority child protection registers
- Area Child Protection Committees
- court or hearings decisions about the need for compulsory measures to protect a child.

Local authorities have been given, by law, the primary role for taking action, though this should be in close consultation with health and other professionals. Police are responsible for investigating whether a crime has been committed. Joint police–social work investigations have become common, in order to overcome some of the problems of multiple interviews for children and of poor inter-agency communication identified in inquiries.

To facilitate the sharing of information between all relevant agencies about particular cases, interdisciplinary case conferences have become routine (Stevenson 1989). For a long time these were restricted to professionals out of fear that the presence of family members would inhibit information sharing and distort decision-making. Within a few years, practice has reversed, so that parents and, less often, older children are now commonly invited to case conferences. Workers now believe that involvement of the family makes planning easier and more likely to succeed (Thoburn *et al.* 1995; 1996). However, involvement of parents often remains marginal and may disguise rather than resolve conflicts of interest (Corby *et al.* 1996). One of the tasks of case conferences is to decide whether a child's name should go on a child protection register – a list which is kept so that when anyone becomes aware of possible abuse s/he may check if incidents are known to have happened previously. The case conference is the main means of collaboration at case level and so front-line workers and middle managers are usually present. Area Child Protection Committees are responsible for strategic planning and comprise senior representatives of the key agencies.

A second element of child protection strategy has had a more universalist and preventive focus. This has consisted of educational programmes for children aiming to give them the information to ascertain and avoid dangerous situations, for example, by refusing to go off with a stranger, saying no to adults who touch them in ways they dislike, and telling someone else about unwanted intrusions (Mayes *et al.* 1992; Gillham 1994; Smith 1996). These can be seen as empowering children and respecting their capacities to think and act in their own interests, although some of the materials take little account of differences amongst children related to disability, ethnic background and so on (Kennedy 1995). In the United States children have reported finding victimisation prevention programmes useful and helpful. Although the programmes increased fear and anxiety, this can be seen as positive in fostering alertness to danger (Dziuba-Leatherman *et al.* 1995). However, especially if seen as the only or main solution, such initiatives risk placing the responsibility for adults' actions onto children and underestimating the physical and persuasive power of adults to overcome children's resistance (Gilbert *et al.* 1989).

Analyses and evaluations of the British approach to child abuse and protection

The most influential theoretical analysis of British child protection has been that of Parton (1991; 1995), using concepts derived from Foucault and Donzelot about the subtle ways in which public service agencies are used to control family behaviour (see also Chapters 1 and 4). The general thrust of the argument is that conformity by individuals and families to patterns of behaviour prescribed by the state are established by means of 'pervasive mechanisms of social regulation' (Parton 1991: 8). In their daily work, health visitors, social workers, teachers and doctors seek to enlist the voluntary cooperation of parents and thereby encourage them to adhere to prevailing expectations about the appropriate care of children. This acts as a form of 'soft' policing of families, but is underpinned by the implicit threat or actual use of court action to enforce compliance. The government has increased control of these professionals, particularly by means of detailed guidance, in order to increase the social control of families – in practice mainly poor families (Donzelot 1980; Hill 1990; Marshall 1995a). This has resulted in a legal–bureaucratic model of child protection.

Parton showed that during the 1960s and 1970s child abuse had been largely framed in the medical discourse of non-accidental injury. The main responses consisted of medical treatment for children and parents. Strongly influenced by child abuse inquiries (often chaired by lawyers), the 1980s saw a shift towards a socio-legal discourse of child protection, with a much more central role played by the police and courts. Doctors no longer have the leadership role they had in the 1970s (Hallett 1996). Child-protection policy and practice has become highly proceduralised, leaving little scope for professional discretion (Howe 1992). Professional time and energy is often dominated by the need to determine whether a child should be registered and to prove in court that abuse has occurred. Positive efforts to help families take second place to the requirements of this legalism. According to Rodger (1996: 175) 'a legal discourse narrowly focused on factual events and relationships very often prevails'. Consequently social and environmental considerations are largely excluded from consideration.

For two decades the main influences on policy have been the inquiries that occurred at the rate of one or two per annum after the death of Maria Colwell (Department of Health and Social Security 1982; Department of Health 1991). Useful lessons have been learned from inquiries, but the focus on exceptional cases has skewed attention (Parton 1985; 1996b). The need for protection has been framed in terms of identifying 'high-risk' individuals and family circumstances, yet typical risk factors are so common that they provide an unreliable guide (Dingwall 1989). Furthermore, inquiries focused on preventing further abuse once it had come to light, rather than attempts to prevent interfamilial abuse from occurring in the first place, taking account of socioeconomic and social value influences (Hill 1990; Boushel 1994).

In the 1970s and 1980s the main inquiry criticism against professionals was that they neglected to impose social control on families and made insufficient use of the law, particularly to remove children from dangerous situations. Although the inquiries dealt only with a small number of the most extreme circumstances leading to the deaths of children, the conclusions were generalised to influence the whole approach to thousands of families. As professionals were said to have been deceived by parents in these cases, they were now expected to be suspicious of any parental accounts (Stevenson 1989). Since workers had been vilified and lost jobs for their failure to protect children from death, agencies were tempted to play safe by removing children whenever there was doubt, leading to a large increase in the numbers of children compulsorily removed from home, often on a temporary basis with place of safety orders (Parton 1991). Parents in difficulties were fearful that their children would be taken away from them, so they were less inclined to trust the social services, which further undermined possibilities for cooperation.

The system was torpedoed from an opposite direction by the so called Cleveland child abuse scandal described earlier. Here the 'instant removal from home' philosophy based on severe physical abuse was applied to situations of alleged and contested sexual abuse. Although the Cleveland Inquiry was to confirm that a considerable (though vague) proportion of the cases had indeed involved sexual abuse, nevertheless doctors and social workers were deemed to have been overzealous in identifying abuse. Just as significantly, the abrupt placement of children away from home had taken little account of the children's wishes or of the potential for non-abusive family members to continue or resume care (Butler-Sloss 1988). A few years later, similar complaints were made about the handling of suspected child sexual abuse in Orkney. Nine children living on the island of South Ronaldsay were taken from their homes in the early hours of the morning and transported to residential and foster homes on the Scottish mainland. It was alleged that they had been victims of organised sexual abuse, but as a result of legal and procedural technicalities they were returned home without the facts of the case ever being tested in court (Clyde 1992; Asquith 1993). The Orkney events illustrated how professionals and carers had been inhibited from attending to children's wishes lest they 'contaminate' evidence required in court. Especially in the case of sexual abuse, where physical signs are rarely conclusive, the chances of achieving a criminal conviction often rest on children's own statements. As a result, discussions with the child about what has happened have come to be determined by the need to provide viable evidence and witnesses in court, rather than respond to her or his feelings and expressed needs, although sensitive professionals will try to attend to these too (Waterhouse and McGhee 1996; Street 1996).

The justification for giving priority to criminal evidence is that the child benefits from knowing that the person who did the harm is punished and their own accounts are publicly affirmed. Unfortunately, the reality is that only a minority of cases reach court and many of these do not result in convictions (Hallett 1995b, 1996). Consequently, children are often exposed to extended investigation and possibly the trauma of giving evidence only to feel that in the end they are not believed sufficiently for the perpetrator to be convicted (Murray 1995). The standards of proof required in criminal cases, together with the attitudes of some defence lawyers and judges, can mean that children's testimony is discounted (Spicer 1996). Video-recording was introduced to save children from courtroom 'grilling', but although thousands have been made, few have been used in court (Murray 1995; Smith 1996). When treatment is available for children, they may receive it only after the full investigation has taken place (Kelly and Hill 1994; Wattam 1995).

During the 1980s criticisms were made of the colour-blind approach to child abuse investigations. Cultural stereotypes decontextualised parental actions. Presumptions about the coping strengths of Afro-Caribbean and Asian families could lead to a failure to provide supportive services which were in fact desperately needed. For instance, in the Tyra Henry case the main protector was her grandmother, but Social Services failed to realise that she was eventually under too much strain to keep Tyra, who returned to her parental home where she was killed (Lambeth 1987; Phillips 1995). In contrast, white workers have been criticised for devaluing the strengths of black families (Modi *et al.* 1995).

Inquiries have repeatedly pointed to failures by different professions and organisations to collaborate effectively (Hallett and Birchall 1992). These criticisms persisted despite the development of mechanisms, policies and training to facilitate understanding and communication. Evaluations of such arrangements indicate that co-ordination and mutual understanding have improved, though differences in role and perspective continue to cause problems (Waterhouse and Carnie 1991; Lloyd and Burman 1996; Moran-Ellis and Fielding 1996). Apparently most professionals are now reasonably satisfied with inter-agency cooperation (Birchall with Hallett 1995; Hallett 1995a). On the other hand, the time taken up in meeting and communicating with other agencies means that less time is available for direct work with children and their families.

Commentators had been warning for some time that services for families have become dominated by investigations and legal action (social control) at the expense of positive family support (for example, Holman 1988). It required a series of research studies before a significant shift in government policy began to occur in the mid-1990s (Department of Health 1995; Hill and Aldgate 1996). It was revealed that large numbers of families were caught up in distressing investigations which did *not* establish that abuse had occurred, but then received no assistance despite their requests and difficult living circumstances (Denman and Thorpe 1993; Parton and Ottway 1995; Bell *et al.* 1995). Hallett (1995a, 1996) also pointed to the 'front-loading' of inter-agency collaboration, which concentrates on determining whether a child is at risk, gives less time to planning for the children's welfare and leaves follow-up work largely to social work services. The government accepted the broad message of the research: that need should form the basis of services as much as risk.

It is not clear, however, that the policies, practices or resources are in place to move from a focus on the identification and management of child protection cases to the provision of accessible, supportive, available services to meet the wider needs of children and their families. (Hallett 1995b: 534)

Alternative models

North America has developed the same kind of approach as that of the UK, which has met with similar criticisms, although the details vary from state to state, province to province (Lindsey 1994; Hudson and Galaway 1995). Different models are followed in other parts of Europe that reflect a fundamentally different approach to child abuse and the law (Hollows and Armstrong 1991).

Much attention has been given to the Confidential Doctor system, which is predominant in the Netherlands, Belgium and parts of Germany (Marneffe 1992; Van Montfoort 1993). Apart from extreme cases, concerns about children are, as the name suggests, dealt with by medical and allied personnel, using courts only rarely and as a last resort. The emphasis is on encouraging cooperation between families and professionals, and on offering help rather than imposing sanctions. Proponents suggest that this approach encourages adults to admit to difficulties and indeed guilt, and concentrates efforts on relieving stress and helping families to change. Critics argue that adults may be absolved from responsibility for ill-treatment and that focused attention on children's suffering and needs can be diluted within concern for the whole family system (Chistopherson 1989; Borthwick and Hutchinson 1996). Childhood is submerged in familism.

In France, the legal system plays a crucial role – as in the UK – but operates quite differently. The local children's magistrate (*Juge des enfants*) has wide discretion to consult, gather information, organise services and, if need be, impose a legal order. Decision-making is more informal, with as much concern for problems and needs as for proving harm (Cooper *et al.* 1995). Multi-disciplinary welfare teams offer a range of practical, financial and counselling services. Workers have a supportive and educative remit (Hetherington 1996).

Ideally cross-national comparisons of outcomes would indicate which systems appear to work better, but it would be very difficult to take into account all the variables which might explain national differences. In any case, such systematic research has not yet been attempted. Study visits by British academics and practitioners have found generally favourable evidence in the Netherlands, Belgium and France of better-resourced, less stigmatised services than in the UK, with removal of children from home avoided if at all possible. On the other hand, the nature and consequences of abusive situations may sometimes be minimalised (Hetherington 1996; Borthwick and Hutchinson 1996). According to Pritchard (1992; 1993; 1996) cross-national comparisons of official data on child homicides suggest that the UK system has succeeded in reducing the number of non-accidental deaths to children. However, Creighton (1995b) wrote that it is not possible to draw such a conclusion. The overall numbers are very small and are difficult to interpret owing to the strong influence on the figures of differing recording criteria and practices.

The experiences and views of children and young people about abuse

Despite the rhetoric of children's rights and user involvement, child protection services have to a considerable degree 'developed without direct references to the prime objects of the exercise, children themselves' (Butler and Williamson 1996: 86). On the other hand, some children have undoubtedly been saved further suffering and gained effective help. In briefly reviewing children's own accounts of their experiences, this section deals with abuse itself and the next with the responses of relevant agencies.

Effects of physical abuse

Empirical assessments of the effects of abuse have usually relied on external measures (such as of depression, anxiety, behaviour problems, self-esteem). These can help show whether children who are officially recognised as having been abused exhibit more difficulties than the average or than a comparison sample of children presumed to be 'non-abused'. Such studies have revealed that children who have been physically abused tend to be less able to form close relationships, whilst their behaviour, self-esteem and school performance are often adversely affected. Not surprisingly, studies have shown that multiple, serious and persistent abuse has the worst effect (Crittenden 1985; Cicchetti and Carlson 1989). Parenting that combines a lack of warmth, critical attitude and frequent resort to physical punishments (that is, both physical and emotional abuse) seems to be particularly harmful (Gibbons *et al.* 1995; Waterhouse and McGhee 1996). In a small number of extreme cases abuse results in the death of the child.

Gibbons *et al.* (1995) assessed the subsequent progress of children who were on child abuse registers in the early 1980s – that is a time when nearly all recorded cases involved physical abuse and neglect, not sexual or emotional abuse. Compared with a non-registered group from similar social backgrounds, the registered children as a whole had more behaviour problems at home and school, did less well on cognitive tests, reported having fewer friends and poorer relationships with their mothers. However, there were a good many registered children who did not share the general pattern of unfavourable outcomes. A review of this research concluded that 'isolated incidents of physical abuse in the context of a non-violent family and in the absence of sexual abuse or neglect did not lead to poor long-term outcomes for children' (Department of Health 1995: 42).

The testimony of children themselves, as might be expected, tends to portray physical abuse as unwanted and harmful. Many feel emotional as well as physical pain:

The worst thing was when my dad hit me for no reason. I never understood it.
He was my Dad. (Girl aged 15, quoted in Butler and Williamson 1996: 91)

Children who contacted ChildLine about beatings at home expressed 'feelings of rage, shame, humiliation, despair, fear, misery and hopelessness' (MacLeod 1995: 7). Not uncommonly, though, children feel ambivalent or even sympathetic towards the abuser, depending on other aspects of their relationship and the context in which the abuse occurred. Children who have experienced severe physical chastisements 'may still have some emotional ties to their parents that prevent them from categorising parental behaviour as negative or abusive' (Cruise *et al.* 1994: 39).

Effects of sexual abuse

With regard to sexual abuse, there is a continuing debate about what proportion, if any, of revelations by children of adult sexual interference are false. On the one hand, it is avowed that children almost never lie about sexual abuse. Many would be unable to describe details of intercourse or being forced to masturbate an adult unless they had direct experience. A contrasting opinion is that some children do make false allegations for reasons including projection of sexual fantasies, a wish to hurt or because of the influence of a parent in a marital dispute.

Part of the problem is how to establish reliably a criterion to judge whether an allegation is true or false, since physical signs of sexual abuse are often absent or ambiguous, whilst the opinion even of 'experts' may be affected by preconceptions (Howitt 1992). There is evidence that children who have been abused may deny this or retract revelations out of fear of the abuser or concern about the repercussions (Summit 1983). An American evaluation of children where sexual abuse was confirmed legally or medically found that denials and recantations were common, but usually ended with 'active disclosure' that the abuse had occurred (Sorenson and Snow 1991). Not only are children with learning difficulties more vulnerable to sexual exploitation, but some lack the communication skills and confidence to report abuse (Kelly 1996).

Knowledge of such findings led some to a presumption that *any* reversal of a claim is probably false. This was even extended to persistent denials by a child when someone else has made an allegation. The Clyde Report (Clyde 1992) on the Orkney cases affirmed the importance for professionals to keep an open mind during interviews with children. Spencer and Flin (1990) reviewed the relevant research and concluded that 'false complaints made by children are very rare' (p. 269). Howitt (1992) doubted that such a strong claim is justified by the evidence, but accepted that children's testimony has been shown to be as reliable as adults.

Findings about the consequences of sexual abuse are affected by the methods used and by the inclusiveness of the definition of sexual abuse. Brief non-contact incidents appear to have few long-term effects, though they are often distressing at the time. A large number of American studies have shown that persistent abuse involving contact can be associated with lasting troubled feelings and behaviour. Children who experienced sexual abuse combined with violence are most likely to have severe problems (Gomes-Schwartz *et al.* 1990). Children seem to feel less bad if non-abusing family members and friends believe them and provide support (Browne *et al.* 1994; Trowell 1996).

Many adult survivors have reported long-term distress and bitterness at having been sexually abused, especially by father-figures or close relatives whose perceived role it should have been to protect not abuse them (Glaser and Frosh 1993). Children attending a Dundee clinic reported fear, anger and confusion as their main reactions to abuse (Roberts *et al.* 1993). Two-thirds described experiencing some degree of depression. As with physical abuse, some felt total hostility to the abuser, while others were ambivalent, especially if the perpetrator was a family member:

I'm sad about not seeing him. I used to play with him. I want Dad to live with me again. (Quoted in Roberts and Taylor 1993: 27)

I feel guilty, excited and confused. (Boy aged 15, quoted in MacLeod 1995)

Painful memories often recur. A girl who was abused sexually by a babysitter when aged six reported five years later how she continued to worry and have nightmares about him (Butler and Williamson 1994). A 15-year old said:

It flashes back, makes me scared. It's like a black pitch. It's a thing you can't forget. (Quoted in Roberts *et al.* 1993a: 30)

While most evidence points to traumatic effects when adults engage children in sexual activities, certain writers have suggested that the experience may not be harmful or salient. Then children may feel under pressure from professionals and their powerful moral discourses to define their experiences retrospectively as abusive (Evans 1993; Stewart 1996).

The experiences and views of children and young people about adults' 'protective' actions

Official responses to identified abuse usually comprise a complex sequence of elements including:

- reactions to the initial allegation or discovery of abuse
- medical examinations and investigatory interviews
- court action
- possibly one or more removal from home
- counselling and services (if available).

In such circumstances, it may be hard to differentiate the effects of attempts to help the child and family from the consequences of separation, family disruption or alternative care. Moreover, in as many as one in four cases, children are re-abused (Department of Health 1995). Most information is available from older children who have been sexually abused. Little is known about the views of children caught up in allegations when they have not been abused.

Several studies have found that children who reported having been abused were pleased to have told, were glad it stopped and felt released from guilt. On the other hand, many have described the investigations and subsequent intervention as puzzling, disturbing and sometimes humiliating (Roberts *et al.* 1993; Farmer 1993; McGee and Westcott 1996). In a minority of cases, the responses were so intrusive or unwished for that the children regretted having spoken out (Roberts and Taylor 1993; Farmer and Owen 1995).

Children have expressed resentment at not being given information or choices about what happens. They spoke of losing control of their lives to adults (Butler and Williamson 1996). Investigations and court appearances can be experienced as adult-led routines imposed on children:

The whole thing was a nightmare. Police report, investigation, medical just as bad. They didn't consult me about whether to report it or have a medical – just turned up. (Quoted in Roberts *et al.* 1993: 24)

I didn't like going to court. I don't like speaking to judges. (Quoted in Roberts *et al.* 1993: 28)

I didn't understand what was going on.

(Girl, aged 12, quoted in Westcott 1995: 181)

Farmer (1993: 43) noted how 'parents and children spoke of feeling swept along by the investigation without being consulted or, in some cases, informed what would happen next'. The majority of children in another study were unprepared for investigative interviews and were not given any choice about where this should take place. Even when interviewers are experienced as sympathetic, children may find the questions difficult to understand and feel pressurised for details they cannot recall or which they see as irrelevant (Westcott and Davies 1995, 1996; McGee and Westcott 1996). A small but significant request from one set of children was to be spared the embarrassment of being called out of class for interviews and discussions at school (Thoburn *et al.* 1995).

Young people have emphasised the importance of being given information at each stage, feeling valued and having their viewpoints listened to.

How can they know your best interests when they don't even know you?

(Girl, aged 14)

They don't really listen. And then they don't believe you.

(Girl, aged 17, both quotes from Butler and Williamson 1996: 94)

Amongst advice proffered to adults were the following (quoted in Roberts and Taylor 1993: 33):

Believe what is said by children.   (Girl, aged 12)

Don't blame the children.   (Girl, aged 13)

Don't just go ahead with the investigation . . . we've got brains and can make decisions. Take account of us. We are people.   (Girl, aged 15)

A major concern is that social workers, teachers and others will not keep confidences (Triseliotis *et al.* 1995; Gallagher 1996b).

I'm scared of telling adults – in case it goes further. The teachers would probably talk about it in the staffroom.

(Girl, aged nine, quoted in Butler and Williamson 1994: 78)

Children also resent not being believed and may sometimes interpret repeated requests to provide information as reflecting doubt on their accounts. Children tend to interpret failure to prosecute or achieve a conviction as meaning they are thought to have lied (Murray 1995).

Most children do not like case conferences taking place without them – 'everyone talking behind my back' (quoted in Farmer 1993: 48). When children do attend, as they increasingly do, they usually feel listened to and taken seriously (Fletcher 1993; McGee and Westcott 1996). Children are often unaware that their names are on a child protection register, whilst those that do know see it as embarrassing and stigmatising (Waterhouse and McGhee 1996). One 11-year old applied to the High Court for her name to be removed from the local authority register (Joseph 1995).

Despite common complaints about investigations and court appearances, children's feedback about professional help 'has been positive, and in most cases they report feeling better after contact' (McGee and Westcott 1996: 175).

I enjoyed going there 'cos it gave me a chance to say what my feelings were like. (Girl, aged 11, quoted in Westcott 1995: 181)

A 15-year old, who had a history of beatings by her mother, described her social worker:

She's really nice. She seems to know what I'm thinking. And she stands up to my mum. Not many people would do that.
(Quoted in Butler and Williamson 1994: 106)

Sometimes abuse results in short- or long-term family separations (see also Chapter 11). Children may dislike the abuse and want it to stop, but may equally disapprove of splitting their families as a solution. Trowell (1996) reported the case of an 11-year-old girl living in a foster home who told her she hated her father having intercourse with her, but did not want him to be in prison, nor herself to be away from her family. Sometimes children go into foster and residential care. This may bring a sense of relief and being cared for (Wilson 1995; Triseliotis *et al.* 1995) or feelings of isolation; for example:

I wouldn't talk to the staff here. They don't treat me seriously.
(Boy, aged nine, quoted in Butler and Williamson 1996: 94–6)

Concerns about the dangers of arrangements to safeguard children doing more harm than good have crystallised around the concept of 'system abuse'. This embodies a number of ways in which children may suffer from processes which are meant to be there to protect them (McGee and Westcott 1996):

- distressing investigations when a child has not in fact suffered familial abuse
- distressing investigations adding to the pain of children who have been abused
- false raising of hopes about successful prosecution of abuser
- failure to give support
- failure to provide services or remove a child at severe risk
- child's needs not being met in alternative care
- exposure to physical or sexual abuse in care.

Conclusions

The present child protection system has grown up to respond to a particular kind of risk – that of significant avoidable harm within the family. It developed in response mainly to criticisms from a series of well-publicised inquiries, which pointed to defects such as inadequate responses to evidence of physical ill-treatment, too-precipitous intervention in cases of alleged sexual abuse and poor inter-agency collaboration. These criticisms have highlighted the difficulties of reconciling conflicting social expectations about the social control roles of state agencies. In particular, there are strong norms of family privacy and parental autonomy, but also assumptions that professionals will be constantly vigilant and take intrusive action to protect children when necessary. Merrick (1996) refers to the conflicting discourses which coexist in child welfare policy of familialism (support of families to prevent abuse) and authoritarian intervention (to protect children from their families). Recent children's legislation has been dominated by considerations of child abuse and protection. The law has sought to achieve a balance of sometimes competing principles (for example, paramountcy of children's welfare, partnership with parents, attending to children's participatory rights, clear justifications for legal intervention) (Harding 1991; 1996a). In particular instances, however, these tenets can be difficult to reconcile.

In view of the creation of child abuse as a recognised social priority over the last 20 years and the large amount of attention given to developing the present formal arrangements, successive UK governments have undoubtedly tried to fulfil their obligations towards safeguarding children. As the United Nations Convention subsequently urged, it has taken 'legislative, administrative, social and educational measures to protect the child from all forms of physical or mental violence, injury or abuse, neglect or negligent treatment, maltreatment or exploitation – including sexual abuse' (Article 19). Whether these measures have been appropriate or effective remains a matter for debate. The system appears to have met some of its internal objectives, including more efficient identification of children at serious risk and greater levels of co-operation between agencies and professionals. Moreover, many agencies have taken steps to incorporate a *rights perspective* in their work, including the National Society for the Prevention of Cruelty to Children (Cloke and Davies 1995).

However, many critics think that the system often does not provide adequate help to meet children's needs, whether in their own right or subsumed within pleas for more 'family support'. Although the law now requires local authorities to assess and meet need (see Chapter 3), services continue to concentrate on their parallel duty to deal with actual or potential 'significant harm'. Considerable resources are devoted to spending time on identifying children 'at risk', leaving inadequate attention and restricted options for responding to the wishes of children and their parents for assistance (Colton *et al.* 1995; Hallett 1996). The stance of the agencies involved has become more oriented to suspicion and legal–bureaucratic actions, often leading to alienation from the wider community which is in a more immediate sense responsible for the care and protection of children. Yet the system even fails some of those it identifies as in need of protection (such as through mystifying or upsetting procedures; delayed or minimal attention to the children's welfare needs; failure to secure cases in court). The high level of proof required for serious allegations casts doubt on whether the child protection–criminal justice system as a whole operates on a truly welfare basis for children.

Public and government attention has focused on intra-familial abuse, partly because of the central importance for society of seeking to preserve a positive image of childhood and family life in a post-modern world of uncertainty by controlling and minimising deviations from family ideals. In addition, the blame for this form of abuse can be readily attributed to defective parents or professionals, so that any demand for broader social changes and reallocation of resources is minimised (Hill 1990; Parton 1991). Many commentators would argue that the dangers children face from both within the family and outside reflect the distribution of power, the availability of resources and conceptions of adult–child relations which operate at a societal level. According to Jenks 'child abuse is nothing new, it has always been an immanent feature of the relationship between adults and young; concretely the potential resides within the differential of both power and status' (1996: 87). Despite a recent shift in legal emphasis from the notion of parental rights to parental responsibilities, it is still generally the case that adults, and especially parents, are seen to have powers to make children do what they want. Control and discipline are regarded as essential needs of children if they are to be protected from the dangers of their own impulses and if society, too, is to be protected from the feared unruliness of youth. Social values support adults' entitlements to impose on children (for the child's own benefit, of course): these may encourage and reinforce the tendency of some adults to indulge in vicious punishments to ensure a child's compliance or to misuse children for their own sexual gratification (Boushel 1994). Images of children as weak, vulnerable and asexual have rightly evoked protective adult concern, but can also devalue the contribution children have to make in determining appropriate responses to adult behaviour which they resent or find harmful. Furthermore, this has perhaps contributed to the comparative neglect until recently of the role of children (usually teenagers) as abusers (Becker 1991; Murphy *et al.* 1992).

In recent years, there has been a useful corrective to the 'stranger danger' emphasis of the 1980s. Professionals and educators now warn that threats to significant numbers of children arise within the hallowed walls of the home. Nevertheless, for the great majority of children, family members remain the principal sources of comfort and security (see Chapter 4). Moreover, many threats to children do in fact come from outside home, yet efforts to tackle them are usually fragmented and weak compared with the child protection measures aimed at intra-familial abuse. Abduction, rape and murder may not be as common as media representations suggest, but to these must be added the risks children face from traffic, unsafe buildings, environmental hazards, bullying and so on (see chapters 5 to 7). A wider view of risk and of risk-factors is required if child protection is genuinely to mean protecting children from significant harm.

Suggestions for further reading

Batty, D. and Cullen, D. (eds) (1996) *Child Protection: The Therapeutic Option*, London: BAAF.

Cloke, C. and Davies, M. (eds) (1995) *Participation and Empowerment in Child Protection*, London: Pitman.

Department of Health (1995) *Child Protection: Messages from Research*, London: HMSO.

National Commission of Inquiry into the Prevention of Child Abuse (1996) *Childhood Matters*, London: Stationery Office.

Parton, N. (1991) *Governing the Family*, London: Macmillan.

Wilson, K. and James, A. (eds) (1995) *The Child Protection Handbook*, London: Bailliere Tindall.

CHAPTER 11

Separated children

Introduction

With varying degrees of willingness and contentment, nearly all children stay away from their parents – with grandparents, friends or at boarding school, for example. This chapter is concerned with different kinds of separations from one or both parents – those which occur on a longer-term basis as a result of difficulties between or involving the parents.

Some parents separate from each other permanently before their child is born or shortly afterwards. Growing numbers of children are affected by their parents parting when the child is old enough to experience the separation or divorce, and remember times when both parents were still together. The United Nations Convention and recent British children's legislation emphasise a child's right to have continuing relationships with both parents after a separation, provided the children's rights to welfare and protection are not jeopardised (for example, Sections 6 and 17 of the Children (Scotland) Act 1995). Similarly, both parents have enduring legal responsibilities towards their children, unless this is restricted by a court in the children's interests.

A much smaller population of children live apart from both original parents, mainly with foster carers or in residential care, normally under the auspices of local authorities (health boards in Northern Ireland). For a long time, such children were said to be 'in care', but this term acquired stigmatising connotations and was thought by some to imply a total takeover of responsibilities from parents. As a result, the Children Act 1989 introduced the phrase 'looked after' to England and Wales (this was subsequently incorporated into Scottish and Northern Irish legislation, too).

In the past, Children Acts and Children & Young Persons Acts have been largely concerned with children 'in care' or at risk of 'reception into care', whilst children whose parents divorce or separate have been affected by separate matrimonial legislation. The 1989 Act broke new ground in bringing together the law affecting both types of situation. Besides a general wish to integrate public and private law in relation to children, this was also due to the recognition that instabilities in parental partnerships are a common though not invariable precursor of placement in local authority care (Packman *et al.* 1986). Previously some children and families experienced complicated interactions between matrimonial and care proceedings. Of course the majority of parental separations and divorces do not result in children having to leave both parents.

On the whole, decisions about where children should live have been seen as a matter for parents to determine, unless there were grounds for a court order or, in Scotland, a hearing requirement to override that right. The rights of children to live away from their parents were not clear, although some did influence adult decisions by behaving in ways which 'forced their hands' (such as by persistently leaving home). The Children Act 1989 introduced a new provision for children to seek to initiate court action so they could live elsewhere or change contact arrangements (Section 8). Parts of the media exaggerated the nature of this new right and spoke in terms of children's entitlement to 'divorce' their parents. In fact, the right is quite limited since in England and Wales the agreement of the court is needed before a child's request for a hearing is acceded to (Children's Rights Office (CRO) 1996; Roche 1996). Adult judgements of children's competence then come into play, as in the case of *Re S* where the Master of the Rolls determined that a boy of 11 did not have the necessary understanding of future possibilities to be granted leave to apply for a Section 8 Order (Lyon and Parton 1995).

Theoretical approaches to separation

The dominant paradigm for considering children's separation from one or both parents has derived from *psychodynamic and attachment theories* (see also Chapter 4). These suggest that any loss of a loved one, even if partial or temporary, has some of the same elements as the experience of total loss through death. Several reactions follow both bereavement and separation, such as sadness, disorientation, anger and denial (Parkes 1972, 1993; Rutter 1981). Not uncommonly, there are typical sequences of emotional response if separation is prolonged, e.g. protest, denial, detachment (Bowlby 1973). In many adoptions, both child and adoptive parent have suffered losses. The child has had to leave the birth family, whilst childless couples mourn the baby they wanted but infertility prevented them having (Brodzinsky and Schechter 1990).

Alternative perspectives concentrate on cognitive and communicative processes, rather than emotional responses. *Social construction theories* of family processes highlight that a child confronted with major separation has to make sense of this event and its implications, firstly to review the child's own perceptions of their identity and life history (biography) and secondly in order to present an account of these to other people (Smith 1984). Thus, following divorce and remarriage, a child needs to reconceptualise her/his self-image to embrace new roles (as a 'child of divorce', 'step-child') and a new constellation of social relationships, just as the adults concerned do (Burgoyne *et al.* 1987).

A child in a foster home similarly has to work out how to relate to two sets of parental figures, decide on appropriate naming and provide answers to questions from schoolmates, teachers and others about discrepancies between their situation and 'the norm' (such as going backwards and forwards between two homes or living with other children who are not your brothers or sisters). When children are given little or no explanation about why their parents split up or how they came to be living away from home, they are likely to be confused. They may then misperceive the causes and implications. Younger children in particular are likely to blame themselves, whereas older children are more likely to attribute responsibility to parents and so direct anger to them (Robinson 1991; Lindon 1996).

Longitudinal approaches emphasise that changes in living situation and household composition are not just single events, but multiple processes over time in which choices are made, both pragmatically (such as about who to live with or have contact with) and in terms of the nature of relationships and identity. Although there are often major external constraints, reflecting in part children's relative powerlessness when adult relationships founder, scope nevertheless exists for children's active influence on events. With regard to marital conflict and divorce, *stress-coping models* emphasise how children's emotional and behavioural responses are affected by their varied appraisals of the nature and significance of relationships and events as they unfold, as well as personal and network resources. Transitions from one family form to another are accompanied by revisions of prior assumptions and changes of role, as a child's expectations about the nature of home life, schooling and community have to shift, sometimes abruptly (Grych and Fincham 1990; Chiriboga *et al.* 1991). The nature of many existing relationships have to be renegotiated (for example, with grandparents, who are also affected by the breakdown in the family) and new ones established (such as with a step-parent or with children at a new school).

The concept of 'care career' has been applied to the experiences of children in residential and foster care, especially those who experience a sequence of moves rather than a single 'care episode'. Like a sequence of transitions during and after divorce, a care career embraces not only a series of placements and interventions, but also a spectrum of settings and activities such as school and peer relationships. Within the care career 'key moments can be identified when options open and close and when important decisions have to be made' (Little *et al.* 1995: 667). Some careers are relatively stable and some involve marked turning points, whilst in the worst cases there can be a downward spiral of rejection and behaviour difficulties culminating in secure accommodation or prison. Pertinent to both stress-coping and career perspectives is that the way a child (or adult) copes with crises or critical periods has crucial long-term effects. Personal strengths and supports may be developed or constructive new patterns of living and behaving established:

I was a loner, but I learned how to make friends.

When I came here I was mental, would do anything. I'm not that bad now, not stealing or truanting.   (Quoted in Triseliotis *et al.* 1995: 173)

Alternatively, the assault on self-esteem, trust in others and perceptions that adults are not worth cooperating with may have persistent deleterious consequences. For example, one young man had been rejected by his family, did not feel settled in residential care and frequently ran away to 'go to parties, steal cars'. Another said 'When I was feeling depressed, I would just run away' (quoted in Triseliotis *et al.* 1995: 182).

Also relevant to arrangements made for separated children are *theories concerned with the state, parents and children*. As the previous chapter showed with respect to child protection, in conventional 'liberal' theory the state has a role to protect children's interests, but acts on the presumption that parents are entitled to look after children as they see fit unless a threshold of harm to the child is reached (Archard 1993). Hence family privacy and autonomy are generally respected and the state should intervene only as a last resort. In relation to divorce, this has meant that on the whole the state (through the law and the courts) has largely ratified prevailing norms and existing arrangements as regards where children should live and whom they should see. When paternal authority was the primary consideration, custody went mainly to the father; in the twentieth century presumptions that women are usually better carers has favoured mothers – a view which engendered and was supported by early versions of attachment theory. The recent position has been to promote shared responsibilities and favour non-intervention unless a court order would be demonstrably better (Harding 1996a). The principle of minimum intervention may promote parental autonomy, but unless a case is heard in court this means that no consultation with children is legally required in England, Wales or Northern Ireland. In Scotland, parents have to consult children under Section 6 of the 1995 Act.

Public law has also exhibited changing mixes of competing principles related to parental autonomy; state intervention justified by appeals to children's welfare; and (usually much more weakly) children's own views (Adler 1985; Harding 1991). Readers may recall the classification into four main perspectives described in Chapter 1, presented here in modified form:

- *laissez-faire* – the state intervenes only in extreme situations
- *parentalist* – the state concentrates on supporting parents in their child-rearing role
- *protectionist* – the state acts readily to assist children and if necessary remove them from home in order to protect them from family ill-treatment
- *child-centred* – much weight is given to children's views

In practice, most laws, policies and individual decisions involve some kind of compromise between more than one of these perspectives. They are more useful for clarifying what considerations should be taken account of rather than simply classifying any specific policy. Also, the classification focuses on the government (central and local), parents and children: it ignores the roles of other parties (such as voluntary agencies and social networks). Nevertheless it can be argued that there have been shifts in balance over time. In the pre-war period, *laissez-faire* principles were strong; the 1980s were a high point for protectionism and legal intervention (in childcare though not economic policy); the 1990s have seen a shift towards both parentalist and child-centred approaches through such concepts as family support, partnership and participation (Holman 1988; Harding 1991; Packman and Jordan 1991).

In the rest of this chapter, consideration is given first to the needs and rights of children affected by parental separation, then to alternatives to birth-family care.

Separation, divorce and children

The nature and incidence of separation and divorce

Separation and divorce are connected but distinct. Couples may cohabit and part without ever marrying, let alone divorcing. A married couple may split without divorcing, whilst commonly the final legal termination of a marriage happens some time after marital separation. Moreover, temporary separations sometimes precede a final separation – and from a child's perspective it may not be clear which is which. Frequently one or both parents form new partnerships which can then lead on to remarriage. When account is also taken of the tensions which typically occur before separation, it is clear that a complicated sequence of relationship changes is involved, rather than a single event. Much more is known about separation accompanying divorce than informal separations because it is easier for researchers to identify families when there is a legal record. Approximately one-quarter of children born to married couples in the UK will experience their parents' divorce before they reach adulthood (Richards 1995). It is estimated that three-quarters of a million children live full-time in stepfamilies, with a further one-quarter of a million born to couples where at least one of the partners has married for a second time (Lindon 1996).

Following separation, it remains rare for children to divide their time evenly between both parents. Over 80 per cent of children live with their mothers for most or all of the time. A minority shift home from one parent to the other at least once (Buchanan *et al.* 1992; Gregory and Foster 1990).

In the majority of cases, contact after divorce with the non-resident parent (usually the father) falls off rapidly, and in up to half the cases becomes non-existent (McLaughlin and Whitfield 1984). Continuing adult hostility, practical difficulties and absorption with a new family all contribute to this. Even some highly participant fathers 'disengage' from their children because they cannot cope with the emotional stress of losing their role or as a result of conflict with the ex-partner (Kruk 1991, 1993; Walker 1996).

Children's needs during and following separation

In assessing the reactions of children and the needs which arise, it should be borne in mind that 'marital separation happens in many different ways and at different points in childhood' (Richards 1996: 37). The responses amongst children and adults are equally diverse. Research has consistently shown that populations of children whose parents divorce have lower mean levels of academic achievement and self-esteem and a higher incidence of psychological and conduct problems. However, these differences refer to averages and are often small. There are many overlaps and similarities in the experiences of children whose parents separate and those whose parents stay together (Burghes 1996; Richards 1996).

Material wellbeing

Family disruption often means that income is reduced, resulting in fewer resources for daily living and a poorer standard of accommodation (see Chapter 8). Occasionally, there may be improvement because the woman gains greater control of finances (Pahl 1989). In any case, mothers often seek to protect children as much as possible from the effects of reduced income. The Child Support Act 1991 was passed ostensibly to increase the flow of resources from 'absent fathers' (and also save government money), but in practice it often resulted in 'considerable financial and emotional costs for children and their mothers' (Clarke *et al.* 1995: 26; Dean 1995). Remarriage often improves the financial lot, but children in re-ordered households tend to have less space and move house more often (Ferri 1993; Ochiltree 1990).

The need to make sense of what is going on

Social construction and stress-coping theories indicate that children will inevitably seek to make sense of what is going on, but this is likely to be a confusing and isolating process unless the child is given adequate knowledge and support. According to Burgoyne *et al.* (1987), two of the principal needs of children experiencing divorce are for, firstly, 'accurate information about what is happening to their parents' marriage and its implications for their own lives' and, secondly, 'opportunities for talking about their experiences and fears and for comparing them with those of others' (p. 137). Children whose parents have divorced often say they did not realise there were major marital problems or foresee the break-up. Some recognised that there was conflict, but saw it as a small part of a basically happy life. Even several years after the final separation some children do not fully understand or accept the divorce. They may still yearn for reconciliation or indeed still see this as quite possible (Wallerstein and Kelly 1980; Mitchell 1985).

In small part this is affected by the child's inability to perceive what is going on, but more important seems to be adults' failure to recognise children's needs for explanations (Cockett and Tripp 1996) or to acknowledge their capacities to understand and cope. Parents are often too preoccupied with their own feelings and actions. Many try to 'protect' children from knowledge of family difficulties in order to avoid upsetting them or undermining their love for the other parent. As we saw in relation to illness (Chapter 7), in practice it seems that children manage the change better when they are given careful explanations which help them accept what has happened (Kurdeck and Siesky 1980; McLaughlin and Whitfield 1984).

Children often keep their parents' separation secret from friends or teachers, because of feelings of shame and stigma (Mitchell 1985). They have a need for a 'cover' story – a way of explaining what has happened that does not open their whole life to examination, yet does not leave them feeling ashamed or secretive. When children are able to tell friends openly, this is linked to signs of better adjustment (Kurdeck and Siesky 1980). Schools have an important role in enabling children to discuss the diversity of family forms and to share ideas and experiences in ways which do not breach confidentiality (Burgoyne *et al.* 1987).

Emotional wellbeing

The responses of children to parental separation are greatly affected by the nature of the prior family relationships and the circumstances of the split. Relief and happiness are common reactions, but so too are sadness, longing, shame and anger as attachment theory suggests. This range is illustrated in quotes from a group of nine year olds:

I am happy that my parents got divorced . . . now I don't have to listen to her cursing him.

I was ashamed when the children at school told me they knew my parents were not living together.

I'm angry with my Mum for agreeing to Dad's leaving home.

I wish my parents would return to each other and we'd all live together.
(All quoted in Ayalon and Flasher 1993: 96–7)

A minority of children are pleased the conflict is over, but most find the separation distressing (McLaughlin and Whitfield 1984; Parkinson 1987). Some writers have identified a grief reaction, with sadness at the loss of accustomed relationships and routines, often combined with missing the absent parent. This can persist for several years, with accompanying behaviour difficulties (poorer concentration or greater impulsiveness compared with matched controls: Hetherington (1989)). In the long run most children adapt quite well and tend to see the divorce as either inevitable or for the best (McLaughlin and Whitfield 1984; Amato 1987). A 17-year old wrote advice to other children based on her experience of her parents' separation when she was 12:

My parents' divorce felt like it was going to be life shattering at first but this feeling does go away. People said this to me when my parents first separated and I didn't believe them – but it DOES get better!

(Quoted in Harrison 1996: 136)

It appears that *persistent* negative consequences for children are mainly related to family discord rather than separation itself (Amato and Keith 1991; see also Chapter 4). Longitudinal studies have shown that adverse effects were already apparent prior to the separation (Rutter 1980; Jenkins and Smith 1991). On the other hand, there is evidence that for a sizable number of children the inner pain of the separation itself is long-lasting and often hidden or not recognised by key adults (Wallerstein and Kelly 1980; Mitchell 1985).

The change to a less conflictual home setting can bring many benefits. McLaughlin and Whitfield (1984) found that half their sample of children thought they got on better at school after divorce (compared to 12 per cent who thought it was worse). Kurdeck and Siesky (1980) noted that some children found new personal strengths and got on better with friends. Adolescents in post-divorce households tend to have more autonomy, spend less time at home and live in more egalitarian households. Some teenagers believe that divorce made them 'grow up more quickly' and become more self-reliant (Noller and Callan 1991). They may benefit from having two homes and 'two of almost everything' (Harrison 1996: 142). They often have increased personal time alone with each parent.

Generally, children affected by parental separation are seen to need and benefit from sharing their feelings with others (Burgoyne *et al.* 1987). A 13-year-old daughter of divorced parents wrote:

. . . it doesn't really matter who you talk to, as long as you do.

(Quoted in Harrison 1996: 147)

Many gain effective support from their parents and others (Sandler *et al.* 1983), but often children have 'difficulties in communicating their emotional needs to their parents' (Mitchell 1985: 191). Satisfactory adjustment is assisted when the caring parent is emotionally supportive and shows interest in the young person's activities, but is not too intrusive nor overprotective (Dunlop and Burns 1983; Buchanan *et al.* 1992). Relations with the kin of custodial parents tend to intensify, whilst contacts with the other parents' relatives diminish, though are rarely completely broken (Furstenberg and Spanier 1984).

As with divorce, the short-term impact on children of becoming part of a reconstituted family can be strongly negative, but a reasonable accommodation is usually achieved over time (Furstenberg and Spanier 1984). Girls appear to have more problems adapting to a stepfather than do boys (Hetherington *et al.* 1985; Vuchinich *et al.* 1991). This seems to be related to resentment at intrusion into previously close mother–daughter relationships.

Children's need for both parents?

In a minority of cases, particularly when there has been violence, children are glad that one party has left the scene and safety considerations may require discontinuation of access (Mullender and Morley 1994). Children usually struggle much more with loyalty to both parents. They feel love towards both and want to see both, yet find it hard to express this without upsetting the other party (Wallerstein and Kelly 1980; Buchanan *et al.* 1992). Amongst the needs expressed by children themselves in a study of Exeter families was to be able to state their views about arrangements, see both parents freely and have flexible contact arrangements (Cockett and Tripp 1996).

Studies of joint residential arrangements have mainly been carried out in North America. They suggest that these tend towards extremes of success and failure depending on the relationship between the adults (Ahrons 1980; Irving *et al.* 1984). When there is little conflict, clear communication and flexibility, then both parent–child relationships and child adjustment are better than for sole residential arrangements, but when there is conflict, the outcomes are worse.

Most often, though, responsibility and daily care are largely carried out by just one of the parents (and their partners, if any). Most mothers and fathers are equally capable of providing appropriate care. Not surprisingly, children tend to fare better when there is good cooperation between the main and secondary parent (Camara and Resnick 1988; Buchanan *et al.* 1992). Several studies have shown children who have continued contact with non-resident fathers have better social–emotional ratings than those without contact (Wallerstein and Kelly 1980; Hetherington 1989). Richards and Dyson (1982) observed that children themselves are most concerned about how much time they can spend with their non-resident parent and less with the frequency of contact, which tends to preoccupy adults. Amongst the benefits which can come from continued contact are that it:

- avoids a sense of rejection
- enables continuing attachment
- dispels erroneous fantasies
- helps with identity and sense of origins
- helps understanding of the separation
- assists contact with both sets of kin
- may free children to develop relationships with step-parents.

The rights of children affected by separation and divorce

The UN Convention makes it clear that children have the rights to express their views and to participate in decisions and proceedings related to separation, as well as to maintain 'direct contact with both parents on a regular basis, except if it is contrary to the child's best interests' (Articles 9 and 12). In this country, such ideas have had little credence until recently. Both the law and court decisions have been based on the dual principles that, where possible, parents should decide what is best (*laissez-faire*) and, if they cannot agree, the state should make decisions on the basis of perceptions of the child's welfare (*child protectionism*). Only since the 1950s have courts been required to satisfy themselves about arrangements for children in matrimonial proceedings (Gibson 1994). Increasingly children have been consulted, but often their views have not been given great weight because of perceptions that:

- children are unable to assess the long-term consequences of decisions about residence and contact
- it is unfair to 'burden' children with the responsibility of making difficult choices
- the outcomes of arrangements depend so much on parents anyway that it is best to go along with what they suggest.

The Family Law Act 1996 included provision for courts to take account of the views of any children of the marriage and to avoid an automatic presumption that children will live with their mother. Children in England and Wales acquired the rights to be a party in divorce proceedings and receive copies of the papers. However, Murch has pointed out that 'no one has the responsibility within the legal framework of divorce to listen to the children, get alongside them and support them' (1995: 26).

Some researchers have also argued against acceding to children's preferences. Wallerstein and Kelly (1980) found that children up to about ten or 11 were prone to polarisation in their attitudes, tending to think of one parent as 'good' and one as 'bad'. The authors' conclusion was *paternalist* – 'children below adolescence are not reliable judges of their own best interests' (p. 314). However children are resentful when their feelings are apparently ignored:

My Mum never said anything about visiting my Dad: I would have wanted to see him.

We supposed he'd gone for a drink instead [when the father failed to keep an appointment to see them].   (Quoted in Mitchell 1985: 131)

Services concerned with divorce and separation have also been mainly oriented to adults. Most legal services respond to the wishes of their (usual) paying customers – the parents. Conciliation and family mediation services are either court-based or independent (voluntary) schemes. For a long time they confined their attention to parents. This often included helping them negotiate arrangements for the children and take more notice of children's wishes and feelings, but children themselves were not directly involved. This approach was based on notions that decisions are likely to be more effective if made by parents; that parents are best able to decide what is best; and that parents should be responsible for decisions (Howard and Shepherd 1987; Parkinson 1987; Walker 1991). Although mainly derived from the principle of parental autonomy from state interference, these ideas also tended to diminish the contribution of children. Further considerations were to protect children from the animosities which often accompany conciliation processes and from 'the additional burden of having to contribute a view of what is in their own best interests' (Simpson 1989: 265). Nowadays it is more common to include children in mediation, although this may still occur mainly at the discretion of conciliators and when parents want it, rather than as a direct result of children's own choice (Garwood 1992). Moreover the reasons for including children vary and may be contradictory, namely to:

• help parents focus on the present and future, not the past
• assist parental decision-making
• give children a voice in the decision
• provide a safe place for children to express their feelings
• identify children who need specialist help.

In any case, the voluntary nature of the service means that it is only available in certain areas. The Family Law Act 1996 introduced an expanded role for family mediation in England and Wales.

Children distressed by parental discord or separation will be hard put to find any specialist counselling services available to them. A high proportion of referrals to child guidance clinics and social work services concern children affected by divorce and separation, but very few are self-referrals and not uncommonly the overt reason for help-seeking is to modify the child's behaviour (Burgoyne *et al.* 1987).

Children living apart from their birth families

The issues dealt with in preceding chapters and the last section – child crime, child abuse, parental separation, step-parent relationships – may all lead, in a minority of cases, to children being looked after away from home under local authority auspices. Coordinated public services for children living away from home were established as one of the less well-known elements of the welfare state, through the Children Act 1948 in Great Britain and the very similar Children and Young Persons Act 1950 in Northern Ireland (Heywood 1978; Murray and Hill 1992; Hendrick 1994; Kelly and Pinkerton 1996). At the heart of this legislation was the duty of local authorities to make decisions based on the perceived interests of children, in other words, official perceptions of need. There were relatively few supportive services for families at this time (apart from child welfare clinics and a small number of day nurseries), so the main decisions were whether or not a child should remain at home. Over the years and particularly since the 1980s there has been a shift to taking more account of both parents' and children's expressed needs and participatory rights. Ideals of partnership and family support have been espoused which may mask tensions between the rights of parents and children.

In the 1960s, various pressures built up in favour of the establishment of integrated, community-based services across the life span. Following legislation covering Scotland in 1968 and England and Wales in 1970, children's departments were effectively absorbed into Social Work and Social Services Departments respectively (Packman 1981; Murphy 1993). Over the following two decades, these have been responsible for local authority provision for separated children (apart from special boarding schools and hospitals). In the 1990s the organisation of services has been affected by both local government reorganisation and internal restructuring (Kendrick 1995). Northern Ireland has a distinct system whereby social services have been incorporated within Health Boards and, more recently, Health Trusts (McColgan 1995).

The profile of children living away from home has changed markedly over the last 20 years (Rowe *et al.* 1989; Bebbington and Miles, 1989; Charles *et al.* 1992; Barn 1993). Amongst the key features are:

- an overall reduction in numbers away from home
- a rise in the proportion of teenagers
- an increased percentage of children in foster care
- over-representation of children of mixed ethnic parentage
- fewer babies adopted, but more older children
- fewer disabled children staying long-term in hospitals and residential care.

The needs of children in foster and residential care

The great majority of children living away from home in public care are in foster homes, children's homes (residential units) and residential schools. Young people who are particularly challenging may be confined in secure accommodation (Kelly 1992; Harris and Timms 1993). Local authorities also register and supervise private foster homes and residential establishments. Certain issues arise whatever the placement, but some are specific to the living situation.

Children away from home share many needs with all other children (e.g. for food, protection), though some of these may take on a special significance. There are also additional needs (Fahlberg 1994; Palmer 1995):

- to handle the effects of separation from familiar people and surroundings
- to manage two or more living situations and sets of relationships i.e. family home and placement(s)
- to establish a sense of identity which takes account of discontinuity and the reasons for separation (for example, rejection, ill-treatment).

A number of children also need to recover from the impact of abuse or ill-treatment by family members or others. It has also become common to refer to some children as having 'special needs' on account of emotional/behaviour problems, learning difficulties or physical disability (see Chapter 3). Afro-Caribbean and Asian children often have to deal with being brought up by white carers in mainly white communities. This generally means that the families are not well equipped to be sensitive to their cultural or identity needs, nor to tackle effectively experiences of racism (Barn 1993). It is important that siblings are not treated just as a 'pair' or 'group', but that their differing needs and separate identities are respected (Kosonen 1994; Hindle 1995).

Typically children who have longer care careers experience a number of moves (Department of Health 1991). These changes of home require further emotional and social adjustments, make continuity of schooling and health care difficult to achieve and may interfere with family contacts (Palmer 1995). Social workers and carers have developed a range of techniques to help meet children's needs for continuity and identity when a move is necessary (Redgrave 1987; Ryan and Walker 1993; Fahlberg 1994). These include direct work with children such as:

- careful preparation for moves with full explanations
- assisting children to develop positive interaction cycles (see Chapter 1)
- life-story work: that is, helping children to make sense of their past through discussion, visits, drawings, photos and so on.

Downes (1992) applied attachment theory to the fostering of young people and suggested that carers' approach should match the young person's needs for closeness or distance, support or autonomy. These needs are linked to insecure attachment patterns resulting from earlier family relationships:

1 *Anxious attachment* – a young person needs constant support and reassurance, especially early on in stressful encounters.
   Suggested response – frequent accompanying and nurturance.
2 *Hostile, ambivalent attachment* – a young person oscillates, sometimes wanting closeness and support, then rejecting it. Tendency to go missing.
   Suggested response – setting limits, consistency, feedback on consequences, avoiding personal reproach.
3 *Emotional detachment* – a young person appears competent and self-sufficient, lacks and resists intimacy.

Suggested response – careful adjustment to the young person's own cues, acceptance of minimal emotional rewards for carers.

How well are children's needs met?

Various scandals from the late 1980s onwards highlighted that children removed from home avowedly for their own benefit ran the risk of physical, emotional or sexual ill-treatment at the hands of carers (Berridge 1996a). These were extreme and exceptional cases, but evidence has accumulated over the years that caring and skilful work is required if out-of-home care is to alleviate and not compound the difficulties which prompted intervention.

Many evaluations have been carried out of the success of public care placements in meeting children's needs. These chiefly assessed children's progress on dimensions related to expert definitions of need. The samples were sometimes compared with 'average children' or children from similar backgrounds. Interpreting the findings is not easy (Parker *et al.* 1991; Ward 1995; Hill *et al.* 1996). For example:

- different criteria can lead to different conclusions
- it may be unclear which elements of the experience have contributed to any particular outcome
- it is difficult to distinguish between problems resulting from earlier experiences and from placement
- short-term and longer-term effects may differ.

The majority of children placed away from home do return home within a matter of days, weeks or months (Rowe *et al.* 1989; Bullock *et al.* 1993a). Surprisingly little is known about the consequences of such short-term care, but the effects are often positive (Triseliotis *et al.* 1995). However, research has identified a number of common consequences when children are away for longer than a few months and these run counter to their needs for continuity, security and identity (Packman *et al.* 1986; Millham *et al.* 1986; Department of Health 1991a). They include high likelihood of:

- unplanned and ill-prepared admission
- several moves of home
- several moves of school
- infrequent or no parental contact
- reduced contact with other significant family members
- changes in household composition or roles at home which make it harder for children to fit back in
- other children coming and going in the placement
- staff changes (in residential care).

Of course some children do receive stable care in the same setting and are able to maintain positive links with their original family and community. When children return home after longer periods, especially when there has been a statutory order indicating significant difficulties of one kind or another, risks are high of further ill-treatment or periods away from home (Farmer and Parker 1991).

In view of the discontinuities which are common experiences, it is not surprising that many of the global appraisals have suggested that longer-term placements away from home often leave children disadvantaged. This may be as much due to prior circumstances and separation effects as the particulars of the placement, but at the very least, care careers often do not compensate for these. Most studies have shown that *on average* children in care have more behaviour, relationship and educational difficulties than their peers (Wolkind 1988), though they may well make progress from a poor start (Triseliotis *et al.* 1995). Those who leave care at the age of 16 to 18 often encounter major difficulties of poverty, isolation and depression (Stein and Carey 1986; Garnett 1992; Biehal *et al.* 1995). Such people often lack family support, educational qualifications and social skills, yet are expected to cope with the transition to adulthood sooner than nearly all of their agemates. It appears that people brought up in care who do well as adults have usually had a close supportive relationship with at least one carer and/or have been able to form a stable partnership (Mann 1984; Quinton and Rutter 1988).

When allowance is made for the fact that residential care caters for more older children with more serious difficulties, there appears to be little difference between residential and foster care in overall outcomes (Berridge 1996b). It is now generally accepted that residential care in the UK is not suited for younger children's long-term upbringing, but can be helpful to older children. Recent evidence suggests that residential schools can be particularly successful, because of the combination of care with education on the same premises and the systematic sharing of care with the child's family (Grimshaw with Berridge 1994; Triseliotis *et al.* 1995). Placements with long-term foster families are subject to high rates of breakdown (Triseliotis 1989), but when they do last, the children generally feel accepted and well integrated (Rowe *et al.* 1984).

Children's expressed needs

We mostly know about the views of older children – partly because adults may assume they are easier to ask and partly because they tend to be more articulate in public. There are various national and local organisations of young people in care (see below) which have given them a voice, whilst a small number of researchers have spoken with children.

Preparation for a move is vital and in the early stages children need to feel they are wanted as individuals. Even brief 'respite' stays for families with disabled children or who want relief from a crisis can cause acute homesickness (Stalker 1990, 1995). On arrival it is important to sort out misconceptions (for example, that the child does not have to share a bed). One seven-year-old was relieved when the foster carer asked about and took account of his food preferences (Aldgate *et al.* 1996).

Several recent studies have reached similar conclusions about young peoples' wishes as regards alternative care (Buchanan *et al.* 1993; Fletcher 1993; Triseliotis *et al.* 1995; Freeman *et al.* 1996). Most young people affirm the need for siblings to stay together when apart from their parents. A common demand is for greater opportunities and choices to maintain social network relationships. The majority are satisfied with existing levels of contact with their parents, but up to one in three would like more frequent contact. Obstacles to contact include:

• agency factors (not being allowed contact; supervised contact)
• practical factors (distance and cost)
• family factors (such as step-parent's hostility).

Some teenagers resent restrictions placed on access to their families, whether for their own protection or as sanctions for unacceptable behaviour. They also criticise social workers for undervaluing the significance to them of knowing what is going on at home. Conversely, others dislike pressure to see their family. Many would like more contact with friends and point to the difficulties of sustaining friendships because of distance and moves (Triseliotis *et al.* 1995).

A recent study of children in foster care highlighted their need for continuity (McAuley 1996). This revealed the intense feelings and loyalties foster children retained towards their birth parents, of which carers and social workers were often little aware. Two children in different families said they thought or dreamed every day about a parent who had died more than a year previously. Others worried greatly about how their parents were getting on or relived in their minds happy family events. Besides missing family, over half expressed sadness or confusion about leaving their previous schools.

Teenagers looked after away from home value three main things from carers (Triseliotis et al. 1995):

• *belonging and trust*: for example, feeling part of a foster family, being listened to and understood by foster carers or residential staff
• *autonomy*: being able to suit themselves about when to come in, see friends and so on
• *helping them change*: for example, to return to school after a period of truancy.

Most appreciate the opportunity to discuss personal issues, including family relationships and the effects of separation, but only if they feel the carers or social workers are genuinely interested and concerned (Hill 1995b). The issues do not have to be addressed explicitly or constantly however:

I like to be by myself and think a bit, when I'm sad. She [her carer] knows though.   (Rosi, aged nine, quoted in Aldgate *et al.* 1996: 154)

When good relationships are established and the need for trust is satisfied, young people are willing to modify their behaviour in response to guidance:

I've kept out of trouble, off the glue.

I enjoyed their company (foster family) and I listened to them and followed their advice. They kind of helped me to mature more.

(Quoted in Triseliotis *et al.* 1995: 173, 188)

I started to go back to school, did my exams, went to college. If I was at home I wouldn't have done any of that. (Quoted in Sinclair and Gibbs 1996: 284)

Young people in residential care like to have well-kept but discreet physical surroundings. They resent stigmatising signs of institutional-isation, such as bulk buying or 'council' vehicles. Negative public atti-tudes mean that often the need for respect goes unmet:

When you say you are in a children's home, people think you are a tramp or something.

. . . lots of people feel sorry for you. I hate that feeling.

(Quoted in Buchanan 1995: 692)

Privacy is a major issue. Children want space to be alone, quietness for homework, private storage space, being able to phone without being overheard by staff (Fletcher 1993; Kahan 1994; Freeman *et al.* 1996). Many children want action taken to stop bullying or abuse (Sinclair and Gibbs 1996).

The rights of children living away from their parental homes

Children subject to public intervention should continue to have the same basic entitlements as those brought up by their families, including the right to love, good-quality care, appropriate education and continu-ity of experiences and relationships. Triseliotis (1983) also highlighted the importance of having an understanding of personal history and of a sense of belonging. Dennington and Pitts (1991) outlined a set of additional rights. These include:

- a personalised response to needs and difficulties
- access to friends and trusted family members
- having views listened to and taken account of
- being involved in key decisions.

British child-care policy and practice has placed increased emphasis on attending to children's views. The duty to take account of children's wishes was included in the Social Work (Scotland) Act 1968 and the Children Act 1975. More recent legislation affirmed the requirement to ascertain children's wishes and feelings, and give due consideration to their views when making any decision. However the 'child's view is just one amongst numerous parties and it is left open as to how the various views and interests are weighed' (Lyon and Parton 1995: 42). There is also a necessary qualification that the child's influence depends on age and understanding. This may mean that professionals downplay the views of younger or less able children. The UN Convention includes rights to express an opinion and to have that taken into account (Article 12); to information and freedom of expression (13); to privacy (16) and to periodic review of placement (25).

Choices and decision-making

Some children enter foster or residential care reluctantly, especially if this happens as a result of a legal order. The majority, however, see it as a positive move, although some only reach this view as time goes by (Triseliotis *et al.* 1995; Kufeldt *et al.* 1996). Many young people have felt they had little choice about *where* they go. Some wanted more choices about placements, though others were fatalistic, recognising that there are usually few or no alternatives (Buchanan *et al.* 1993; Triseliotis *et al.* 1995). Some moves occur with minimal warning let alone consultation:

One time I got five minutes' notice – it was scary stuff I can tell you.

It happened in the night – I didn't know anything about it.

(Quoted in Fletcher 1993: 58)

When children are consulted, this is much appreciated:

Well I thought 'I have to go, don't I?' But she really did ask what I thought and what I wanted. (Quoted in Aldgate *et al.* 1996: 154)

Substantial numbers of teenagers have a strong preference for residential care and similar numbers prefer foster care, so it is clearly important to have both options available (Cliffe with Berridge 1991; Hill *et al.* 1996b).

The main forum for decision-making concerning children looked after away from home is the child-care review. This is a planning meeting attended by social work personnel, carers and sometimes family members or teachers. (The Scottish children's hearings also encourage more informal discussion with young people and parents than English youth courts do and they hold periodic reviews as well). In recent years, it has become routine rather than exceptional to involve young people in child-care reviews. Some agencies also facilitate preparation, for example by asking youngsters to write down their views or arranging for the chairperson to speak with them beforehand. Perhaps in consequence, the majority of young people asked about reviews have expressed satisfaction about them and say they are listened to. Dissatisfaction mostly centred on feelings of exclusion or disagreement with the outcome. Some have voiced deep resentment when adults discussed their personal lives and made crucial decisions as if the young person was not there (Kendrick and Mapstone 1991; Fletcher 1993). Many young people would like to have more choice about who attends, so that fewer people are involved and only people they know are present (Triseliotis *et al.* 1995; Freeman *et al.* 1996). Some of the reasons why young people feel they are inhibited or ignored were conveyed to Buchanan (1995: 689):

I couldn't really say what I wanted in case I upset my key worker.

When I found out things did not change, I did not bother to go.

They are not speaking to you, they are just telling you what you have to do.

Some young people believe it is important to be assertive, even uncompromising, in order to ensure their view point is responded to. Many recognise the value of having someone to help represent their wishes, but depending on the individual, this may be a parent, a friend, a teacher, a social worker or whoever they have confidence in. It is important not to have a standard figure, but:

Someone you trust and who takes the time to understand your point of view.
(Quoted in Triseliotis *et al.* 1995: 215)

Young people in care have their own national and local organisations for mutual support, advice and advocacy. Increasing numbers of social services departments have established Children's Rights Officer posts, since Leicestershire first did so in 1987. These have had multiple roles, including policy development, establishment of complaints procedures and individual consultation (Rae 1996). Unless these posts are able to influence attitudes and policies more generally, there is a danger that concern about rights may be marginalised. Other staff may feel their own positions threatened or assume that the issues are satisfactorily covered (Ellis and Franklin 1995). Moreover, it appears that most authorities have not developed guidance or training on how to ascertain the wishes of disabled children (Social Services Inspectorate 1994).

The perspectives of foster carers' children

Most foster families include children by birth and sometimes by adoption in addition to the children they foster. These children have a distinctive role and perspective in relation to alternative family care. It might well be supposed that the company and support of children similar in age would be helpful, but one of the most consistent research findings over several decades has been that the presence of children close in age significantly increases the risk of placement breakdown (Trasler 1960; Parker 1966; Berridge and Cleaver 1987; Fenyo *et al.* 1989). It appears that rivalry and tension are more likely to result from this than positive relationships. On the other hand, the presence of other children is often helpful when there is a considerable age gap (Wedge and Mantle 1991).

Amongst children brought together in the same home by fostering, the variety and ambiguity of sibling relationships in general (see Chapter 4) seem to be intensified. Interviews with children in families currently fostering have revealed that most like being part of a foster family and that there are many skills which 'young people are quietly contributing to the fostering process' (Pugh 1996: 35). The main benefits stated were companionship, the pleasure of looking after younger children and helping others who were worse off:

The best thing is when we get babies because I like playing with them.
(Boy, aged 12, quoted in Part 1993: 28)

Partially through the experiences of fostering I believe I have matured and become more responsible.   (Boy, aged 15, quoted in Part 1993: 28)

Every achievement gives me a buzz.   (Quoted in Ames-Reed 1994: 169)

We're so much closer as a family than we would have been otherwise.
(Girl, aged 14, quoted in Pugh 1996: 38)

Amongst the disadvantages described were coping with difficult behaviour, resentment at differential treatment and lack of privacy:

They cry all the time.   (Girl, aged eight)

They get away with things that I would never be allowed to do.
(Girl, aged fifteen)

I don't usually get on with them which isn't much fun having someone in your home that you don't like.   (Girl, aged 11, all quoted in Part 1993: 29–30)

It's upsetting when things vanish from your own room. I then have to lock things away, but feel I shouldn't have to.   (Quoted in Cameron 1996: 33)

In one study, three-quarters were mainly positive, but an important minority were extremely negative about the irritation, disruption and lack of privacy and attention (Ames-Reed 1994).

Not uncommonly, separated children confide in their foster siblings before or instead of the foster carers. This can shock children and cause them worries they are ill-prepared for, especially when they are told about sexual abuse or extreme violence:

It's difficult because I don't know what to say to them. It's never happened to me so I don't know how they're feeling. But they're getting it out, so it's helping I suppose.   (Quoted in Cameron 1996: 36)

Birth children in foster families have expressed wishes for more information and preparation, mainly by their parents. They welcome opportunities to share their experiences in groups and would like to be included more in discussions with social workers (Pugh 1996; Cameron 1996). Given the significant contribution they often make to the lives of separated children, it is important that they receive greater recognition and that their rights to privacy and attention are not ignored.

The needs of adopted children

Adopted children share with foster children the fact that they are members of two families, but with adoption all legal ties to birth parents are irrevocably transferred to a new family, except in the rare circumstance when the court order includes maintenance of contact. (The present discussion is not concerned with the distinctive group of children adopted by a parent and step-parent – see, for example, Phillips 1995). Unlike birth parents, both foster carers and adopters have to be approved formally by social work agencies according to professionals' views on their capacities to meet children's needs, although in recent years this has become more of a two-way process in which applicants assess their own strengths and weaknesses and help define which kinds of children they are most suited to adopt. For adopters, judgements are also made about their ability to assist the child in making sense of the reasons why s/he could not be brought up by her/his birth parents and in achieving a coherent, positive identity taking account of a history of dual family membership. By law adopters must be married or single, so cohabiting and gay couples cannot adopt jointly, despite evidence reviewed in Chapter 4 that marital status and sexual orientation have no necessary bearing on the ability to offer love and stability to children (see also Sullivan 1995).

For most of the time since legal adoption was introduced into England and Wales in 1926 and in Scotland in 1930 it has been assumed that all contact with the birth family should and would be severed. Not only has contact been discouraged, but adopted children had no right to their original birth certificate and birth information at all in England and Wales up to the 1980s, though in Scotland that right was available to adult adoptees (Triseliotis 1973). This contrasts with adoptions in many other parts of the world which were 'open', i.e. it was expected or even encouraged that children would maintain contact (O'Collins 1984; France 1990). Open forms of adoption have been normal in several of the traditional cultures of black British families too (Dutt and Sanyal 1991).

Only since the late 1980s has mainstream British adoption practice become more 'open', prompted partly by developments overseas (especially New Zealand) and also because more older children have been adopted (Fratter 1996). Most commonly, ongoing contact is confined to occasional exchanges of information between the adults – both birth and adoptive parents (Argent 1988; Arton and Clark 1996). Regular face-to-face contact occurs in a few cases, however:

She (birth mother) comes round once a month, we ring each other, comes for special things like school plays, and yes she's just like a family friend or maybe a sister I haven't seen for a while.

(Girl, aged 13, quoted in Ryburn 1994: 148)

Proposals to facilitate greater openness by law have been strongly opposed by many adopters and adoptees, who fear this will threaten the security of adoptive families (Paterson with Hill 1994).

According to Kirk (1964; 1981) the key task for adopted children is management of the fact that their biological family and genetic inheritance differ from their social family and its influences. This has several aspects, including the needs to:

- make sense of the reasons why their original parents did not keep them (easily interpreted as rejection – Why did they not want me?)
- clarify what traits, if any, they might inherit – such as appearance, physical or mental illness, 'bad' behaviour
- respond to the feelings and attitudes of the adoptive parents about the birth family
- have a suitable explanation for other people or else keep secret a vital part of identity
- sort out the sense of self involved in having dual family membership
- handle negative stereotypes about adopted children (for example, 'bad blood', only birth children are really 'your own').

Adoptive families vary in their attitudes to communication about the adoption and in their feelings about it. Research suggests it is very important for children's identity and trust to have free and full discussions about the circumstances of their adoption, but it is unhelpful to dwell on it or constantly use it to explain a child's misdemeanours (Brodzinsky 1987; Kaye 1990; Ryburn 1995).

Until the 1980s, nearly all adoptions (other than step-parent adoptions) concerned children adopted in infancy – mainly white, healthy babies. Since then, adoption has diversified, with significant numbers of older children, black children and children with disabilities being adopted (Triseliotis *et al.* 1997). Such children were originally called 'hard to place', since at that time their characteristics did not fit with the wishes of most would-be adopters. However, more open information and recruitment strategies showed that it was possible to locate adopters for these children, so the term 'special needs' became current, in recognition that they required more than basic love and care (for example, mobility aids, medication, ointments, psychological help). For children adopted trans-racially or intercountry (which is usually trans-racial too), there are issues concerned with growing up in a household of a different racial group and with a different culture from the original family (Small 1991). It may also be necessary to come to terms with racism in the country of adoption and apparent indifference in the country of origin (Sjogren 1996).

This all means that a small but increasing proportion of adoptees recall a life prior to adoption. They know what it is like to *become* adopted, whereas those adopted in infancy have experienced only the status of *being* adopted (Hill and Triseliotis 1989). On the one hand, their loyalties to the past and established patterns of behaviour can make adjustment to a new family more difficult. On the other hand, they may feel less stigma. Whereas most people adopted as infants have been conscious that their status is viewed more negatively than that of birth children, older children usually feel positive about belonging permanently to an adoptive family compared with being a foster child or living in a children's home (Hill *et al.* 1989).

How well are the needs of adopted children met?

There are many ways of judging the success of adoptions. These include:

- duration – does the child remain part of the family for life?
- reported satisfactions of adopters and adoptees
- developmental indicators, such as, how well the children do at school, measures of self-esteem, social performance, and so on
- measures of family and community integration
- referrals to specialist services.

Most of the early assessments were inevitably concerned with the outcomes of 'baby adoptions' and only recently has the opportunity arisen to assess significant numbers of placements of older children.

Some cross-sectional studies have found no differences between adopted and non-adopted children's development or adjustment; others have indicated an above-average incidence of behavioural and emotional problems. These have not usually been of a serious nature (Brodzinsky 1987; Kadushin and Martin 1988). Longitudinal surveys which include large numbers of adopted children have consistently shown that the great majority appear to do very well (Seglow *et al.* 1972; Bohman and Sigvardsson 1990). Indeed on most criteria they seem to do significantly better than children with comparable starts in life, because in general the material and social circumstances of adoptive homes are highly favourable. The National Child Development Study cohort revealed adopted persons to have done particularly well educationally at age 23 (Maughan and Pickles 1991).

Similar conclusions have been reached in relation to children placed trans-racially (McRoy 1991a; Simon and Altstein 1992). It also appears that many such children have faced racism, have a weak sense of their ethnic and cultural identity, and have few contacts with other people of similar backgrounds (Gill and Jackson 1983; Dalen and Saetersdal 1987). Thus there is evidence to support both sides of the debate on whether trans-racial adoption is desirable or not, though research findings are not the only considerations (Triseliotis 1991; Triseliotis *et al.* 1997).

Older children, at least up to the age of 11, have a very good chance of integrating happily in adoptive families, although it is likely that early insecurities and school-related difficulties will not disappear altogether (Tizard 1977; Hodges and Tizard 1989). This is also true for children placed internationally after severe early traumas and with the need to learn a new language and culture (Hoksbergen 1986; Verhulst *et al*. 1992). Adoptions which involve continued face-to-face contact with birth relatives can be successful too, although it is probable that careful selection and preparation of adopters is vital (Berry 1991; McRoy 1991b; Fratter *et al*. 1991).

On the other hand, it has become clear that the higher the age of the child at placement, the greater the risk that the adoption will break down (Barth and Berry 1987; O'Hara and Hoggan 1988). Older children have usually had a long history of instability in their lives which makes it hard for them to integrate with a new family at this late stage and they often behave in a challenging way which adopters find hard to cope with. Current attempts to help families in these circumstances apply techniques derived from attachment, behavioural and systems theories (Archer 1996; Roberts 1996).

Howe (1995b; 1996a) found that relationships in the teens and early adulthood described by adoptive parents were greatly affected by children's initial attachment histories. Those placed for adoption as babies or following relatively stable and loving care had few problems later. Children who had been abused or emotionally neglected were challenging in the early years and often had major difficulties in adolescence, though some appeared much more settled by the time they reached their early twenties.

The increased proportions of adoptions which are not straightforward has altered the view that adoptive families want and need to get on with their lives independent of any official contacts. Partly in response to demands from adoptive parents and adult adoptees, post-adoption services have been developed, although their availability is variable. They include allowances, specialist services and self-help initiatives (Hill *et al*. 1989; O'Hara 1991; Phillips and McWilliam 1996).

The rights of adopted children

In the past adoption was often regarded as serving adults' interests – initially to create heirs and later so that childless couples could satisfy their wish to be parents (Benet 1976). Increasingly the child's best interests have become central and now the law in Britain requires that the paramount consideration must be the child's welfare, not only at the time of adoption but into adulthood. Some argue, though, that the very concept of adoption runs counter to the rights of children and not to have legal ties with birth parents fully severed. This is linked to social structural analyses arguing that adoption represents a transfer of children from the poor to the better off, for which a better solution would be material and other support for families under stress (Ryburn 1995).

Adoption practices are seen by some to violate certain rights of children. For example the UN Convention includes rights to preserve knowledge of parents, identity, name and family relations (Article 8).

When ratifying the Convention, the UK government interpreted this to mean that 'parents' meant legal parents, so that in the case of adopters this would exclude an entitlement to know about birth parents (Children's Rights Office 1996). Consequently, adopted children have no legal right to know details of their birth families or to seek contact, if they wish. This applies to siblings and other relatives, as well as parents. Only at the age of 16 (Scotland) or 18 (England and Wales) are young people entitled to have access to their original birth certificate and adoption court records (Lambert *et al.* 1990). Adopted children are therefore dependent on the knowledge and discretion of their adoptive parents for their own understanding of their origins. Up to 20 to 30 years ago many adopters did not tell children they were adopted until adolescence or later, often with traumatic consequences (McWhinnie 1967; Raynor 1980). Such secrecy now seems to be a thing of the past, but even when told, children may not understand or integrate the facts of adoption. As with other complex, sensitive matters like divorce or sex education, brief one-off explanations are inadequate. Inhibitions and over-optimism about their abilities to give adequate explanations may mean that adopters fail to realise that communication needs to be repeated, two-way and adjusted to the age of the child (Brodzinsky *et al.* 1984; Hill *et al.* 1989; Ryburn 1995). When children are adopted from abroad, very little background information may be available (Selman and Wells 1996).

Reports to the courts in cases of adoption should convey the wishes of the child, which judges are obliged to take into account according to their age and understanding. However, it seems that communication with children and inclusion of their views in reports are often done in a cursory fashion (Selwyn 1996). Children's consent is required for adoption after the age of twelve in Scotland (McNeill 1986).

One of the arguments against trans-racial adoption is that this is likely to rob children of an accurate, positive and coherent sense of identity (Ahmad 1989, 1990; Banks 1992; Macey 1995). Matching should entail taking careful account of a child's precise cultural heritage and self-image (Banks 1995). In contrast to the Children Act 1989, the government was reluctant to include in the Adoption Bill 1996 a right to have ethnic background taken into account (Ball 1996).

Conclusions

In considering substantial separations from one or both parents, it is important to take a longitudinal perspective. In the majority of cases, the child's household circumstances and companions change more than once, whether it be from birth family to lone-parent household to reconstituted family or from one foster home or residential unit to another. The 'career' of successive transitions in living situation is accompanied by 'psycho-social pathways' which comprise the responses and socio-emotional development of the child (Lewis 1996). Most often separations are distressing and affect the child's relationships, schooling, self-esteem and so on, but recovery occurs sooner or later. With a few exceptions, continuity of contact with parents who live elsewhere is important for children's coping and sense of identity.

Children who experience separation have **needs** for emotional and social support. They also wish to understand as fully as possible what is going on and to be helped to explain this to the outside world in a way which preserves their self-respect. The systems and services which have been set up to deal with parental separation have by and large not been sensitive to such needs. Divorce proceedings and mediation services have not usually been proactive as regards children's welfare, but tended to confirm the status quo. Services for children separated briefly from both parents are usually experienced as helpful, but too often when children have been in care in the longer term, their needs for continuity of personalised care and attention have not been met, whilst educational and health deficits are more likely to be perpetuated than compensated for (Heath *et al.* 1994; Ward 1995).

Children's interests have been embodied in legislation and practice for many years, but only gradually have their participatory **rights** gained ground. Despite piecemeal developments in consulting with young people individually and collectively, children's views often remain marginal when critical decisions are made which affect the nature and extent of contact with separated family members, including siblings. A number of elements are necessary for exercising rights in relation to key decisions (Duquette 1992; Triseliotis *et al.* 1993; Lockyer 1994):

1 Procedures for consulting young people.
2 Access to information, skills and processes which enable young people to express themselves well.
3 Decision-making which genuinely takes account of their expressed views.
4 The right to be assisted or represented by a trusted person of their choice.
5 Opportunities for complaint or appeal.

Although these requirements have been documented for separated children, they are applicable to all children – at home, in school and elsewhere.

Suggestions for further reading

Ayalon, O. and Flasher, A. (1993) *Chain Reaction: Children and Divorce*, London: Jessica Kingsley.
Harding, L. F. (1991) *Perspectives in Child Care Policy*, London: Longman.

Hill, M. and Aldgate, J. (eds) (1996) *Child Welfare Services*, London: Jessica Kingsley.

Parkinson, L. (1987) *Separation, Divorce and Families*, London: Macmillan.

Triseliotis, J., Borland, M., Hill, M. and Lambert, L. (1995) *Teenagers and the Social Work Services*, London: HMSO.

Triseliotis, J., Shireman, J. and Hundleby, M. (1997) *Adoption: Theory, Policy and Practice*, London: Cassell.

CHAPTER 12

Children's lives: re-evaluating concepts and policies

Considering how the social science literature is written about children – what it emphasises, what it ignores, its trends and patterns – seems almost as informative as what the literature itself contains. For example, certain topics have an immense and ever-growing literature. The wealth of material on child protection and juvenile delinquency/ young offenders may suggest the difficulties these issues present for adults' concepts of 'childhood', as well as the social concerns they represent. Other topics are written about extensively, but are located within a set literature. For example, a great deal has been written on young people with 'special educational needs', yet rarely does mainstream literature on education include them as a matter of course. In some ways, the segregation in the literature replicates the segregation in reality for many young disabled people. Certain topics are very difficult to locate anywhere in the social science literature. We have, for example, found accessing the direct views of children a particular challenge, especially the views of children under the age of 12.

While a great deal has been written about children, we still know far more about what adults think about children than we do directly from children themselves. Academic traditions have often resulted in the abstraction of children's views and their absorption into qualitative variables, with the accompanying loss of directness and sometimes meaning. This is changing. Certain areas of literature (such as bullying, truancy, juvenile delinquency) are now replete with direct quotations from young people. Sources outside academia – for example, the media or advocacy agencies' publications – were often fruitful for finding the direct views of 'ordinary' young people.

Knowledge about today's 'childhood' has grown substantially in recent years, largely thanks to the continued work of child psychology and the burgeoning sociology of childhood. Both have made their different contributions. Child psychology has the longer tradition, with particular sensitivity to the gradations of maturity/stage as young people develop. The sociology of childhood looks at 'childhood' as a social group. It particularly emphasises children as actors, and not always as 'objects of concern'. As such, it closely parallels – and undoubtedly has been influenced by – the movement for children's rights.

Just as other rights' movements have gathered force in this century (such as feminism, civil rights, disability rights), the calls for children's rights have gained momentum. The United Nations (UN) Convention on the Rights of the Child, since its acceptance by the UN Assembly in 1989, provides a touchstone for many children's rights advocates. The UN Convention's requirement that children's views be given due regard has supported the sociological conclusion that children are active participants in society.

Adults' views of 'childhood' tell us almost as much about the social category of 'adulthood' as they do about 'childhood'. When the sociology of childhood concludes that 'childhood' is defined largely by children's *dependence* on adults, this illuminates the tendency for adults to devalue and fear dependence, and to deny inter-dependence (tendencies much discussed in the disability literature), and to equate 'children' with babies and younger children. When worries are expressed about the faulty socialisation of children – that families, that education, that society is failing to socialise children into worthy citizens – what is most revealed are adults' worries for society and its future, about losing control. The ideology of the family tells us as much about adults' desire and desperate need to find meaning in the parent–child relationship as about children's actual dependence. Definitions of 'childhood' and 'adulthood' are intertwined.

This concluding chapter will bring together the theoretical issues central to this book:

- how 'childhood' is perceived and 'socially constructed'
- notions of children's rights
- ideas about children's needs.

Common and contrasting themes, from the topics covered in this book, will be outlined. While much of academic literature is divided between separate theories and orientations, this book has sought to consider the various merits and deficits of these, and how they can work to create a 'patchwork quilt' depicting children's lives. Such an approach has dangers – some theories or orientations may be seen as incompatible with others, for example – but has potential advantages of avoiding the traditional competition between different viewpoints and considering how most can fill in a certain perspective of children's lives and experiences.

Questions of policy will be addressed: how far can the law deal with children's social realities? How can policy be altered to best meet the needs and rights of children? Finally, we will return to the issue of children's citizenship: can and should children be 'full' citizens?

'Childhood'

Society is fearful and we look inwardly; everything is formalised and schools take on roles they should not need to shoulder. Our children need their minds to be occupied. They need to play with one another and not be locked in rooms with blinking computers and the wallpaper of anodyne antipodean soap operas. They need to be set free to be children again.

(Editorial, *The Scotsman* 28.10.96)

Where should children be? When should they be there? What should they be doing? As with the quotation above, the literature covered in this book has clear messages about how adults think children *should* spend their time, where they *should* be and what they *should* be doing. Children should, for the most part, be in the 'family' or at school. Their education is their primary work – although it is seldom acknowledged as 'real' work, in terms of social or monetary value – and, for those of school age, it is supposed to take up much of their waking day. Children's place is typically in school or at home, and not in the labour market. Children should play, but only in particular ways. Many adults, as the above editorial stated, feel that children should not be playing with 'blinking' computers nor watching soap operas. They should play with each other. They should be set free from the 'real world', to be 'children again'.

'Childhood' is perhaps not so easy to identify as *The Scotsman*'s editorial would suggest. For example, the term 'child' is itself contentious. Under the UN Convention, a child is defined as any human being under the age of 18. Yet in the older age range, say over 15 years, many would resent being called 'children'. The sociology of childhood has widened the conceptual horizons in considering childhood as a social group, but it has not always taken with it sensitivity to differences within the group. Some of the contributions of psychology, for example, have been left behind. These contributions remind us to consider how children may have different lives, different values, different cultures as they develop physically and experientially. Feminist and cultural research remind us to give attention to differences by gender and by cultural or ethnic background. Children can be seen as a social group – but they also have other identities and are members of other groups.

Ecological and network theories bring out the social connectedness of children's lives: that they do live in intersecting relationships with their families, with other children, and with adult members of their communities. What research is available on children's daily lives sug- gests that children can have their own sense of space and time, their own cultures and ways of thinking. For example, children can have very different priorities from those of their parents. In research with 5- to 12-year-olds, children did not replicate concerns adults frequently express (e.g. the dangers of drugs or of environmental hazards). The children were most distressed by personal relationships with their siblings and other children, and what they wanted most from their parents was their time and attention (see Chapter 3). Research on children's play described the competency and richness of children's creative and social lives, as it does the vibrancy and creativity in many areas of youth culture (see Chapter 5). Children are an integral part of communities, providing a considerable amount of adult employment, influencing not only children's or youth cultures but also adults' cultures.

Children may be part of their communities, but their physical access to different parts of their environments may be decreasing. Children are increasingly encouraged to be indoors, as the dangers of the outdoors (abduction, traffic accidents, deviant peer groups, and so on) become more and more feared:

I don't know if the world is more violent than when my parents were younger but my Mum says there were more police walking about then. I'm scared to go out the door really, because I'm scared that I'm being followed.
(Lisa Jackman, 13-year-old, quoted in Grant 1996)

While at times adults deplore the limited freedom of children to explore their environment independently, the priorities of the economy, modern transport and adult society predominate. For example, no serious consideration has been given to restricting car use substantially in the UK, so that children can walk to school without fear of traffic accidents (see Chapter 7).

Girls have often been confined to their homes, in adults' concern to protect (and control?) them. Some girls, though, have long had their own place on the streets and in the neighbourhoods (see Chapter 5). For girls from certain cultural backgrounds, though, venturing out can make them especially vulnerable. For example, young Muslim women reported being the targets for racial harassment outside their homes, but often felt unable to report it to their families for fear they might be blamed for inviting or provoking such attacks (Webster 1996). The adult perception that girls *should* be indoors seems evident in the media hype about girls on the streets being 'gangs' and their supposed violence – despite little evidence that girls feel part of 'gangs', let alone carry out the crimes associated with such a label (see Chapter 9). Children are potential victims if they are outdoors; they are also potential threats.

The perception of children as threats, as potential criminals, has led to suggestions of curfews for children (see Chapter 9). Such suggestions ignore children's rights to use public space. Curfews could 'criminalise' children even before they commit property or violent crimes or could penalise parents already having difficulty in caring for their children. Too little financial commitment has been put into providing recreational and social opportunities that young people actually say they want and considerably more commitment exerted in forbidding those activities some young people find most attractive (such as raves). Children are more easily seen as threats by the state, than as people who are being excluded from, or uncatered for in, recreation, leisure and public space.

Curfews ignore why some children are on the streets in the first place. The idealisation of the family does not recognise that some children may actually find it safer to be on the streets than at home. When young people over 16 are homeless on the street, the government

has insisted that their first option should be to return to their families
– and young people's residual option is financial assistance for shared
accommodation. For some young people (and one can think particularly of young women and/or those who have been abused), shared
accommodation may hardly seem a safer option than the streets. The
funding for homeless hostels, homeless projects and housing benefits is
welcome, but is truly only a bandaid for the young people's situations.
The funding certainly has not 'solved' the homelessness of young people, which appears only to be increasing. It does not address the lack
of suitable, affordable and quality housing for young people and their
lack of employment and other funds to afford housing themselves.
While young people at age 16 can take on employment as 'adults' –
and thus contribute financially to society – they are not recognised as
adults having full claims on society when they are unable to find such
employment (see Chapter 8).

In many respects, 'childhood' is becoming increasingly controlled.
As described above, the perceived risk of children as threats has led
to suggestions such as curfews or increased criminal penalties. Similarly, the perceived risk of children being victimised has led to their
enrolment in adult-supervised activities: after-school clubs, sports activities, holiday schemes. Children are monitored and evaluated in school
and by health services, by a large range of professionals (from psychologists to health visitors to teachers). Some countervailing trends
can be observed. State schools cannot administer corporal punishment
(although periodically strong calls are made to reintroduce it, and certain
independent schools have never ceased). Children's participation has
been encouraged in certain areas, such as residential care and peer education. But, compared to any other social group, children do seem to be
the most governed, as social control increases both by overt physical
means and more covert psycho-sociological ones.

Perhaps part of the 'governance' of children comes from fears that
they are 'out of control'. For example, in Chapter 3 we describe how
young people's access to modern technology and media provides a
means of socialising them that is increasingly out of the control of three
traditional socialising agents (parents, schools and community). The
adult reaction most often seeks to restrict access to such technology,
through various regulatory and physical means of censorship aimed at
children. The reaction does not acknowledge that the modern technology increasingly cannot be controlled successfully in this way. Rather
than seeking to give children the tools to deal with the new technology – through media awareness, through sex education, through opportunities to discuss their reactions – the prevalent approach is to try and
protect a 'childhood' that is increasingly unable to be so protected. It
ignores the competencies of many young people in using technology in
ways many adults find difficult to do. In such ways, adults can be seen
to be denying the fact that many children already are active participants
in an increasingly globalised society.

To be socialised into a 'good citizen' is a task commonly ascribed to childhood in the academic literature and policy documents. In this way, children are typically seen as 'human becomings', that is, valued for what they will be and do in the future rather than for their current selves and contributions. At times, this may provide them with greater protection and provision. For example, Allen (1996) disagreed with the growing criminal policy orientation towards punishing children if they offend, and suggested a more positive approach. His reasoning was based on children's greater malleability:

... as human beings who have not yet completed their growth and development to adulthood, the prospects for influencing children to change for the better are much greater than for adults and the mechanisms for bringing about that change – in families, schools and communities – having more influence than they do with adults. (Allen 1996: 12)

At the same time, Allen's particular phrasing brings home the extent of social control over children. Greater protection can mean greater control.

A less protective approach can be found in the concept of 'careers'. While this sometimes still has overtones of children as 'human becomings', the concept also has associations with adult employment careers. The notion of career thus brings with it ideas of transition and change along with underlying continuity of the individual. It has been increasingly applied to various areas of children's lives, giving recognition to the pasts and futures of young people: so that the concept of a 'care career' for young people 'looked after' by local authorities recognises that many experience a sequence of living situations which pose emotional, social and identity challenges; the concept of a 'delinquent career' helps illuminate certain turning points where services might try to influence young people to desist from offending. It could be usefully applied to other areas of children's lives, as suggested by Farrington (1993), such as bullying. The concept of careers helps adults not just to see isolated incidents in children's lives, but to see possible connections between past and present events.

But the concept of careers has not often been used to help adults perceive the 'whole child'. So while researchers might use the concept of a 'delinquent career', little is noted about what children do with the rest of their time. Most young people are not spending all their waking time offending but, as Foster (1990) eloquently described, their offending tends to be a 'moral holiday'. The concept of 'lifestyles' could provide more opportunities to see the 'wholeness' of young people's lives, but remains largely restricted to descriptions of youth (sub)cultures and young people's recreational pursuits.

Services are not particularly good at seeing the 'whole child'. As the chapters before have demonstrated, children can be perceived differently, depending on the labels they have gained or the situation they are in. The differences between child protection and criminal law are often held up as exemplifying such disparities:

Child victims are different people from child offenders. Whereas the former are considered highly vulnerable, and, therefore, in need of protection from the rigours of courtroom examination, the latter are seen in most jurisdictions as quite competent to give evidence in court and to be examined on that evidence. Of course, very young children are exempt from prosecution but the protection offered to child witnesses in sex abuse cases extends to children well beyond the minimum age of criminal responsibility.   (King and Piper 1990: 59)

Children with the same types of symptoms or problems can be found in very different types of services, dependent on their referral careers: services such as mental health, special education or for offenders (see Chapter 7). Mayall (1994b) wrote of the discrepancies between the negotiating style of the family and the authoritarian style of education, to which children must quickly learn to distinguish and adapt their behaviour. Children can become caught between systems:

I've never had any money since New Year. Something to do with my claim, opening a fresh claim, or something like that. Cos I'm 17 they want me to go to Careers. Right, went down to Careers. Careers said, 'No, you don't get a B1 form from here, ya have to go back to DSS [Department of Social Security]'. Went back to DSS, right? 'I get a B1 form from here, don't I?' 'No, you have to go and sign on with Careers'. So I get pissed off then, ya know what I mean? Them sending me back to Careers and Careers sending me back to the DSS. So I fucked it off and came back here. And I've got an interview with them on Thursday . . . but it does your head in.

(Ron, 17-year-old, quoted in Carlen 1996: 92)

The research on numerous issues – on crime, on poverty, on educational attainment, on truancy, on health – shows the correlations, if not connections, between different aspects of children's lives. Yet adults find it difficult not to compartmentalise services into different categories, with their different criteria, their different thresholds, and their different parameters, and thus sometimes fail to address the needs of the 'whole child'. This is not a new finding. The calls for improved inter-agency cooperation and collaboration have been persistent for many years. What is more difficult is finding effective solutions – and solutions that actually meet the needs of the children.

Children's needs – or evaluating risk?

Even the most basic needs – for food, for water safe to drink, for adequate shelter – are not met for some children in the UK today. Doctors report increasing concerns about children's nutrition: not only in terms of poor eating habits, but also of inadequate diets (Jones 1996). In some parts of the UK, households' water can be shut off because of parents' inability to pay for it. One in 13 houses in the UK are 'unfit to live in', and one in four houses in Scotland have damp conditions considered detrimental to health. Of the various age groups, children are one of the poorest by even the most basic definition of absolute poverty (see Chapter 8).

The improvements for some children should not be forgotten. Over the past century, a wide range of services has improved for children, so that infant mortality has gone down, child abuse is a recognised reality, and opportunities for education have widened. Inclusion of disabled children is now a rallying cry, and their potential and competencies are recognised. More attention is being paid to children's cultural, religious and linguistic identities in social services. When children were asked, they felt their needs were generally well met (see Chapter 3). Many teenagers, too, were content with their lot (Hendry *et al.* 1993). Perhaps what may be a more accurate description, particularly over the past two decades, would be the polarisation between the 'haves' and the 'have nots'. Some children's needs may be extremely well met, but others may find it less and less likely. Whether this will change after the 1997 election of the Labour Government remains to be seen.

Increasing numbers of young people are being excluded from school, and their access to quality education is often greatly curtailed if not completely cut off. A disproportionate number of children from Afro-Caribbean and mixed parentage backgrounds are 'looked after' in England and Wales. Adoption remains 'closed', legally tending to sever children's ties to their birth families despite children's potential need to maintain them. Children's needs to socialise and establish peer relationships are typically not treated on the same par as children's needs for adult–child relationships. So, for example, much of the family law legislation is written in relation to children and parents – not directly addressing children's wishes or needs for sibling contact. Refugee children and gypsy and traveller children seem to be penalised because they are not in the 'right place'. The increased limitations on benefits for refugees, and the increased criminalisation of the travelling lifestyle, have seriously detrimental effects on these children's needs.

Traditionally, needs have been the criteria for welfare services and state intervention. Now, access to services is being increasingly determined by the criterion of 'risk' (see discussions in Chapters 7 and 10). Sentences for young offenders are more and more influenced by the perceived 'risk to the community'; child protection agencies make decisions based on the risk of 'significant harm'; health promotion concentrates on potential risks to (mainly future) health. The concept of 'risk' brings with it difficult questions: how does one assess 'risk'? when do concerns step over the threshold to become a 'risk' that requires intervention or action? The 'gatekeepers' to the services must seek to make some calculation of harm and benefits. But these calculations clearly only contain some information about certain 'risks' and not others. For example, in Chapter 10 we reported on the considerable personnel and service resources expended on investigating the risk of 'significant harm' for child protection. Yet many of these resources are typically withdrawn after this crisis decision is made – ignoring the 'risks' children (and their families) still might face.

These queries about the definition of 'risk' are not new. The very same questions could be, and have been, asked about 'needs'. The greatest

distinction between 'risks' and 'needs' may simply be that 'risk' allows
a more targeted or limited approach to state intervention and support
than even the discourse of 'needs'. While all children (and adults, for
that matter) have needs, only some are 'at risk' or 'a risk'. Just as social
security benefits are becoming more means-tested and public housing
is becoming more residual, the discourse of 'risk' may be further lim-
iting who has claims on the welfare state.

When services act in 'children's welfare', a 'child's best interests'
or to 'protect those most at risk', the questioning of such actions
can be muted by these beneficent claims. Services can be seen to not
only serve the needs of their clients or service users. Services can also
be seen to meet the needs of their staff, society or the economy. The
clients or services users may not be the ones at 'risk', but professional
power, staff jobs or society's sense of control, order or safety. Education, for example, can be seen as primarily organised to develop the
potential of each child, but it can also be seen to meet the needs of the
economy (for docile and/or skilled workers); to meet the needs of society
(for model active citizens); or to meet the needs of employed parents
(to 'warehouse' their children). In the past, adoption tended to be a
service for the adoptive parents rather than one for the adopted child.
The reaction to young people who offend can be influenced as much by
the desires for retribution, for punishment, for public safety, to better
to socialise young people, as it is by concern for young people's own
welfare. The 'needs' and 'risk' discourses can put a heavy claim on
a society's resources, but they can also camouflage very disparate
motivations and power relationships. The 'needs' and 'risks' discourses
may well result in dominance of certain professional perspectives. On
the other hand, such discourses link claims to outcomes, so that services can be more open to testing and evaluation than rights' claims,
which can be less clear on the desired outcomes.

Children's rights

Different discourses often frame similar issues and claims in a different
language, which may or may not result in divergent practical implications. For example, a rights discourse can include needs and risks;
needs or risk discourses can also include rights. Similarly, a needs or
risk discourse can include child advocacy and children's agency, just
as a rights discourse can maintain adult power and question children's
agency.

The UN Convention largely does not dispute the dependency concept of childhood. It emphasises the position of children in the 'family',
the primary responsibility of parents to meet children's needs, and the
primacy of a child's best interests (whatever those may be). The child's
right to have his or her views given due regard is subject to others'
judgement of their 'maturity', and some would say completely subser-

vient to their 'best interests' as defined by adults (see Lücker-Babel 1995). Adults remain the primary advocates for children's rights, just as they are for children's needs. What the UN Convention clearly does is *incorporate* ideas about children's needs, about protecting children from risks and harm, along with ideas about children as social actors.

A discourse that does combine elements of needs, risks and rights might best meet the social and psychological realities of children today. Children may indeed need some protection; they may need to be protected from being fully responsible for directing their lives at times of stress; they may not always know what is in their best interests. What is (potentially) different between the discourses of needs and rights, and rights discourse is emphasis. For example, rights are in danger of being consumed by discourses of need or risk:

> . . . consultations with the child, expressing their wishes, either directly or indirectly, are treated as an addition to the child's assumed needs. Children *need* to be consulted, to express their feelings, and any parent who denies this is failing to recognize the child's needs.
> (King and Piper 1990: 62. Emphasis in original)

Research findings do suggest that children *need* to be listened to (see Chapter 3). A need, however, is not the same as a right. People who make claims in terms of their needs have less power than people who are considered 'rights-holders'. Needs is a discourse about deficiency. Rights is a discourse about equality, dignity and respect. The power relationship suggested by the rights discourse is fundamentally different from that suggested by the discourse on needs. To base children's participation rights on the evaluation of a child's 'needs' risks undermining children's claims to their rights.

The UN Convention is arguably not radical in its limited forays into civil and political rights for children. At its most basic, no mention is made in the UN Convention of children's rights to vote or hold political office. Children's freedom to thought, conscience and religion (Article 14(1)) can easily be overwhelmed by parents' rights (Article 14(2)) and by education's duty to direct and develop a child's respect for the parents' culture, religion and values. How, then, would the issue be resolved of parents who want to send their child to a religious school when the child does not want to go? In seeking to protect children from sexual exploitation, Article 19 can lead to denial of a young person's own sexuality (Ennew 1995). Where the UN Convention can be considered radical is in its insistence on comprehensiveness, that the rights be applied in all areas of a child's life and without discrimination, and its requirement that states put forward 'the maximum extent of their available resources' (Article 4) to meet the rights outlined in the Convention.

In the UK, perhaps the most progress has been made on the rights of children to participation. For example, children 'looked after' by local authorities now regularly attend their care reviews; research is starting to bring the direct views of children to policy makers' attention; parents in Scotland will now have a duty to give 'due regard' to their children's views, when making decisions in relation to parental responsibilities. Some of this progress may be due to the probably mistaken view that such rights are cost-free. Clearly children's recently increased right to legal aid in Scotland could have a considerable cost, and procedures to ascertain children's views (say in court decisions) do have financial implications. At times, the rhetoric of participation is stronger than the reality; in such cases, participation can be nearly cost-free. For example, one 14-year old complained about 'consultation' in school:

We want to be consulted about the running of the school and discuss issues, not just asked for ideas for stupid things like school concerts.
(Quoted in Children's Rights Development Unit (CRDU) 1994: 13)

In this case, the 'consultation' seemed stuck between the third and fourth steps of Hart's participation ladder (see Chapter 2, figure 2.1), with at least four steps to go to the top. The rhetoric of children's participation is easier and cheaper than its effective implementation.

The UK's implementation of the UN Convention is questionable. The UK may even be going backwards in meeting the rights of children to protection and provision. More and more children seem to be in poverty. More and more young people can be found homeless on the street. Large numbers of young people face unemployment and under-employment. The young people quoted in the CRDU (1994) evaluation of the UK's progress have definitive criticisms of adult society's priorities:

There's cuts going on everywhere, like through the Government. Like in the youth service, where are the kids supposed to go if the youth club gets closed down? . . . There's no other youth club in the area, where are they going to go? What are they going to do? They're going to turn to violence. They're going to turn to crime.   (17-year old, quoted p. 181)

It's an ongoing cycle of deprivation; our parents are unemployed, we are unemployed and it will go onto a third generation and a really bad situation of debt and malnutrition.   (17-year old, quoted p. 25)

Social rights, such as the right to an adequate standard of living, may be particularly difficult to claim. It is illuminating that, even in countries where the UN Convention is part of (and above) domestic law, social rights can be the hardest to claim through the courts. The criticism is that social rights are too vague, that they cannot adequately be specified in legal terms. When stated rights contain such discretionary phrases as 'best interests', 'appropriate', or 'necessary', they risk a vagueness and discretion that is incompatible with legal enforcement through the courts.

The rhetorical power of children's rights is strong in many quarters of the UK. It has led to re-conceptualisations of 'children' as social actors in certain areas of policy; it has mobilised many adults to place a greater priority on children. Yet, as the reaction of the UN Committee on the Rights of the Child to the UK's report (1995) demonstrated, there are numerous and serious gaps in meeting children's rights.

Policy on children

The rights' discourse usually entails the individualisation of social problems. In the UK, only individuals can take a case to court, and the American option of 'class action' suits is not even possible. King and Piper (1990) wrote of the 'reductionist nature' of rights in law, which constructs a tight definition of the problem and a limited allowance for the context of the situation to be considered. The approach to young people who offend in English and Welsh law is an example of this individualisation: the problem of offending is increasingly located in the individual child who offends, who then must be subject to punishment. The concept of 'welfare' has been summarised into a checklist for English and Welsh courts, which, as King and Piper (1990) pointed out, contrasts sharply with the wider concepts of social welfare in social policy or the UN Convention. As law is used to deal increasingly with 'social problems', this individualisation of 'social problems' is increasing as well.

Whilst legislation has its limitations, it does provide the *possibility* of making spaces for more holistic considerations. For example, Scottish children's legislation allows for the welfare-based children's hearings and New Zealand's legislation supports the family group conferences. Both of these systems consider the social context of the child beyond the child's reason for referral. At the same time, neither of these examples truly takes on the complete social rights of the child, as neither can make claims to society's resources to address coherently the child's poverty, or the social situation of children in general. In this way, such legislation does continue to individualise the problem, albeit in a slighter wider way than English and Welsh legislation.

Does a rights' discourse, however, only exist as a legal discourse? Rights have become closely tied to law, as the primary means to resolve conflicts and to enforce them. Yet the roots of rights' discourse can be found in philosophy, and thus arguably have a place in moral discourse as well. The rights discourse has permeated our society, and has increasingly been used by groups (such as disabled people) to empower themselves. The discourse has been picked up by services and has influenced some service providers to change their perspectives. For example, children themselves have come together in their own advocacy groups, such as Who Cares? Scotland or Article 12. Children deemed to be 'Gillick' competent can at least now ask for confidential medical advice (although children's right to refuse medical treatment is more questionable). Bullying councils, made up of students, have been organised in some schools. Procedures have been set up in civil courts, for children's views to be heard in certain types of cases which affect them. Some of these changes are possibly cosmetic, but some changes may have made at least some difference. The rhetoric of children's rights did influence the range of new children's legislation across the UK, with new provisions particularly emphasising children as social actors. Whether the new provisions will actually make a difference in children's lives will largely depend on their implementation by adults – but the possibilities exist.

New children's legislation was propelled by other pressures as well. Families have changed in the past decades, with increased diversity and pressures. The legislation in many ways came about due to inquiries and crises, which played a heavy part in altering social work services in the 1980s and 1990s (see Chapter 10). The revised children's legislation sought to address the constant criticisms about lack of inter-agency co-operation, but without the legal mandate to require all agencies to work together (so that the duty to co-operate has already been found wanting in English courts). The principles introduced in the new legislation at times seem stronger on paper than they have worked out in practice. At the same time, perhaps this new children's legislation has been asked to take on too much responsibility for implementing children's rights and reflecting the changing needs and realities for children. Almost all services affect children, and almost all legislation has an influence on children's lives. All legislation and policy must consider the rights of children.

Harding wrote of the 'holes' and 'knots' caused by the range of policies that affect families and their lack of co-ordination:

'Holes' occur where a void is left in the provision of needed care, support or family maintenance because state assistance is withheld on the assumption of family obligations which cannot be enforced, and the result is an *absence* of care/support/maintenance. 'Knots' occur where policies convey contradictory messages and conflicting rewards/penalties, resulting perhaps in a 'no-win' situation where any options may be penalised.

(1996b: 223, emphasis in original)

For many activists, the plethora of 'holes' and 'knots' have led to declarations that greater coordination is needed, that government structures need to take a holistic view of the family. A coherent 'family policy' has been advocated by some, sometimes specifying the need for a ministry, or at least a minister, for the family in central government.

Harding (1996b), however, outlined major reservations to such solutions. Greater coherence could result in a narrow and inflexible definition of 'family'. This could lead to increasing familialisation of children, with their needs and rights considered indistinguishable from the family unit. Rather than coherent family policy, children's rights advocates have often suggested the need for coherent children's policy. The use of 'child impact' statements and the principles of the UN Convention itself, could provide ways to 'vet' all legislation and policy and not just those overtly concerned with children. A recent committee report on effective government structures (Hodgkin and Newell 1996) advocated a:

- Minister of State for Children
- senior Cabinet member with a responsibility for children
- Cabinet Office Children's Unit
- Cabinet Committee, or Sub-Committee, for Children or a Standing Inter-Ministerial Group on Children
- House of Commons Select Committee on Children.

The report also advocated establishing a Children's Commissioner as an independent body influential on, but outside, central government. This combination of power within the ruling government and parliament, with the civil service and an 'outside' office independent of party politics, would ensure greater attention is given to children. At the time of going to press, it remained to be seen what the 1997 Labour Government would do.

Children's citizenship

Such government structures may indeed provide more effective policies for children and may truly enhance and support children's rights. But they largely leave with adults the power to recognise rights, the power to make decisions, the power of discretion. Children would not have full civil or political rights. Without these rights, can children truly be considered 'citizens'?

Children can certainly be 'citizens' in the common usage of the term: that is, they can have a right to residence in a country or a right to hold a certain country's passport. But theorisation of citizenship reaches beyond such usage, to consider a citizen's claims to certain rights, the links between citizenship and responsibilities, and the status of a citizen in relation to his or her community (see Chapter 2). At least according to Marshall's theorisation so often referred to in the literature, citizens have civil, political and social rights, they have certain responsibilities, and they have the status of being full members of their communities. By such theorisation, children would not be citizens because they do not have equal civil and political rights with other, adult, citizens. They therefore would then not have the same responsibilities, nor would they have the status of being full members of their communities.

Marshall's theorisation need not be accepted. Perhaps there can be different kinds of citizenship, such as social citizenship, which are not dependent on also being political or civil citizens. While citizenship may have been originally conceptualised around an adult propertied male, concepts change. While much of traditional rights' theory was based on some concept of a rational, 'independent' adult, feminist and disability research has demonstrated the dependency within all human relationships. The analysis of Qvortrup *et al.* (1994) pointed out that children are already a social group *within* our communities, as they contribute their work and play a critical role in our economy.

Maybe children can be considered social citizens with rights to provision and protection, they may be privileged citizens, but in practice they are not full and equal citizens. King (1997) wrote of the paradox:

> . . . giving children rights has the effect of drawing attention to the fact that children cannot be expected to have equal rights to adults. . . . It is the very inequality and the continuation of this inequality between children and adults which gives children, so to speak, a right to rights. Children have rights because they do not have, and cannot be expected to have, full citizen's rights.
>
> (212–13)

Children may indeed by unequal to adults in certain ways. Children may need more protection than most adults, they may have more capabilities of change, and they may be more easily influenced. Giving children the same and equal rights to adults, and their full status as civil, political and social citizenship, might actually ignore children's realities and actively disadvantage them.

This represents the views of most children's rights proponents in the 1990s and the UN Convention on the Rights of the Child. If perspectives on children's rights can be seen on a continuum between those who think children have no rights but only needs, and those who think they should have equal rights to adults, most proponents can be found somewhere mid-way, seeking to find a *balance* between a child's welfare rights and concerns for their 'best interests', and a child's rights to agency and freedom. As adults, we seem only to be at the beginning of our exploration of what 'childhood' and 'children's rights' could mean. We still know little about what such concepts mean to children. How do children conceptualise 'childhood'? How do they conceptualise 'adulthood'? What do they think should be their rights?

In Chapter 9, we cited authors who worried that the typical compromises between justice and welfare approaches to juvenile crime brought together the worst of both approaches rather than creating an ideal combination. Similarly, the balance sought between a child's needs and their rights to agency or freedom may bring together the worst of both orientations, and be inevitably contradictory. The submersion of a child's views into an adult's consideration of their best interests, as discussed earlier in this chapter, could be such an example.

Part of the difficulty may lie in the rights discourse itself. Because rights are typically 'trump cards', reconciling different rights of one individual or between individuals may be impossible. A rights discourse tends to individualise social problems and is strongly connected to law and seeking legal solutions. Ultimately, another more preferable discourse might be found that does not have these disadvantages. But the rights discourse still has a fundamental advantage, which discourses of 'obligation', of 'communities' or of 'needs' do not usually have: it encourages questions to be asked about the power adults have over children. It can recognise that children have competencies and make contributions to their communities, which often go unacknowledged by adults. It illuminates how adult concerns can subordinate those of children and young people, serving only to exclude them from 'mainstream' society.

Adults and children should more openly explore the power relationships between them, and question whether they are justified. It might be worthwhile giving more power to children to make decisions, to decide what their own needs are and actually have some control and some say in how those needs are met. Certainly services for children are likely to be more effective if they are created and evaluated on the basis of their service users' views. The National Commission of Inquiry into the Prevention of Child Abuse surveyed 1,000 children from the ages of eight to 16 (1996), asking them what they would like most to change about adults. Overwhelmingly the children asked for more positive attitudes and behaviour towards children. Eighteen per cent asked for adults 'to listen more', 16 per cent asked for greater understanding and more support and an equal number asked adults to 'be nicer and more friendly', to pay them more attention and to talk to them more. Wherever one stands on children's rights to vote, children's participation and involvement can be expressed in a wide variety of ways, and even young children can express their views clearly.

It would seem naive to think that the results of children's greater participation would bring some utopia. Children, like adults, are diverse. In attitudinal surveys (albeit done by adults), children as a group often tend to be at least as conservative or more so than adults – for example, their support of capital punishment or harsher sentences for people who offend (Furnham and Gunter 1989). But children have viewpoints and they have contributions that are too often ignored.

It is appropriate to end this book where it began: with the words of a young person. Julia Press wrote in the preface:

Children want and need to be heard – this is their right. If adults continue to assume that children don't have valid opinions, children will never be heard. Let's rule out the saying, 'Children should be seen and not heard.' Children should be seen *and* heard.

Suggestions for further reading

Children's Rights Development Unit (CRDU) (1994) *UK Agenda for Children*, London: CRDU.

Hodgkin, R. and Newell, P. (1996) *Effective Government Structures for Children. Report of a Gulbenkian Foundation Inquiry*, London: Gulbenkian Foundation.

King, M. (1997) *A Better World for Children? Explorations in Morality and Authority*, London: Routledge. Draft. Forthcoming.

United Nations Committee on the Rights of the Child (1995) 'Concluding Observations of the Committee on the Rights of the Child: United Kingdom of Great Britain and Northern Ireland', *Consideration of Reports Submitted by State Parties under Article 44 of the Convention*, Eighth Session. CRC/C/15/Add.34.

REFERENCES

Abramovitch, R., Pepler, D. and Corter, C. (1982) 'Patterns of sibling interaction among pre-school children', in M. E. Lamb and B. Sutton-Smith (eds) *Sibling Relationships: Their Nature and Significance Across the Life Span*, Hillsdale (NJ): Lawrence Erlbaum.

Adams, R. (1986) 'Juvenile Justice and Children's and Young People's Rights', in B. Franklin (ed.) *The Rights of Children*, Oxford: Basil Blackwell.

Adams, R. (1991) *Protest by Pupils: Empowerment, Schooling and The State*, London: Falmer Press.

Adler, M., Petch, A. and Tweedie, J. (1989) *Parental Choice and Educational Policy*, Edinburgh: Edinburgh University Press.

Adler, R. M. (1985) *Taking Juvenile Justice Seriously*, Edinburgh: Scottish Academic Press.

Ahmad, B. (1989) 'Child care and ethnic minorities', in B. Kahan (ed.) *Child Care: Research, Policy and Practice*, London: Hodder and Stoughton.

Ahmad, B. (1990) *Black Perspectives in Social Work*, Venture Press: Birmingham.

Ahonnen, R., Kalpio, O., Vaskilampi, T. and Hallia, O. (1996) 'Self-medication among families with children in Jyvaskyla, Finland', in Bush, P. J., Trakas, D. J., Sanz, E. J., Wirsing, R. L., Vaskilampi, T. and Prout, A. (eds) (1996) *Children, Medicines and Culture*, New York: Haworth Press.

Ahrons, C. R. (1980) 'Joint custody arrangements in post divorce families', *Journal of Divorce*, 3 (3): 189–205.

Ainslie, R. C. (1985) *The Psychology of Twinship*, Lincoln: University of Nebraska Press.

Alderson, P. (1990) *Choosing for Children*, Oxford: Oxford University Press.

Alderson, P. (1995) *Listening to Children*, London: Barnardos.

Aldgate, J., Bradley, M. and Hawley, D. (1996) 'Respite accommodation: A case study of partnership under the Children Act 1989', in M. Hill and J. Aldgate (eds) *Child Welfare Services*, London: Jessica Kingsley.

Aldgate, J., Tunstill, J., McBeath, G. and Ozolins, R. (1995) *Implementing Section 17 of the Children Act – the first 18 months,* University of Leicester: Report for the Department of Health.

Aldridge, J. and Becker, S. (1994) *Children who Care*, Loughborough: University of Loughborough.

Aldridge, J. and Becker, S. (1995) 'The rights and wrongs of children who care', in B. Franklin (ed.) *The Handbook of Children's Rights*, London: Routledge.

Allan, G. (1979) *The Sociology of Friendship and Kinship*, London: George Allen & Unwin.

Allatt, P. (1996) 'Conceptualising parenting from the standpoint of children: Relationship and transition in the life course', in J. Brannen and M. O'Brien (eds) *Children in Families*, London: Falmer Press.

Allen, R. (1996) *Children and Crime: Taking Responsibility*, London: IPPR.

Amato, P. R. (1987) 'Children's reactions to parental separation and divorce: The views of children and custodial mothers', *Australian Journal of Social Issues*, **22** (4): 610–23.

Amato, P. R. and Keith, B. (1991) 'Parental divorce and well-being of children: A meta-analysis', *Psychological Bulletin*, **110** (1): 26–46.

Ambert, A-M. (1986) 'Sociology of socialisation: The place of children in North American sociology', in Adler, P. A. and Adler, P. (eds) *Sociological Studies of Children: Volume 7*, Greenwich (Conn.): Jai Press.

Ames-Reed, J. (1994) 'We live here too: Birth children's perspectives on fostering someone with learning disabilities', *Children & Society*, **8** (2): 164–73.

Amin, K. with Oppenheim, C. (1992) *Poverty in Black and White: Deprivation and Ethnic Minorities*, London: Child Poverty Action Group.

Ampofo-Boateng, K. and Thomson, J. A. (1991) 'Children's perception of safety and danger on the road', *British Journal of Psychology*, **82**: 487–505.

Anderson, D. and Dawson, G. (eds) (1986) *Family Portraits*, London: The Social Affairs Unit.

Anderson, E. M. and Clarke, L. (1982) *Disability in Adolescence*, London: Methuen.

Anderson, R., Britton, J., Esmail, A., Hollowell, J. and Strachan, D. (1995) 'Respiratory disease and Sudden Infant Death Syndrome', in Botting, B. (ed.) *The Health of our Children*, London: HMSO.

Anonymous (1990) 'Easing a childhood nightmare', *British Medical Journal*, **301**: 244.

Antonovsky, A. (1987) *Unraveling the Mystery of Health*, San Francisco: Jossey-Bass.

Appleton, P. (1995) 'Young people with disability: aspects of social empowerment', in Cloke, C. and Davies, M. (eds) *Participation and Empowerment in Child Protection*, London: Pitman.

Appleton, P. L. and Minchom, P. E. (1988) 'Models of parent partnership and child development centres'. Paper presented to a conference on *Child Development Centres: Current and Future Trends*, Leeds.

Archard, D. (1993) *Children: Rights and Childhood*, London: Routledge.

Archer, C. (1996) 'Attachment disordered children', in Phillips, R. and McWilliam, E. (eds) *After Adoption*, London: BAAF.

Archer, J. (1992) 'Childhood gender roles: Social context and organisation', in H. McGurk (ed.) *Childhood Social Development*, Hove: Lawrence Erlbaum.

Argent, H. (ed.) (1988) *Keeping the Doors Open: A Review of Post-adoption Services,* London: BAAF.

Argent, H. (1996) 'Children in need: Unaccompanied refugees', *Adoption & Fostering*, **20** (2): 24–9.

Argyle, M. and Henderson, M. (1986) *The Anatomy of Relationships*, Harmondsworth: Penguin.

Ariès, P. (1973) *Centuries of Childhood*, first published 1960. Harmondsworth: Penguin.

Armstrong, D. and Galloway, G. (1994) 'Special educational needs and problem behaviour: making policy in the classroom', in Riddell, S. and Brown, S. (eds) *Special Educational Needs Policy in the 1990s*, London: Routledge.

Armstrong, D. K., Galloway, D. and Tomlinson, S. (1993) 'Assessing Special Educational Needs: the child's contribution', *British Educational Research Journal*, **19** (2): 121–31.

Arnett, J. J. (1995) 'Adolescents' Uses of Media for Self-Socialization', *Journal of Youth and Adolescence*, **24** (5): 519–33.

Aronsson, K. and Rundstrom, B. (1988) 'Child discourse and parental control', *Text*, **8** (3): 159–89.

Arton, K. and Clark, I. (1996) 'Managing open adoption arrangements', in Phillips, R. and McWilliam, E. (eds) *After Adoption*, London: BAAF.

Asher, S. R, and Renshaw, P. D. (1981) 'Children without friends: social knowledge and social skill training', in Asher, S. R. and Gottman, J. M. (eds) *The Development of Children's Friendships*, Cambridge: Cambridge University Press.

Asher, S. R. and Coie, J. D. (eds) (1991) *Peer Rejection in Childhood*, Cambridge: Cambridge University Press.

Ashworth, K., Hill, M. and Walker, R. (1994) 'Patterns of Childhood Poverty: New Challenges for Policy', *Journal of Policy Analysis and Management*, **13** (4): 658–80.

Asquith, S. (1983) 'Justice, retribution and children', in A. Morris and H. Giller (eds) *Providing Criminal Justice for Children*, London: Edward Arnold.

Asquith, S. (ed.) (1993) *Protecting Children, Cleveland to Orkney: More Lessons to Learn*, Edinburgh: SCAFA/NCB.

Asquith, S. (1996) 'Children, crime and society', in M. Hill and J. Aldgate (eds) *Child Welfare Services: Developments in Law, Policy, Practice and Research*, London: Jessica Kingsley.

Audit Commission (1994) *Seen But Not Heard*, London: HMSO.

Audit Commission (1996) *Misspent Youth: Young People and Crime*, London: Audit Commission.

Audit Commission and HMI for Schools (1992) *Getting in on the Act: Provision for Pupils with Special Educational Needs: The National Picture*, London: HMSO.

Avineri, S. and de-Shalit, A. (1992) *Communitarianism and Individualism*, Oxford: Oxford University Press.

Ayalon, O. and Flasher, A. (1993) *Chain Reaction: Children and Divorce*, London: Jessica Kingsley.

Backett, K. C. (1982) *Mothers and Fathers*, London: Macmillan.

Backett, K. C. (1990) 'Image and reality: Health enhancing behaviours in middle class families', *Health Education Journal*, **49** (2): 61–3.

Backett, K. C. (1992) 'Taboos and excesses: lay health moralities in middle class families', *Sociology of Health and Illness*, **14**, 2, 255–73.

Backett, K. C. and Alexander, H. (1991) 'Talking to young children about health: Methods and findings', *Health Education Journal*, **50** (1): 34–8.

Bailleau, F. (1996) 'Social crime prevention: Juvenile delinquency', in S. Asquith (ed.) *Children and Young People in Conflict with the Law*, London: Jessica Kingsley.

Ball, C. (1996) 'Adoption: A service for children?', *Adoption & Fostering*, **20** (2): 27–31.

Banks, M., Bates, I., Breakwell, G., Brynner, J., Emler, N., Jamieson, L. and Roberts, K. (1992) *Careers and Identities*, Milton Keynes: Open University Press.

Banks, N. (1992) 'Techniques for direct identity work with Black children' *Adoption & Fostering*, **16** (3): 19–25.

Banks, N. (1995) 'Children of black mixed parentage their placement needs', *Adoption & Fostering*, **19** (2): 19–24.

Barham, V., Boadway, R., Marchand, M. and Pestieau, P. (1995) 'Education and the poverty trap', *European Economic Review*, **39**: 1257–75.

Barn, R. (1993a) 'Black and white child care careers: a different reality', in Marsh, P. and Triseliotis, J. (eds) *Prevention and Reunification in Child Care,* London: Batsford.

Barn, R. (1993b) *Black Children in the Public Care System*, London: Batsford.

Barnard, M., Forsyth, A. and McKeganey, N. (1996) 'Levels of drug use among a sample of Scottish schoolchildren', *Drugs: education, prevention and policy*, **3** (1): 81–9.

Barry, H. and Paxson, L. N. (1971) 'Infancy and early childhood', *Ethnology*, **16:** 191–230.

Barsh, R. L. (1989) 'The Draft Convention on the Rights of the Child: A Case of Eurocentricism in standard-setting', *Nordic Journal of International Law*, **58**: 24–34.

Barth, R. P. and Berry, M. (1987) 'Outcomes of welfare services under permanency planning', *Social Service Review*, **61** (1): 71–90.

Baskett, L. M. (1984) 'Ordinal differences in children's family interactions', *Developmental Psychology*, **20** (6): 1026–31.

Battitstelli, P. and Farneti, A. (1991) 'Grandchildren's images of their grandparents: A psychodynamic perspective', in Smith, P. K. (ed.) *The Psychology of Grandparenthood*, London: Routledge.

Beail, N. and McGuire, J. (eds) (1982) *Fathers – Psychological Perspectives*, London: Junction Books.

Bebbington, A. and Miles, J. (1989) 'The background of children who enter Local Authority Care', *British Journal of Social Work*, **19** (5): 349–68.

Beck, U. (1992) *Risk Society*, London: Sage.

Becker, J. M. T. (1977) 'A learning analysis of the development of peer-oriented behaviour in nine month infants', *Developmental Psychology*, **13** (5): 481–91.

Becker, J. V. (1991) 'Working with perpetrators', in K. Murray and D. Gough (eds) *Intervening in Child Sexual Abuse*, Edinburgh: Scottish Academic Press.

Becker, S. and MacPherson, S. (1988) *Public Issues and Private Pain*, London: Social Services Insight.

Bee, H. (1995) *The Developing Child*, New York: HarperCollins.

Beijing Rules (1985) See United Nations (1985).

Bell, A. and Gibson, P. (1991) 'Tackling the Dilemmas for policy and practice in justice systems divided by age', in T. Booth (ed.) *Juvenile Justice in the New Europe*, Social Services Monographs: Research in Practice, Sheffield: University of Sheffield, Joint Unit for Social Services Research, pp. 97–104.

Bell, C., Conroy, S. and Gibbons, J. (1995) *Operating the Child Protection System*, London: HMSO.

Bell, R. Q. (1970) 'A reinterpretation of the direction of effects in studies of child socialisation', in K. Danziger (ed.) *Socialisation*, Harmondsworth: Penguin.

Belle, D. (1989) *Children's Social Networks and Social Supports*, New York: John Wiley.

Belsky, J. (1984) 'The determinants of parenting: A process model', *Child Development*, **55**: 83–95.

Belson, P. (1993) 'The care of children in hospital', in G. Pugh (ed.) *30 Years of Change for Children*, London: National Children's Bureau.

Benedict, R. (1935) *Patterns of Culture*, London: Routledge & Kegan Paul.

Benet, M. (1976) *The Challenge of Adoption*, London: Jonathan Cape.

Bengston, V. L. and Robertson, J. F. (eds) (1985) *Grandparenthood*, Beverley Hills: Sage.

Bennathan, M. (1992) 'The Care and Education of Troubled Children' *Therapeutic Care and Education* **1** (1): 37–49.

Bennet, D. L. (1985) 'Young people and their health needs', *Seminars in Adolescent Medicine*, **1** (1): 1–14.

Bennett, L. (1991) 'Adolescent girls' experience of witnessing marital violence: a phenomenological study', *Journal of Advanced Nursing*, **16**: 431–38.

Bennett, L. and Westera, D. (1994) 'The primacy of relationships for teens: Issues and responses', *Community Health*, **17** (3): 60–9.

Bentham, J. (1970) 'Anarchical fallacies', in A. I. Melden (ed.) *Human Rights*, Belmont CA: Wadsworth Publishing Company, Inc.

Berg, M. and Medrich, E. A. (1980) 'Children in four neighbourhoods', *Environment and Behaviour*, **12** (3): 320–48.

Berger, P. and Luckmann, T. (1971) *The Social Construction of Reality*, Harmondsworth: Penguin.

Berndt, T. J. (1986) 'Children's comments about their friendships', in M. Perlmutter (ed.) *Cognitive Perspectives on Children's Social and Behavioural Development*, Hillsdale (NJ): Lawrence Erlbaum.

Berndt, T. J. and Bulleit, T. N. (1985) 'Effects of sibling relationships on pre-schoolers' behaviour at home and at school', *Developmental Psychology*, **21** (5): 761–67.

Bernheimer, L. P. (1986) 'The use of qualitative methodology in child health research', *Child Health Care*, **14** (4): 224–32.

Berridge, D. (1994) 'Foster and residential care reassessed: A research perspective', *Children & Society*, **8** (2): 132–50.

Berridge, D. (1995) 'Families in need: crisis and responsibility', in H. Dean (ed.) *Parents' Duties, Children's Debts*, Aldershot: Arena.

Berridge, D. (1996a) 'A successful partnership: Child care research in England', *Community Alternatives*, **7** (2): 99–108.

Berridge, D. (1996b) 'Residential child care in England and Wales: The inquiries and after', in M. Hill and J. Aldgate (eds) *Child Welfare Services*, London: Jessica Kingsley.

Berridge, D. (1996c) *Foster Care: A Research Review*, London: HMSO.

Berridge, D. and Cleaver, H. (1987) *Foster Home Breakdown*, Oxford: Basic Blackwell.

Berry, M. (1991) 'The effects of open adoption on biological and adoptive parents and the children: The arguments and the evidence', *Child Welfare*, **70** (6): 637–51.

Berti, A. E. and Bombi, A. S. (1988) *The Child's Construction of Economics*, Cambridge, Cambridge University Press.

Beveridge, S. (1993) *Special Educational Needs in Schools*, London: Routledge.

Bibace, R. and Walsh, M. (1980) 'Development of children's concepts of illness', *Pediatrics*, **66** (6): 912–17.

Biehal, N., Clayden, J., Stein, M. and Wade, J. (1995) *Moving On: Young People and Leaving Care Schemes*, London: HMSO.

Bigelow, B. J. and La Gaipa, J. J. (1980) 'The development of friendship values and choice', in Foot, H. C., Chapman, A. J. and Smith, J. R. (eds) *Friendship and Social Relations in Children*, Chichester: John Wiley.

Bigelow, B. J., Tesson, G. and Lewko, J. H. (1996) *Learning the Rules*, New York: Guilford Press.

Billis, D. and Harris, M. (1996) *Voluntary Agencies*, London: Macmillan.

Binns, D. and Mars, G. (1984) 'Family, community and unemployment: A study in change', *Sociological Review*, **32**: 662–95.

Birchall, E. with Hallett, C. (1995) *Working Together in Child Protection*, London: HMSO.

Björklid, P. (1985) 'Children's outdoor environment from the perspectives of environmental and developmental psychology', in Gärling, T. and Valsiner, J. (eds) *Children within Environments*, New York: Plenum Press.

Black, D. (1990) 'What do children need from parents', *Adoption & Fostering*, **14** (1): 43–51.

Black, J. (1985) *The New Paediatrics: Child Health in Ethnic Minorities*, London: British Medical Journal.

Blatchford, P., Creeser, R. and Mooney, A. (1991) 'Playground games and playtime: the children's view', in Woodhead, M., Light, P. and Carr, R. (eds) *Growing up in a Changing Society*, London: Routledge.

Blaxter, M. and Paterson, E. (1982) *Mothers and Daughters*, London: Heinemann.

Blom-Cooper, L. (1986) *A Child in Trust*, London: L. B. Brent.

Bluebond-Langner, M. (1978) *The Private Worlds of Dying Children*, Princeton, New Jersey: Princeton University Press.

Bluebond-Langner, M. (1991) 'Living with cystic fibrosis: The well sibling's perspective', *Medical Anthropology Quarterly*, **5** (2): 133–52.

Blyth, E. and Milner, J. (1993) 'Exclusion from school: A first step in exclusion from society', *Children & Society*, **7** (3): 255–68.

Blyth, E. and Milner, J. (1994) 'Exclusion from school and victim-blaming', *Oxford Review of Education*, **20** (3): 293–306.

Boer, F. (1990) *Sibling Relationships in Middle Childhood*, Leiden: DSWO Press.

Boëthius, U. (1995) 'Youth, the media and moral panics', in J. Fornäs and G. Bolin (eds) *Youth Culture in Late Modernity*, London: Sage.

Bohman, M. and Sigvardsson, S. (1990) 'Outcome in adoption: Lessons from longitudinal studies', in Brodzinsky, D. and Schechter, M. (eds) *The Psychology of Adoption*, Oxford: Oxford University Press.

Borland, M. and Hill, M. (1997) 'Teenagers in Britain: Empowered or embattled', *Youth & Policy*, **55**: 56–68.

Borland, M., Brown, J., Hill, M. and Buist, M. (1996) *Parenting in Middle Childhood*, Glasgow: Report to Health Education Board for Scotland.

Borland, M., Laybourn, A., Hill, M. and Brown, J. (forthcoming in 1997) *Middle Childhood*, London: Jessica Kingsley.

Borthwick, S. and Hutchinson, B. (1996) 'The Confidential Doctor system: An appraisal', in Batty, D. and Cullen, D. (eds) *Child Protection: The Therapeutic Option*, London: BAAF.

Boswell, G. R. (1996) 'The needs of children who commit serious offences', *Health and Social Care in the Community*, **4** (1): 21–29.

Boswell, J. (1991) *The Kindness of Strangers*, Harmondsworth: Penguin.

Bott, E. (1971) *Family and Social Network*, London: Tavistock.

Botting, B. (1995) *The Health of Our Children*, London: HMSO.

Botting, B. and Crawley, R. (1995) 'Trends and patterns in childhood mortality and morbidity', in Botting, B. (ed.) *The Health of our Children*, London: HMSO.

Boulton, M. (1995) 'Patterns of bully/victim problems in mixed race groups of children', *Social Development*, **4** (3): 277–93.

Boulton, M. J. (1992) 'Participation in playground activities at middle school', *Educational Research*, **34** (3): 167–82.

Boushel, M. (1994) 'The protective environment of children: towards a framework for anti-oppressive, cross-cultural and cross-national understanding', *British Journal of Social Work*, **24**: 173–90.

Boushel, M. and Lebacq, M. (1992) 'Towards empowerment in child protection work', *Children & Society*, **6** (1): 38–50.

Bowlby, J. (1956) *Child Care and the Growth of Love*, Harmondsworth: Penguin.

Bowlby, J. (1969) *Attachment*, Harmondsworth: Penguin.

Bowlby, J. (1973) *Separation*, Harmondsworth: Penguin.

Bowlby, J. (1988) *A Secure Base*, London: Routledge.

Bowles, S. and Gintis, H. (1976) *Schooling in Capitalist America*, London: Routledge.

Bradshaw, J. (1972) 'The concept of social need', *New Society*, **19**: 640–43.

Bradshaw, J. (1990) *Child Poverty and Deprivation in the UK*, London: National Children's Bureau.

Braithwaite, J. (1989) *Crime, Shame and Reintegration*, Cambridge: Cambridge University Press.

Braithwaite, J. and Daly, K. (1994) 'Masculinities, violence and communitarian control', in T. Newburn and E. Stanko (eds) *Just Boys Doing Business? Men, Masculinities and Crime*, London: Routledge.

Braithwaite, J. and Mugford, S. (1994) 'Conditions of successful reintegration ceremonies. dealing with juvenile offenders', *British Journal of Criminology*, **34** (2): 139–71.

Brandon, M. (1996) 'Attachment in child protection assessment: Implications for helping', in Howe, D. (1996) *Attachment Theory and Child and Family Social Work*, Aldershot: Avebury.

Brannen, J. (1996) 'Discourses of adolescence: Young people's independence and autonomy within families', in J. Brannen and M. O'Brien (eds) *Children in Families*, London: Falmer Press.

Brannen, J. and Storey, P. (1996) *Child Health in Social Context*, London: Health Education Authority.

Brannen, J., Dodd, D., Oakley, A. and Storey, P. (1994) *Young People: Health and Family Life*, Buckingham: Open University Press.

Bright, J. (1996) 'Preventing youth crime in high crime areas: Towards a strategy', in S. Asquith (ed.) *Children and Young People in Conflict with the Law*, London: Jessica Kingsley.

Brodzinsky, D. M. (1987) 'Adjustment to adoption; A psycho-social perspective', *Clinical Psychology Review*, **7**: 25–47.

Brodzinsky, D. and Schechter, M. (1990) *The Psychology of Adoption*, Oxford: Oxford University Press.

Brodzinsky, D. M., Singer, L. M. and Braff, A. M. (1984) 'Children's understanding of adoption', *Child Development*, **55**: 869–76.

Bronfenbrenner, U. (1979) *The Ecology of Human Development*, Cambridge, Mass.: Harvard University Press.

Brown, J. C. (1992) 'Which way for the family: choices for the 1990s', in N. Manning and R. Page (eds) *Social Policy Review 4*, London: Social Policy Association.

Brown, S. and Riddell, S. (eds) (1992) *Class, Race and Gender in Schools: A New Agenda for Policy and Practice in Scottish Education*, Edinburgh: Scottish Council for Research in Education.

Brown, U. and Tait, L. (1992) *Working Miracles: Experiences of Jobs and Childcare*, Glasgow: Scottish Low Pay Unit.

Browne, K. (1995) 'Child abuse: Defining, understanding, intervening', in Wilson, K. and James, A. (eds) *The Child Protection Handbook*, London: Bailliere Tindall.

Browne, K. and Lynch, M. A. (1995) 'Guessing at the extent of child sexual abuse', *Child Abuse Review*, 4: 79–83.

Bruner, J. (1990) *Acts of Meaning*, Cambridge, Mass.: Harvard University Press.

Bryant, B. K. (1982) 'Sibling relationships in middle childhood', in M. E. Lamb and B. Sutton-Smith (eds) *Sibling Relationships: Their Nature and Significance Across the Life Span*, Hillsdale, NJ: Lawrence Erlbaum.

Buchanan, A. (1993) 'The Dolphin Project: the impact of the Children Act', in C. Cloke and M. Davies (eds) *Participation and Empowerment in Child Protection*, London: Pitman.

Buchanan, A. (1995) 'Young people's views on being looked after in out-of-home-care under the Children Act 1989', *Children and Youth Services Review*, 17, 5/6, 681–96.

Buchanan, C. M., Maccoby, E. E. and Dornbusch, S. M. (1991) 'Caught between parents: Adolescents' experience in divorced homes', *Child Development*, 62: 1008–29.

Buchanan, A., Wheal, A. and Coker, R. (1993) *Answering Back*, (1992) (Dolphin Project), University of Southampton: Department of Social Work Studies.

Bullock, R. (ed.) (1993) 'The United Kingdom', in M. Colton and W. Hellinckx (eds) *Child Care in the EC*, Aldershot: Ashgate.

Bullock, R., Little, M. and Millham, S. (1993a) *Going Home*, Aldershot: Dartmouth.

Bullock, R., Little, M. and Millham, S. (1993b) *Residential Care: A Review of the Research*, London: HMSO.

Burghes, L. (1993) *One-parent Families: Policy Options for the 1990s*, York: Joseph Rowntree Foundation.

Burghes, L. (1996) 'Discontinuities and disruptions in parenting', in J. Brannen and R. Edwards (eds) *Perspectives on Parenting and Childhood: Looking Back and Moving Forward*, London: South Bank University.

Burgoyne, J. and Clark, D. (1984) *Making a Go of It*, London: Routledge & Kegan Paul.

Burgoyne, J., Ormrod, R. and Richards, M. (1987) *Divorce Matters*, Harmondsworth: Penguin.

Burman, E. (1994) *Deconstructing Developmental Psychology*, London: Routledge.

Burman, E. (1996) 'Local, global or globalized? Child development and international child rights legislation', *Childhood*, 3 (1): 45–66.

Burnham, J. B. (1986) *Family Therapy*, London: Tavistock.

Burroughs, S. and Evans, R. (1986) *Play, Language and Socialisation: Perspectives on Adult Roles*, London: Gordon and Breach.

Busfield, J. and Paddon, M. (1977) *Thinking About Children*, Cambridge: Cambridge University Press.

Bush, P. J., Trakas, D. J., Sanz, E. J., Wirsing, R. L., Vaskilampi, T. and Prout, A. (eds) (1996) *Children, Medicines and Culture*, New York: Haworth Press.

Butler, I. and Williamson, H. (1994) *Children Speak: Children, Trauma and Social Work*, London: NSPCC/Longman.

Butler, I. and Williamson, H. (1996) 'Safe? Involving children in child protection', in I. Butler and I. Shaw (eds) *A Case of Neglect? Children's Experiences and the Sociology of Childhood*, Aldershot: Avebury.

Butler-Sloss, E. Lord Justice (1988) *Report of the Inquiry into Child Abuse in Cleveland*, (The Cleveland Report) London: HMSO.

Cadranel, J. A. (1991) 'Paediatrics', in H. Davis and L. Fallowfield (eds) *Counselling and Communication in Health Care*, Chichester: Wiley.

Camara, K. A. and Resnick, G. (1988) 'Interparental conflict and cooperation: Factors affecting children's post-divorce adjustment', in E. M. Hetherington and J. D. Arasteh (eds) *Impact of Divorce, Single Parenting and Stepparenting on Children*, Hillsdale, NJ: Lawrence Erlbaum.

Cameron, S. E. (1996) *Fostering Good Relations*, University of Reading: MA Dissertation.

Campbell, J. D. (1975) 'Illness is a point of view: The development of children's concepts of illness', *Child Development*, **46**: 92–100.

Campbell, T. H. (1977) 'Punishment in juvenile justice', *British Journal of Law and Society*, **4**: 76–86.

Campion, M. J. (1995) *Who's Fit to be a Parent?*, London: Routledge.

Carlen, P. (1996) *Jigsaw – a Political Criminology of Youth Homelessness*, Buckingham: Open University Press.

Carlen, P., Gleeson, D. and Wardhaugh, J. (1992) *Truancy. The Politics of Compulsory Schooling*, Buckingham: Open University Press.

Casey, B. and Smith, D. (1995) *Truancy and Youth Transitions*, England and Wales Youth Cohort Study, London: Policy Studies Institute.

Central Statistical Office (1996) *Social Trends 26*, 1996 Edition, London: HMSO.

Chafel, J. A. (1993) 'Conclusion: Integrating themes about child poverty in search of a solution', in J. A. Chafel (ed.) *Child Poverty and Public Policy*, Washington, DC: The Urban Institute Press.

Chamberlain, R. (1989) *Free Children and Democratic Schools: A Philosophical Study of Liberty and Education*, London: The Falmer Press.

Charles, M., Rashid, S. and Thoburn, J. (1992) 'The placement of black children with permanent new families', *Adoption & Fostering*, **16** (3): 13–18.

Charles, S. and Webb, A. (1986) *The Economic Approach to Social Policy*, Brighton: Wheatsheaf Books.

Chasty, H. and Friel, J. (1993) *Children with Special Needs*, London: Jessica Kingsley.

Chazan, M., Laing, A. F. and Davies, D. (1994) *Emotional and Behavioural Difficulties in Middle Childhood*, London: Falmer Press.

Cheal, D. (1991) *Family and the State of Theory*, Hemel Hempstead: Harvester Wheatsheaf.

Children's Rights Development Unit (CRDU) (1994) *UK Agenda for Children*, London: CRDU.

Children's Rights Office (CRO) (1996) *Building Small Democracies*, London: CRO.

Chiriboga, D. A., Catron, L. S. and associates (1991) *Divorce: Crisis, Challenge or Relief?*, New York: New York University Press.

Christensen, P. H. (1993) 'The social construction of help among Danish children: The intentional act and the actual content', *Sociology of Health and Illness*, **15** (4): 488–502.

Christopherson, J. (1989) 'European child-abuse management systems', in O. Stevenson (ed.) *Child Abuse: Professional Practice and Public Policy*, Hemel Hempstead: Harvester Wheatsheaf.

Cicchetti, D. and Carlson, V. (1989) *Child Maltreatment*, Cambridge: Cambridge University Press.

Claflin, C. J. and Barbarin, O. A. (1991) 'Does "telling" less protect more? Relationships among age, information disclosure and what children with cancer see and feel', *Journal of Pediatric Psychology*, **16** (2): 169–91.

Clark, D. (ed.) (1991) *Marriage, Domestic Life and Social Change*, London: Routledge.

Clarke, J., Hall, S., Jefferson, T. and Roberts, B. (1976) 'Subcultures, cultures and class: a theoretical overview', in S. Hall and T. Jefferson (eds) *Resistance through Rituals: Youth Subcultures in Post-War Britain*, London: Hutchinson.

Clarke, K., Craig, G. and Glendinning, C. (1995) 'Money isn't everything. Fiscal policy and family policy in the Child Support Act', *Social Policy and Administration*, **29** (1): 26–39.

Cleland, A. (1995) 'Legal solutions for children: Comparing Scots Law with other jurisdictions', *Scottish Affairs*, **10**: 6–24.

Cliffe, D. with Berridge, D. (1991) *Closing Children's Homes: An End to Residential Childcare?*, London: National Children's Bureau.

Cloke, C. and Davies, M. (eds) (1995) *Participation and Empowerment in Child Protection*, London: Pitman.

Cloward, R. and Ohlin, E. (1961) *Delinquency and Opportunity*, London: Routledge.

Clulow, C. and Mattinson, J. (1989) *Marriage Inside Out*, Harmondsworth: Penguin.

Clyde, Lord (1992) *Report of the Inquiry into the Removal of Children from Orkney*, Edinburgh: Scottish Office.

Cobbett, S. (1993) *Parent-held Records – Improving Communication Between Parents and Professionals*, Edinburgh: Project Report.

Cochran, M., Larner, D., Riley, D., Gunnarson, L. and Henderson, C. R. (1990) *Extending Families: The Social Networks of Parents and their Children*, Cambridge: Cambridge University Press.

Cockett, M. and Tripp, J. (1996) 'Divorce, mediation and the rights of the child', in John, M. (ed.) *Children in Our Charge: The Child's Right to Resources*, London: Jessica Kingsley.

Cohen, B. and Hagen, O. (1997) *Children's Services: Shaping Up for the Millennium*, Edinburgh: HMSO.

Cohen, D. (1993) *The Development of Play*, London: Routledge.

Cohen, S. (1972) *Folk Devils and Moral Panics: the Creation of the Mods and Rockers*, Oxford: Basil Blackwell.

Coie, J. D. (1991) 'Towards a theory of peer rejection', in S. R. Asher and J. D. Coie (eds) *Peer Rejection in Childhood*, Cambridge: Cambridge University Press.

Coleman, J. (ed.) (1992) *The School Years*, London: Routledge.

Coleman, J. C. and Hendry, L. (1990) *The Nature of Adolescence*, London: Routledge, Chapman and Hall.

Coles, B. (1995) *Youth and Social Policy: Youth Citizenship and Young Careers*, London: UCL Press.

Colin, B. (1996) 'Most important people in the house', *The Scotsman*, 23.10.96.

Collings, W. A., Harris, M. L. and Susman, A. (1995) 'Parenting during Middle Childhood', in M. H. Bornstein (ed.) *Handbook of Parenting: Children and Parenting* Vol. 1, Hillsdale, NJ: Lawrence Erlbaum.

Colton, M., Drury, C. and Williams, M. (1995) 'Children in Need: Definition, Identification and Support', *British Journal of Social Work*, **25**: 711–28.

Commission of the European Communities (1994) *European Social Policy – A Way Forward for the Union*, Com (94) 333. 27th July 1994.

Commission on Children and Violence (1995) *Children and Violence*, London: Calouste Gulbenkian Foundation.

Community Care (1996) 'Families. The Cost of Children', 25–31 January: 31.

Cooper, A., Hetherington, R., Baistow, K., Pitts, J. and Spriggs, A. (1995) *Positive Child Protection: A View from Abroad*, Lyme Regis: Russell House Publishing.

Cooper, D. M. (1993) *Child Abuse Revisited*, Buckingham: Open University Press.

Copeland, I. C. (1994) 'Exclusion From School: The Agenda and the Players', *Education Today*, **44** (4): 13–20.

Coppock, V. (1996) 'Mad, Bad or Misunderstood? A Critical Analysis of State Responses to Children and Young People Whose Behaviour is Defined as "Disturbed" or "Disturbing" ', *Youth & Policy*, **53**: 53–65.

Corby, B. (1993) *Child Abuse: Towards a Knowledge Base*, Buckingham: Open University Press.

Corby, B., Millar, M. and Young, L. (1996) 'Parental participation in child protection work: Rethinking the rhetoric', *British Journal of Social Work*, **26**: 475–92.

Corsaro, W. A. (1981) 'Friendship in a nursery school', in S. R. Asher and J. M. Gottman (eds) *The Development of Children's Friendships*, Cambridge: Cambridge University Press.

Corsaro, W. A. (1992) 'Interpretive reproduction of children's peer cultures', *Social Psychology Quarterly*, **55** (2): 160–77.

Court, D. and Alberman, E. (1988) 'Worlds apart', in Forfar, D. (ed.) *Child Health in a Changing Society*, Oxford: Oxford University Press.

Cox, M. V. (1980) *Are Young Children Egocentric?*, London: Batsford.

Cranston, M. (1967) 'Human Rights, Real and Supposed', in D. D. Raphael (ed.) *Political Theory and the Rights of Man*, London: Macmillan and Co. Ltd.

CRDU *see* Children's Rights Development Unit.

Creighton, S. J. (1995a) 'Patterns and outcomes', in Wilson, K. and James, A. (eds) *The Child Protection Handbook*, London: Bailliere Tindall.

Creighton, S. J. (1995b) 'Fatal child abuse – how preventable is it?', *Child Abuse Review*, **4**: 318–28.

Creighton, S. J. and Russell, N. (1995) *Voices from Childhood*, London: NSPCC.

Cresson, G. and Pitrou, A. (1991) 'The role of the family in creating and maintaining healthy lifestyles', in Badura, B. and Kickbusch, I. (eds) *Health Promotion Research: Towards a new Social Epidemiology*, Copenhagen: WHO.

Crittenden, P. M. (1985) 'Social networks, quality of child-rearing and child development', *Child Development*, **56**: 1299–1313.

Croce, O., Hill, B. and Williams, M. (1996) 'Running Our School', in M. John (ed.) *Children in Charge. The Child's Right to a Fair Hearing*, London: Jessica Kingsley.

Croll, P. and Moses, D. (1985) *One in Five: The Assessment and Incidence of Special Educational Needs*, London: Routledge & Kegan Paul.

Crompton, M. (1995) 'Individual work with children', in Wilson, K. and James, A. (eds) *The Child Protection Handbook*, London: Bailliere Tindall.

Cross, W. E. (1992) *Black Identity: Theory and Practice*, Philadelphia: Temple University Press.

Cruise, K. R., Jacobs, J. E. and Lyons, P. M. (1994) 'Definitions of physical abuse: A preliminary inquiry into children's perceptions', *Behavioural Sciences and the Law*, **12**: 35–48.

Cunningham, H. (1995) *Children and Childhood in Western Society since 1500*, Harlow, Essex: Longman.

Cunningham-Burley, S. and MacLean, U. (1991) 'Dealing with children's illness: mothers' dilemmas', in S. Wyke and J. Hewison (eds) *Child Health Matters*, Milton Keynes: Open University Press.

Dahlberg, G. (ed.) (1981) *Woman the Gatherer*, New Haven: Yale University Press.

Dahlberg, G. (1996) 'Negotiating modern childrearing and family life in Sweden', in J. Brannen and R. Edwards (eds) *Perspectives on Parenting and Childhood: Looking Back and Moving Forward*, London: South Bank University.

Dalen, M. and Saetersdal, B. (1987) 'Transracial adoption in Norway', *Adoption & Fostering*, **11** (4): 44–6.

Dalley, G. (1993) 'Familist ideology and possessive individualism', in A. Beattie, M. Gott, L. Jones and M. Siddell (eds) *Health and Well-being: A Reader*, London: Macmillan.

Dallos, R. (1995) 'Constructing family life: Family belief systems', in J. Muncie, M. Wetherell, R. Dallos and A. Cochrane (eds) *Understanding the Family*, London: Sage.

Dallos, R. and McLaughlin, E. (1993) *Social Problems and the Family*, London: Sage.

Dalrymple, J. and Burke, B. (1995) *Anti-Oppressive Practice*, Buckingham: Open University Press.

Dartington Social Research Unit (1996) *Matching Needs and Services*, Totnes: Dartington Social Research Unit.

Datar, C. (1995) 'Democratising the family', *Indian Journal of Social Work*, **56** (2): 211–24.

Davenport, C., Browne, K. and Palmer, R. (1994) 'Opinions on the traumatizing effects of child sexual abuse: Evidence for consensus', *Child Abuse & Neglect*, **18** (9): 725–38.

David, D. (1994a) 'From poverty to exclusion', *The Courier*, **143**: 41–2.

David, D. (1994b) 'Fighting poverty and exclusion', *The Courier*, **143**: 40.

David, D. (1994c) 'Child Labour. Poverty is not the whole story', *The Courier*, **143**: 56–8.

Davidson, R. (1991) 'Financial assistance from social workers', in R. Davidson and A. Erskine (eds) *Social Work Response to Poverty and Deprivation*, London: Jessica Kingsley.

Deakin, N. (1991) 'Some Limits to Active Citizenship', *Waverley Papers*, Edinburgh: University of Edinburgh.

Dean, H. (1995) 'Paying for children: procreation and financial liability', in H. Dean (ed.) *Parents' Duties, Children's Debts*, Aldershot: Arena.

Delamont, S. (1990) *Sex Roles and The School*, 2nd Edition, London: Routledge.

DeMause, L. (1982) 'The evolution of childhood', in C. Jenks (ed.) *The Sociology of Childhood*, London: Batsford.

Denman, G. and Thorpe, D. (1993) *Family Participation and Patterns of Child Protection in Gwent*, Lancaster: University of Lancaster.

Dennington, J. and Pitts, J. (1991) *Developing Services for Young People in Crisis*, London: Longman.

Dennis, N. and Erdos, G. (1992) *Families Without Fatherhood*, London: IEA Health and Welfare Unit.

Denzin, N. K. (1977) *Childhood Socialisation*, London: Jossey-Bass.

Department for Education (DfE) (1994) *Code of Practice on the Identification and Assessment of Educational Needs*, London: DfE.

Department for Education (DfE) and the Welsh Office (1992) *Choice and Diversity: A New Framework for Schools*, Cm 2021, London: HMSO.

Department for Education and Employment (1996) 'Work-Related Skills and Attitudes for Pupils – Shephard sets out agenda for higher education', Press Release 140/96, 26.4.96.

Department of Health (1991a) *Patterns and Outcomes in Child Placement*, London: HMSO.

Department of Health (1991b) *Guidance on the Children Act 1989*, London: HMSO.

Department of Health (1992) *Health of a Nation*, White Paper, London: HMSO.

Department of Health (1995) *Child Protection: Messages from Research*, London: HMSO.

Department of Health and Social Security (1992) *Child Abuse: A Study of Inquiry Reports*, London: HMSO.

Department of Social Security (DSS) (1995) *Social Security Statistics 1995*, London: HMSO.

Dickens, J. and Watts, J. (1996) 'Developing alternatives to residential care in Romania', *Adoption & Fostering*, **20** (3): 8–13.

Dingwall, R. (1989) 'Some problems about predicting child abuse and neglect', in Stevenson, O. (ed.) *Child Abuse*, Hemel Hempstead: Harvester Wheatsheaf.

Dingwall, R. and Robinson, K. M. (1990) 'Policing the family? Health visiting and the public surveillance of private behaviour', in J. F. Gubrium and S. Sankar (eds) *The Home Care Experience*, Newbury Park: Sage.

Dobash, R., Dobash, R. E. and Gutteridge, S. (1986) *The Imprisonment of Women*, Oxford: Basil Blackwell.

Dobson B., Beardsworth A. and Walker R. (1994) *Diet, Choice and Poverty*, London: Family Policy Studies Centre.

Dodge, K. A., Pettit, G. S., McClaskey, C. L. and Brown, M. M. (1986) 'Social competence in children', *Monographs of the Society for Research in Child Development*, **51** (2).

Donaldson, M. (1978) *Children's Minds*, London: Fontana.

Donzelot, J. (1980) *The Policing of Families*, London: Hutchinson.

Dowler, C. and Calvert, C. (1995) *Nutrition and Diet in Lone Parent Families in London*, London: Family Policy Studies Centre.

Downes, C. (1992) *Separation Revisited*, Aldershot: Ashgate.

Downie, R. S., Fyfe, C. and Tannahill, A. (1990) *Health Promotion: Models and Values*, Oxford: Oxford University Press.

Downs, R. M. and Stea, D. (1977) *Maps in Minds*, New York: Harper and Row.

Doyal, L. and Gough, I. (1991) *A Theory of Human Need*, London: Macmillan.

Draper, G. (1995) 'Cancer', in Botting, B. (ed.) *The Health of our Children*, London: HMSO.

Dreitzel, P. (ed.) (1973) *Childhood and Socialisation*, London: Macmillan.

Duck, S. (ed.) and Gilmour, R. (1981) *Personal Relationships*, London: Academic Press.

Duncan, G., Brooks-Gunn, J. and Klebanov, P. K. (1994) 'Economic Deprivation and Early Childhood Development', *Child Development*, **65**: 296–318.

Dunlop, R. and Burns, A. (1983) 'Adolescents and divorce', *Proceedings of the Australian Family Research Conference*, Melbourne: Australian Institute of Family Studies.

Dunn, J. (1984) *Brothers and Sisters*, London: Fontana.

Dunn, J. (1988) 'Relationships among relationships', in S. Duck (ed.) *Handbook of Personal Relationships*, New York: Wiley.

Dunn, J. (1993) *Young Children's Close Relationships*, London: Sage.

Dunn, J. and Kendrick, C. (1982) *Siblings: Love, Envy and Understanding*, London: Grant McIntyre.

Dunn, J. and Munn, P. (1986) 'Sibling quarrels and maternal intervention: Individual differences in understanding and aggression', *Journal of Child Psychology and Psychiatry*, **27** (5): 583–95.

Dunn, J. and Plomin, R. (1990) *Separate Lives*, New York: Basic Books.

Dunn, K., Ruddock, J. and Cowie, H. (1989) 'Developing group work in the secondary schools' & 'Cooperation and the ideology of individualism in schools', in C. Harber and R. Meighan (eds) *The Democratic School*, Ticknall: Education Now Books.

Dunn, T. (1986) 'The evolution of cultural studies', in D. Punter (ed.) *Introduction to Contemporary Cultural Studies*, London: Longman.

Dunst, C., Trivette, C. and Deal, A. (1988) *Enabling and Empowering Families*, Cambridge (Mass.): Brookline.

Duquette, D. (1992) 'Child protection legal process: Comparing the United States and Great Britain', *University of Pittsburgh Law Review*, **54** (1): 241–94.

Dutt, R. and Sanyal, A. (1991) 'Openness in adoption or open adoption – a black perspective', *Adoption & Fostering*, **15** (4): 111–15.

Dwivedi, K. N. (1996) 'Culture and personality', in K. N. Dwivedi and V. P. Varma (eds) *Meeting the Needs of Ethnic Minority Children*, London: Jessica Kingsley.

Dwivedi, K. N. and Varma, V. P. (1996) *Meeting the Needs of Ethnic Minority Children*, London: Jessica Kingsley.

Dworkin, R. (1978) *Taking Rights Seriously*, 2nd Edition. London: Gerald Duckworth & Co. Ltd.

Dziuba-Leatherman, J., Finkelhor, D. and Asdigian, N. (1995) 'Consulting children about the effectiveness of school-based victimisation prevention programmes', in C. Cloke and M. Davies (eds) *Participation and Empowerment in Child Protection*, London: Pitman.

Ecob, R., McIntyre, S. and West, P. (1993) 'Reporting by parents of long-standing illness in their adolescent children', *Soc. Sci. Med.*, **36** (8): 1017–22.

Editorial (1996) 'Kids stuff', *The Scotsman*, 28.10.96.

Education Committee, House of Commons (1996) *Special Educational Needs: The Working of The Code of Practice and The Tribunal*, Second Report, No. 205, London: HMSO.

Eekelaar, J. (1992) 'The Importance of Thinking that Children Have Rights', *International Journal of Law and the Family*, **6**: 221–35.

Eekelaar, J. (1994) 'The Interests of the Child and the Child's Wishes: The Role of Dynamic Self-Determinism', *International Journal of Law and the Family*, **8**: 42–61.

Eisenberg, A. R. (1988) 'Grandchildren's perspectives on relationships with grandparents: The influence of gender across generations', *Sex Roles*, **19** (3/4): 205–17.

Eiser, C. (1989) 'Children's concepts of illness: Towards an alternative to the "stage" approach', *Psychology and Health*, **3** (1): 93–101.

Eiser, C., Patterson, D. and Eiser, J. R. (1983) 'Children's knowledge of health and illness: implications for health education', *Child: care, health and development*, **9**: 285–92.

Ekeh, P. (1974) *Social Exchange Theory: The Two Traditions*, London: Heinemann.

Elliot, I. R. (1986) *The Family: Change or Continuity*, London: Macmillan.

Ellis, S. and Franklin, A. (1995) 'Children's Rights Officers: righting wrongs and promoting rights', in B. Franklin (ed.) *The Handbook of Children's Rights*, London: Routledge.

Ennew, J. (1986) *The Sexual Exploitation of Children*, London: Polity Press.

Ennew, J. (1994) 'Time for children or time for adults', in J. Qvortrup, M. Bardy, G. Sgritta and H. Wintersberger (eds) *Childhood Matters*, Aldershot: Avebury.

Ennew, J. (1995) 'Outside childhood: Street children's rights', in B. Franklin (ed.) *The Handbook of Children's Rights*, London: Routledge.

Ericksen, J. R. and Henderson, A. D. (1992) 'Witnessing family violence: the children's experience', *Journal of Advanced Nursing*, **17**: 1200–9.

Erickson, P. G. (1982) 'The Client's Perspective', in F. M. Martin and K. Murray (eds) *The Scottish Juvenile Justice System,* Edinburgh: Scottish Academic Press.

Erikson, E. H. (1963) *Childhood and Society*, Harmondsworth: Penguin.

Erwin, P. (1992) *Friendship and Peer Relations in Children*, Chichester: Wiley.

Esping-Andersen, G. (1990) *The Three Worlds of Welfare Capitalism*, Princeton, NJ: Princeton University Press.

Evans, D. T. (1993) *Sexual Citizenship*, London: Routledge.

Evans, D. T. (1994) 'Falling angels? – the material construction of children as sexual citizens', *International Journal of Children's Rights*, **2**: 1–33.

Fahlberg, V. (1994) *A Child's Journey Through Placement*, London: BAAF.

Falbo, T. (1984) *The Single Child Family*, New York: Guildford Press.

Farmer, E. (1993) 'The impact of child protection interventions: the experiences of parents and children', in L. Waterhouse (ed.) *Child Abuse and Child Abusers*, London: Jessica Kingsley.

Farmer, E. and Owen, M. (1995) *Child Protection Practice: Private Risks and Public Remedies*, London: HMSO.

Farmer, E. and Parker, R. (1991) *Trials and Tribulations*, London: HMSO.

Farrell, C. (1978) *My Mother Said . . . The Way Young People Learned about Sex and Birth Control*, London: Routledge.

Farrington, D. (1993) 'Understanding and Preventing Bullying', in M. Tonry (ed.) *Crime and Justice. A Review of Research*, Vol. 17, Chicago: University of Chicago Press.

Feiring, C. and Lewis, M. (1992) 'The child's social network from three to six years', in S. Salzinger, J. Antrobus and M. Hammer (eds) *Social Networks of Children, Adolescents and College Students*, Hillsdale, NJ: Lawrence Erlbaum.

Fenyo, A., Knapp, M. and Baines, B. (1989) *Foster Care Breakdown: A Study of a Special Teenager Fostering Scheme*, Canterbury: PSSRU, University of Kent.

Ferri, E. (1984) *Step-children*, London: NFER-Nelson.

Ferri, E.(1993) (ed.) *Life at 33*, London: National Children's Bureau.

Finch, J. and Mason, J. (1993) *Negotiating Family Responsibilities*, London: Routledge.

Fischer, J. L., Sollie, D. L. and Morrow, K. B. (1986) 'Social networks in male and female adolescents', *Journal of Adolescent Research*, **6** (1): 1–14.

Fletcher, B. (1993) *Not Just a Name: The Views of Young People in Foster and Residential Care*, London: National Consumer Council/Who Cares? Trust.

Fogelman, K. (1975) *Britain's Sixteen Year Olds*, London: National Children's Bureau.

Fonagy, P., Steele, M., Steele, H., Higgitt, A. and Target, M. (1994) 'The theory and practice of resilience', *Journal of Child Psychology and Psychiatry*, **35** (2): 231–57.

Foot, H. C., Chapman, A. J. and Smith, J. R. (eds) (1980) *Friendship and Social Relations in Children*, Chichester: John Wiley.

Foster, J. (1990) *Villains. Crime and Community in the Inner City*, London: Routledge.

Fox, R. (1977) *Kinship and Marriage*, Harmondsworth: Penguin.

France, E. (1990) *International Perspectives*, Background Paper No. 1 to the Interdepartmental Review of Adoption Law, London: Department of Health.

Francis, D. and Henderson, P. (1992) *Working with Rural Communities*, London: Macmillan.

Franklin, B. (1995a) 'Children's Rights: an overview', in B. Franklin (ed.) *The Handbook of Children's Rights*, London: Routledge.

Franklin, B. (ed.) (1995b) *The Handbook of Children's Rights*, London: Routledge.

Fraser, N. (1989) 'Talking about Needs', *Ethics*, **99**: 291–313.

Fratter, J. (1996) *Adoption with Contact*, London: BAAF.

Fratter, J., Rowe, J., Sapsford, D. and Thoburn, J. (1991) *Permanent Family Placement: A Decade of Experience*, London: BAAF.

Frazer, E. (1996) 'Political and Social Participation and Citizenship' Framework paper, draft for British Youth Research: the new agenda, Conference (January 1996).

Freeden, M. (1991) *Rights*, Milton Keynes: Open University Press.

Freeman, D. (1983) *Margaret Mead and Samoa*, Cambridge, Mass: Harvard University Press.

Freeman, I., Morrison, A., Lockhart, F. and Swanson, M. (1996) 'Consulting service users: The views of young people', in M. Hill and J. Aldgate (eds) *Child Welfare Services: Developments in Law, Policy Practice and Research*, London: Jessica Kingsley.

Freeman, M. D. A. (1983) 'The Rights of Children Who Do Wrong', in *The Rights and Wrongs of Children*, London: Frances Pinter.

Fulcher, G. (1989) *Disabling Policies? A Comparative Approach to Education Policy and Disability*, London: The Falmer Press.

Funder, K. and Kinsella, S. (1991) 'Divorce, Change and Children', *Family Matters*, **30**: 20–3.

Furman, W. and Buhrmeister, D. (1985) 'Children's perceptions of the personal relationships in their social networks', *Developmental Psychology*, **21** (6): 1016–24.

Furnham, A. and Gunter, B. (1989) *The Anatomy of Adolescence: Young People's Social Attitudes in Britain*, London: Routledge.

Furnham, A. and Stacey, B. (1991) *Young People's Understanding of Society*, London: Routledge.

Furniss, T. (1991) *The Multi-professional Handbook of Child Sexual Abuse*, London: Routledge.

Furstenberg, F. F. and Spanier, G. B. (1984) *Recycling the Family: Remarriage after Divorce*, Beverley Hills: Sage.

Furth, H. (1980) *The World of Grown Ups*, Elsevier, New York.

Galbo, J. J. (1986) 'Adolescents' perceptions of significant adults', *Children & Youth Services Review*, **8**: 37–51.

Gallagher, R. (1996a) 'Legal Proceedings and the Children (Scotland) Act 1995. A Children's Rights Perspective'. Paper to the Centre for the Study of the Child, the Family and the Law, University of Liverpool. Available from Glasgow; Scottish Child Law Centre.

Gallagher, R. (1996b) *Confidentiality in Schools*, Unpublished Report, Glasgow: Scottish Child Law Centre.

Galloway, D., Armstrong, D. and Tomlinson, S. (1994) *The Assessment of Special Educational Needs: Whose Problem?* London: Longman.

Gambe, D., Gomes, J., Kapur, V., Rangel, M. and Stubbs, P. (1992) *Improving Practice with Children and Families*, London: CCETSW.

Ganetz, H. (1995) 'The shop, the home and femininity as a masquerade', in J. Fornäs and G. Bolin (eds) *Youth Culture in Late Modernity*, London: Sage.

Garbarino, J. and Stott, F. M. (1992) *What Children Can Tell Us*, San Francisco: Jossey-Bass.

Gärling, T. and Valsiner, J. (eds) (1985) *Children within Environments*, New York: Plenum Press.

Garmezy, N. (1987) 'Stress, competence and development', *American Journal of Orthopsychiatry*, **57** (2): 159–74.

Garnett, L. (1992) *Leaving Care and After*, London: National Children's Bureau.

Garratt, D., Roche, J. and Tucker, S. (eds) (1997) *Changing Experiences of Youth*, London: Sage.

Garrett, P., Ng'andu, N. and Ferron, J. (1994) 'Poverty Experiences of Young Children and the Quality of their Home Environments', *Child Development*, **65**: 331–45.

Garwood, F. (1992) 'Conciliation: A forum for children's views?', *Children & Society*, **6** (4): 353–63.

Genders, E. and Player, E. (1986) 'Women's Imprisonment: The Effects of Youth Custody', *British Journal of Criminology*, **26** (4): 357–71.

Gersch, I. S. with Moyse, S., Nolan, A. and Pratt, G. (1996) 'Listening to Children in Educational Contexts', in R. Davie, G. Upton and V. Varma (eds) *The Voice of the Child*, London: Falmer Press.

Gersch, I. S. and Nolan, A. (1994) 'Exclusions: What the Children Think', *Educational Psychology in Practice*, **10** (1): 35–45.

Gibbons, J. (1995) 'Family support in Child Protection', in Hill, M., Hawthorne-Kirk, R. and Part, D. (eds) *Supporting Families*, Edinburgh: HMSO.

Gibbons, J., Gallagher, B., Bell, C. and Gordon, D. (1995) *Development After Physical Abuse in Early Childhood*, London: HMSO.

Gibson, C. S. (1994) *Dissolving Wedlock*, Routledge, London.

Giddens, A. (1987) *Social Theory and Modern Sociology*, Cambridge: Polity.

Gil, D. G. (1970) *Violence against Children*, Cambridge, Mass: Harvard University Press.

Gill, O. and Jackson, B. (1983) *Adoption and Race*, London: Cassell.

Gillham, B. (1991) *The Facts About Child Abuse*, Cassell, London.

Gillham, B. (1994) *The Facts About Child Physical Abuse*, London: Cassell.

Gilmore, J. B. (1971) 'Play: A special behaviour', in R. E. Herron and B. Sutton-Smith (eds) *Child's Play*, New York: Wiley.

Ginsburg, N. (1992) *Divisions of Welfare: A Critical Approach to Comparative Social Policy,* London: Sage.

Giroux, H. A. (1994) 'Doing Cultural Studies: Youth and the Challenge of Pedagogy', *Harvard Educational Review*, **64** (3): 278–308.

Gittins, D. (1993) *The Family in Question*, London: Macmillan.

Glaser, D. and Frosh, S. (1993) *Child Sexual Abuse*, London: Macmillan.

Glassner, B. (1995) 'In the name of health', in R. Bunton, S. Nettleton and R. Burrows (eds) (1995) *The Sociology of Health Promotion*, London: Routledge.

Glendinning, C. and Millar, J. (eds) (1987) *Women and Poverty in Britain*, Brighton: Wheatsheaf.

Gold, D. and Andres, D. (1978) 'Relations between maternal employment and development of nursery school children', *Canadian Journal of Behavioural Science*, **10** (2): 116–29.

Golding, J., Hull, D. and Rutter, M. (1988) 'Child health and environment', in Forfar, D. (ed.) *Child Health in a Changing Society*, Oxford: Oxford University Press.

Goldschmied, E. and Jackson, S. (1994) *People Under Three*, London: Routledge.

Golombok, S., Spencer, A. and Rutter, M. (1983) 'Children in lesbian and single-parent households: Psychosexual and psychiatric appraisal', *Journal of Child Psychology and Psychiatry*, **24**: 551–72.

Gomes-Schwartz, B., Horowitz, J. M. and Cardarelli, A. P. (1990) *Child Sexual Abuse: The Initial Effects*, Newbury Park: Sage.

Goodin, R. E. (1990) 'Relative needs', in A. Ware and R. E. Goodin (eds) *Needs and Welfare*, London: Sage

Goodnow, J. J. and Collins, W. A. (1990) *Development According to Parents*, Hillsdale (NJ): Lawrence Erlbaum.

Goody, E. (1970) 'Kinship fostering in Gonja', in P. Mason (ed.) *Socialisation: The Approach from Social Anthropology*, London: Tavistock.

Goonesekere, S. (1994) 'National policies on children's rights and international norms', in Asquith, S. and Hill, M. (eds) (1994) *Justice for Children*, Dordrecht: Martinus Nijhoff.

Gorard, S. A. C. (1996) 'Fee-paying schools in Britain – a peculiarly English phenomenon', *Educational Review*, **48** (1): 89–93.

Gottlieb, B. (1993) *The Family in the Western World*, Oxford: Oxford University Press.

Gottlieb, J. and Leyser, Y. (1981) 'Friendship between mentally retarded and nonretarded children', in S. R. Asher and J. M. Gottman (eds) *The Development of Children's Friendships*, Cambridge: Cambridge University Press.

Gottman, J. M. and Parker, J. G. (eds) (1986) *Conversations of Friends*, Cambridge: Cambridge University Press.

Gould, P. and White, R. (1986) *Mental Maps*, Boston: Allen & Unwin.

Government Green Paper (1992) *The Health of the Nation*, London: HMSO.

Graham, H. (1996) 'Researching women's health work', in P. Bywaters and E. McLeod (eds) *Working for Equality in Health*, London: Routledge.

Graham, J. (1988) *Schools, Disruptive Behaviour and Delinquency: A Review of Research*, Home Office Research Study No. 96, London: HMSO.

Graham, J. and Bowling, B. (1995) *Young People and Crime*, Research Study 145, London: Home Office Research and Statistics Department.

Grant, L. (1996) 'Cares of the world', *The Guardian*, 15.5.96.

Green, J. (1995) 'Accidents and the risk society: some problems with prevention', in R. Bunton, S. Nettleton and R. Burrows (eds) *The Sociology of Health Promotion*, London: Routledge.

Gregory, J. and Foster, K. (1990) *The Consequences of Divorce*, OPCS, HMSO, London.

Grimshaw, R. with Berridge, D. (1994) *Educating Disruptive Children*, London: National Children's Bureau.

Grootaert, C. and Kanbur, R. (1995) 'Child labour: An economic perspective', *International Labour Review*, **134** (2): 187–203.

Grych, J. H. and Fincham, F. D. (1990) 'Marital conflict and children's adjustment: A cognitive-contextual framework', *Psychological Bulletin*, **108** (2): 267–90.

Guardian (1996) 'Young Lives', 15.5.96.

Hadley, R. and Wilkinson, H. (1995) 'Integration and its future: a case study of primary education and physical disability', *Disability and Society*, **10** (3): 309–23.

Hakim, C. (1996) *Key Issues in Women's Work: Female Heterogeneity and the Polarisation of Women's Employment*, London: Athlone Press.

Hallett, C. (1995a) *Interagency Coordination in Child Protection*, London: HMSO.

Hallett, C. (1995b) 'Taking stock: Past developments and future directions in child protection', in K. Wilson, and A. James (eds) *The Child Protection Handbook*, London: Bailliere Tindall.

Hallett, C. (1996) 'From investigations to help', in D. Batty and D. Cullen (eds) (1996) *Child Protection: The Therapeutic Option*, London: BAAF.

Hallett, C. and Birchall, E. (1992) *Coordination and Child Protection: A Review of the Literature*, Edinburgh: HMSO.

Halsey, A. H. (1993) 'Changes in the family', in G. Pugh, (ed) *30 Years of Change for Children*, London: National Children's Bureau.

Hammarberg, T. (1990) 'The UN Convention on the Rights of the Child – and How to make It Work', *Human Rights Quarterly*, **12**: 97–105.

Hannan, A. (1996) 'Equality Assurance, Children's Rights and Education', in M. John (ed.) *Children in Our Charge. The Child's Right to Resources*, London: Jessica Kingsley.

Hantrais, L. (1994) 'Family policy in Europe', in R. Page and J. Baldock (eds) *Social Policy Review 6*, Canterbury: Social Policy Association.

Hantrais, L. (1995) *Social Policy in the European Union*, London: Macmillan.

Hardiker, P. (1996) 'The legal and social construction of significant harm', in M. Hill and J. Aldgate (eds) *Child Welfare Services: Developments in Law, Policy, Practice and Research*, London: Jessica Kingsley.

Harding, L. F. (1991) *Perspectives in Child Care Policy*, London: Longman.

Harding, L. F. (1996a) 'Recent developments in "children's rights": liberation for whom?', *Child and Family Social Work*, **1** (3): 141–50.

Harding, L. F. (1996b) *Family, State and Social Policy*, Basingstoke: Macmillan.

Hardyment, C. (1983) *Dream Babies*, London: Jonathan Cape.

Harris, C. C. (1990) *Kinship*, Buckingham: Open University Press.

Harris, P. L. (1992) *Children and Emotion*, Oxford: Blackwell.

Harris, R. (1995) 'Child protection, child care and child welfare', in K. Wilson and A. James (eds) *The Child Protection Handbook*, London: Bailliere Tindall.

Harris, R. and Timms, N. (1993a) 'The Lost Key: secure accommodation and juvenile crime: an English and Welsh perspective', *Australia and New Zealand Journal of Criminology*, **26**: 219–31.

Harris, R. and Timms, N. (1993b) *Secure Accommodation in Child Care: Between Hospital and Prison or Thereabouts,* London: Routledge.

Harrison, S. (1996) 'Piggy in the middle: What happens to you when your parents separate', in M. Long (ed.) *Children in Charge: The Child's Right to a Fair Hearing*, London: Jessica Kingsley.

Hart, R. (1979) *Children's Experience of Place*, New York: Irvington.

Hart, R. A. (1992) *Children's Participation. From Tokenism to Citizenship*, Innocenti Essays, No. 4. Florence: UNICEF International Child Development Centre.

Hart, S. N. (1991) 'From Property to Person Status: Historical Perspective on Children's Rights', *American Psychologist*, **46** (1): 53–9.

Harter, S. (1983) 'Developmental perspectives on the self system', in E. M. Hetherington (ed.) *Handbook of Child Psychology: Socialisation, Personality and Social Development* (Vol. 4) New York: Wiley.

Hartup, W. W. (1992) 'Friendships and their developmental significance', in H. McGurk (ed.) *Childhood Social Development*, Hove: Lawrence Erlbaum.

Hartup, W. W. (1996) 'The company they keep: Friends and their developmental significance', *Child Development*, **67**: 1–13.

Hartzema, A. G. (1996) 'Implications for health policy', in P. J. Bush, D. J. Trakas, E. J. Sanz, R. L. Wirsing, T. Vaskilampi and A. Prout (eds) (1996) *Children, Medicines and Culture*, New York: Haworth Press.

Haskey, J. (1994a) 'Stepfamilies and stepchildren in Great Britain', *Population Trends*, **76**: 17–28.

Haskey, J. (1994b) 'Estimated numbers of one-parent families and their prevalence in Great Britain in 1991', *Population Trends*, **78**: 5–19.

Hawthorne-Kirk, R. (1995) 'Social support and early years centres', in M. Hill, R. H. Kirk and D. Part (eds) (1995) *Supporting Families*, Edinburgh: HMSO.

Hawthorne-Kirk, R. and Part, D. (1995) 'The Impact of Changing Social Policies on Families', in M. Hill, R. H. Kirk and D. Part (eds) (1995) *Supporting Families*, Edinburgh: HMSO.

Heath, A. F., Colton, M. J. and Aldgate, J. (1994) 'Failure to escape: A longitudinal study of foster children's educational attainment', *British Journal of Social Work*, 24, 241–60.

Hebdige, D. (1988) 'Hiding in the Light: Youth Surveillance and Display', in *Hiding in the Light*, London: Routledge.

Henderson, P. (ed.) (1995) *Children and Communities*, London: Pluto Press.

Hendrick, H. (1990) 'Constructions and reconstructions of British childhood: An interpretative survey, 1800 to the present', in A. James and A. Prout (eds) *Constructing and Reconstructing Childhood: Contemporary Issues in the Sociological Study of Childhood*, London: The Falmer Press.

Hendrick, H. (1994) *Child Welfare: England 1872–1989*, London: Routledge.

Hendry, L., Shucksmith, J., Love, J., and Glendinning, A. (1993) *Young People's Leisure and Lifestyles*, London: Routledge.

Henggeler, S. W., Melton, G. B. and Rodrigue, J. R. (1992) *Pediatric and Adolescent AIDS*, Newbury Park: Sage.

Herbert, M. (1987) *Conduct Disorders of Childhood and Adolescence*, London: John Wiley.

Hernon, I. (1996) 'An Act of Shame', *Community Care*, 8–14 February: 11.

Herrenkohl, E. C., Herrenkohl, R. C. and Egolf, M. A. (1994) 'Resilient early school-age children from maltreating homes: Outcomes in late adolescence', *American Journal of Orthopsychiatry*, **64** (2): 301–9.

Hetherington, E. M. (1989) 'Coping with family transitions: Winners, losers and survivors', *Child Development*, **66**: 1–14.

Hetherington, E. M., Cox, M. and Cox, R. (1985) 'Long-term effects of divorce and remarriage on the adjustment of children', *Journal of the American Academy of Child Psychiatry*, **24** (5): 518–30.

Hetherington, R. (1996) 'Prevention and education in work with children and families', in Batty, D. and Cullen, D. (eds) *Child Protection: The Therapeutic Option*, London: BAAF.

Hewitt, M. (1992) *Welfare, Ideology and Need*, Hemel Hempstead: Harvester Wheatsheaf.

Heywood, J. (1978) *Children in Care,* London: Routledge and Kegan Paul.

Hill, F. and Michelson, W. (1981) 'Towards a geography of urban children and youth', in D. T. Herbert and R. J. Johnston (eds) *Geography and the Urban Environment,* Vol. IV, London: Wiley.

Hill, M. (1987), *Sharing Child Care in Early Parenthood,* London: Routledge & Kegan Paul.

Hill, M. (1990) 'The manifest and latent lessons of child abuse inquiries', *British Journal of Social Work,* **20** (3): 197–213.

Hill, M. (1991) 'Concepts of parenthood and their application to adoption', *Adoption & Fostering,* **15** (4): 16–23.

Hill, M. (1992) 'Children's role in the domestic economy', *Journal of Consumer Studies and Home Economics,* **16**: 33–50.

Hill, M. (1995a) 'Family Policies in Western Europe', in M. Hill, R. Hawthorne-Kirk and D. Part (eds) *Supporting Families,* Edinburgh: HMSO.

Hill, M. (1995b) 'Young people's views of social work and care services', *Child Care in Practice,* **2** (1): 49–59.

Hill, M. and Aldgate, J. (1996) 'The Children Act 1989 and recent developments in research in England and Wales', in M. Hill and J. Aldgate (eds) *Child Welfare Services,* London: Jessica Kingsley.

Hill, M. and Triseliotis, J. (1989) 'The Transition from Foster Care to Adoption', in J. Hudson and B. Galaway (eds) *The State as Parent,* Dordrecht: Kluwer.

Hill, M., Hawthorne-Kirk, R. and Part, D. (1995) 'Supporting families: changes, challenges and dilemmas', in M. Hill, R. Kirk and D. Part (eds) *Supporting Families,* Edinburgh: HMSO.

Hill, M., Lambert, L. and Triseliotis, J. (1989) *Achieving Adoption with Love and Money,* London: National Children's Bureau.

Hill, M., Laybourn, A. and Borland, M. (1995) *Children's Well-Being,* University of Glasgow: Report to the Health Education Board for Scotland.

Hill, M., Laybourn, A. and Borland, M. (1996a) 'Engaging with primary-aged children about their emotions and well-being: Methodological considerations', *Children & Society,* **10** (2): 129–44.

Hill, M., Laybourn, A. and Borland, M. (1996b) *Children's Well-Being,* Final Report, University of Glasgow: Centre for the Child & Society.

Hill, M., Murray, K. and Rankin, J. (1991) 'The early history of Scottish child welfare', *Children & Society,* **5** (2): 182–95.

Hill, M., Murray, K. and Tisdall, K. (forthcoming) 'Services for children and their families', in J. English (ed.) *Social Services in Scotland,* Revised Edition, Edinburgh: Mercat Press.

Hillman, M. (ed.) (1993) *Children, Transport and the Quality of Life,* London: Policy Studies Institute.

Hindle, D. (1995) 'Thinking about siblings who are fostered together', *Adoption & Fostering,* **19** (1): 14–20.

Hirschi, T. (1969) *Causes of Delinquency,* Berkeley: University of California Press.

Hirst, M. and Baldwin, S. (1994) *Unequal Opportunities: Growing Up Disabled,* London: HMSO.

Hobbes, T. (1994) *The Correspondence,* N. Malcolm (ed.), Oxford: Clarendon Press.

Hock, E. (1978) 'Working and non-working mothers with infants: Perceptions of their careers, their infants' needs and satisfaction with mothering', *Developmental Psychology,* **14** (1): 37–43.

Hock, E. (1980) 'Working and non-working mothers and their infants', *Merrill-Palmer Quarterly*, **26**: 79–101.

Hockenberry-Eaton, M. and Minick, P. (1994) 'Living with cancer: children with extraordinary courage', *Oncology Nursing Forum*, **21** (6): 1025–31.

Hodges, J. and Tizard, B. (1989) 'IQ and behavioural adjustment of ex-institutional adolescents', *Journal of Child Psychology and Psychiatry*, **30**: 53–75.

Hodgkin, R. and Newell, P. (1996) *Effective Government Structures for Children*, Report of a Gulbenkian Foundation Inquiry. London: Gulbenkian Foundation.

Hogan, V. (1996) 'Consulting children about play', in John, M. (ed.) *Children in Our Charge: The Child's Right to Resources*, London: Jessica Kingsley.

Hoksbergen, R. (ed.) (1986) *Adoption in Worldwide Perspective*, Lisse: Swets and Zeitlinger.

Holden (1996) 'Tomorrow's Europeans: Human rights education in the Primary School', in M. Long (ed.) *Children in our Charge*, London: Jessica Kingsley.

Hollands, R. G. (1990) *The Long Transition. Class, Culture and Youth Training*, London: Macmillan.

Hollows, A. and Armstrong, H. (1991) 'Responses to child abuse in the EC', in M. Hill (ed.) *Social Work and the European Community*, London: Jessica Kingsley.

Holman, B. (1988) *Putting Families First*, London: Macmillan.

Holmes, J. (1993) *John Bowlby and Attachment Theory*, London: Routledge.

Holstein-Beck, S. (1995) 'Consistency and change in the lifeworld of young women', in J. Fornäs and G. Bolin (eds) *Youth Culture in Late Modernity*, London: Sage.

Holt, J. (1974) *Escape from Childhood. The Needs and Rights of Children*, London: Penguin Books.

Homel, R. and Burns, A. (1985) 'Through a child's eyes: quality of neighbourhood and quality of life', in I. Burney and J. Forrest (eds) *Living in Cities*, London: Allen & Unwin.

Hood, S., Kelley, P. and Mayall, B. (1996a) 'Children as research subjects: A risky enterprise', *Children & Society*, **10** (2): 117–29.

Hood, S., Kelley, P., Mayall, B., Oakley, A. with Morrell, R. (1996b) *Children, Parents and Risk*, London: Institute of Education.

Howard, J. and Shepherd, G. (1987) *Conciliation, Children and Divorce*, London: Batsford.

Howe, D. (1992) 'Child abuse and the bureaucratisation of social work', *The Sociological Review*, **40** (3): 491–508.

Howe, D. (1995a) *Attachment Theory for Social Work Practice*, London: Macmillan.

Howe, D. (1995b) 'Adoption and attachment', *Adoption & Fostering*, **19** (4): 7–15.

Howe, D. (1996a) 'Adopters' relationships with their adopted children from adolescence to early adulthood', *Adoption & Fostering*, **20** (3): 35–43.

Howe, D. (ed.) (1996b) *Attachment Theory and Child and Family Social Work*, Aldershot: Avebury.

Howitt, D. (1992) *Child Abuse Errors*, Hemel Hempstead: Harvester Wheatsheaf.

Hudson, B. and McDonald, G. (1986) *Behavioural Social Work*, London: Macmillan.

Hudson, J. and Galaway, B. (1995) *Child Welfare in Canada: Research and Policy Implications*, Toronto: Thompson Educational Publishing.

Hughes, C. (1991) *Stepparents: Wicked or Wonderful*, Aldershot: Avebury.

Hughes, M. and Lloyd, E. (1996) 'Young people: stakeholders in the educational system', in H. Roberts and D. Sachdev (eds) *Having Their Say – The Views of 12–19 Year Olds*, Essex: Barnardos.

Hurrelmann, K. and Losel, F. (1990) *Health Hazards in Adolescence*, Berlin: Walter de Gruyter.

Hutson, A. C., McLoyd, V. C. and Coll, C. G. (1994) 'Children and Poverty: Issues in Contemporary Research', *Child Development*, **65**: 275–82.

Hutson, S. and Cheung, W. (1992) 'Saturday Jobs: Sixth-formers in the labour market and the family', in C. Marsh and S. Arber (eds) *Families and Households: Divisions and Change*, British Sociological Association, Explorations in Sociology 42, London: Macmillan Press Ltd.

Imich, A. J. (1994) 'Exclusions from school: current trends and issues', *Educational Research*, **36** (1): 3–11.

International Labour Organization (ILO) (1996) 'ILO Calls for Immediate Action Against Intolerable Forms of Child Labour', Press Release, http://www.ilo.org/english/235press/pr/96-38.htm.

Ireland, L. and Holloway, I. (1996) 'Qualitative health research with children', *Children & Society*, **10** (2): 155–65.

Irving, B. A. and Parker-Jenkins, M. (1995) 'Tackling Truancy: an examination of persistent non-attendance amongst disaffected school pupils and positive support strategies', *Cambridge Journal of Education*, **25** (2): 225–35.

Irving, H. H., Benjamin, M. and Trocme, N. (1984) 'Shared parenting: An empirical analysis utilizing a large data base', *Family Process*, **23**: 561–569.

Jackson, A. A. (1995) 'The Health of the Nation: the population perspective', in D. Davies (ed.) *Nutrition in Child Health*, London: Royal College of Physicians.

Jackson, B. and Jackson, S. (1979) *Childminder*, London: Routledge and Kegan Paul.

Jackson, S. (1989) 'Education of Children in Care', in B. Kahan (ed.) *Child Care: Research, Policy and Practice*, London: Hodder and Stoughton.

Jahoda, G. (1982) *Psychology and Anthropology*, London: Academic Press.

James, A. (1993) *Childhood Identities*, Edinburgh: Edinburgh University Press.

James, A. and Prout, A. (eds) (1990) *Constructing and Reconstructing Childhood*, London: Falmer Press.

James, J. (1996) 'From negative perceptions to positive well-being: The young people's health project', *Children UK*, Summer 1996, 3.

Jarvis, S., Towner, E. and Walsh, S. (1995) 'Accidents', in Botting, B. (ed.) *The Health of our Children*, London: HMSO.

Jeffs, T. (1986) 'Children's Rights at School', in B. Franklin (ed.) *The Rights of Children*, Oxford: Basil Blackwell.

Jeffs, T. (1995) 'Children's educational rights in a new ERA?', in B. Franklin (ed.) *The Handbook of Children's Rights*, London: Routledge.

Jeffs, T. and Smith, M. K. (1996) '"Getting the Dirtbags Off The Streets" Curfews & Other Solutions to Juvenile Crime', *Youth & Policy*, **53**: 1–14.

Jenkins, J. M. and Smith, M. A. (1991) 'Marital disharmony and children's behaviour problems: Aspects of a poor marriage that affect children adversely', *Journal of Child Psychology and Psychiatry*, **32** (5): 793–810.

Jenks, C. (ed.) (1982) *The Sociology of Childhood*, London: Batsford.

Jenks, C. (1996) *Childhood*, London: Routledge.

Johnson, N. (1990) *Reconstructing the Welfare State*, Hemel Hempstead: Harvester Wheatsheaf.

Johnstone, A. (1996) 'A poor view of the world', *The Herald*, 18th April.

Jones, C. (ed.) (1993) *New Perspectives on the Welfare State in Europe*, London: Routledge.

Jones, G. (1992) 'Short-term Reciprocity in Parent-Child Economic Exchanges', in C. Marsh and S. Arber (eds) *Families and Households: Divisions and Change*, British Sociological Association, Explorations in Sociology 42, London: Macmillan Press Ltd.

Jones, G. and Wallace, C. (1992) *Youth, Family and Citizenship*, Buckingham: Open University Press.

Jones, J. (1996) 'Poverty triggers UK diet crisis', *The Observer*, 21.1.96.

Jones, P. (1994) *Rights*, London: Macmillan.

Jones, R. A. (1995) *The Child–School Interface*, London: Cassell.

Jones, T. (1993) *Britain's Ethnic Minorities: An Analysis of the Labour Force Survey*, London: Policy Studies Institute.

Jordan, B., Redley, M. and James, S. (1994) *Putting the Family First*, London: UCL Press.

Joseph, Y. (1995) 'Child protection rights: can an international declaration be an effective instrument for protecting children?', in C. Cloke and M. Davies (eds) *Participation and Empowerment in Child Protection*, London: Pitman.

Jowell, R., Curtice, J., Park, A., Brook, L. and Ahrendt, D. (eds) (1995) *British Social Attitudes. The 12th Report*, 1995/96 Edition, Aldershot: Dartmouth Publishing Company Ltd.

Jowett, S. (1995) *Health and Well-being in the 1990s*, Slough: NFER.

Kadushin, A. and Martin, J. A. (1988) *Child Welfare Services*, New York: Macmillan.

Kahan, B. (1994) *Growing up in Groups*, London: HMSO.

Kahana, B. and Kahana, J. (1970) 'Grandparenthood from the perspective of the developing child', *Developmental Psychology*, **3** (1): 98–105.

Kahana, J. and Kahana, B. (1971) 'Theoretical and research perspectives on grandparenthood', *Aging and Human Development*, **2**: 261–8.

Kalnins, I., McQueen, D. V., Backett, K. C., Curtice, L. and Currie, C. A. (1992) 'Children, empowerment and health promotion: New directions in research and practice', *Health Promotion International*, **7** (1): 53–9.

Karrby, G. (1990) 'Children's conceptions of their own play', *Early Child Development*, **58**: 81–5.

Katz, C. (1993) 'Growing girls/Closing circles', in C. Katz and J. Monk (eds) *Full Circles: Geographies of Women over the Life Course*, London: Routledge.

Katz, I. (1996a) *The Construction of Racial Identity in Children of Mixed Parentage*, London: Jessica Kingsley.

Katz, I. (1996b) 'How do young Asian and white people view their problems? A step towards child-focused research', in I. Butler and I. Shaw (eds) *A Case of Neglect? Children's experiences and the sociology of childhood*, Aldershot: Avebury.

Kaye, K. (1990) 'Acknowledgement or rejection of differences?', in D. Brodzinsky and M. Schechter (eds) *The Psychology of Adoption*, Oxford: Oxford University Press.

Kegerreis, S. (1993) 'Independent mobility and children's mental and emotional development', in M. Hillman (ed.) *Children, Transport and the Quality of Life*, London: Policy Studies Institute.

Keith, L. and Morris, J. (1995) 'Easy targets: a disability rights perspective on the 'children as carers' debate', *Critical Social Policy*, **44/5**: 36–57.

286 Children and Society

Kelly, A. (1996) Introduction to the Scottish Children's Panel, Winchester: Waterside Press.

Kelly, B. (1992) Children Inside: A Study of Secure Provision, London: Routledge.

Kelly, B. and Hill, M. (1994) 'Working together to help children and families', Research, Policy and Planning, 12 (3): 1–5.

Kelly, G. and Pinkerton, G. (1996) 'The Children (Northern Ireland) Order 1995: Prospects for Progress', in M. Hill and J. Aldgate (eds) Child Welfare Services, London: Jessica Kingsley.

Kendrick, A. (1995) 'Residential Care in the Integration of Child Care Services', Research Findings No 5, Edinburgh: Scottish Office Central Research Unit.

Kendrick, A. and Mapstone, E. (1991) 'Who decides? Child care reviews in two Scottish social work departments', Children & Society, 5 (2): 1.

Kennedy, M. (1995a) 'Perceptions of abused disabled children', in K. Wilson and A. James (eds) The Child Protection Handbook, London: Bailliere Tindall.

Kennedy, M. (1995b) 'Rights for children who are disabled', in B. Franklin (ed.) The Handbook of Children's Rights, London: Routledge.

Kerr, S. (1983) Making Ends Meet, London: Bedford Square Press.

Kersten, J. (1990) 'A Gender Specific Look at Patterns of Violence in Juvenile Institutions: or Are Girls Really "More Difficult to Handle"?', International Journal of the Sociology of Law, 18: 473–93.

Khan, A. (1996) 'Give us direction for future', The Herald, 29.10.96.

Kiernan, K. (1992) 'The impact of family disruption in childhood on transitions in young adulthood', Population Studies, 46: 213–21.

Kiernan, K. and Wicks, M. (1990) Family Change and Future Policy, London: Family Policy Studies Centre.

Kilbrandon Report. Scottish Home and Health Department and the Scottish Education Department (1964) Children and Young Persons Scotland. Report by the Committee Appointed by the Secretary of State for Scotland. Presented to Parliament April 1964. Cm 2306. Edinburgh: HMSO.

King, M. (1994) 'Law's healing of children's hearings: the paradox moves north', Journal of Social Policy, 24 (3): 315–40.

King, M. (1997) A Better World for Children? Explorations in Morality and Authority, London: Routledge.

King, M. and Piper, C. (1990) How the Law Thinks About Children, Aldershot: Gower.

King, P. (1984) 'Decision-Makers and Decision-Making in the English Criminal Law, 1750–1800', The Historic Journal, 27 (1): 25–58.

Kirk, D. (1964) Shared Fate: A Theory of Adoption and Mental Health, London: Macmillan.

Kirk, D. (1981) Adoptive Kinship – a modern institution in need of reform, Toronto: Butterworth.

Kitwood, T. (1983) 'Self-conception among young British–Asian Muslims: Confutation of a stereotype', in G. Breakwell (ed.) Threatened Identities, Chichester: John Wiley.

Klein, D. M. and White, J. M. (1996) Family Theories, London: Sage.

Kline, S. (1993) Out of the Garden: Toys, TV, and Children's Culture in the Age of Marketing, London: Verso.

Knight, B. (1993) Voluntary Action, London: Centris.

Kohlberg, L. A. (1969) 'Stage and sequence: The cognitive developmental approach to socialization', in D. Goslin (ed.) Handbook of Socialisation, Chicago: Rand McNally.

Konner, M. (1975) 'Relations among infants and juveniles in comparative perspective', in M. Lewis and L. A. Rosenblum (eds) *The Effects of the Infant on its Caregiver*, New York: Wiley.

Kosonen, M. (1994) 'Sibling relationships for children in the care system', *Adoption & Fostering*, **18** (3): 30–5.

Kosonen, M. (1996a) 'Maintaining sibling relationships – neglected dimension in child care practice', *British Journal of Social Work*, **26** (6): 809–22.

Kosonen, M. (1996b) 'Siblings as providers of support and care during middle childhood: Children's perceptions', *Children & Society*, **10** (4): 267–79.

Kruk, E. (1991) 'Discontinuity between pre- and post-divorce father-child relationships: New evidence regarding paternal disengagement', in Everett, C. A. (ed.) (1991) *The Consequences of Divorce*, London: Haworth Press.

Kruk, E. (1993) *Divorce and Disengagement*, Halifax (Nova Scotia): Fenwood.

Kufeldt, K., Armstrong, J. and Dorosh, M. (1996) 'Connection and continuity in foster care', *Adoption & Fostering*, **20** (2): 14–20.

Kurdeck, L. A. and Siesky, A. E. (1980) 'Effects of divorce on children', *Journal of Divorce*, **1**: 222–46.

Kurtz, Z. and Tomlinson, J. (1991) 'How do we value our children today? As reflected by children's health, health care and policy?' *Children & Society*, **5** (3): 207–24.

Lafreniere, P. J. and Sroufe, L. A. (1985) 'Profiles of peer competence in the preschool: Interrelations between measures, influence of social ecology and relation of attachment history', *Developmental Psychology*, **21** (1): 56–69.

Lamb, M. (1987) *The Father's Role: Cross-national Perspectives*, Hillsdale, NJ: Lawrence Erlbaum.

Lambert, L., Buist, M., Triseliotis, J. and Hill, M. (1990) *Freeing Children For Adoption*, London: BAAF.

Lambeth (1987) *Whose Child?* Report of the Inquiry into the Death of Tyra Henry, London: London Borongh of Lambeth.

Lansdown, G. (1994) 'Children's Rights', in B. Mayall (ed.) *Children's Childhood: Observed and Experienced*, London: The Falmer Press.

Lansdown, G. (1995) 'The Children's Rights Development Unit', in B. Franklin (ed.) *The Handbook of Children's Rights*, London: Routledge.

Lansdown, G. (1996) 'Implementation of the UN Convention on the Rights of the Child in the UK', in M. Long (ed.) *Children in our Charge*, London: Jessica Kingsley.

Lasch, C. (1977) *Haven in a Heartless World*, New York: Basic Books.

Lasko, J. K. (1954) 'Parent behaviour towards first and second children', *Genetic Psychology Monographs*, **49**: 97–134.

Laslett, P. and Wall, R. (1972) *Household and Family in Past Time*, Cambridge: Cambridge University Press.

Lavalette, M. (1994) *Child Employment in the Capitalist Labour Market*, Aldershot: Avebury.

Laybourn, A. (1994) *The Only Child*, Edinburgh: HMSO.

Laybourn, A. and Cutting, E. (1996) *Young People with Epilepsy: Supports and Services – Existing and Desired*, Glasgow; Report for Enlighten (Action for Epilepsy Edinburgh, Mid and East Lothian).

Laybourn, A. and Hill, M. (1994) 'Children with epilepsy and their families: needs and services', *Child: care, health and development*, **20**: 1–14.

Laybourn, A., Brown, J. and Hill, M. (1996) *Hurting on the Inside: Children, Families and Alcohol*, Aldershot: Avebury.

Leach, S., Davis, H. and Associates (1996) *Enabling or Disabling Local Government*, Buckingham: Open University Press.

Leather, P., Mackintosh, S. and Rolfe, S. (1994) *Papering over the cracks. Housing conditions and the nation's health*, London: National Housing Forum.

Lees, L. H. (1994) 'Educational Inequality and Academic Achievement in England and France', *Comparative Education Review*, **38** (1): 65–87.

Lees, S. (1993) *Sugar and Spice: Sexuality and Adolescent Girls*, Harmondsworth: Penguin.

Leibfried, S. (1991) 'European Models of Welfare and the Wider International Order', in G. Room (ed.) *Towards a European Welfare State*, Bristol: SAUS Publications.

Leira, A. (1993) 'Mothers, markets and the State: A Scandinavian model?', *Journal of Social Policy*, **22** (3): 329–48.

Leonard, D. (1990) 'Persons in their own right: Children and sociology in the UK', in L. Chisholm, P. Buchner, H. H. Kruger and P. Brown (eds) *Childhood, Youth and Social Change: A Comparative Perspective*, London: Falmer Press.

Leshied, A. W., Jaffe, P. G. and Willis, W. (1991) *The Young Offenders Act: A Revolution in Canadian Juvenile Justice*, Toronto: University of Toronto Press.

Lestor, J. (1995) 'A Minister for Children', in B. Franklin (ed.) *The Handbook of Children's Rights*, London: Routledge.

Levačič, R. (1993) 'Assessing the Impact of Formula Funding on Schools', *Oxford Review of Education*, **19** (4): 435–57.

Levin, I. (1995) 'Children's perceptions of their family', *Annale dell'Istituto di Dirritto e Procedura penale*, 55–74.

Levitt, R., Wall, A. and Appleby, J. (1992) *The Reorganised National Health Service*, London: Chapman and Hall.

Lewis, A. (1995) *Children's Understanding of Disability*, London: Routledge.

Lewis, C. (1996) 'Psychological research', in J. Brannen and R. Edwards (eds) *Perspectives on Parenting and Childhood: Looking Back and Moving Forward*, London: South Bank University.

Lewis, C. and O'Brien, M. (eds) (1987) *Reassessing Fatherhood*, London: Sage.

Ley, D. (1983) *A Social Geography of the City*, New York: Harper Row.

Lindley, R. (1991) 'Teenagers and other children', in G. Scarre (ed.) *Children, Parents and Politics*, Cambridge: Cambridge University Press.

Lindon, J. (1996) *Growing Up: from Eight Years to Young Adulthood*, London: National Children's Bureau.

Lindsey, D. (1994) *The Welfare of Children*, New York: Oxford University Press.

Lishman, J. (ed.) (1983) *Collaboration and Conflict*, Aberdeen: Aberdeen University Press.

Liss, P-E. (1993) *Health Care Need: Meaning and Measurement*, Aldershot: Avebury.

Lister, R. (1990a) 'Women, Economic Dependency and Citizenship', *Journal of Social Policy*, **19** (4): 445–67.

Lister, R. (1990b) *The Exclusive Society. Citizenship and the Poor*, London: Child Poverty Action Group.

Little, M. (1990) *Young Men in Prison: The Criminal Identity Explored Through the Rules of Behaviour*, Aldershot: Dartmouth Publishing.

Little, M., Leitch, H. and Bullock, R. (1995) 'The care careers of long-stay children: The contribution of new theoretical approaches', *Children and Youth Services Review*, **17** (5/6) 665–79.

Littlewood, P. (1996) 'Secure units', in S. Asquith (ed.) *Children and Young People in Conflict with the Law*, London: Jessica Kingsley.

Littlewood, P. (1997) 'Education', in J. English (ed.) *Social Services in Scotland*, Edinburgh: Mercat Press.

Lloyd, S. and Burman, M. (1996) 'Specialist Police Units and the Joint Investigation of Child Abuse', *Child Abuse Review*, **5**: 4–17.

Lockyer, A. (1992) *Citizen's Service and Children's Panel Membership*. A research study on behalf of the Children's Panel Chairmen's Group. A report presented to the Social Work Services Group. Edinburgh: The Scottish Office.

Lockyer, A. (1994) 'The Scottish Children's Hearings System: Internal Developments and the UN Convention', in S. Asquith and M. Hill (eds) *Justice for Children*, Dordrecht: Martinus Nijhoff.

Lombroso, C. and Ferrero, W. (1895) *The Female Offender*, with an introduction by W. D. Morrison, London: T. Fisher Unwin.

Long, G. (1995) 'Family Poverty and the Role of Family Support Work', in M. Hill, R. Hawthorne-Kirk, and D. Part (eds) *Supporting Families*, Children in Society Series, Edinburgh: HMSO.

Long, G., Macdonald, S. and Scott, G. (1996) *Children and Family Poverty in Scotland: the Facts*, 2nd Edition, Glasgow: Glasgow Caledonian University and Save the Children Fund.

Long, M. (1996a) *Children in Charge: The Child's Right to a Fair Hearing*, London: Jessica Kingsley.

Long, M. (1996b) *Children in Our Charge: The Child's Right to Resources*, London: Jessica Kingsley.

Lorenz, W. (1994) *Social Work in a Changing Europe*, London: Routledge.

Lücker-Babel, M. (1995) 'The right of the child to express views and to be heard: An attempt to interpret Article 12 of the UN Convention on the Rights of the Child', *The International Journal of Children's Rights*, **3**: 391–404.

Lukes, S. (1974) *Power: A Radical View*, London: Macmillan.

Lyon, C. and Parton, N. (1995) 'Children's rights and the Children Act 1989', in B. Franklin (ed.) *The Handbook of Children's Rights*, London: Routledge.

Macaskill, C. (1985) *Against the Odds*, London: BAAF.

Maccoby, E. E. and Martin, J. A. (1983) 'Socialisation in the context of the family: Parent–child interaction', in E. M. Hetherington (ed.) *Handbook of Child Psychology: Socialisation, Personality and Social Development* (Vol. 4) New York: Wiley.

McAleer, M. (1994) 'The school fax', *Nursing Times*, **90** (31): 9–31.

McArthur, C. (1956) 'Personalities of first and second children', *Psychiatry*, **19**: 47–54.

McAuley, C. (1996) 'Children's perspectives on long-term foster care', in M. Hill and J. Aldgate (eds) *Child Welfare Services*, London: Jessica Kingsley.

McBain, B. (1995) 'A clear case of comeback kids', *The Herald*, 14.12.95.

McColgan, M. (1995) 'The Children (Northern Ireland) Order 1995: Considerations of the legislative, economic and political, organisational and social policy contexts', *Children and Youth Services Review*, **17** (5/6): 637–49.

McCormick, A. and Hall, S. (1995) 'Infectious diseases in childhood', in B. Botting (ed.) *The Health of our Children*, London: HMSO.

MacCormick, N. (1982) *Legal Right and Social Democracy. Essays in Legal and Political Philosophy*, Oxford: Clarendon Press.

MacDonald, P. (1989) 'What is Sociology? What is the Sociology of Education?', in M. Cole (ed.) *The Social Contexts of Schooling*, London: Falmer Press.

McEwen, A. and Salters, M. (1995) 'Public policy and education in Northern Ireland', *Research Papers in Education*, **10** (1): 131–41.

Macey, M. (1995) '"Same Race" Adoption Policy: Anti-racism or racism?', *Journal of Social Policy*, **24** (4): 473–91.

MacDonald, G. (1993) 'Defining the goals and raising the issues in mental health promotion' in Trent, D. and Reed, C. (eds), *Prompting Mental Health*, Avebury, Aldershot.

MacFarlane, A. and Mitchell, R. (1988) 'Health services for children and their relationship to the educational and social services', in D. Forfar (ed.) *Child Health in a Changing Society*, Oxford: Oxford University Press.

McGee, C. and Westcott, H. L. (1996) 'System abuse: towards greater understanding from the perspectives of children and parents', *Child & Family Social Work*, **1** (3): 169–80.

McGillicuddy-De Lisi, A. V. (1982) 'Parental beliefs about developmental processes', *Human Development*, **25**: 192–200.

McGillivray, A. (1994) 'Why children do have equal rights: in reply to Laura Purdy', *The International Journal of Children's Rights*, **2** (3): 243–58.

McGuire, J. (ed.) (1995) *What Works: Reducing Reoffending. Guidelines from Research and Practice*, Chichester: Wiley.

McIntosh, J. (1992) 'The perception and use of child health clinics in a sample of working class families', *Child: care, health and development*, **18**: 133–50.

Macintyre, S., Annandale, E., Ecob, R., Ford, G., Hunt, K., Jamieson, B., Maciver, S., West, P. and Wyke, S. (1989) 'The West of Scotland Twenty-07 Study: Health in the Community', in C. J. Martin and D. V. McQueen (eds) *Readings for New Public Health*, Edinburgh: Edinburgh University Press.

Mack, J. and Lansley, S. (1985) *Poor Britain*, London: Allen & Unwin.

McKechnie, J., Lindsay, S. and Hobbs, S. (1994) *Child Employment in Dumfries and Galloway. Still Forgotten*, Glasgow: Scottish Low Pay Unit.

McKechnie, J., Lindsay, S. and Hobbs, S. (1996) 'Child employment: a neglected topic?', *The Psychologist*, **May**: 219–222.

McKillip, J. (1987) *Need Analysis*, Newbury Park: Sage.

McLanahan, S. and Booth, K. (1989) 'Mother-only families: Problems, prospects and politics', *Journal of Marriage and the Family*, **51**: 557–80.

McLaughlin, D. and Whitfield, R. (1984) 'Adolescents and their experience of parental divorce', *Journal of Adolescence*, **7**: 155–70.

MacLeod, M. (1995) *What Children Tell us about Being Abused*, London: ChildLine.

MacLeod, M. and Saraga, E. (1988) 'Challenging the orthodox: towards a feminist theory and practice' *Feminist Review*, **28**: 16–55.

MacLeod, M. and Saraga, E. (1991) 'Clearing a path through the undergrowth: a feminist reading of recent literature on child sexual abuse', in P. Carter, T. Jeffs and M. K. Smith (eds) *Social Work and Social Welfare: Yearbook 3*, Buckingham: Open University Press.

McLoyd, V. C. and Wilson, L. (1991) 'The strain of living poor: Parenting, social support and child mental health', in A. C. Huston (ed.) *Children in Poverty: Child Development and Public Policy*, Cambridge: Cambridge University Press.

Macmillan, J. (1991) 'Social information and decision-making in juvenile liaison panels', in T. Booth (ed.) *Juvenile Justice in the New Europe*, Social Services Monographs: Research in Practice, Sheffield: University of Sheffield, Joint Unit for Social Services Research.

McNeill, P. (1986) *Adoption of Children in Scotland*, Edinburgh: Green & Son.

McNeish, D. (1996) 'Young people, crime, justice and punishment', in H. Roberts and D. Sachdev (eds) *Young People's Social Attitudes. Having Their Say – The Views of 12–19 Year Olds*, Essex: Barnardo's.

McNeish, D. and Roberts, H. (1995) *Playing it Safe: Today's Children at Play*, Barkingside: Barnardo's.

Macnicol, J. (1978) 'Family allowances and less eligibility', in P. Thane (ed.) *The Origins of British Social Policy,* Croom Helm: London.

Magill, J. and Hurlbut, N. (1986) 'The self-esteem of adolescents with cerebral palsy', *The American Journal of Occupational Therapy*, **40** (6): 402–7.

McQuoid, J. (1996) 'Brief Report. The ISRD Study – Self-report findings from N. Ireland', *Journal of Adolescence*, **19** (1): 95–98.

McRobbie, A. and Garber, J. (1991) 'Girls and Subcultures', in *Feminism and Youth Culture: From 'Jackie' to 'Just Seventeen'*, Basingstoke: Macmillan.

McRoy, R. (1991a) 'American experience and research on openness', *Adoption & Fostering*, **15** (4): 99–110.

McRoy, R. (1991b) 'Significance of ethnic and racial identity in inter-country adoption within the United States', *Adoption & Fostering*, **15** (4): 53–60.

McWhinnie, A. (1967) *Adopted Children, How They Grow Up*, London: Routledge and Kegan Paul.

Makrinioti, D. (1994) 'Conceptualisation of Childhood in a Welfare State: A critical reappraisal', in J. Qvortrup, M. Bardy, G. Sgritta and H. Wintersberger, (eds) *Childhood Matters*, Aldershot: Avebury.

Malek, M. (1991) *Psychiatric admissions: A report on young people entering psychiatric care*, London: The Children's Society.

Malik, N. M. and Furman, W. (1993) 'Practitioner review: Problems in children's peer relations: What can the clinicians do?', *Journal of Child Psychology and Psychiatry*, **34** (8): 1303–26.

Mann, P. (1984) *Children in Care Revisited*, London: Batsford.

Marneffe, C. (1992) 'The Confidential Doctor Centre – a new approach to child protection work', *Adoption & Fostering*, **16** (4): 23–8.

Marshall, K. (1995a) 'Families and the Law: Policing or social support', in M. Hill, R. Hawthorn-Kirk and D. Part (eds) (1995) *Supporting Families*, Edinburgh: HMSO.

Marshall, K. (1995b) *Children's Rights in the Balance. Reconciling Views and Interests*, A Report. December 1995.

Marshall, T. H. (1963) 'Citizenship and Social Class', in *Sociology at the Crossroads and Other Essays*, London: Heinemann.

Marshall, T. H. (1981) *The Right to Welfare and Other Essays*, with an introduction by Robert Pinker. London: Heinemann Educational Books Ltd.

Martin, F. M., Fox, S. F. and Murray, K. (1981) *Children out of Court*, Edinburgh: Scottish Academic Press.

Martin, J. and Roberts, C. (1984) *Women and Employment: A Lifetime Perspective*, London: HMSO.

Martinson, F. M. (1994) *The Sexual Life of Children*, Westport, Conn: Bergin and Garvey.

Maslow, A. (1970) *Motivation and Personality*, New York: Harper and Row.

Mason, D. (1995) *Race and Ethnicity in Modern Britain*, Oxford: Oxford University Press.

Masson, H. and O'Byrne, P. (1990) 'The family systems approach: A help or a hindrance', in *Violence Against Children Group: Taking Child Abuse Seriously*, London: Unwin Hyman.

Matthews, M. H. (1992) *Making Sense of Place*, Hemel Hempstead: Harvester Wheatsheaf.

Maughan, B. and Pickles, A. (1991) 'Adopted and illegitimate children growing up', in L. Robbins and M. Rutter (eds) *Straight and Deviant Pathways from Childhood to Adulthood*, Cambridge: Cambridge University Press.

Maxime, J. (1986) 'Some psychological models of black self-concept', in S. Ahmed, J. Cheetham and J. Small (eds) *Social Work with Black Children and their Families*, London: Batsford/BAAF.

Maxwell, W. (1990) 'The nature of friendship in the primary school', in C. Rogers and P. Kutnik (eds) *The Psychology of the Primary School*, London: Routledge.

May, T. (1996) *Situating Social Theory*, Buckingham: Open University Press.

Mayall, B. (1986) *Keeping Children Healthy*, London: Allen & Unwin.

Mayall, B. (ed.) (1994a) *Children's Childhoods*, London: Falmer Press.

Mayall, B. (1994b) 'Children in Action at Home and School', in B. Mayall (ed.) *Children's Childhoods: Observed and Experienced*, London: Falmer Press.

Mayall, B. (1994c) *Negotiating Health: Primary School Children at Home and School*, London: Cassell.

Mayall, B. (1995) 'The changing context of childhood: children's perspectives on health care resources including services', in B. Botting (ed.) *The Health of our Children*, London: HMSO.

Mayall, B. (1996) *Children, Health and the Social Order*, Buckingham: Open University Press.

Mayes, G., Currie, E. F., MacLeod, L., Gillies, J. B. and Warden, D. A. (1992) *Child Sexual Abuse*, Edinburgh: Scottish Academic Press.

MBise, A. (1990) 'The changing perspective of childrearing in Tanzania', in J. Ross and V. Bergum (eds) *Through the Glass Darkly*, Ottawa: Canadian Public Health Association.

Mead, M. (1942) *Growing Up in New Guinea*, Edinburgh: Pelican.

Mead, M. (1961) *Coming of Age in Samoa*, Harmondsworth: Penguin.

Mead, M. (1962) *Male and Female*, Harmondsworth: Penguin.

Mead, M. and Wolfenstein, M. (1954) *Childhood in Contemporary Cultures*, Chicago: University of Chicago Press.

Meadows, R. (1988) 'Time past and time present for children and their doctors', in D. Forfar (ed.) *Child Health in a Changing Society*, Oxford: Oxford University Press.

Meadows, S. (1993) *The Child as Thinker*, London: Routledge.

Measor, L. and Sikes, P. (1992) *Gender and Schools*, London: Cassell.

Mehra, H. (1996) 'Residential care for ethnic minorities' children', in K. N. Dwivedi and V. P. Varma (eds) *Meeting the Needs of Ethnic Minority Children*, London: Jessica Kingsley.

Melden, A. I. (ed.) (1970) *Human Rights*, Belmont CA: Wadsworth Publishing Company Inc.

Mellor, A. (1990) *Bullying in Scottish Secondary Schools*, Spotlights 23, Edinburgh: Scottish Council for Research in Education (SCRE).

Merchant, J. and Macdonald, R. (1994) 'Youth and the Rave Culture, Ecstasy & Health', *Youth and Policy*, **45**: 16–38.

Merrett, F. and Jones, L. (1994) 'Rules, Sanctions and Rewards in Primary Schools', *Educational Studies*, **20** (3): 345–56.

Merrett, F., Wilkins, J., Houghton, S. and Wheldall, K. (1988) 'Rules, Sanctions and Rewards in Secondary Schools', *Educational Studies*, **14** (2): 139–49.

Merrick, D. (1996) *Social Work and Child Abuse*, London: Routledge.

Merton, R. K. (1957) *Social Theory and Social Structure*, Glencoe, Ill: Free Press.

Middleton, S., Ashworth, K. and Walker, R. (eds) (1994) *Family Fortunes: Pressures on Parents and Children in the 1990s*, London: Child Poverty Action Group.

Milburn, K. (1996) *Peer Education*, HEBS Working Paper No. 2, Edinburgh: Health Education Board for Scotland.

Miles, S. (1996) 'Use and consumption in the construction of identities', paper given at *British Youth Research: The New Agenda*, 26–28 January 1996, Glasgow.

Miller, J. B. (1993) 'Learning from early relationship experience', in S. Duck (ed.) *Learning about Relationships*, London: Sage.

Miller, S. A., Davis, T. L., Wilde, C. A. and Brown, J. (1993) 'Parents' knowledge of their children's preferences', *International Journal of Behavioural Development*, **16** (1): 35–60.

Millham, S., Bullock, R., Hosie, K. and Haak, M. (1986) *Lost in Care*, Aldershot: Gower.

Millstein, S. G. and Litt, I. F. (1990) 'Adolescent Health', in S. E. Feldman and G. R. Elliott (eds) *At the Threshold*, Cambridge, Mass: Harvard University Press.

Milne, R. (1992) *Who's Hearing? A summary of a one day seminar on children's hearings in Scotland*, Edinburgh: The Scottish Office, Social Work Services Group.

Mitchell, A. (1985) *Children in the Middle*, London: Tavistock.

Mitchell, J. C. (1969) *Social Networks in Urban Situations*, Manchester: Manchester University Press.

Mitchell, L. and West, P. (1996) 'Peer pressure to smoke: the meaning depends on the method', *Health Education Research*, **11**, 1, 39–49.

Mizen, P. (1995) *The State, Young People and Youth Training: In and Against the Training State*, London: Mansell.

Modi, P., Marks, C. and Wattley, R. (1995) 'From the margin to the centre: empowering the black child', in C. Cloke and M. Davies (eds) *Participation and Empowerment in Child Protection*, London: Pitman.

Modood, T., Beishon, S. and Virdee, S. (1994) *Changing Ethnic Identities*, London: Policy Studies Institute.

Monck, E. (1991) 'Patterns of confiding relationships among adolescent girls', *Journal of Child Psychology and Psychiatry*, **32** (2): 333–45.

Moore, R. C. (1986) *Children's Domain: Play and Place in Child Development*, London: Croom Helm.

Moore, T. (1975) 'Exclusive early mothering and its alternatives: the outcome to adolescence', *Scandinavian Journal of Psychology*, **16**: 255–72.

Moran-Ellis, J. and Fielding, N. (1996) 'A national survey of the investigation of child sexual abuse', *British Journal of Social Work*, **26**: 337–56.

Morgan, D. H. (1985) *The Family, Politics and Social Theory*, London: Routledge and Kegan Paul.

Morris, A. (1974) 'Scottish Juvenile Justice: A Critique', in R. Hood (ed.) *Crime, Criminology and Public Policy*, London: Heinemann.

Morris, A. and Giller, H. (1987) *Understanding Juvenile Justice*, London: Croom Helm.

Morris, A. and Maxwell, G. M. (1993) 'Juvenile Justice in New Zealand: A New Paradigm', *Australia and New Zealand Journal of Criminology*, **26** (1): 72–90.

Morrison, M. (1995) 'Researching food consumers in school. Recipes for concern', *Educational Studies*, **21**, 2, 239–63.

Morrow, V. (1994) 'Responsible children? Aspects of children's work and employment outside school in contemporary UK', in B. Mayall (ed.) *Children's Childhood: Observed and Experienced*, London: The Falmer Press.

Morrow, V. and Richards, M. (1996) 'The ethics of social research with children: An overview', *Children & Society*, **10** (2): 90–105.

Moss, P. (1988/9) 'The indirect costs of parenthood: A neglected issue in social policy', *Critical Social Policy*, **20** (2): 110–17.

Moss, P. (ed.) (1996) *Father Figures*, London: HMSO.

Mount, F. (1982) *The Subversive Family*, London: Jonathan Cape.

Mullender, A. and Morley, R. (eds) (1994) *Children Living with Domestic Violence: Putting Men's Abuse of Women on the Child Care Agenda*, London: Whiting and Birch.

Mulvey, E. P., Arthur, M. W. and Reppucci, N. D. (1993) 'The Prevention and Treatment of Juvenile Delinquency: A Review of the Research', *Clinical Psychology Review*, **13** (2): 133–67.

Muncie, J., Wetherell, M., Dallos, R. and Cochrane, A. (eds) (1995) *Understanding the Family*, London: Sage.

Munn, P. and Johnstone, M. (1992) *Truancy and Attendance in Scottish Secondary Schools*, Spotlights No. 38, Edinburgh: Scottish Council for Research in Education.

Munro, E. (1996) 'Avoidable and unavoidable mistakes in child protection work', *British Journal of Social Work*, **26** (6): 795–810.

Murch, M. (1995) 'Listening to the voice of the child – critical transitions, support and child representations for children', *Representing Children*, **8** (2): 19–27.

Murphy, J. (1993) *British Social Services: The Scottish Dimension*, Scottish Academic Press, Edinburgh.

Murphy, W. D., Haynes, M. R. and Page, I. J. (1992) 'Adolescent Sex Offenders', in W. O'Donohue and J. H. Geer (eds) *The Sexual Abuse of Children: Clinical Issues, Volume 2*, Hillsdale, NJ: Lawrence Erlbaum.

Murray, K. (1995) *Live Television Links in Court*, Edinburgh: Scottish Office Central Research Unit.

Murray, K. and Hill, M. (1992) 'The recent history of Scottish child welfare', *Children & Society*, **5** (3): 266–81.

Musick, J. S. (1993) 'Profiles of Children and Families in Poverty', in J. A. Chafel (ed.) *Child Poverty and Public Policy*, Washington, DC: The Urban Institute Press.

Nadelbaum, L. and Begun, A. (1982) 'The effects of the newborn on the older sibling', in M. E. Lamb and B. Sutton-Smith (eds) *Sibling Relationships: Their Nature and Significance Across the Life Span*, Hillsdale, NJ: Lawrence Erlbaum.

Näsman, E. (1994) 'Individualization and institutionalization of childhood in today's Europe', in J. Qvortrup, M. Bardy, G. Sgritta and H. Wintersberger (eds) *Childhood Matters. Social Theory, Practice and Politics*, European Centre, Vienna. Aldershot: Avebury.

National Commission of Inquiry into the Prevention of Child Abuse (1996) *Childhood Matters*, London: The Stationery Office.

Naylor, H. (1986) 'Outdoor play and play equipment', in Smith, P. (ed.) *Children's Play*, London: Gordon and Breach.

Nestmann, F. and Hurrelmann, K. (eds) (1994) *Social Networks and Social Support in Childhood*, Berlin: De Gruyter.

Netting, N. S. (1992) 'Sexuality in Youth Culture: Identity and Change', *Adolescence*, **27** (108): 961–76.

Newell, P. (1991) *The UN Convention and Children's Rights in the UK*, London: National Children's Bureau.

Newman, J. L., Roberts, L. R. and Syre, C. R. (1993) 'Concepts of family among children and adolescents: effect of cognitive level, gender and family structure', *Developmental Psychology*, **29** (6): 951–62.

Nielson, R. (1996) 'Young Lives', *The Guardian*, 15.5.96.

Noller, P. and Callan, V. (1991) *The Adolescent in the Family*, London: Routledge.

Norrie, K. (1995) *Children (Scotland) Act 1995*, Edinburgh: W. Green.

Noschis, K. (1992) 'Child development through play and planning', *Children's Environments*, **9** (2): 3–9.

O'Brien, M. (1995) 'Health and lifestyle a critical mess? Notes on the differentiation of health', in R. Bunton, S. Nettleton and R. Burrows (eds) *The Sociology of Health Promotion*, London: Routledge.

O'Brien, M., Alldred, P. and Jones, D. (1996) 'Children's constructions of family and kinship', in J. Brannen and M. O'Brien (eds) *Children in Families*, London: Falmer Press.

O'Collins, M. (1984) 'The influence of western adoption on customary adoption in the Third World', in P. Bean (ed.) *Adoption: Essays in Social Policy, Law and Sociology*, London: Tavistock.

O'Hara, G. (1991) 'Placing children with special needs – outcomes and implications for practice', *Adoption & Fostering*, **15** (4): 24–30.

O'Hara, G. and Hoggan, P. (1988) 'Permanent substitute family care in Lothian – placement outcome', *Adoption & Fostering*, **12** (3): 35–8.

O'Neill, J. (1994) *The Missing Child in Liberal Theory*, Toronto: University of Toronto Press.

O'Neill, J. (1995) 'On the liberal culture of child risk: A covenant critique of contractarian theory', in Ambert, A-M. (ed.) *Sociological Studies of Children: Volume 7*, Greenwich, Conn: Jai Press.

Oakley, A. (1980) *Women Confined: Towards a Sociology of Childbirth*, Oxford: Martin Robertson.

Oakley, A. (1994) 'Women and children first and last: Parallels and differences between children's and women's studies', in B. Mayall (ed.) *Children's Childhoods*, London: Falmer Press.

Oakley, A., Bendelow, G., Barnes, J, Buchanan, M. and Nasseem Husain, O. A. (1995) 'Health and cancer prevention: knowledge and beliefs of children and young people', *British Medical Journal*, **310**: 1029–33.

Ochiltree, G. (1990) *Children in Stepfamilies*, Englewood Cliffs: Prentice Hall.

Office of Population Censuses and Surveys (OPCS) (1995) *1993 General Household Survey*, London: HMSO.

Oldfield, N. and Yu, A. C. S. (1993) *The Cost of a Child. Living Standards for the 1990s*, London: Child Poverty Action Group.

Oldman, D. (1994) 'Adult-child relations as class relations', in J. Qvortrup, M. Bardy, G. Sgritta and H. Wintersberger (eds) *Childhood Matters*, Aldershot: Avebury.

Oliver, M. (ed.) (1991) *Social Work: Disabled People and Disabling Environments*, London: Jessica Kingsley.

Olsen, F. (1992) 'Social legislation. Sex bias in international law: The UN Convention on the Rights of the Child', *Indian Journal of Social Work*, **53** (3): 491–516.

Olsson, S. and McMurphy, S. (1993) 'Social policy in Sweden: The Swedish model in transition', in R. Page and J. Baldock (eds) *Social Policy Review 5*, Canterbury: Social Policy Association.

Olweus, D. (1991) 'Bully/Victim Problems among school children: basic facts and effects of a school-based intervention program', in D. Pepler and K. Rubin (eds) *The Development and Treatment of Childhood Aggression*, London: Lawrence Erlbaum Associates.

OPCS (1995) *General Household Survey 1993*, London: HMSO.

Opie, I. (1993) *The People in the Playground*, Oxford: Oxford University Press.

Opie, I. and Opie, P. (1959) *The Language and Lore of Schoolchildren*, Oxford: Oxford University Press.

Opie, I. and Opie, P. (1969) *Children's Games in Street and Playground*, Oxford: Clarendon Press.

Oppenheim, C. (1996) *Poverty: The Facts*, London: Child Poverty Action Group.

Osborne, R. D., Cormack, R. J. and Miller, R. L. (1987) *Education and Policy in Northern Ireland*, Belfast: Policy Research Unit.

Packman, J. (1981) *The Child's Generation*, Oxford: Blackwell.

Packman, J. and Jordan, B. (1991) 'The Children Act: Looking Forward, Looking Back', *British Journal of Social Work*, **21**: 315–27.

Packman, J., Randall, J. and Jacques, N. (1986) *Who Needs Care?*, Oxford: Blackwell.

Pahl, J. (1989) *Money and Marriage*, London: Macmillan.

Palmer, S. E. (1995) *Maintaining Family Ties: Inclusive Practice in Foster Care*, Washington DC: Child Welfare League of America.

Parffrey, V. (1994) 'Exclusion: failed children or systems failure?', *School Organisation*, **14** (2): 107–20.

Parke, R. D. (1981) *Fathering*, Glasgow: Fontana.

Parke, R. D. and Stearns, P. N. (1993) 'Fathers and child-rearing', in G. H. Elder, J. Modell and R. D. Parke (eds) (1993) *Children in Place and Time*, Cambridge: Cambridge University Press.

Parker, D. (1995) *Through Different Eyes: The Cultural Identity of Young Chinese People in Britain*, Aldershot: Avebury.

Parker, J. G. and Asher, R. (1987) 'Later personal adjustment: Are low-accepted children at risk?' *Psychological Bulletin*, **102** (3): 357–89.

Parker, R. (1966) *Decision in Child Care*, London: Allen & Unwin.

Parker, R. (1988) 'Residential Care for Children', in I. Sinclair (ed.) *The Research Reviewed*, London: HMSO.

Parker, R., Ward, H., Jackson, S., Aldgate, J. and Wedge, P. (1991) *Assessing Outcomes in Child Care*, London: HMSO.

Parkes, C. M. (1972) *Bereavement – Studies of Grief in Adult Life*, London: Tavistock.

Parkes, C. M. (1993) 'Bereavement as a psychosocial transition: Processes of adaptation to change', in D. Dickenson and M. Johnson (eds) *Death, Dying and Bereavement*, London: Sage.

Parkes, C. M., Stevenson-Hinde, J. and Marris, P. (eds) (1991) *Attachment Across the Life Cycle*, London: Routledge.

Parkinson, L. (1987) *Separation, Divorce and Families*, London: Macmillan.

Parsons, T. and Bales, R. F. (1956) *Family, Socialization and Interaction Process*, London: Routledge and Kegan Paul.

Parsons, T. C. (1980) 'The isolated conjugal family', in M. Anderson (ed.) *The Sociology of the Family*, Harmondsworth: Penguin.

Part, D. (1993) 'Fostering as seen by the carers' children', *Adoption & Fostering*, **17** (1): 26–31.

Parten, M. B. (1932) 'Social participation among pre-school children', *Journal of Abnormal and Social Psychology*, **24**: 243–69.

Parten, M. B. (1933) 'Social play among pre-school children', *Journal of Abnormal and Social Psychology*, **28**: 136–47.

Parton, N. (1985) *The Politics of Child Abuse*, London: Macmillan.

Parton, N. (1991) *Governing the Family*, London: Macmillan.

Parton, N. (1996a) 'Child protection, family support and social work: A critical appraisal of the Department of Health research studies in child protection', *Child and Family Social Work*, **1**: 3–11.

Parton, N. (1996b) 'Social work, risk and the blaming system', in N. Parton (ed.) *Social Theory, Social Change and Social Work*, London: Routledge.

Parton, N. and Otway, O. (1995) 'The contemporary state of child protection policy and practice in England and Wales', *Children and Youth Services Review*, **17** (5/6): 599–617.

Pasternicki, G., Wakefield, D., Robertson, J. and Edwards, L. (1993) 'A school-based action research project on truancy: Within-school factors', *Support for Learning*, **8** (1): 3–6.

Paterson, L. with Hill, M. (1994) *Opening and Reopening Adoption: Views from Adoptive Families*, Central Research Unit Paper, Edinburgh: Scottish Office.

Patterson, G. (1971) *Families: Application of Social Learning to Family Life*, Champaign, Ill: Research Press.

Pavlovic, Z. (1996) 'Children's Parliament in Slovenia', in M. John (ed.) *The Child's Right to a Fair Hearing,* London: Jessica Kingsley Publishers.

Pearson, S. (1994) *Baking Cakes at 60: Young Disabled People in Transition*, Edinburgh: Access Ability Lothian.

Percy-Smith, J. (1996) *Needs Assessments in Public Policy*, Buckingham: Open University Press.

Petersen, A, C. (1988) 'Adolescent development', *Annual Review of Psychology*, **39**: 583–607.

Petrie, P. (1994) *Play and Care After School*, London: HMSO.

Phillips, M. (1994) 'Habermas, Rural Studies and Critical Social Theory', in P. Cloke, M. Doel, D. Matless, M. Phillips and N. Thrift (eds) *Writing the Rural: Five Cultural Geographies*, London: Paul Chapman.

Phillips, M. (1995) 'Issues of ethnicity and culture', in K. Wilson and A. James (eds) *The Child Protection Handbook*, London: Bailliere Tindall.

Phillips, M. (1996) *All Must Have Prizes*, London: Little, Brown and Co.

Phillips, R. and McWilliam, E. (1996) *After Adoption*, London: BAAF.

Piachaud, D. (1987) 'Problems in the Definition and Measurement of Poverty', *Journal of Social Policy*, **16** (2): 147–64.

Piaget, J. (1959) *The Language and Thought of the Child*, London: Routledge and Kegan Paul.

Piche, D. (1981) 'The spontaneous geography of the urban child', in D. T. Herbert and R. J. Johnston (eds) *Geography and the Urban Environment*, Vol. IV, London: Wiley.

Pickin, C. and St. Leger, S. (1993) *Assessing Health Need Using the Life Cycle Framework*, Buckingham: Open University Press.

Pilkington, B. and Kremer, J. (1995) 'A review of the epidemiological research on child sexual abuse', *Child Abuse Review*, **4**: 84–98.

Pitts, J. (1988) *The Politics of Juvenile Crime*, London: Sage.

Plant, M. and Plant, M. (1992) *Risk-takers: Alcohol, drugs, sex and youth*, London: Routledge.

Pollak, O. (1950) *The Criminality of Women*, Philadelphia: University of Pennsylvania Press.

Pollard, A. (1985) *The Social World of the Primary School*, London: Holt, Rinehart and Winston.

Pollock, L. (1983) *Forgotten Children: Parent-Child Relations from 1500 to 1900*, Cambridge: Cambridge University Press.

Polnay, L. and Roberts, H. (1989) 'Evaluation of an easy to read parent-held information and record booklet of child health', *Children & Society*, **3** (3): 255–60.

Polnay, L. and Hull, D. (1992) *Community Paediatrics*, Edinburgh: Churchill Livingstone.

Power, C. (1995) 'Health related behaviour', in B. Botting (ed.) *The Health of our Children*, London: HMSO.

Pringle, M. K. (1980) *The Needs of Children*, London: Hutchinson.

Pritchard, C. (1992) 'Children's homicide as an indicator of effective child protection: A comparative study of Western European statistics', *British Journal of Social Work*, **22**: 663–84.

Pritchard, C. (1993) 'Re-analysing children's homicide and undetermined death rates as an indication of improved child protection: A reply to Creighton', *British Journal of Social Work*, **23**: 645–52.

Pritchard, C. (1996) 'Search for an indicator of Effective Child Protection in a Re-analysis of Child Homicide in the major western countries 1973–1992', *British Journal of Social Work*, **26**: 545–63.

Prochaska, J. M. and Prochaska, J. O. (1985) 'Children's views of the causes and "cures" of sibling rivalry', *Child Welfare*, **64**: 427–33.

Prout, A. (1986) ' "Wet children" and "little actresses": going sick in primary school', *Sociology of Health and Illness*, **8**: 111–36.

Prout, A. (1996) *Families, Cultural Bias and Health Promotion*, London: Health Education Authority.

Prout, A. and Christensen, P. (1996) 'Hierarchies, boundaries and symbols: medicine use and the cultural performance of childhood sickness', in P. J. Bush, D. J. Trakas, E. J. Sanz, R. L. Wirsing, T. Vaskilampi and Prout, A. (eds) (1996) *Children, Medicines and Culture*, New York: Haworth Press.

Prout, A. and James, A. (1990) 'A New Paradigm for the Sociology of Childhood? Provenance, Promise and Problems', in A. James and A. Prout (eds) *Constructing and Reconstructing Childhood: Contemporary Issues in the Sociological Study of Childhood*, London: The Falmer Press.

Pugh, G. (1996) 'Seen but not heard: Addressing the needs of children who foster', *Adoption & Fostering*, **20** (1): 35–41.

Pugh, G., De'Ath, E. and Smith C. (1995) *Confident Parents, Confident Children*, London: National Children's Bureau.

Purdy, L. (1992) *In Their Best Interest? The Case against Equal Rights for Children*, Ithaca and London: Cornell University Press.

Purdy, L. (1994) 'Why children shouldn't have equal rights', *The International Journal of Children's Rights*, **2**: 223–41.

Putallaz, M. and Heflin, A. H. (1986) 'Towards a model of peer acceptance', in J. M. Gottman and J. G. Parker (eds) *Conversations of Friends*, Cambridge: Cambridge University Press.

Quinton, D. and Rutter, M. (1988) *Parenting Breakdown*, Aldershot: Avebury.

Qvortrup, J. (1991) *Childhood as Social Phenomenon: An Introduction to a Series of International Reports*, Budapest: Publicitas.

Qvortrup, J. (1994) 'Childhood Matters: An Introduction', in J. Qvortrup, M. Bardy, G. Sgritta and H. Wintersberger (eds) *Childhood Matters*, Aldershot: Avebury.

Qvortrup, J., Bardy, M., Sgritta, G. and Wintersberger, H. (eds) (1994) *Childhood Matters*, Aldershot: Avebury.

Rae, R. (1996) 'Researching Children's Rights Officers', in M. Long (ed.) *Children in our Charge*, London: Jessica Kingsley.

Raleigh, V. S. and Balajaran, R. (1995) 'The health of infants and children among ethnic minorities', in B. Botting (ed.) *The Health of our Children*, London: HMSO.

Rashid, S. P. (1996) 'Attachment reviewed through a cultural lens', in D. Howe (ed.) *Attachment Theory and Child and Family Social Work*, Aldershot: Avebury.

Rayner, M. (1995) 'Children's Rights in Australia', in B. Franklin (ed.) *The Handbook of Children's Rights. Comparative Policy and Practice*, London: Routledge.

Raynor, L. (1980) *The Adopted Child Comes of Age*, London: Allen & Unwin.

Rechner, M. (1990) 'Adolescents with cancer: Getting on with life', *Journal of Pediatric Oncology Nursing*, **7** (4): 139–44.

Reddy, N. (1995) 'Child Labour: A Hidden Form of Child Abuse', *Child Abuse Review*, **4**: 207–13.

Reder, P., Duncan, S. and Gray, M. (1993) *Beyond Blame: Child Abuse Tragedies Revisited*, London: Routledge.

Redgrave, K. (1987) *Child's Play*, Manchester: Boys and Girls Welfare Society.

Reed, J. (1995) 'Young Carers', *Highlight No 37*, London: National Children's Bureau.

Rees, A. M. (1995) 'The Promise of Social Citizenship', *Policy and Politics*, **23** (4): 313–25.

Regis, (1996) 'The voice of the children in health education: Use of the Just a Tick method to consult children over curriculum content', in M. Long (ed.) *Children in our Charge*, London: Jessica Kingsley.

Reid, R. (1994) 'Children's Rights: Radical Remedies for Critical Needs', in S. Asquith and M. Hill (eds) *Justice for Children*, London: Martinus Nijhoff Publishers.

Reimers, S. and Treacher, A. (1995) *Introducing User-friendly Family Therapy*, London: Routledge.

Reppucci, N. D. and Crosby, C. A. (1993) 'Law, Psychology and Children. Overarching Issues', *Law and Human Behaviour*, **17** (1): 1–10.

Rhodes, M. (1996) 'Globalization and West European welfare states', *Journal of European Social Policy*, **6** (4): 305–27.

Richards, M. (1995) 'Changing Families', in M. Hill, R. Kirk and D. Part (eds) *Supporting Families*, Edinburgh: HMSO.

Richards, M. (1996) 'Long-term implication for children of disruptions in parental relations', in J. Brannen and R. Edwards (eds) *Perspectives on Parenting and Childhood: Looking Back and Moving Forward*, London: South Bank University.

Richards, M. and Dyson, M. (1982) *Separation, Divorce and the Development of Children: A Review*, London: DHSS.

Riddell, S. and Brown, S. (1994) 'Special educational needs provision in the United Kingdom – the policy context', in S. Riddell and S. Brown (eds) *Special Educational Needs Policy in the 1990s*, London: Routledge.

Riddell, S. and Brown, S. (eds) (1994) *Special Educational Needs Policy in the 1990s*, London: Routledge.

Roberts, H., Smith, S. J. and Bryce, C. (1995) *Children at Risk? Safety as a Social Value*, Milton Keynes: Open University Press.

Roberts, J. (1996) 'Behavioural and cognitive-behavioural approaches', in Phillips, R. and McWilliam, E. (eds) *After Adoption*, London: BAAF.

Roberts, J. and Taylor, C. (1993) 'Sexually abused children and young people speak out', in Waterhouse, L. (ed.) *Child Abuse and Child Abusers*, London: Jessica Kingsley.

Roberts, J., Taylor, C., Dempster, H., Bonnar, S. and Smith, C. (1993) *Sexually Abused Children and their Families*, Edinburgh: Child and Family Trust.

Robertson, W. (1995) 'Scots children cash in on feel-good factor', *The Scotsman*, 18.4.95.

Robins, L. and Rutter, M. (eds) (1991) *Straight and Deviant Pathways from Childhood to Adulthood*, Cambridge: Cambridge University Press.

Robinson, M. (1991) *Family Transformation Through Divorce and Remarriage*, London: Routledge.

Roche, J. (1996) 'Children's rights: A lawyer's view', in M. Long (ed.) *Children in our Charge*, London: Jessica Kingsley.

Roche, J. and Tucker, S. (eds), (1997), *Youth in Society*, London: Sage.

Rodger, J. J. (1996) *Family Life and Social Control*, London: Macmillan.

Roeyers, H. and Mycke, K. (1995) 'Siblings of a child with autism, with mental retardation and with a normal development', *Child: care, health and development*, **21** (5): 305–19.

Rogers, R. S. and Rogers, W. S. (1994) *Stories of Childhood*, Toronto: University of Toronto Press.

Rogers, W. S., Hevey, D., Roche, J. and Ash, E. (1992) *Child Abuse and Neglect: Facing the Challenge*, Milton Keynes: Open University Press.

Roker, D. (1996) 'Understanding health risk in adolescence', in A. Sigston, P. Curran, A. Labram and S. Wolfendale (eds) *Psychology in Practice with Young People, Families and Schools*, London: David Fulton.

Roll, J. (1991) 'One in ten: lone parent families in the European Community', in N. Manning (ed.) *Social Policy Review 1990–91*, London: Longman.

Roll, J. (1992) *Understanding Poverty: A guide to the concept and measures*, London: Family Policy Studies Centre.

Rowe, J., Cain, H., Hundleby, M. and Keane, A. (1984) *Long Term Foster Care*, Batsford, London.

Rowe, J., Hundleby, M. and Garnett, L. (1989) *Child Care Now: A Survey of Placement Patterns*, London: BAAF.

Rubin, Z. (1980) *Children's Friendships*, Glasgow: Fontana.

Ruefle, W. and Reynolds, K. M. (1995) 'Curfews and delinquency in major American cities', *Crime & Delinquency*, **41** (3): 347–63.

Rutter, M. (1981) *Maternal Deprivation Reassessed*, Harmondsworth: Penguin.

Rutter, M. (1985) 'Resilience in the face of adversity', *British Journal of Psychiatry*, **147**: 598–611.

Rutter, M. and Giller, J. (1983) *Juvenile Delinquency: Trends and Perspectives*, Harmondsworth: Penguin.

Rutter, M. and Rutter, M. (1993) *Developing Minds*, Harmondsworth: Penguin.

Ryan, T. and Walker, R. (1993) *Life Story Work*, London: BAAF.

Ryburn, M. (1994) *Open Adoption: Research, Theory and Practice*, Aldershot: Avebury.

Ryburn, M. (ed.) (1994) *Contested Adoption: Research, Law, Policy and Practice*, Aldershot: Arena.

Ryburn, M. (1995) 'Adopted children's identity and information needs', *Children & Society*, **9**, 3, 41–64.

Salzinger, S. (1990) 'Social networks in child rearing and child development', *Annals of the New York Academy of Sciences*, 171–88.

Sameroff, A. (1975) 'Transactional models in early social relations', *Human Development*, **18**, 65–79.

Samuel, E. and Tisdall, K. (1996) 'Female Offenders in Scotland: Implications for Theory', in S. Asquith (ed.) *Children and Young People in Conflict with the Law*, London: Jessica Kingsley.

Sandel, M. J. (1982) *Liberalism and the Limits of Justice*, Cambridge: Cambridge University Press.

Sandler, I., Wolchik, S. and Braver, S. (1983) 'Social support and children of divorce', in I. G. Sarason and B. R. Sarason (eds) *Social Support: Theory, Research and Applications*, Dordrecht: Martinus Nijhoff.

Sanghera, P. (1994) 'Identity politics & young Asian people', *Youth and Policy*, **45**: 39–45.

Saraga, E. (1993) 'The abuse of children', in R. Dallos and E. McLaughlin (eds) *Social Problems and the Family*, London: Sage.

Sartorius, N. (1992) 'The promotion of mental health: meaning and tasks', in D. Trent (ed.) *Promoting Mental Health*, Volume 1, Aldershot: Avebury.

Savin-Williams, R. C. and Berndt, T. C. (1990) 'Friendship and peer relations', in S. E. Feldman and G. R. Elliott (eds) *At the Threshold*, Cambridge, Mass: Harvard University Press.

Scanzoni, J. and Szinovacz, M. (1980) *Family Decision-Making*, Newbury Park: Sage.

Scarr, S. (1992) 'Developmental theories for the 1990s: The Development of Individual Differences', *Child Development*, **63**: 1–19.

Scarr, S. and Dunn, J. (1987) *Mother Care/Other Care*, Harmondsworth: Pelican.

Scarr, S. and Grajek, S. (1982) 'Similarities and differences among siblings', in M. E. Lamb and B. Sutton-Smith (eds) *Sibling Relationships: Their Nature and Significance Across the Life Span*, Hillsdale, NJ: Lawrence Erlbaum.

Schaffer, H. R. (1990) *Making Decisions about Children*, Oxford: Blackwell.

Schaffer, H. R. (1992) 'Joint involvement episodes as contexts for development', in H. McGurk (ed.) *Childhood Social Development*, Hove: Lawrence Erlbaum.

Schaffer, H. R. and Emerson, P. (1964) *The Development of Social Attachments in Infancy*, Chicago: University of Chicago Press.

Schweinhart, L. J., Barnes, H. V. and Weikart, D. P. (eds) (1993) *Significant Benefits: The High/Scope Perry Preschool Study through age 27*, Ypsilanti, MI: High/Scope Press.

Scottish Office (1994a) *Scotland's Children. Speaking Out. Young People's Views on Child Care Law in Scotland*, Edinburgh: Social Work Services Group, the Scottish Office.

Scottish Office (1994b) *Referrals of Children to Reporters and Children's Hearings 1993*, SWK/CH/1994/18, Edinburgh: HMSO.

Scottish Office Education and Industry Department (SOEID) (1996) *Children and Young Persons with Special Educational Needs. Assessment and Recording*, Circular 4/96, Edinburgh: The SOEID.

Scottish Office Guidance (1995) *Child Protection: Guidance for Social Workers in Scotland*, SWSI, Edinburgh.

Sears, R. R. (1950) 'Ordinal position in the family as psychological variable', *American Sociological Review*, **15**: 397–401.

Secombe, W. (1974) 'The housewife and her labour under capitalism', *New Left Review*, **83**: 3–26.

Segal, L. (1995) 'A feminist looks at the family', in J. Muncie, M. Wetherell, R. Dallos and A. Cochrane (eds) *Understanding the Family*, London: Sage.

Seglow, J., Pringle, M. K. and Wedge, P. (1972) *Growing Up Adopted*, Windsor: NFER.

Selman, P. and Wells, S. (1996) 'Post-adoption issues in intercountry adoption', in Phillips, R. and McWilliam, E. (eds) *After Adoption*, London: BAAF.

Selwyn, J. (1996) 'Ascertaining wishes and feelings in relation to adoption', *Adoption & Fostering*, **20** (3): 14–21.

Sen, A. (1984) *Resources, Values and Development*, Oxford: Basil Blackwell.

Sex Education Forum (1994) *Developing and Reviewing a School Sex Education Policy: A Positive Strategy*, London: National Children's Bureau.

Shahar, S. (1992) *Childhood in the Middle Ages*, Paperback Edition. Translated by C. Galai, London: Routledge.

Shamgar-Handelman, L. (1994) 'To Whom Does Childhood Belong?', in J. Qvortrup, M. Bardy, G. Sgritta, H. Wintersberger (eds) *Childhood Matters. Social Theory, Practice and Politics*, European Centre, Vienna. Aldershot: Avebury.

Shams, M. and Williams, R. (1995) 'Differences in perceived parental care and protection and related psychological distress between British Asian and non-Asian adolescents', *Journal of Adolescence*, **18**: 329–48.

Sharpe, S., Mauthner, M. and France-Dawson, M. (1996) *Family Health: A Literature Review*, London: Health Education Authority.

Shaw, I. (1996) 'Unbroken voices: Children, young people and qualitative methods', in I. Butler and I. Shaw (eds) *A Case of Neglect? Children's experiences and the Sociology of Childhood*, Aldershot: Avebury.

Short, G. (1991) 'Children's grasp of controversial issues', in M. Woodhead, P. Light and R. Carr (eds) *Growing up in a Changing Society*, London: Routledge.

Shorter, E. (1976) *The Making of the Modern Family*, London: Collins.

Shucksmith, J., Hendry, L. B. and Glendinning, A. (1995) 'Models of parenting: Implications for adolescent well-being within different types of family contexts', *Journal of Adolescence*, **18**: 253–70.

Silverman, D. (1987) *Communication and Medical Practice*, London: Sage.

Simon, R. J. and Altstein, H. (1992) *Adoption, Race, and Identity*, New York: Praeger.

Simpson, B. (1989) 'Giving children a voice in divorce: The role of family conciliation', *Children & Society*, **3** (3): 261–74.

Sinclair, I. and Gibbs, I. (1996) *Quality of care in Children's Homes*, Report to the Department of Health, University of York.

Sinclair, R., Garnett, L. and Berridge, D. (1995) *Social Work Assessment with Adolescents*, London: National Children's Bureau.

Sinclair, R., Grimshaw, R. and Garnett, L. (1994) 'The Education of Children in Need: The impact of the Education Reform Act 1988, The Education Act 1993 and the Children Act 1989', *Oxford Review of Education*, **20** (3): 281–92.

Sjögren, J. S. (1996) 'A ghost in my own country', *Adoption & Fostering*, **20** (2): 32–5.

Skolnick, A. (1975) 'The Limits of Childhood', *Law and Contemporary Social Problems*, **39** (3): 38–9.

Skolnick, A. (1989) 'Children in their own right: The view from developmental psychology', in E. Verhellen and F. Spiesschaert (eds) *Ombudswork for Children*, Leuven: Acco.

Slee, R. (1995) *Changing Theories and Practices of Discipline*, London: The Falmer Press.

Sluckin, A. (1981) *Growing up in the Playground*, London: Routledge and Kegan Paul.

Small, J. (1991) 'Ethnic and racial identity in adoption within the United Kingdom', *Adoption & Fostering*, **15** (4): 61–8.

Smith, C. (1984) *Adoption and Fostering*, London: Macmillan.

Smith, D. J. (1995) 'Youth Crime and Conduct Disorders: Trends, Patterns and Causal Explanations', in M. Rutter and D. Smith (eds) *Psychosocial Disorders in Young People. Time Trends and Their Causes*, Chichester: John Wiley & Sons.

Smith, G. (1980) *Social Need: Policy, Practice and Research*, London: Routledge and Kegan Paul.

Smith, G. (1996) 'Reassessing protectiveness', in Batty, D. and Cullen, D. (eds) *Child Protection: The Therapeutic Option*, BAAF; London.

Smith, G. D., Bartley, M. and Blane, D. (1990) 'The Black Report on socio-economic inequalities in health 10 years on', *British Medical Journal*, **301**: 373–7.

Smith, G., Williamson, H. and Platt, L. (1996) *Youth in an Age of Uncertainty: An Overview of Recent Research on Young People aged 11–25*, London: Paper presented to the Carnegie UK Trust 'Years of Decision' Conference, May 1996.

Smith, P. K. (1979) 'How many people can a young child feel secure with?', *New Society*, 504–6.

Smith, P. K. (1980) 'Shared care of young children: Alternative models to monotropism', *Merrill-Palmer Quarterly*, **26** (4): 371–87.

Smith, P. K. (1990) 'The role of play in the nursery and primary school curriculum', in C. Rogers and P. Kutnik (eds) *The Psychology of the Primary School*, London: Routledge.

Smith, P. K. (ed.) (1986) *Children's Play*, London: Gordon and Breach.

Smith, P. K. (ed.) (1991) *The Psychology of Grandparenthood*, London: Routledge.

Smith, P. K. and Cowie, H. (1991) *Understanding Children's Development*, Oxford: Blackwell.

Smith, P. K. and Sharp, S. (eds) (1994) *School Bullying: Insights and Perspectives*, London: Routledge.

Smyth, M. and Robus, N. (1989) *OPCS surveys of disability in Great Britain: the financial circumstances of families with disabled children living in private households*, Report 5, London: HMSO.

Social Security Committee (1993) *The Operation of the Child Support Act*, First Report. Session 1993–94. London: HMSO.

Social Services Inspectorate (1994) *Services to Disabled Children and their Families*, London: Department of Health.

Social Work Services Group (1993) *Scotland's Children: Proposals for Child Care Policy and Law*, Cm 2286, Edinburgh: HMSO.

Somers, M. R. (1994) 'Rights, relationality, and membership: Rethinking the making and meaning of citizenship', *Law and Social Inquiry*, **19** (1): 63–112.

Song, M. (1996) ' "Helping Out": Children's labour participation in Chinese take-away businesses in Britain', in J. Brannen and M. O'Brien (eds) *Children in Families: Research and Policy*, London: Falmer Press.

Soper, K. (1993a) 'Review of "A Theory of Human Need" ', *New Left Review*, **197**: 113–28.

Soper, K. (1993b) 'The thick and thin of human needing', in G. Drover and P. Kerans (eds) *New Approaches to Welfare Theory*, Aldershot: Edward Elgar.

Sorensen, T. and Snow, B. (1991) 'How children tell: The process of disclosure in child sexual abuse', *Child Welfare*, **70** (1): 3–15.

Spector, M. and Kitsuse, J. I. (1987) *Constructing Social Problems*, New York: Aldine de Gruyter.

Spencer, J. R. and Flin, R. (1990) *The Evidence of Children*, London: Blackstone Press.

Spencer, N. (1996a) 'Reducing child health inequalities: insights and strategies for health workers', in P. Bywaters and E. McLeod (eds) *Working for Equality in Health*, London: Routledge.

Spencer, N. (1996b) *Poverty and Child Health*, Oxford: Radcliffe Medical Press.

Spencer, N. J. (1990) 'Poverty and child health', *Children & Society*, **4** (4): 352–64.

Spicer, D. (1996) 'An injudicious approach to child protection', in D. Batty. and D. Cullen (eds) *Child Protection: The Therapeutic Option*, London: BAAF.

Stalker, K. (1990) *'Share the Care' : An Evaluation of a Family-based Respite Care Service*, London: Jessica Kingsley.

Stalker, K. (ed.) (1995) *Developments in Short-term Care*, London: Jessica Kingsley.

Stanley, C. (1995) 'Teenage kicks: Urban narratives of dissent not deviance', *Crime, Law and Social Change*, **23**: 91–119.

Stein, M. and Carey, K. (1986) *Leaving Care*, Oxford: Basil Blackwell.

Stephenson, H. (1995) 'Message in the bottle', *The Scotsman*, 19.6.95.

Stevenson, O. (ed.) (1989) *Child Abuse*, London: Harvester Wheatsheaf.

Stewart, K. (1996) 'Sexual abuse as a moral event', *British Journal of Social Work*, **26**: 293–308.

Stewart, R. B. (1983) 'Sibling attachment relationships: Child–infant interactions in the Strange Situation', *Developmental Psychology*, **19** (2): 192–9.

Stirling, M. (1992) 'How Many Pupils are being Excluded?', *British Journal of Special Education*, **19** (4): 128–30.

Stocker, C. M. and McHale, S. M. (1992) 'The nature and family correlates of preadolescents' perceptions of their sibling relationships', *Journal of Social and Personal Relationships*, **9**: 179–95.

Stoll, P. (1994) 'Truancy in English Secondary Schools', *Education Today*, **44** (1): 35–37.

Stolz, L. M. (1967) *Influences on Parent Behaviour*, London: Tavistock.

Stone, L. (1977) *The Family, Sex and Marriage in England 1500–1800*, London: Weidenfeld and Nicolson.

Strathclyde Region Social Work Department (1995) *Child Protection Statistics*, Unpublished data.

Street, H. (1996) 'Is it possible to establish the truth of a child's statement alleging sexual abuse?', *Adoption & Fostering*, **20** (4).

Sugarman, L. (1986) *Life-span Development*, London: Methuen.

Sullivan, A. (1995) 'Policy issues in gay and lesbian adoption', *Adoption & Fostering*, **19** (4): 21–5.

Summers, C. R. (1994) 'Siblings of children with a disability: A review and analysis of the empirical literature', *Journal of Social Behaviour and Personality*, **9** (5): 169–84.

Summit, R. (1983) 'The child sexual abuse accommodation syndrome', *Child Abuse & Neglect*, **7**: 177–93.

Sutton-Smith, B. and Rosenberg, R. G. (1970) *The Sibling*, New York: Holt, Rinehart and Winston.

Sweeting, H. (1995) 'Reversals of fortune'. Sex differences in childhood and adolescense, Soc. Sci. Med., **60** (1): 77–90.

Sweeting, H. and West, P. (1995) 'Family life and health in adolescence: A role for culture in the health inequalities debate?', *Social Science and Medicine*, **40** (2): 163–75.

Sweeting, H. and West, P. (1996) *The Health of 11 Year Olds in the West of Scotland*, Glasgow: MRC Medical Sociology Unit.

Taylor, D. (1989) 'Citizenship and social power', *Critical Social Policy*, 26, **9** (2): 19–31.

Taylor, R. and Ford, J. (1989), *Social Work and Health Care*, London: Jessica Kingsley.

Tesson, G. and Youniss, J. (1995) 'Micro-sociology and psychological development: A sociological interpretation of Piaget's theory', in Ambert, A-M. (ed.) (1995) *Sociological Studies of Children: Volume 7*, Greenwich (Conn.): Jai Press.

Thoburn, J. (1986) *Child Placement: Principles and Practice*, Aldershot: Gower.

Thoburn, J. (1994) *Child Placement: Principles and Practice*, Aldershot: Wildwood House.

Thoburn, J., Lewis, A. and Shemmings, D. (1995) *Paternalism or Partnership? Family Involvement in the Child Protection Process*, London: HMSO.

Thomas, A. and Chess, S. (1977) *Temperament and Development*, New York: Brunner/Mazel.

Thompson, A. (1995) 'No Place Like Home', *Community Care*, 26 October–1 November: 14–15.

Thomson, G. (1987) *Needs and Desires*, London: Routledge and Kegan Paul.

Thomson, G. O. B., Riddell, S. I. and Dyer, S. (1990) 'The Placements of Pupils Recorded as Having Special Educational Needs; An Analysis of Scottish Data 1986–1988', *Oxford Review of Education*, **16** (2): 159–78.

Thomson, G. O. B., Stewart, M., and Ward, K. M. (1995) *Criteria for Opening Records of Needs*, Report to the Scottish Office Education Department. Edinburgh: Department of Education, University of Edinburgh.

Thorne, B. (1993) *Gender Play*, Buckingham: Open University Press.

Thornton, S. (1995) *Club Culture. Music, Media and Subcultural Capital*, Cambridge: Polity Press.

Thorpe, D. (1995) 'Some implications of recent child protection research', *Representing Children*, **8** (3): 27–31.

Thrasher, S. P. and Mowbray, C. T. (1995) 'A Strengths Perspective: An Ethnographic Study of Homeless Women with Children', *Health and Social Work*, **20** (2): 93–101.

Tietjen, A. M. (1982) 'The social networks of preadolescent children in Sweden', *International Journal of Behavioural Development*, **5**: 111–30.

Tisdall, E. K. M. (1990) *Conflicts in Participation – Narratives of Young People who are Physically Disabled in Ontario*, Unpublished Honors Thesis, Cambridge MA: Harvard University.

306   *Children and Society*

Tisdall, E. K. M. (1994) 'Why Not Consider Citizenship? A critique of post-school transitional models for young disabled people', *Disability and Society*, **9**: 3–17.

Tisdall, E. K. M. (1997) *Children (Scotland) Act 1995* Edinburgh: HMSO.

Tisdall, E. K. M. with E. Donnaghie (1995) *Scotland's Families Today*. Children in Scotland. Edinburgh: HMSO.

Tisdall, E. K. (1996) 'From the Social Work (Scotland) Act 1968 to the Children (Scotland) Act 1995: Pressures for change', in M. Hill and J. Aldgate (eds) *Child Welfare Services*, London: Jessica Kingsley.

Tite, R. (1993) 'How teachers define and respond to child abuse: The distinction between theoretical and reportable cases', *Child Abuse & Neglect*, **17**: 591–603.

Titmuss, R. (1958) *Essays on the Welfare State*, London: Allen and Unwin.

Tizard, B. (1977) *Adoption: A Second Chance*, London: Open Books.

Tizard, B. (1986) *The Care of Young Children: The Implications of Recent Research*, London: Thomas Coram Foundation.

Tizard, B. and Phoenix, A. (1993) *Black, White or Mixed Race*, London: Routledge.

Tomlinson, S. (1982) *A Sociology of Special Education*, London: Routledge and Kegan Paul.

Toope, S. (1996) 'The Convention on the Rights of the Child: Implications for Canada', in M. Freeman (ed.) *Children's Rights: A Comparative Perspective*, Aldershot: Dartmouth.

Townsend, P. (1979) *Poverty in the United Kingdom. A Survey of Household Resources and Standards of Living*, Middlesex: Penguin Books.

Townsend, P., Davidson, N. and Whitehead, M. (1992) *The Health Divide*, Harmondsworth: Penguin.

Trasler, G. (1960) *In Place of Parents*, London: Routledge and Kegan Paul.

Trevarthen, C. (1992) 'The self born in intersubjectivity', in U. Neisser (ed.) *Ecological and Interpersonal Knowledge of the Self*, Cambridge: Cambridge University Press.

Triseliotis, J. (1973) *In Search of Origins*, London: Routledge and Kegan Paul.

Triseliotis, J. (1983) 'Identity and security in adoption and long-term fostering', *Adoption & Fostering*, **9** (1): 22–31.

Triseliotis, J. (1989) 'Foster care outcomes', *Adoption & Fostering*, **13** (3): 5–16.

Triseliotis, J. (1991) 'Inter-country adoption: A brief overview of the research evidence', *Adoption & Fostering*, **15** (4): 46–52.

Triseliotis, J., Borland, M., Hill, M. and Lambert, L. (1993) 'The rights and responsibilities of adolescents in need or in trouble', *International Journal of Children's Rights*, **1**: 315–30.

Triseliotis, J., Borland, M., Hill, M. and Lambert, L. (1995) *Teenagers and the Social Work Services*, London: HMSO.

Triseliotis, J., Sellick, C. and Short, R. (1995) *Foster Care*, London: Batsford.

Triseliotis, J., Shireman, J. and Hundleby. M. (1997) *Adoption: Theory, Policy and Practice*, London: Cassell.

Trowell, J. (1996) 'Understanding the child: The importance of thinking about the child's feelings', in D. Batty and D. Cullen (eds) (1996) *Child Protection: The Therapeutic Option*, London: BAAF.

Tudor, K. (1992) 'Community mental health promotion: a paradigm approach', in D. Trent (ed.) *Promoting Mental Health Volume 1*, Aldershot: Avebury.

Tunstill, J. (1995) 'The concept of children in need: The answer or the problem for family support', *Children and Youth Services Review*, **17** (5/6): 651–64.

Tunstill, J. (1996) 'Family support: past, present and future challenges', *Child & Family Social Work*, **1** (3): 151–58.

Turner, B. S. (1986) *Citizenship and Capitalism: The Debate over Reformism*, Controversies in Sociology 21, London: Allen and Unwin.

Turner, B. S. (1990) 'Outline of a theory of citizenship', *Sociology*, **24**: 189–217.

UNICEF (1996) 'Convention watch begins' http://www.unicef.org/pon96/cowatch.htm.

United Nations (1985) *United Nations Standard Minimum Rules for the Administration of Juvenile Justice (The 'Beijing Rules')*, A/RES/40/33, 29th November, 96th plenary meeting.

United Nations Committee on the Rights of the Child (1995) 'Concluding Observations of the Committee on the Rights of the Child: United Kingdom of Great Britain and Northern Ireland', *Consideration of Reports Submitted by State Parties under Article 44 of the Convention*, Eighth Session. CRC/C/15/Add.34.

Vagaro, D. (1995) 'Health inequalities as policy issues – reflections on ethics, policy and public health', *Sociology of Health and Illness*, **17** (1): 1–19.

Valios, N. (1997) 'Government to review "misinterpreted" Act', *Community Care*, **1152**: 1, 9–15 January.

Van Loon, J. H. A. (1990) *Report on Intercountry Adoption*, The Hague: Permanent Bureau of the Conference on Private International Law.

Van Montfoort, A. (1993) 'The protection of children in the Netherlands: Between justice and welfare', in H. Ferguson, R. Gilligan and R. Torode (eds) *Surviving Childhood Adversity: Issues for Policy and Practice*, Dublin: Social Studies Press.

Vandell, D. L. and Bailey, M. D. (1992) 'Conflicts between siblings', in C. U. Schantz and W. W. Hartup (eds) (1992) *Conflict in Child and Adolescent Development*, Cambridge: Cambridge University Press.

Vandell, D. L. and Mueller, E. C. (1980) 'Peer play and friendship during the first two years', in H. C. Foot, A. J. Chapman and J. R. Smith (eds) *Friendship and Social Relations in Children*, Chichester: John Wiley.

Vaskilampi, T., Kalpio, O. and Hallia, O. (1996) 'From catching a cold to eating junk food: Conceptualisations of illness among Finnish children', in P. J. Bush, D. J. Trakas, E. J. Sanz, R. L. Wirsing, T. Vaskilampi and A. Prout (eds) (1996) *Children, Medicines and Culture*, New York: Haworth Press.

Veerman, P. E. (1992) *The Rights of the Child and the Changing Image of Childhood*, Dordrecht: Martinus Nijhoff.

Verhulst, F. C., Althaus, M. and Versluis-den Bieman, H. J. M. (1992) 'Damaging backgrounds: Later adjustments of international adoptees', *Journal of American Academy of Child and Adolescent Psychiatry*, 31, 518–24.

Vuchinich, S., Hetherington, E. M., Vuchinich, R. A. and Clingempeel, W. G. (1991) 'Parent-child interaction and gender differences in early adolescents' adaptation to stepfamilies', *Developmental Psychology*, **27** (4): 618–26.

Wade, B. and Moore, M. (1993) *Experiencing Special Education. What Young People with Special Educational Needs Can Tell Us*, Buckingham: Open University Press.

Wadsworth, M. (1986) 'Evidence from three birth cohort studies for long-term and cross-generational effects on the development of children', in M. Richards and P. Light (eds) *Children of Social Worlds*, Oxford: Blackwell.

Wagner, M. E., Schubert, H. J. P. and Schubert, D. S. P. (1985) 'Effect of sibling spacing on intelligence, interfamilial relations, psychosocial characteristics and mental and physical health', *Advances in Child Development and Behaviour*, **19**: 149–206.

Waksler, F. C. (1991) *Studying the Social Worlds of Children*, London: Falmer Press.

Waldrop, M. F. and Halverson, C. S. (1975) 'Intensive and extensive peer behaviour: longitudinal and cross-sectional analysis', *Child Development*, **46**: 19–26.

Walford, G. (1990) 'Developing Choice in British Education', *Compare*, **20** (1): 67–81.

Walgrave, L. (1995) 'Restorative Justice for Juveniles: Just a Technique or a Fully Fledged Alternative', *The Howard Journal of Criminal Justice*, **34** (3): 228–49.

Walker, J. (1991) 'Interventions in families', in D. Clark (ed.) *Marriage, Domestic Life and Social Change*, London: Routledge.

Walker, J. (1996) 'Re-negotiating fatherhood', in E. De'Ath (ed.) *Families in Transition*, London: Stepfamily Publications.

Wallerstein, J. S. and Kelly, J. B. (1980) *Surviving the Break-up*, London: Grant McIntyre.

Walmsley, D. J. and Lewis, G. J. (1993) *People and Environment: Behavioural Approaches in Human Geography*, London: Longman.

Ward, C. (1978) *The Child in the City*, London: Architectural Press.

Ward, H. (1995) *Looking After Children: Research into Practice*, London: HMSO.

Ward, K., Riddell, S., Dyer, M. and Thomson, G. (1991) *The Transition to Adulthood of Young People with Recorded Special Educational Needs*. The Departments of Education of the Universities of Edinburgh and Stirling: Final Report to the Scottish Office Education Department.

Ware, A. and Goodin, R. E. (1990) *Needs and Welfare*, Sage, London.

Warnock Report: Report of the Committee of Enquiry into the Education of Handicapped Children and Young People (1978) *Special Educational Needs*, Cmnd. 7212, London: HMSO.

Waterhouse, L. and Carnie, J. (1991) 'Research note: Social work and police responses to child sexual abuse in Scotland', *British Journal of Social Work*, **21**: 373–9.

Waterhouse, L. and McGhee, J. (1996) 'Families, social workers' and police perspectives on child abuse investigations', in M. Hill and J. Aldgate (eds) *Child Welfare Services: Developments in Law, Policy, Practice and Research*, London: Jessica Kingsley.

Waterhouse, L., Dobash, R. P. and Carnie, J. (1994) *Child Sexual Abusers*, Edinburgh: Scottish Office Central Research Unit.

Wattam, C. (1995) 'The investigative process', in Wilson, K. and James, A. (eds) *The Child Protection Handbook*, London: Bailliere Tindall.

Weale, A. (1983) *Political Theory and Social Policy*, London: Macmillan.

Webster, C. (1996) 'Local Heroes. Violent Racism, Localism and Spacism among Asian and White Young People', *Youth & Policy*, **53**: 15–27.

Wedge, P. and Mantle, G. (1991) *Sibling Groups and Social Work*, Avebury, Aldershot.

Weigert, A. J., Teitge, J. S. and Teitge, D. W. (1986) *Society and Identity*, Cambridge: Cambridge University Press.

Weisner, T. S. and Gallimore, R. (1977) 'My brothers' keeper: Child and sibling caretaking', *Current Anthropology*, **18** (2): 169–90.

Weisner, T. S. (1987) 'Socialisation for parenthood in sibling caretaking societies', in J. Lancaster, A. Rossi and L. Sherrod (eds) *Parenting across the Lifespan*, New York: Aldine De Gruyter.

Wellings, K. and Bradshaw, S. (1994) 'First Intercourse between Men and Women', in A. Johnson, J. Wadsworth, K. Wellings, J. Field, with S. Bradshaw (eds) *Sexual Attitudes and Lifestyles*, Oxford: Blackwell Scientific Publications.

Wellings, K., Field, J. and Whitaker, L. (1994) 'Sexual Diversity and Homosexual Behaviour', in A. Johnson, J. Wadsworth, K. Wellings, J. Field, with S. Bradshaw (eds) *Sexual Attitudes and Lifestyles*, Oxford: Blackwell Scientific Publications.

Wendelken, C. (1983) *Children In and Out of Care*, Aldershot: Wildwood House.

Werner, E. E. and Smith, R. S. (1992) *Overcoming the Odds*, Ithaca: Cornell University Press.

Westcott, H. (1995) 'Perceptions of child protection casework: views from children, parents and practitioners', in C. Cloke and M. Davies (eds) *Participation and Empowerment in Child Protection*, London: Pitman.

Westcott, H. L. and Davies, G. M. (1995) 'Children's help-seeking behaviour', *Child: care, health and development*, **21** (4): 255–70.

Westcott, H. L. and Davies, G. M. (1996) 'Sexually abused children's and young people's perspectives on investigative interviews', *British Journal of Social Work*, 26, 451–74.

White, D. and Woollett, A. (1992) *Families: A Context for Development*, London: Falmer Press.

White, R. (1994) 'A case of significant harm?' *New Law Journal*, March 4, 329–30.

Whitney, B. (1994) *The Truth about Truancy*, London: Kogan Page.

Whitney, I. and Smith, P. K. (1993) 'A survey of the nature and extent of bullying in junior/middle and secondary schools', *Educational Research*, **35** (1): 3–25.

Widdicombe, S. and Woofit, R. (1995) *The Language of Youth Subcultures. Social Identity in Action*, London: Harvester Wheatsheaf.

Wilkinson, S. R. (1988) *The Child's World of Illness*, Cambridge: Cambridge University Press.

Willemsen, T. and Van Schie, E. C. M. (1989) 'Sex Stereotypes and Responses to Juvenile Delinquency', *Sex Roles*, **20** (11/12): 623–38.

Williams, T., Wetton, N. and Moon, A. (1989) *A Way In*, Southampton: Health Education Authority/University of Southampton.

Willis, P. (1977) *Learning to Labour: How Working Class Kids Get Working Class Jobs*, Hants: Saxon House.

Willis, P. with Jones, S., Cannan, J. and Hurd, G. (1990) *Common Culture. Symbolic Work at Play in the Everyday Cultures of the Young*, Milton Keynes: Open University Press.

Willow, C. (1990) *Hear! Hear! Promoting Children and Young People's Democratic Participation in Local Government*, London: Local Government Information Unit.

Wilson, A. (1980) 'The Infancy of The History of Adulthood: An Appraisal of Philippe Ariès', *History and Theory*, **19**: 132–53.

Wilson, A. (1987) *Mixed Race Children*, London: Allen & Unwin.

Wilson, C. (1995) 'Issues for children and young people in local authority accommodation', in C. Cloke and M. Davies (eds) *Participation and Empowerment in Child Protection*, London: Pitman.

Wilson, K. and James, A. (eds) (1995) *The Child Protection Handbook*, London: Bailliere Tindall.

Winnicott, D. W. (1957) *The Child and the Family*, London: Tavistock.

Wintersberger, H. (1994) 'Costs and benefits – The economics of childhood', in J. Qvortrup, M. Bardy, G. Sgritta and H. Wintersberger (eds) *Childhood Matters. Social Theory, Practice and Politics*, European Centre, Vienna. Aldershot: Avebury.

Wolkind, S. (1988) *The Mental Health Needs of Children in Care*, London: ESRC.

Woodhead, M. (1990) 'Psychology and the cultural construction of children's needs', in A. James and A. Prout (eds) *Constructing and Deconstructing Childhood*, London: Falmer Press.

Woodhead, M., Light, P. and Carr, R. (1991) *Growing up in a Changing Society*, London: Routledge.

Woodroffe, C. and Glickman, M. (1993) 'Trends in child health', in G. Pugh (ed.) *30 Years of Change for Children*, London: National Children's Bureau.

Woodroffe, C., Glickman, M., Barker, M. and Power, C. (1993) *Children, Teenagers and Health: The Key Facts*, Milton Keynes: Open University Press.

Wulff, H. (1995a) 'Inter-racial friendship. Consuming youth styles, ethnicity and teenage femininity in South London', in V. Amit-Talai and H. Wulff (eds) *Youth Cultures. A Cross-cultural Perspective*, London: Routledge.

Wulff, H. (1995b) 'Introducing youth culture in its own right. The state of the art and new possibilities', in V. Amit-Talai and H. Wulff (eds) *Youth Cultures. A Cross-cultural Perspective*, London: Routledge.

Yoos, H. L. (1994) 'Children's illness concepts: Old and new paradigms', *Pediatric Nursing*, **20** (2): 134–45.

Youniss, J. and Smollar, J. (1985) *Adolescent Relations with Mothers, Fathers and Friends*, Chicago: University of Chicago Press.

Zajonc, R. A. and Marcus, G. B. (1975) 'Birth order and intellectual development', *Psychological Review*, **82**: 74–88.

Zeitlin, H. (1996) 'Adoption of children from minority groups', in K. N. Dwivedi and V. P. Varma (eds) *Meeting the Needs of Ethnic Minority Children*, London: Jessica Kingsley.

The United Nations Convention on the Rights of the Child

BACKGROUND TO THE CONVENTION

Children's international rights, as distinct from human rights, have been recognised since the early part of this century. In 1924 the League of Nations, fore-runner to the United Nations, adopted the Declaration of the Rights of the Child. This codified a growing sense that children need special protection, which had been expressed in 1923 by Eglantyne Jebb, founder of Save the Children: 'I believe we should claim certain rights for children and labour for their universal recognition'.

The League of Nations was replaced, after World War II, by the United Nations. This new body quickly produced its famous Universal Declaration of Human Rights, and not long afterwards a second Declaration on the Rights of the Child (20 November 1959).

This was a step forward for children's rights, but as a declaration, this new set of principles was not legally binding and did not carry a procedure to ensure its implementation. During the International Year of the Child (1979) Poland proposed that a convention should be drafted.

The Convention on the Rights of the Child was passed unanimously by the United Nations General Assembly on 20 November 1989 – exactly 30 years after the second Declaration on the Rights of the Child.

A UN convention is binding on those countries which agree to ratify. By ratifying, a country shows that it is prepared to meet the provisions and obligations set out in the convention. On ratification the country becomes a State Party to the convention. A State Party can, within reason, enter declarations and reservations on the convention. A declaration clarifies the country's interpretation of a section of the convention. A reservation indicates where a particular provision or Article is not acceptable to the State Party. Declarations and reservations can be challenged by other States Parties.

Within the UN convention there is normally a mechanism for monitoring compliance with its Articles. In the case of the Convention on the Rights of the Child, this is undertaken by a committee of ten experts on children's rights from around the world – the Committee on the Rights of the Child.

The Committee on the Rights of the Child monitors the progress of States Parties in fulfilling their obligations. The States Parties must submit a national report two years after ratification and thereafter each five years. These reports are to be given widespread distribution, as part of the obligation to promote awareness of the Convention. The Committee acts on the reports in various ways: it may ask States Parties to add to their report; make recommendations and suggestions to the government concerned; make recommendations to the United Nations General Assembly; pass to other States Parties requests for support and assistance.

The Committee on the Rights of the Child will not make its assessment of each country dependent only on the governmental report. Views will be sought from specialised agencies such as UNICEF and from a wide range of non-governmental organisations (NGOs).

The Convention on the Rights of the Child consists of 54 Articles. 'Child' is defined as every human being below the age of 18. The key principles of the Convention are: that all the rights guaranteed by it must be available to all children without discrimination of any kind (Article 2); that the best interests of the child must be a primary consideration in all actions concerning children (Article 3); and that children's views must be considered and taken into account in all matters affecting them (Article 12).

The other Articles are often defined within three categories – Participation, Provision and Protection.

Participation

These articles including civil and political rights, are based on the concept of the child as an active and contributing participant in society and not merely as a passive recipient of good or bad treatment.

BACKGROUND TO THE CONVENTION

Provision

These articles cover the basic rights of children to survive and develop. These range through health care, food and clean water to education and an environment which allows children to develop. The Convention is clear that the best place for a child is with its parents, and that the State has a duty to support and assist parents in this responsibility where necessary.

Protection

These articles deal with exploitation of children at work; physical, sexual and psychological abuse; discrimination and other mistreatments which many still suffer, including UK children. In other parts of the world children are suffering the effects of war. The Convention makes it a duty for States Parties to protect children and, where necessary, to provide rehabilitation for them.

The Convention on the Rights of the Child was ratified by the UK Government on 16 December 1991. British ratification included several declarations and reservations which have been reprinted at the back of this book (appendix 1).

The Children's Rights Development Unit (CRDU)

The Children's Rights Development Unit was set up in March 1992 as a three-year independent project to promote the fullest possible implementation of the UN Convention on the Rights of the Child. The work of the Unit falls into two broad interlinked areas.

First, it aims to produce a National Agenda for Children. This Agenda will identify, Article by Article, where current law, policy and practice in the UK fails to meet the standards embodied in the Convention and will develop detailed policy proposals which, if implemented, would bring the UK in line with those standards. It will undertake this work through a wide ranging collaborative process with statutory and voluntary organisations, professional associations and interested individuals. The Unit will also be working to ensure that the views and experiences of young people are incorporated in the Agenda and will be recruiting a youth development officer to develop this work.

The rights of children throughout the UK will be represented in the Unit's work. Posts have been established in Scotland and Northern Ireland and the Unit will also be working in close collaboration will the Children in Wales organisation.

Second, the Unit will take an active role in promoting awareness of the Convention and working with local and health authorities, voluntary and professional bodies to develop strategies for applying the principles contained in the Convention to their policies and practice. It will achieve this through the production of guidance documents, policy papers, articles and participation in and organisation of conferences and seminars.

If you wold like to find out more about the Children's Rights Development Unit, write to us, enclosing a large stamped addressed envelope (address on page 346).

THE CONVENTION ON THE RIGHTS OF THE CHILD

Adopted by the United Nations General Assembly on 20 November 1989 and entered into force on 2 September 1990

Text	Unofficial summary of main provisions
PREAMBLE	**PREAMBLE**
The States Parties to the present Convention,	*The preamble: recalls the basic principles of the United Nations and specific provisions of certain relevant human rights treaties and proclamations; reaffirms the fact that children, because of their vulnerability, need special care and protection; and places special emphasis on the primary caring and protective responsibility of the family, the need for legal and other protection of the child before and after birth, the importance of respect for the cultural values of the child's community, and the vital role of international cooperation in achieving the realization of children's rights.*
Considering that, in accordance with the principles proclaimed in the Charter of the United Nations, recognition of the inherent dignity and of the equal and inalienable rights of all members of the human family is the foundation of freedom, justice and peace in the world,	
Bearing in mind that the peoples of the United Nations have, in the Charter, reaffirmed their faith in fundamental human rights and in the dignity and worth of the human person, and have determined to promote social progress and better standards of life in larger freedom,	
Recognizing that the United Nations has, in the Universal Declaration of Human Rights and in the International Covenants on Human Rights, proclaimed and agreed that everyone is entitled to all the rights and freedoms set forth therein, without distinction of any kind, such as race, colour, sex, language, religion, political or other opinion, national or social origin, property, birth or other status,	
Recalling that, in the Universal Declaration of Human Rights, the United Nations has proclaimed that childhood is entitled to special care and assistance,	
Convinced that the family, as the fundamental group of society and the natural environment for the growth and well-being of all its members and particularly children, should be afforded the necessary protection and assistance so that it can fully assume its responsibilities within the community,	

Recognizing that the child, for the full and harmonious development of his or her personality, should grow up in a family environment, in an atmosphere of happiness, love and understanding,

Considering that the child should be fully prepared to live an individual life in society, and brought up in the spirit of the ideals proclaimed in the Charter of the United Nations, and in particular in the spirit of peace, dignity, tolerance, freedom, equality and solidarity,

Bearing in mind that the need to extend particular care to the child has been stated in the Geneva Declaration on the Rights of the Child of 1924 and in the Declaration of the Rights of the Child adopted by the General Assembly on 20 November 1959 and recognized in the Universal Declaration of Human Rights, in the International Covenant on Civil and Political Rights (in particular in articles 23 and 24), in the International Covenant on Economic, Social and Cultural Rights (in particular in article 10) and in the statutes and relevant instruments of specialized agencies and international organizations concerned with the welfare of children,

Bearing in mind that, as indicated in the Declaration of the Rights of the Child, "the child, by reason of his physical and mental immaturity, needs special safeguards and care, including appropriate legal protection, before as well as after birth",

Recalling the provisions of the Declaration on Social and Legal Principles relating to the Protection and Welfare of Children, with Special Reference to Foster Placement and Adoption Nationally and Internationally; the United Nations Standard Minimum Rules for the Administration of Juvenile Justice (The Beijing Rules); and the Declaration on the Protection of Women and Children in Emergency and Armed Conflict,

Recognizing that, in all countries in the world, there are children living in exceptionally difficult conditions, and that such children need special consideration,

Taking due account of the importance of the traditions and cultural values of each people for the protection and harmonious development of the child,

Recognizing the importance of international co-operation for improving the living conditions of children in every country, in particular in the developing countries,

Have agreed as follows:

THE CONVENTION ON THE RIGHTS OF THE CHILD

Text	Unofficial summary of main provisions
Part I	
Article 1	**Definition of a child**
For the purposes of the present Convention, a child means every human being below the age of eighteen years unless, under the law applicable to the child, majority is attained earlier.	All persons under 18, unless by law majority is attained at an earlier age.
Article 2	**Non-discrimination**
1. States Parties shall respect and ensure the rights set forth in the present Convention to each child within their jurisdiction without discrimination of any kind, irrespective of the child's or his or her parent's or legal guardian's race, colour, sex, language, religion, political or other opinion, national, ethnic or social origin, property, disability, birth or other status.	The principle that all rights apply to all children without exception, and the State's obligation to protect children from any form of discrimination. The State must not violate any right, and must take positive action to promote them all.
2. States Parties shall take all appropriate measures to ensure that the child is protected against all forms of discrimination or punishment on the basis of the status, activities, expressed opinions, or beliefs of the child's parents, legal guardians, or family members.	
Article 3	**Best interests of the child**
1. In all actions concerning children, whether undertaken by public or private social welfare institutions, courts of law, administrative authorities or legislative bodies, the best interests of the child shall be a primary consideration.	All actions concerning the child should take full account of his or her best interests. The State is

2. States Parties undertake to ensure the child such protection and care as is necessary for his or her well-being, taking into account the rights and duties of his or her parents, legal guardians, or other individuals legally responsible for him or her, and, to this end, shall take all appropriate legislative and administrative measures.

3. States Parties shall ensure that the institutions, services and facilities responsible for the care or protection of children shall conform with the standards established by competent authorities, particularly in the areas of safety, health, in the number and suitability of their staff as well as competent supervision.

to provide adequate care when parents or others responsible fail to do so.

Article 4

States Parties shall undertake all appropriate legislative, administrative, and other measures, for the implementation of the rights recognized in the present Convention. With regard to economic, social and cultural rights, States Parties shall undertake such measures to the maximum extent of their available resources and, where needed, within the framework of international co-operation.

Implementation of rights

The State's obligation to translate the rights in the Convention into reality.

Article 5

States Parties shall respect the responsibilities, rights and duties of parents or, where applicable, the members of the extended family or community as provided for by local custom, legal guardians or other persons legally responsible for the child, to provide, in a manner consistent with the evolving capacities of the child, appropriate direction and guidance in the exercise by the child of the rights recognized in the present Convention.

Parental guidance and the child's evolving capacities

The State's duty to respect the rights and responsibilities of parents and the wider family to provide guidance appropriate to the child's evolving capacities.

Article 6

1. States Parties recognize that every child has the inherent right to life.

2. States Parties shall ensure to the maximum extent possible the survival and development of the child.

Survival and development

The inherent right to life, and the State's obligation to ensure the child's survival and development.

THE CONVENTION ON THE RIGHTS OF THE CHILD

Text	Unofficial summary of main provisions
Article 7 1. The child shall be registered immediately after birth and shall have the right from birth to a name, the right to acquire a nationality and, as far as possible, the right to know and be cared for by his or her parents. 2. States Parties shall ensure the implementation of these rights in accordance with their national law and their obligations under the relevant international instruments in this field, in particular where the child would otherwise be stateless.	**Name and nationality** *The right to have a name from birth and to be granted a nationality.*
Article 8 1. States Parties undertake to respect the right of the child to preserve his or her identity, including nationality, name and family relations as recognized by law without unlawful interference. 2. Where a child is illegally deprived of some or all of the elements of his or her identity, States Parties shall provide appropriate assistance and protection, with a view to speedily re-establishing his or her identity.	**Preservation of identity** *The State's obligation to protect and, if necessary, re-establish the basic aspects of a child's identity (name, nationality and family ties).*
Article 9 1. States Parties shall ensure that a child shall not be separated from his or her parents against their will, except when competent authorities subject to judicial review determine, in accordance with applicable law and procedures, that such separation is necessary for the best interests of the child. Such determination may be necessary in a particular case such as one involving abuse or neglect of the child by the parents, or one where the parents are living separately and a decision must be made as to the child's place of residence.	**Separation from parents** *The child's right to live with his/her parents unless this is deemed incompatible with his/her best interests; the right to maintain contact with both parents if separated from one or*

both: the duties of States in cases where such separation results from State action.

2. In any proceedings pursuant to paragraph 1 of the present article, all interested parties shall be given an opportunity to participate in the proceedings and make their views known.

3. States Parties shall respect the right of the child who is separated from one or both parents to maintain personal relations and direct contact with both parents on a regular basis, except if it is contrary to the child's best interests.

4. Where such separation results from any action initiated by a State Party, such as the detention, imprisonment, exile, deportation or death (including death arising from any cause while the person is in the custody of the State) of one or both parents or of the child, that State Party shall, upon request, provide the parents, the child or, if appropriate, another member of the family with the essential information concerning the whereabouts of the absent member(s) of the family unless the provision of the information would be detrimental to the well-being of the child. States Parties shall further ensure that the submission of such a request shall of itself entail no adverse consequences for the person(s) concerned.

Article 10

Family reunification

The right of children and their parents to leave any country and to enter their own in order to be reunited or to maintain the child-parent relationship.

1. In accordance with the obligation of States Parties under article 9, paragraph 1, applications by a child or his or her parents to enter or leave a State Party for the purpose of family reunification shall be dealt with by States Parties in a positive, humane and expeditious manner. States Parties shall further ensure that the submission of such a request shall entail no adverse consequences for the applicants and for the members of their family.

2. A child whose parents reside in different States shall have the right to maintain on a regular basis, save in exceptional circumstances, personal relations and direct contacts with both parents. Towards that end and in accordance with the obligation of States Parties under article 9, paragraph 2, States Parties shall respect the right of the child and his or her parents to leave any country, including their own, and to enter their own country. The right to leave any country shall be subject only to such restrictions as are prescribed by law and which are necessary to protect the national security, public order (*ordre public*), public health or morals or the rights and freedoms of others and are consistent with the other rights recognized in the present Convention.

THE CONVENTION ON THE RIGHTS OF THE CHILD

Text	Unofficial summary of main provisions
Article 11	**Illicit transfer and non-return**
1. States Parties shall take measures to combat the illicit transfer and non-return of children abroad.	The State's obligation to try to prevent and remedy the kidnapping or retention of children abroad by a parent or third party.
2. To this end, States Parties shall promote the conclusion of bilateral or multilateral agreements or accession to existing agreements.	
Article 12	**The child's opinion**
1. States Parties shall assure to the child who is capable of forming his or her own views the right to express those views freely in all matters affecting the child, the views of the child being given due weight in accordance with the age and maturity of the child.	The child's right to express an opinion, and to have that opinion taken into account, in any matter or procedure affecting the child.
2. For this purpose, the child shall in particular be provided the opportunity to be heard in any judicial and administrative proceedings affecting the child, either directly, or through a representative or an appropriate body, in a manner consistent with the procedural rules of national law.	
Article 13	**Freedom of expression**
1. The child shall have the right to freedom of expression; this right shall include freedom to seek, receive and impart information and ideas of all kinds, regardless of frontiers, either orally, in writing or in print, in the form of art, or through any other media of the child's choice.	The child's right to obtain and make known information, and to express his or her views, unless this would violate the rights of others.
2. The exercise of this right may be subject to certain restrictions, but these shall only be such as are provided by law and are necessary:	

(a) For respect of the rights or reputations of others; or

(b) For the protection of national security or of public order *(ordre public)*, or of public health or morals.

Article 14

1. States Parties shall respect the right of the child to freedom of thought, conscience and religion.

2. States Parties shall respect the rights and duties of the parents and, when applicable, legal guardians, to provide direction to the child in the exercise of his or her right in a manner consistent with the evolving capacities of the child.

3. Freedom to manifest one's religion or beliefs may be subject only to such limitations as are prescribed by law and are necessary to protect public safety, order, health or morals, or the fundamental rights and freedoms of others.

Article 15

1. States Parties recognize the rights of the child to freedom of association and to freedom of peaceful assembly.

2. No restrictions may be placed on the exercise of these rights other than those imposed in conformity with the law and which are necessary in a democratic society in the interests of national security or public safety, public order *(ordre public)*, the protection of public health or morals or the protection of the rights and freedoms of others.

Article 16

1. No child shall be subjected to arbitrary or unlawful interference with his or her privacy, family, home or correspondence, nor to unlawful attacks on his or her honour and reputation.

2. The child has the right to the protection of the law against such interference or attacks.

Freedom of thought, conscience and religion

The child's right to freedom of thought, conscience and religion, subject to appropriate parental guidance and national law.

Freedom of association

The right of children to meet with others and to join or set up associations, unless the fact of doing so violates the rights of others.

Protection of privacy

The right to protection from interference with privacy, family, home and correspondence, and from libel/slander.

THE CONVENTION ON THE RIGHTS OF THE CHILD

Text	Unofficial summary of main provisions
Article 17	**Access to appropriate information**
States Parties recognize the important function performed by the mass media and shall ensure that the child has access to information and material from a diversity of national and international sources, especially those aimed at the promotion of his or her social, spiritual and moral well-being and physical and mental health. To this end, States Parties shall:	*The role of the media in disseminating information to children that is consistent with moral well-being and knowledge and understanding among peoples, and respects the child's cultural background. The State is to take measures to encourage this and to protect children from harmful materials.*
(a) Encourage the mass media to disseminate information and material of social and cultural benefit to the child and in accordance with the spirit of article 29;	
(b) Encourage international co-operation in the production, exchange and dissemination of such information and material from a diversity of cultural, national and international sources;	
(c) Encourage the production and dissemination of children's books;	
(d) Encourage the mass media to have particular regard to the linguistic needs of the child who belongs to a minority group or who is indigenous;	
(e) Encourage the development of appropriate guidelines for the protection of the child from information and material injurious to his or her well-being, bearing in mind the provisions of articles 13 and 18.	
Article 18	**Parental responsibilities**
1. States Parties shall use their best efforts to ensure recognition of the principle that both parents have common responsibilities for the upbringing and development of the child. Parents or, as the	*The principle that both parents have joint primary responsibility*

case may be, legal guardians, have the primary responsibility for the upbringing and development of the child. The best interests of the child will be their basic concern.

2. For the purpose of guaranteeing and promoting the rights set forth in the present Convention, States Parties shall render appropriate assistance to parents and legal guardians in the performance of their child-rearing responsibilities and shall ensure the development of institutions, facilities and services for the care of children.

3. States Parties shall take all appropriate measures to ensure that children of working parents have the right to benefit from child-care services and facilities for which they are eligible.

for bringing up their children, and that the State should support them in this task.

Article 19

1. States Parties shall take all appropriate legislative, administrative, social and educational measures to protect the child from all forms of physical or mental violence, injury or abuse, neglect or negligent treatment, maltreatment or exploitation, including sexual abuse, while in the care of parent(s), legal guardian(s) or any other person who has the care of the child.

2. Such protective measures should, as appropriate, include effective procedures for the establishment of social programmes to provide necessary support for the child and for those who have the care of the child, as well as for other forms of prevention and for identification, reporting, referral, investigation, treatment and follow-up of instances of child maltreatment described heretofore, and, as appropriate, for judicial involvement.

Protection from abuse and neglect

The State's obligation to protect children from all forms of maltreatment perpetrated by parents or others responsible for their care, and to undertake preventive and treatment programmes in this regard.

Article 20

1. A child temporarily or permanently deprived of his or her family environment, or in whose own best interests cannot be allowed to remain in that environment, shall be entitled to special protection and assistance provided by the State.

2. States Parties shall in accordance with their national laws ensure alternative care for such a child.

3. Such care could include, *inter alia*, foster placement, *kafalah* of Islamic law, adoption or if necessary placement in suitable institutions for the care of children. When considering solutions, due regard shall be paid to the desirability of continuity in a child's upbringing and to the child's ethnic, religious, cultural and linguistic background.

Protection of children without families

The State's obligation to provide special protection for children deprived of their family environment and to ensure that appropriate alternative family care or institutional placement is made available to them, taking into account the child's cultural background.

THE CONVENTION ON THE RIGHTS OF THE CHILD

Text	Unofficial summary of main provisions
Article 21 States Parties which recognize and/or permit the system of adoption shall ensure that the best interests of the child shall be the paramount consideration and they shall: *(a)* Ensure that the adoption of a child is authorized only by competent authorities who determine, in accordance with applicable law and procedures and on the basis of all pertinent and reliable information, that the adoption is permissible in view of the child's status concerning parents, relatives and legal guardians and that, if required, the persons concerned have given their informed consent to the adoption on the basis of such counselling as may be necessary; *(b)* Recognize that inter-country adoption may be considered as an alternative means of child's care, if the child cannot be placed in a foster or an adoptive family or cannot in any suitable manner be cared for in the child's country of origin; *(c)* Ensure that the child concerned by inter-country adoption enjoys safeguards and standards equivalent to those existing in the case of national adoption; *(d)* Take all appropriate measures to ensure that, in inter-country adoption, the placement does not result in improper financial gain for those involved in it; *(e)* Promote, where appropriate, the objectives of the present article by concluding bilateral or multilateral arrangements or agreements, and endeavour, within this framework, to ensure that the placement of the child in another country is carried out by competent authorities or organs. **Article 22** 1. States Parties shall take appropriate measures to ensure that a child who is seeking refugee status or who is considered a refugee in accordance with applicable international or domestic law	**Adoption** *In countries where adoption is recognized and/or allowed, it shall only be carried out in the best interests of the child, with all necessary safeguards for a given child and authorization by the competent authorities.* **Refugee children** *Special protection to be granted to children who are refugees or*

seeking refugee status, *and the State's obligation to cooperate with competent organizations providing such protection and assistance.*

and procedures shall, whether unaccompanied or accompanied by his or her parents or by any other person, receive appropriate protection and humanitarian assistance in the enjoyment of applicable rights set forth in the present Convention and in other international human rights or humanitarian instruments to which the said States are Parties.

2. For this purpose, States Parties shall provide, as they consider appropriate, co-operation in any efforts by the United Nations and other competent intergovernmental organizations or non-governmental organizations co-operating with the United Nations to protect and assist such a child and to trace the parents or other members of the family of any refugee child in order to obtain information necessary for reunification with his or her family. In cases where no parents or other members of the family can be found, the child shall be accorded the same protection as any other child permanently or temporarily deprived of his or her family environment for any reason, as set forth in the present Convention.

Handicapped children

The right of handicapped children to special care, education and training designed to help them to achieve greatest possible self-reliance and to lead a full and active life in society.

Article 23

1. States Parties recognize that a mentally or physically disabled child should enjoy a full and decent life, in conditions which ensure dignity, promote self-reliance, and facilitate the child's active participation in the community.

2. States Parties recognize the right of the disabled child to special care and shall encourage and ensure the extension, subject to available resources, to the eligible child and those responsible for his or her care, of assistance for which application is made and which is appropriate to the child's condition and to the circumstances of the parents or others caring for the child.

3. Recognizing the special needs of a disabled child, assistance extended in accordance with paragraph 2 of the present article shall be provided free of charge, whenever possible, taking into account the financial resources of the parents or others caring for the child, and shall be designed to ensure that the disabled child has effective access to and receives education, training, health care services, rehabilitation services, preparation for employment and recreation opportunities in a manner conducive to the child's achieving the fullest possible social integration and individual development, including his or her cultural and spiritual development.

4. States Parties shall promote, in the spirit of international co-operation, the exchange of appropriate information in the field of preventive health care and of medical, psychological and functional

THE CONVENTION ON THE RIGHTS OF THE CHILD

Text

treatment of disabled children, including dissemination of and access to information concerning methods of rehabilitation, education and vocational services, with the aim of enabling States Parties to improve their capabilities and skills and to widen their experience in these areas. In this regard, particular account shall be taken of the needs of developing countries.

Article 24

1. States Parties recognize the right of the child to the enjoyment of the highest attainable standard of health and to facilities for the treatment of illness and rehabilitation of health. States Parties shall strive to ensure that no child is deprived of his or her right of access to such health care services.

2. States Parties shall pursue full implementation of this right and, in particular, shall take appropriate measures:

(a) To diminish infant and child mortality;

(b) To ensure the provision of necessary medical assistance and health care to all children with emphasis on the development of primary health care;

(c) To combat disease and malnutrition, including within the framework of primary health care, through, *inter alia*, the application of readily available technology and through the provision of adequate nutritious foods and clean drinking-water, taking into consideration the dangers and risks of environmental pollution;

(d) To ensure appropriate pre-natal and post-natal health care for mothers;

(e) To ensure that all segments of society, in particular parents and children, are informed, have access to education and are supported in the use of basic knowledge of child health and nutrition,

Unofficial summary of main provisions

Health and health services

The right to the highest level of health possible and to access to health and medical services, with special emphasis on primary and preventive health care, public health education and the diminution of infant mortality. The State's obligation to work towards the abolition of harmful traditional practices. Emphasis is laid on the need for international cooperation to ensure this right.

the advantages of breast-feeding, hygiene and environmental sanitation and the prevention of accidents;

(f) To develop preventive health care, guidance for parents, and family planning education and services.

3. States Parties shall take all effective and appropriate measures with a view to abolishing traditional practices prejudicial to the health of children.

4. States Parties undertake to promote and encourage international co-operation with a view to achieving progressively the full realization of the right recognized in the present article. In this regard, particular account shall be taken of the needs of developing countries.

Article 25

States Parties recognize the right of a child who has been placed by the competent authorities for the purposes of care, protection, or treatment of his or her physical or mental health, to a periodic review of the treatment provided to the child and all other circumstances relevant to his or her placement.

Periodic review of placement

The right of children placed by the State for reasons of care, protection or treatment to have all aspects of that placement evaluated regularly.

Article 26

1. States Parties shall recognize for every child the right to benefit from social security, including social insurance, and shall take the necessary measures to achieve the full realization of this right in accordance with their national law.

2. The benefits should, where appropriate, be granted, taking into account the resources and the circumstances of the child and persons having responsibility for the maintenance of the child, as well as any other consideration relevant to an application for benefits made by or on behalf of the child.

Social security

The right of children to benefit from social security.

Article 27

1. States Parties recognize the right of every child to a standard of living adequate for the child's physical, mental, spiritual, moral and social development.

Standard of living

The right of children to benefit from an adequate standard of

THE CONVENTION ON THE RIGHTS OF THE CHILD

Text	Unofficial summary of main provisions
2. The parent(s) or others responsible for the child have the primary responsibility to secure, within their abilities and financial capacities, the conditions of living necessary for the child's development.	living, the primary responsibility of parents to provide this, and the State's duty to ensure that this responsibility is first fulfillable and then fulfilled, where necessary through the recovery of maintenance.
3. States Parties, in accordance with national conditions and within their means, shall take appropriate measures to assist parents and others responsible for the child to implement this right and shall in case of need provide material assistance and support programmes, particularly with regard to nutrition, clothing and housing.	
4. States Parties shall take all appropriate measures to secure the recovery of maintenance for the child from the parents or other persons having financial responsibility for the child, both within the State Party and from abroad. In particular, where the person having financial responsibility for the child lives in a State different from that of the child, States Parties shall promote the accession to international agreements or the conclusion of such agreements, as well as the making of other appropriate arrangements.	
Article 28	**Education**
1. States Parties recognize the right of the child to education, and with a view to achieving this right progressively and on the basis of equal opportunity, they shall, in particular:	The child's right to education, and the State's duty to ensure that primary education at least is made free and compulsory. Administration of school discipline is to reflect the child's human dignity. Emphasis is laid on the need for international cooperation to ensure this right.
(a) Make primary education compulsory and available free to all;	
(b) Encourage the development of different forms of secondary education, including general and vocational education, make them available and accessible to every child, and take appropriate measures such as the introduction of free education and offering financial assistance in case of need;	
(c) Make higher education accessible to all on the basis of capacity by every appropriate means;	

(d) Make educational and vocational information and guidance available and accessible to all children;

(e) Take measures to encourage regular attendance at schools and the reduction of drop-out rates.

2. States Parties shall take all appropriate measures to ensure that school discipline is administered in a manner consistent with the child's human dignity and in conformity with the present Convention.

3. States Parties shall promote and encourage international co-operation in matters relating to education, in particular with a view to contributing to the elimination of ignorance and illiteracy throughout the world and facilitating access to scientific and technical knowledge and modern teaching methods. In this regard, particular account shall be taken of the needs of developing countries.

Article 29

1. States Parties agree that the education of the child shall be directed to:

(a) The development of the child's personality, talents and mental and physical abilities to their fullest potential;

(b) The development of respect for human rights and fundamental freedoms, and for the principles enshrined in the Charter of the United Nations;

(c) The development of respect for the child's parents, his or her own cultural identity, language and values, for the national values of the country in which the child is living, the country from which he or she may originate, and for civilizations different from his or her own;

(d) The preparation of the child for responsible life in a free society, in the spirit of understanding, peace, tolerance, equality of sexes, and friendship among all peoples, ethnic, national and religious groups and persons of indigenous origin;

(e) The development of respect for the natural environment.

2. No part of the present article or article 28 shall be construed so as to interfere with the liberty of individuals and bodies to establish and direct educational institutions, subject always to the

Aims of education

The State's recognition that education should be directed at developing the child's personality and talents, preparing the child for active life as an adult, fostering respect for basic human rights and developing respect for the child's own cultural and national values and those of others.

THE CONVENTION ON THE RIGHTS OF THE CHILD

Text	Unofficial summary of main provisions
observance of the principles set forth in paragraph 1 of the present article and to the requirements that the education given in such institutions shall conform to such minimum standards as may be laid down by the State.	
Article 30	**Children of minorities or of indigenous peoples**
In those States in which ethnic, religious or linguistic minorities or persons of indigenous origin exist, a child belonging to such a minority or who is indigenous shall not be denied the right, in community with other members of his or her group, to enjoy his or her own culture, to profess and practise his or her own religion, or to use his or her own language.	*The right of children of minority communities and indigenous peoples to enjoy their own culture and to practice their own religion and language.*
Article 31	**Leisure, recreation and cultural activities**
1. States Parties recognize the right of the child to rest and leisure, to engage in play and recreational activities appropriate to the age of the child and to participate freely in cultural life and the arts.	*The right of children to leisure, play and participation in cultural and artistic activities.*
2. States Parties shall respect and promote the right of the child to participate fully in cultural and artistic life and shall encourage the provision of appropriate and equal opportunities for cultural, artistic, recreational and leisure activity.	
Article 32	**Child labour**
1. States Parties recognize the right of the child to be protected from economic exploitation and from performing any work that is likely to be hazardous or to interfere with the child's education, or to be harmful to the child's health or physical, mental, spiritual, moral or social development.	*The State's obligation to protect children from engaging in work that constitutes a threat to their*

health, education or development, to set minimum ages for employment, and to regulate conditions of employment.

2. States Parties shall take legislative, administrative, social and educational measures to ensure the implementation of the present article. To this end, and having regard to the relevant provisions of other international instruments, States Parties shall in particular:

(a) Provide for a minimum age or minimum ages for admissions to employment;

(b) Provide for appropriate regulation of the hours and conditions of employment;

(c) Provide for appropriate penalties or other sanctions to ensure the effective enforcement of the present article.

Drug abuse

The child's right to protection from the use of narcotic and psychotropic drugs and from being involved in their production or distribution.

Article 33

States Parties shall take all appropriate measures, including legislative, administrative, social and educational measures, to protect children from the illicit use of narcotic drugs and psychotropic substances as defined in the relevant international treaties; and to prevent the use of children in the illicit production and trafficking of such substances.

Sexual exploitation

The child's right to protection from sexual exploitation and abuse, including prostitution and involvement in pornography.

Article 34

States Parties undertake to protect the child from all forms of sexual exploitation and sexual abuse. For these purposes, States Parties shall in particular take all appropriate national, bilateral and multilateral measures to prevent:

(a) The inducement or coercion of a child to engage in any unlawful sexual activity;

(b) The exploitative use of children in prostitution or other unlawful sexual practices;

(c) The exploitative use of children in pornographic performances and materials.

Sale, trafficking and abduction

The State's obligation to make every effort to prevent the sale, trafficking and abduction of children.

Article 35

States Parties shall take all appropriate national, bilateral and multilateral measures to prevent the abduction of, the sale of or traffic in children for any purpose or in any form.

THE CONVENTION ON THE RIGHTS OF THE CHILD

Text	Unofficial summary of main provisions

Article 36

States Parties shall protect the child against all other forms of exploitation prejudicial to any aspects of the child's welfare.

Other forms of exploitation

The child's right to protection from all other forms of exploitation not covered in articles 32, 33, 34 and 35.

Article 37

States Parties shall ensure that:

(a) No child shall be subjected to torture or other cruel, inhuman or degrading treatment or punishment. Neither capital punishment nor life imprisonment without possibility of release shall be imposed for offences committed by persons below eighteen years of age;

(b) No child shall be deprived of his or her liberty unlawfully or arbitrarily. The arrest, detention or imprisonment of a child shall be in conformity with the law and shall be used only as a measure of last resort and for the shortest appropriate period of time;

(c) Every child deprived of liberty shall be treated with humanity and respect for the inherent dignity of the human person, and in a manner which takes into account the needs of persons of his or her age. In particular, every child deprived of liberty shall be separated from adults unless it is considered in the child's best interest not to do so and shall have the right to maintain contact with his or her family through correspondence and visits, save in exceptional circumstances;

(d) Every child deprived of his or her liberty shall have the right to prompt access to legal and other appropriate assistance, as well as the right to challenge the legality of the deprivation of his

Torture and deprivation of liberty

The prohibition of torture, cruel treatment or punishment, capital punishment, life imprisonment, and unlawful arrest or deprivation of liberty. The principles of appropriate treatment, separation from detained adults, contact with family and access to legal and other assistance.

or her liberty before a court or other competent, independent and impartial authority, and to a prompt decision on any such action.

Article 38

1. States Parties undertake to respect and to ensure respect for rules of international humanitarian law applicable to them in armed conflicts which are relevant to the child.

2. States Parties shall take all feasible measures to ensure that persons who have not attained the age of fifteen years do not take a direct part in hostilities.

3. States Parties shall refrain from recruiting any person who has not attained the age of fifteen years into their armed forces. In recruiting among those persons who have attained the age of fifteen years but who have not attained the age of eighteen years, States Parties shall endeavour to give priority to those who are oldest.

4. In accordance with their obligations under international humanitarian law to protect the civilian population in armed conflicts, States Parties shall take all feasible measures to ensure protection and care of children who are affected by an armed conflict.

Armed conflicts

The obligation of States to respect and ensure respect for humanitarian law as it applies to children. The principle that no child under 15 take a direct part in hostilities or be recruited into the armed forces, and that all children affected by armed conflict benefit from protection and care.

Article 39

States Parties shall take all appropriate measures to promote physical and psychological recovery and social reintegration of a child victim of: any form of neglect, exploitation, or abuse; torture or any other form of cruel, inhuman or degrading treatment or punishment; or armed conflicts. Such recovery and reintegration shall take place in an environment which fosters the health, self-respect and dignity of the child.

Rehabilitative care

The State's obligation to ensure that child victims of armed conflicts, torture, neglect, maltreatment or exploitation receive appropriate treatment for their re-covery and social re-integration.

Article 40

1. States Parties recognize the right of every child alleged as, accused of, or recognized as having infringed the penal law to be treated in a manner consistent with the promotion of the child's sense of dignity and worth, which reinforces the child's respect for the human rights and fundamental

Administration of juvenile justice

The right of children alleged or recognized as having committed an offence to respect for their

THE CONVENTION ON THE RIGHTS OF THE CHILD

Text	Unofficial summary of main provisions
freedoms of others and which takes into account the child's age and the desirability of promoting the child's reintegration and the child's assuming a constructive role in society. 2. To this end, and having regard to the relevant provisions of international instruments. States Parties shall, in particular, ensure that: *(a)* No child shall be alleged as, be accused of, or recognized as having infringed the penal law by reason of acts or omissions that were not prohibited by national or international law at the time they were committed; *(b)* Every child alleged as or accused of having infringed the penal law has at least the following guarantees: *(i)* To be presumed innocent until proven guilty according to law; *(ii)* To be informed promptly and directly of the charges against him or her, and, if appropriate through his or her parents or legal guardian, and to have legal or other appropriate assistance in the preparation and presentation of his or her defence; *(iii)* To have the matter determined without delay by a competent, independent and impartial authority or judicial body in a fair hearing according to law, in the presence of legal or other appropriate assistance and, unless it is considered not to be in the best interest of the child, in particular, taking into account his or her age or situation, his or her parents or legal guardians; *(iv)* Not to be compelled to give testimony or to confess guilt; to examine or have examined adverse witnesses and to obtain the participation and examination of witnesses on his or her behalf under conditions of equality; *(v)* If considered to have infringed the penal law, to have this decision and any measures imposed in consequence thereof reviewed by a higher competent, independent and impartial authority or judicial body according to law;	*human rights and, in particular, to benefit from all aspects of the due process of law, including legal or other assistance in preparing and presenting their defence. The principle that recourse to judicial proceedings and institutional placements should be avoided wherever possible and appropriate.*

(vi) To have the free assistance of an interpreter if the child cannot understand or speak the language used;

(vii) To have his or her privacy fully respected at all stages of the proceedings.

3. States Parties shall seek to promote the establishment of laws, procedures, authorities and institutions specifically applicable to children alleged as, accused of, or recognized as having infringed the penal law, and in particular:

(a) The establishment of a minimum age below which children shall be presumed not to have the capacity to infringe the penal law;

(b) Whenever appropriate and desirable, measures for dealing with such children without resorting to judicial proceedings, providing that human rights and legal safeguards are fully respected.

4. A variety of dispositions, such as care, guidance and supervision orders; counselling; probation; foster care; education and vocational training programmes and other alternatives to institutional care shall be available to ensure that children are dealt with in a manner appropriate to their well-being and proportionate both to their circumstances and the offence.

Article 41

Nothing in the present Convention shall affect any provisions which are more conducive to the realization of the rights of the child and which may be contained in:

(a) The law of a State Party; or

(b) International law in force for that State.

PART II

Article 42

States Parties undertake to make the principles and provisions of the Convention widely known, by appropriate and active means, to adults and children alike.

Respect for existing standards

The principle that, if any standards set in national law or other applicable international instruments are higher than those of this Convention, it is the higher standard that applies.

Implementation and entry into force

The provisions of articles 42–54 notably foresee:

THE CONVENTION ON THE RIGHTS OF THE CHILD

Text	Unofficial summary of main provisions
Article 43 1. For the purpose of examining the progress made by States Parties in achieving the realization of the obligations undertaken in the present Convention, there shall be established a Committee on the Rights of the Child, which shall carry out the functions hereinafter provided. 2. The Committee shall consist of ten experts of high moral standing and recognized competence in the field covered by this Convention. The members of the Committee shall be elected by States Parties from among their nationals and shall serve in their personal capacity, consideration being given to equitable geographical distribution, as well as to the principal legal systems. 3. The members of the Committee shall be elected by secret ballot from a list of persons nominated by States Parties. Each State Party may nominate one person from among its own nationals. 4. The initial election to the Committee shall be held no later than six months after the date of the entry into force of the present Convention and thereafter every second year. At least four months before the date of each election, the Secretary-General of the United Nations shall address a letter to States Parties inviting them to submit their nominations within two months. The Secretary-General shall subsequently prepare a list in alphabetical order of all persons thus nominated, indicating States Parties which have nominated them, and shall submit it to the States Parties to the present Convention. 5. The elections shall be held at meetings of States Parties convened by the Secretary-General at United Nations Headquarters. At those meetings, for which two-thirds of States Parties shall constitute a quorum, the persons elected to the Committee shall be those who obtain the largest number of votes and an absolute majority of the votes of the representatives of States Parties present and voting.	*(i) the State's obligation to make the rights contained in this Convention widely known to both adults and children.* *(ii) the setting up of a Committee on the Rights of the child composed of ten experts, which will consider reports that States Parties to the Convention are to submit two years after ratification and every five years thereafter. The Convention enters into force – and the Committee would therefore be set up – once 20 countries have ratified it.* *(iii) States Parties are to make their reports widely available to the general public.* *(iv) The Committee may propose that special studies be undertaken on specific issues relating to the rights of the child, and may make its evaluations known to*

each State Party concerned as well as to the UN General Assembly.

(v) In order to 'foster the effective implementation of the Convention and to encourage international cooperation', the specialized agencies of the UN (such as the ILO, WHO and UNESCO) and UNICEF would be able to attend the meetings of the Committee. Together with any other body recognized as 'competent', including NGOs in consultative status with the UN and UN organs such as the UNHCR, they can submit pertinent information to the Committee and be asked to advise on the optimal implementation of the Convention.

6. The members of the Committee shall be elected for a term of four years. They shall be eligible for re-election if renominated. The term of five of the members elected at the first election shall expire at the end of two years; immediately after the first election, the names of these five members shall be chosen by lot by the Chairman of the meeting.

7. If a member of the Committee dies or resigns or declares that for any other cause he or she can no longer perform the duties of the Committee, the State Party which nominated the member shall appoint another expert from among its nationals to serve for the remainder of the term, subject to the approval of the Committee.

8. The Committee shall establish its own rules of procedure.

9. The Committee shall elect its officers for a period of two years.

10. The meetings of the Committee shall normally be held at the United Nations Headquarters or at any other convenient place as determined by the Committee. The Committee shall normally meet annually. The duration of the meetings of the Committee shall be determined, and reviewed, if necessary, by a meeting of the States Parties to the present Convention, subject to the approval of the General Assembly.

11. The Secretary-General of the United Nations shall provide the necessary staff and facilities for the effective performance of the functions of the Committee under the present Convention.

12. With the approval of the General Assembly, the members of the Committee established under the present Convention shall receive emoluments from United Nations resources on such terms and conditions as the Assembly may decide.

Article 44

1. States Parties undertake to submit to the Committee, through the Secretary-General of the United Nations, reports on the measures they have adopted which give effect to the rights recognized herein and on the progress made on the enjoyment of those rights:

(a) Within two years of the entry into force of Convention for the State Party concerned;

(b) Thereafter every five years.

THE CONVENTION ON THE RIGHTS OF THE CHILD

Text	Unofficial summary of main provisions
2. Reports made under the present article shall indicate factors and difficulties, if any, affecting the degree of fulfilment of the obligations under the present Convention. Reports shall also contain sufficient information to provide the Committee with a comprehensive understanding of the implementation of the Convention in the country concerned.	
3. A State Party which has submitted a comprehensive initial report to the Committee need not in its subsequent reports submitted in accordance with paragraph 1(b) of the present article, repeat basic information previously provided.	
4. The Committee may request from States Parties further information relevant to the implementation of the Convention.	
5. The Committee shall submit to the General Assembly, through the Economic and Social Council, every two years, reports on its activities.	
6. States Parties shall make their reports widely available to the public in their own countries.	
Article 45	
In order to foster the effective implementation of the Convention and to encourage international co-operation in the field covered by the Convention:	
(a) The specialized agencies, the United Nations Children's Fund and other United Nations organs shall be entitled to be represented at the consideration of the implementation of such provisions of the present Convention as fall within the scope of their mandate. The Committee may invite the specialized agencies, the United Nations Children's Fund and other competent bodies as it may consider appropriate to provide expert advice on the implementation of the Convention in areas	

falling within the scope of their respective mandates. The Committee may invite the specialized agencies, the United Nations Children's Fund and other United Nations organs to submit reports on the implementation of the Convention in areas falling within the scope of their activities;

(b) The Committee shall transmit, as it may consider appropriate, to the specialized agencies, the United Nations Children's Fund and other competent bodies, any reports from States Parties that contain a request, or indicate a need, for technical advice or assistance along with the Committee's observations and suggestions, if any, on these requests or indications;

(c) The Committee may recommend to the General Assembly to request the Secretary-General to undertake on its behalf studies on specific issues relating to the rights of the child;

(d) The Committee may make suggestions and general recommendations based on information received pursuant to articles 44 and 45 of the present Convention. Such suggestions and general recommendations shall be transmitted to any State Party concerned and reported to the General Assembly, together with comments, if any, from States Parties.

PART III

Article 46

The present Convention shall be open for signature by all States.

Article 47

The present Convention is subject to ratification. Instruments of ratification shall be deposited with the Secretary-General of the United Nations.

Article 48

The present Convention shall remain open for accession by any State. The instruments of accession shall be deposited with the Secretary-General of the United Nations.

THE CONVENTION ON THE RIGHTS OF THE CHILD

Text	Unofficial summary of main provisions
Article 49 1. The present Convention shall enter into force on the thirtieth day following the date of deposit with the Secretary-General of the United Nations of the twentieth instrument of ratification or accession. 2. For each State ratifying or acceding to the Convention after the deposit of the twentieth instrument of ratification or accession, the Convention shall enter into force on the thirtieth day after the deposit by such State of its instrument of ratification or accession. **Article 50** 1. Any State Party may propose an amendment and file it with the Secretary-General of the United Nations. The Secretary-General shall thereupon communicate the proposed amendment to States Parties, with a request that they indicate whether they favour a conference of States Parties for the purpose of considering and voting upon the proposals. In the event that, within four months from the date of such communication, at least one third of the States Parties favour such a conference, the Secretary-General shall convene the conference under the auspices of the United Nations. Any amendment adopted by a majority of States Parties present and voting at the conference shall be submitted to the General Assembly for approval. 2. An amendment adopted in accordance with paragraph (1) of the present article shall enter into force when it has been approved by the General Assembly of the United Nations and accepted by a two-thirds majority of States Parties. 3. When an amendment enters into force, it shall be binding on those States Parties which have accepted it, other States Parties still being bound by the provisions of the present Convention and any earlier amendments which they have accepted.	

Article 51

1. The Secretary-General of the United Nations shall receive and circulate to all States the text of reservations made by States at the time of ratification or accession.

2. A reservation incompatible with the object and purpose of the present Convention shall not be permitted.

3. Reservations may be withdrawn at any time by notification to that effect addressed to the Secretary-General of the United Nations, who shall then inform all States. Such notification shall take effect on the date on which it is received by the Secretary-General.

Article 52

A State Party may denounce the present Convention by written notification to the Secretary-General of the United Nations. Denunciation becomes effective one year after the date of receipt of the notification by the Secretary-General.

Article 53

The Secretary-General of the United Nations is designated as the depositary of the present Convention.

Article 54

The original of the present Convention, of which the Arabic, Chinese, English, French, Russian and Spanish texts are equally authentic, shall be deposited with the Secretary-General of the United Nations.

In witness thereof the undersigned plenipotentiaries, being duly authorized thereto by their respective Governments, have signed the present Convention.

APPENDIX 1 – UK DECLARATION & RESERVATIONS

UN Convention on the Rights of the Child UK Ratification

The Instrument of ratification contained the following reservations and declarations:

(a) The United Kingdom interprets the Convention as applicable only following a live birth.

(b) The United Kingdom interprets the reference in the Convention to 'parents' to mean only those persons who, as a matter of national law, are treated as parents. This includes cases where the law regards a child as having only one parent, for example where a child has been adopted by one person only and in certain cases where a child is conceived other than as a result of sexual intercourse by the woman who gives birth to it and she is treated as the only parent.

(c) The United Kingdom reserves the right to apply such legislation, in so far as it relates to the entry into, stay in and departure from the United Kingdom of those who do not have the right under the law of the United Kingdom to enter and remain in the United Kingdom, and to the acquisition and possession of citizenship, as it may deem necessary from time to time.

(d) Employment legislation in the United Kingdom does not treat persons under 18, but under the school-leaving age as children, but as 'young people'. Accordingly the United Kingdom reserves the right to continue to apply Article 32 subject to such employment legislation.

(e) Where at any time there is a lack of suitable accommodation or adequate facilities for a particular individual in any institution in which young offenders are detained, or where the mixing of adults and children is deemed to be mutually beneficial, the United Kingdom reserves the right not to apply Article 37(c) in so far as those provisions require children who are detained to be accommodated separately from adults.

(f) In Scotland there are tribunals (known as 'children's hearings') which consider the welfare of the child and deal with the majority of offences which a child is alleged to have committed. In some cases, mainly of a welfare nature, the child is temporarily deprived of its liberty for up to seven days prior to attending the hearing. The child and its family are, however, allowed access to a lawyer during this period. Although the decisions of the hearings are subject to appeal to the courts, legal representation is not permitted at the proceedings of the children's hearings themselves. Children's hearings have proved over the years to be a very effective way of dealing with the problems of children in a less formal, non-adversarial manner. Accordingly, the United Kingdom, in respect of Article 37(d), reserves its right to continue the present operation of children's hearings.

USEFUL CONTACTS

Children's Rights Development Unit (CRDU) **London**	235, Shaftesbury Avenue London WC2H 8EL Tel: 071 240 4449
Scotland	Lion Chambers 170, Hope Street Glasgow G2 2TU Tel: 041 353 0206
Northern Ireland	c/o John Pinkerton Department of Social Work Queen's University Belfast B17 1NN Tel: 0232 245133
Children in Wales	7, Cleave House Lanbourne Crescent Cardiff CF4 5GJ Tel: 0222 761177

Scottish Child Law Centre

Lion Chambers
170, Hope Street
Glasgow G2 2TU
Tel: 041 333 9305

Department of Health
(who have responsibility for co-ordinating the Government report to the UN Committee on the Rights of the Child on the UK's progress towards implementation)

Community Services Division
Department of Health
Wellington House
133/135, Waterloo Road
London SE1 8UG
Tel: 071 972 4416

UNA

3 Whitehall Court
London SW1A 2EL
Tel: 071 930 2931/2

UNICEF-UK

55 Lincoln's Inn Fields
London WC2A 3NB
Tel: 071 405 5592

INDEX

Page numbers in **bold** denote major section/chapter devoted to subject.